Remapping Sovereignty

Remapping Sovereignty

DECOLONIZATION AND SELF-DETERMINATION IN NORTH AMERICAN INDIGENOUS POLITICAL THOUGHT

David Myer Temin

THE UNIVERSITY OF CHICAGO PRESS
CHICAGO AND LONDON

The University of Chicago Press, Chicago 60637
The University of Chicago Press, Ltd., London
© 2023 by The University of Chicago
All rights reserved. No part of this book may be used or reproduced in any manner whatsoever without written permission, except in the case of brief quotations in critical articles and reviews. For more information, contact the University of Chicago Press, 1427 E. 60th St., Chicago, IL 60637.
Published 2023
Printed in the United States of America

32 31 30 29 28 27 26 25 24 23   1 2 3 4 5

ISBN-13: 978-0-226-82726-1 (cloth)
ISBN-13: 978-0-226-82728-5 (paper)
ISBN-13: 978-0-226-82727-8 (e-book)
DOI: https://doi.org/10.7208/chicago/9780226827278.001.0001

Library of Congress Cataloging-in-Publication Data
Names: Temin, David Myer, author.
Title: Remapping sovereignty : decolonization and self-determination in North American indigenous political thought / David Myer Temin.
Description: Chicago : The University of Chicago Press, 2023. | Includes bibliographical references and index.
Identifiers: LCCN 2022049632 | ISBN 9780226827261 (cloth) | ISBN 9780226827285 (paperback) | ISBN 9780226827278 (ebook)
Subjects: LCSH: Decolonization—United States. | Decolonization—Canada. | Indians of North America—United States—Government relations. | Indians of North America—Canada—Government relations.
Classification: LCC E91 .T46 2023 | DDC 323.1197—dc23/eng/20221026
LC record available at https://lccn.loc.gov/2022049632

Contents

INTRODUCTION
Remapping Sovereignty · *1*

CHAPTER ONE
Indigenous Self-Determination against Political Slavery
Zitkala-Ša and Vine Deloria Jr. on the Colonialism of US Sovereignty and Citizenship · *27*

CHAPTER TWO
The Struggle for Treaty
Ella Cara Deloria and Vine Deloria Jr. on Anticolonial Relations · *63*

CHAPTER THREE
"The Land Is Our Culture"
George Manuel on the Fourth World and the Politics of Resurgence · *101*

CHAPTER FOUR
Indigenous Marxisms
Howard Adams and Lee Maracle on Colonial-Racial Capitalism · *141*

Conclusion *183*
Acknowledgments *191*
Notes *195*
Bibliography *231*
Index *257*

[INTRODUCTION]

Remapping Sovereignty

Who has the right to make the earth anew, and how is it made so?
Winona LaDuke (White Earth Anishinaabe)[1]

In 2014, Dakota Access, LLC (later Energy Transfer Partners) proposed to build the $3.78 billion Dakota Access Pipeline (DAPL). The pipeline would run a half-million barrels of crude oil a day from the Bakken oil fields in western North Dakota to another pipeline near the Gulf of Mexico. The company diverted the pipeline to run ten miles upstream of the Standing Rock Sioux Reservation, with the likelihood that any spill could poison the tribe's primary water sources at Lake Oahe and the Missouri River.

Igniting a saga followed across the globe, young tribal citizens first initiated the NODAPL movement to stop Dakota Access from building the pipeline on unceded treaty lands. In April 2016, twenty-five Standing Rock Sioux citizens gathered to protect their relative of the water nation, Mní Oyate, at the first Sacred Stone Camp.[2] The Očhéthi Šakówiŋ (Great Sioux Nation) and allied water protectors announced their responsibilities to defend the water in proclaiming that water is life, Mní wičóni—a maxim that bridges deeply context-specific and universal meanings. The encampments grew to four thousand people, including representatives there in solidarity from some three hundred Indigenous nations, until police dismantled the camps in February 2017.[3]

NODAPL was an anticolonial movement that directly rejected the institutions and conceptual logic of colonial sovereignty. The water protectors enacted a refusal of sovereignty *for* decolonization by cultivating resurgent reciprocities with land and water. Against the building of extractive infrastructure on occupied lands, they sought to emancipate themselves and the earth itself from sovereignty. Such reciprocities conceive the basis for alternative forms of self-determining authority rooted in Indigenous jurisdiction.

This brief summary of the confrontation between the NODAPL water protectors and Energy Transfer Partners helps to introduce two of this book's main contentions. The first is that there is an enduring interplay between political thought and practice within Indigenous societies, which accounts for the prominence and distinctiveness of orienting political action in certain ways—notably here, to care for and defend the water. The lineages emergent from this interplay unfortunately have played a negligible role in academic political theory's telling of the contours of twentieth-century thought (this, even with the turn over the last twenty-five years to a more comparative and globalized political theory). Notwithstanding their erasure in academic political theorizing up until very recently, thinkers from Indigenous societies in North America have nevertheless produced a rich, diverse field of anticolonial political thought. This is already attested to in the fact that many such thinkers are cited—and subject to detailed interpretation—as canonical to the interdisciplinary field of Indigenous studies.

With this in mind, the first task of this book is historical: to reconstruct some key figures and conceptual frameworks from Indigenous societies in North America as interlocutors forming independently valuable but relatively occluded bodies of anticolonial thinking. I use the term "anticolonial" here because my interpretive focus sheds light on modes of political theorizing that reflect on the agencies, strategies, and transformative horizons of struggles against colonial conquest, and for something beyond it. To be sure, NODAPL as a gathering was impressive and even generational in scale, which led some media observers to treat it as springing up from nowhere. But it was far from an outlier. In fact, it was among the most prominent and forceful recent illustrations of the depth and specificity of Indigenous anticolonialism(s) in North America. The water protectors drew right from these lineages. The first premise this book works from, then, is that these lineages demand careful reconstruction as modes of thinking worthy of systematic attention, both in their own right and as prelude to understanding present-day resistance to colonization.

My second contention is conceptual and political: anticolonial practices employed in NODAPL are rooted in a specific set of political-theoretical debates about what "decolonization" does (as a practice) and what it means (as a concept). At the center of my focus here is the role of sovereignty in (de)colonization.

Why decolonization? To zoom much further out, the short answer is that colonialism has played a formative role in shaping the basic hierarchical systemic architecture of the modern world order. As a result, it becomes an indispensable core of the work of critical and emancipatory politics to dismantle—that is, to decolonize—the vast structural (and cultural, epistemic, etc.) imprint of colonialism (and capitalism). In line with diverse approaches that likewise historicize political modernity as a colonial modernity, I define decolonization in quite general terms as this project of fundamentally reshaping these colonial systemic architectures through restitution, repair, and radical transformation—with the aim of transfiguring and replacing those architectures entirely.

Within this initial very expansive formulation of the significance of (de)colonization, I adduce that the Očhéthi Šakówiŋ water protectors articulated what decolonization does and means along more specific lines. To wit, consider that they articulated "decolonization" as the creation of a social world shared by multiple peoples, whose collective and individual freedoms and flourishing are integrally bound up with the realization of reciprocal responsibilities to land and water. In so doing, the water protectors used one of the central frameworks of decolonization the world over: the concept of "self-determination." Yet I want to suggest that they also made an implicit argument about how to transform—or, more accurately, how Lakota-Dakota philosophical notions had already transformed—the idea of self-determination. That is, they theorized the *concepts* of self-determination and decolonization in innovative ways.

Specifically, what is innovative here is the effort to unsettle and reimagine sovereignty, in defiance of the state's claim to unilateral authority. In seeking to shape how the public would understand this mobilization, they not only expose the *colonial* faces of the sovereign state, but they also reach for political epistemologies (e.g., territory understood as a richly meaningful meeting place for practices of care) that frame alternatives to the most basic features of modern political rule: that political order just is, by definition, forged through a monopoly of violence projected over territory.

Through these practices, sovereignty moves to the center of decolonizing praxis as a question, not as the self-evident container or normative aspiration for anticolonial struggles. Drawing on archival research, *Remapping Sovereignty* traces the deep roots of diverse anticolonial efforts to reconfigure sovereignty for decolonization by assembling histories of twentieth-century political thought crafted in and from Indigenous societies in North America. Through close readings of the following key Indigenous thinkers, I weave together a series of genealogies of Indigenous political thought in North America: Zitkala-Ša (Yankton Dakota), Ella Deloria (Yankton Dakota), Vine Deloria Jr. (Yankton Dakota), George Manuel (Secwépmec), Lee Maracle (Stó:lō), and Howard Adams (Métis).

By drawing on and interpreting the work of these thinkers in context, I show how sovereignty is materially embedded in and conceptually constituted *through* colonial projects. As a result of its deep, enduring centrality to colonial domination, sovereignty takes on multiple meanings as a dilemma for projects of Indigenous decolonization: it becomes all at once a problem of vast accumulated state powers to face; a question-begging assertion of the validity of the hegemonic order; an impure discursive weapon in Indigenous anticolonial struggles; and a synecdoche or an overarching proxy to mark who can (properly) wield authoritative speech, action, and violence.

To capture the relationship between sovereignty and (de)colonization that I elucidate at the center of these thinkers' work, I develop an interpretive lens I call "remapping sovereignty." Remapping sovereignty brings into view how projects of Indigenous decolonization make sovereignty into a question (and what the political entailments of that question are). My conception of "remapping" draws on Tonawanda Seneca theorist Mishuana Goeman's influential account of Native women writers "(re)mapping" their nations, against the destructive incursions of ongoing colonization. I retain Goeman's focus on how "settler colonial society is built on the violent erasure of alternative modes of spatial practice and geographic understanding."[4] Yet whereas Goeman studies spatial violence and (in)justice in literature, I attend to the work the *concept* of sovereignty does to organize collective practices in settler-colonial societies. To do so, I elucidate the commonalities among several through lines across Indigenous anticolonial thought, which construe decolonization as those material practices and constructive visions that *disentangle* Indigenous self-determination from sovereignty.

Remapping Sovereignty is a work of political theory and conceptually driven intellectual history that explores the relationship between (de)colonization and sovereignty by assembling an archive of Indigenous thinkers that I interpret in the material contexts of anticolonial politics in North American settler societies. The reason that I turn to an intellectual-historical archive is that I aim to explore a long historical and conceptual arc of how thinkers from different Indigenous societies throughout the twentieth century dealt with these questions. I systematically reconstruct how this problem of sovereignty and the decolonial alternatives to it surfaced throughout the twentieth century as core concerns of various strands of Indigenous anticolonialisms. Projects of remapping sovereignty are not one ideologically singular framework. They encompass a variety of *antistatist*, *nonstatist*, and *treaty-based federalist* strategies for refiguring the state and planetary order, so as to contest and model alternatives that fashion anticolonial and decolonial futures.[5]

What is more, I reconstruct these thinkers as contributors to a set of debates that I will refer to as *political theories of Indigenous decolonization*.[6] By "Indigenous decolonization," I mean a set of political theories and constructive projects of self-government proposed over the course of the "long red power movement."[7] These projects centrally aim to address global white supremacy, empire, and especially settler-colonial conquest by drawing on the political and ethical articulations of Indigenous societies themselves. In this way, political theories of Indigenous decolonization are not reducible to what some theorists have called "settler decolonization," or decolonization primarily (or only) understood as a response to the specific structural and institutional contexts of settler-colonial societies like the United States and Canada.[8]

Power and context are of course crucial, but it is insufficient to treat these bodies of thought as simply reactive responses whose terms are capitulated only in relation to this particular axis of colonial domination (characterized primarily by settler expansionism and the theft of land, not labor). Instead, I underscore how these thinkers imagine independence in inheriting, reinventing, and actively making *Indigenous societies'* political outlooks as core to decolonizing struggle. Put otherwise, my analysis focuses on the meaning-making practices forged in the contexts of deliberating the substance and entailments of decolonization *for* Indigenous societies.

To further sketch out the core arguments of the book in what follows, I first expand on my approach to the concept of sovereignty. By laying out the historical co-constitution of settler colonialism and state formation, I motivate how sovereignty becomes the kind of question and problem that it is for the thinkers in this book. This section in turn vivifies the political stakes of *remapping sovereignty* I derive from these bodies of anticolonial thought. Second, I then turn to what I call *earthmaking,* or political projects that seek to structurally transform domestic and international institutions so as to create nonexploitative and reciprocity-oriented relationships between humans and the earth, on terms that sustain and rebuild Indigenous self-determination.

Third, I turn briefly to what I call *transnational internationalism.* Transnational internationalism is an interpretive framework I use to illustrate how Indigenous (relational) self-determination as theory and practice counters the (antirelational) projection of settler-colonial sovereignty, and, so too, the role of sovereignty in the reproduction of a hegemonic international order of states. Finally, I comment briefly on my methodological approach, laying out the structure of the book as a series of connected close readings of thinkers from which I derive and explicate these core theoretical frameworks.

Sovereignty in/as Colonization

To conceive of decolonization as a project of remapping sovereignty requires an analysis of two connected modes of decolonizing praxis: first, projects of (re)theorizing the sovereign state as a colonial institution embedded in an imperial and colonial world order and, second, practical enactments and imaginative invocations of self-determination that reconfigure the basic logics of sovereignty framing the very notion of "politics" in Western political thought. In short, the water protectors embody some of the many ways that Indigenous societies' anticolonial practices seek to disentangle the meaning of self-determination from state sovereignty—both from the *institutions* of the state and the conceptual *logics* of sovereignty. In studying the back and forth here among these thinkers between critique and constructive vision, I explore how intergenerational projects of Indigenous self-government systematically recast the overarching political and conceptual relationship between (de)colonization and sovereignty. Decolonization entails strategies for remapping sovereignty; in turn, remapping sovereignty (re)constitutes what decolonization means as an orientation toward political futures.

To advance this line of argument, however, it is first necessary to provide some conceptual scaffolding to contextualize my discussion of sovereignty. To this end, I first sketch how the term's stakes and meanings diverge vastly between debates in political theory and Indigenous studies. Here, my intention is to bridge differences between two disciplinary audiences by specifying how I theorize the concept of sovereignty. As such, I then contend that the context of (settler-)colonial domination shapes the concept and materiality of sovereignty, in ways evaded in standard accounts of the concept in Western political thought. The lineages of situated anticolonial thought and mobilization I reconstruct center this disavowed constitutive context of sovereignty in theorizing political strategies and dilemmas of decolonization.

To begin with its history in political theory and political science, sovereignty is an "essentially contested concept."[9] Every attempt to define sovereignty is already suffused with contingent and controversial mixtures of empirical assumptions and evaluative judgments. For my purposes, a useful point of departure is to define sovereignty as a concept that proposes the normative centrality and perceived necessity of the claim to final and ultimate authority over a bounded space.

There are already multiple elements within this preliminary definition that bear spelling out. On the one hand, sovereignty here refers to a set of normative justifications and material practices that order, or provide a rationale for, the forces of violence and domination specific to the modern state form. In this sense, sovereignty is the justificatory apparatus that licenses the state institutions that claim ultimate, final authority over a bounded territory. On the other hand, political theorists in particular have used the term sovereignty in ways that rely less directly on this familiar package of institutional logics associated with the sovereign state. In this latter regard, I also use sovereignty to mean those *conceptual logics* that conceive a particular "worldview" about how political authority must be organized (independent of whether the resulting "sovereign" institutions are actually described as "states").[10] Tracking with sovereignty as "worldview"—or "logic" as I often shorthand it here—is the idea that the fabrication and enforcement of social order *within* a bounded space requires an unlimited, undivided, and unaccountable power.[11]

In abstract terms, then, sovereignty means drawing a set of borders around territory in which the "self" of self-determination is separated out. The self is represented as putatively independent of competing forces and authorities, so as to portray and assert itself as the ultimate arbiter. Accordingly, the very notion of sovereignty requires the active elimination/suppression and disavowal of the interdependence through which the self is always materially and figuratively constituted. In this sense, to self-legislate *as* a sovereign requires sustaining the illusion that there are no outside forces that empirically or normatively constitute *any form of* selfhood (collective or individual); it is to stand outside of and subordinate those other sources of power and the interdependencies to which they are bound.

In this very claim to final, ultimate, and self-contained authority over decision making, sovereignty is a concept that my interlocutors in this text allow me to analyze as dependent upon the disavowal of relationships and accountability. In sum, sovereignty is a relation (or web of relations) that is constituted by a *refusal of relation*. It is inherently antirelational as a conceptual logic, even as sovereignty is actually brought into material form in relation to other forces represented as nonsovereign. (My later discussion of earthmaking shows that this suppression of relationality extends to the very concept of territory, which disavows relations to the other-than-human, too—to the earth itself.)

This insight into what a sovereign has to suppress and/or incorporate to become (or "figure itself" as) sovereign is made far sharper not only in examining the practices by which the colonized are "constitutively excluded" under this notion of the sovereign state or sovereign people,[12] but also by looking toward those alternative models of political community that refuse sovereignty in forging anticolonial relational social practices.

With this in mind, it is not surprising that Indigenous studies scholars and Indigenous activists have used the terms "Indigenous sovereignty" or "tribal sovereignty" in a number of other ways. These latter usages are at odds with (or otherwise just orthogonal to) sovereignty as a term of art in Western political thought. As Chickasaw scholar Jodi A. Byrd writes: "If there is one unifying principle that the field of Indigenous studies asserts as foundational, inviolable, and central, it is the concept of sovereignty," which is used "to assert Indigenous difference, persistence, and authority."[13] The resulting "sovereignty debate" within Indigenous studies has revolved around whether sovereignty is actually an appropriate language to orient the political aspirations of Indigenous societies.

In particular, debates over "sovereignty" in Native studies are about how best to craft spaces of autonomy across arenas of social life, spaces whose possibilities are defined by Indigenous societies as inherently sovereign *polities* themselves. This affirmation of tribal nations in the US and Aboriginal peoples in Canada as sovereigns with the capacities and rights to govern themselves against colonization counters the way that indigeneity is otherwise apprehended ideologically through a litany of predominant paradigms in North American politics, including multicultural pluralism, ethnic group assimilation, and civil rights and integration.[14] The deployment of sovereignty has real world effects for Indigenous societies who conceive sovereignty as a way to refuse the material encroachments of (claims to) *settler sovereignty*.[15] All this is also to say that, when Indigenous struggles cite "sovereignty," they claim a flexible idiom distinct from Western political epistemologies.[16]

For my purposes, it then becomes important to bridge the stakes of these separate disciplinary arenas of meaning making. Conceptually speaking, my own use of the notion of "Indigenous self-determination" throughout the book hinges on an interpretation of "Indigenous sovereignty" as a way to powerfully *name* this refusal of dominant colonial notions of sovereignty. As such, I theorize Indigenous self-determination as advanced through projects that are aimed at disentangling the very idea of collective self-determination from the antirelational lineages of sovereignty in the history of Western political thought (not, of course, as the term has evolved in Indigenous studies). More terminologically speaking, I intentionally refer to Indigenous "self-determination" throughout to underscore these contrasts between Indigenous sovereignty and colonial sovereignty.[17]

The sovereign state and the concept of sovereignty are often standardly portrayed as having displaced archaic accounts of rule, including imperial and colonial politics. In what sense, then, can sovereignty be theorized as "colonial"? These standard accounts are first of all based on the mistaken assumption that colonialism is a phenomenon of the past rather than an enduring structure in settler contexts.

Counter to this narrative, sovereignty and the state form are central to the *continued* creation and reproduction of the colonial domination of Indigenous societies in and by settler-colonial societies like the United States and Canada.[18] How? In short, sovereignty is colonial in North American settler societies like Canada and the United States, first, because the state is a core set of ideologies and institutions central to the practices of securing conquest, where conquest here means the territorial dispossession of and colonial rule over Indigenous societies. In a more discursive and conceptual vein, sovereignty is a self-fulfilling premise: expansionism is posited as an inevitable outgrowth of the very logic of political rule (e.g., manifest destiny), which then contributes to the material realization of conquest.

Second, sovereignty and the state form are themselves an outcome or product of those material practices of colonial conquest. As a historical outcome that must naturalize its own origins and parry modes of countermemory that center the unmistakable facts of conquest,[19] sovereignty normalizes these constitutively coercive foundations of the polity by representing them as necessarily progressive and consensually formed. Sovereign legitimacy is always projected backward either by shrouding or justifying the material realities of colonization as the present's past. Likewise, the juridical vindication of all kinds of extralegal violence through the retrospective assertion and creation of institutions of sovereignty and property markets in land are enabled alongside diffusely circulated ideologies that affirm the post hoc legitimacy of those geopolitical foundations of the settler state.[20] Sovereignty is part of colonization in the sense that it is a core institutional mechanism in realizing colonization. Sovereignty also just *is* colonization in the sense that it establishes a structure of domination that erases alternatives in the form of Indigenous self-determination and jurisdiction.[21]

Transnational practices of genocidal replacement, dispossession, and violent atrocities extending from kidnapping to endemic sexual and gender violence constitute and are constituted by sovereignty. In this regard, sovereignty lives a "double life" when considered from the perspective of Indigenous decolonization: it is both the source (as in both cause and premise) and outcome (as in both result and conclusion) of a massive project of transnationally racialized population movement and replacement—one that is engineered so successfully, so completely, as to normalize and naturalize its own genocidal preconditions (but only for some). This dialectic between sovereignty as the *subject making* colonial power and sovereignty as the *object resulting* from colonial power continues into the "settler colonial present."[22] Colonial sovereignty is a self-positing mode of colonial erasure, one that alternates between sustaining hierarchical domination and the genocidal elimination of Indigenous societies. Sovereignty's antirelationality comes out of these colonial roots.

Does a more democratic practice, or even pluralistic "ethos of sovereignty," serve to unsettle sovereignty's embeddedness in structural colonial domination?[23] I argue "no," or at least not as a point of departure. In Western political thought, the pathologies of sovereignty are often equated with the command-and-control models associated with a formally authoritarian regime type (or, say, the more authoritarian institutional sides of a state),[24] as is the case with the lineage that runs through Hobbes, Schmitt, Arendt, Agamben, and Derrida. Yet, settler-colonial and other axes of racial, colonial, and gendered domination sharply attest to the notion that democratically constituted peoples can serve as—and define their own experience of citizenship as comprising—a form of collective self-sovereignty that is consistently conflated with and bound to sovereign domination over subjected others. That is, this sovereign (collective) subjectivity enacts itself through the incorporation and domination of racialized others, via coercive practices that are justified over time by representing those others as paradigmatically and naturally nonsovereign and unfree.

Democratic theorists are accustomed to the notion that "the people" subject *themselves* to laws that they author. Colonial sovereignty, however, creates this bounded space of authorship through the material realization of paradigmatic experiences of sovereignty that are forged through the subjection of racialized and gendered subjects, who are rendered nonsovereign or antisovereign. Indeed, a small army of political theorists have now shown how white supremacy and settler colonialism shaped modern conceptions of freedom in the West as expressed via liberalism, republicanism, and even more collectivizing conceptions of popular or democratic sovereignty, by perversely tying together *self-legislation* with *other-domination*. That is, "white freedom" or "settler freedom" has been enacted in various historical configurations on terms that presume the rightful capacity to exercise power and outright violence over subordinated and other-defined groups, including the coercive seizure of land and resources, racialized labor exploitation, and control of migration and mobility.[25]

Put in more institutional terms, the enactment of colonial sovereignty can accrue to technically nonstate and para-state actors such as relatively self-organized settler militias, the white lynch mob, the police, plantation owners, and other institutions whose rule is nevertheless upheld or ultimately vindicated by the state in helping to drive territorial expansionism and enforcing racial apartheid for the settler republic. As a result, whereas scholars of political development may find in settler-colonial peripheries a *lack* of (traditional Weberian) sovereignty in the form of weak state capacity,[26] my own approach analyzes the *concept* of sovereignty as a fungible symbolic and material claim that can inhere in the "sovereign people" and in the sovereign state alike (often, with each making a claim on the other). This inherence is made to "stick" through the continual invasion of nonsovereign or "quasi-sovereign" others, whose labor, land, and bodies are rendered terra nullius or otherwise available by right to settler sovereignty.

Put otherwise, the interplay between local self-rule and centralization both in governmental processes and the discursive construction of a white-settler demos (the latter bearing an expansionist prerogative in its own radical democratic capacities, its "constituent power") is not the undoing of sovereignty.[27] It is part of the *making* of sovereignty. Concretely, this is the colonial mobility of frontier violence, land grabs, and other modes of gendered colonial violence against Indigenous societies, which are both projected *outward* and folded *into* formal juridical and political institutions.[28] So, the very chaotic and disordered colonial extraterritoriality that is a theoretical hallmark of the kind of "problem" (typically, threat) that sovereignty is supposed to resolve in fact becomes systematically integrated into sovereignty's actual project of ordering space.

Sovereignty is a colonial process and concept. It is this deeply antirelational structure that is realized in this specific ensemble of practices of colonial sovereignty that the water protectors contested. Next, I turn to remapping sovereignty, earthmaking, and transnational internationalism as modes of decolonial self-determination that aim to structurally negate and transform sovereignty's colonial antirelationality.

Remapping Colonial Sovereignty

What are the aspirations of worldly anticolonial projects that articulate themselves against and for something other than this antirelational colonial sovereignty? What is the relationship between (de)colonization and sovereignty for anticolonial thinkers and movements who seek to counter and even transcend this seemingly intractable structure of settler-colonial domination?

To begin to answer these questions, I spell out two closely related political-theoretic interventions—two forms of remapping sovereignty. As I suggested of the NODAPL movement, there is really a twofold challenge proposed in the water protectors' articulation of alternatives to the modern Western conception of sovereignty: (1) the state's claim to sovereignty and (2) the conceptual entailments of sovereignty as a form of political rule expressed as absolute and independent mastery or domination over a bounded space. Stated otherwise: on the one hand, we can see NODAPL's practice of self-defense and reclamation as a struggle over *the terms of sov-*

ereignty; on the other, we can interpret the movement's deep philosophical underpinnings in claiming the responsibility to protect water as the source of life as a struggle over the *conceptual logics* of sovereignty.

To call this first axis a struggle over the *terms* of sovereignty is to highlight how the water protectors challenged who has and ought to have sovereignty over the land and water, in the face of state violence (blurring public-private lines, just like its nineteenth-century antecedents) that enforced the "criminalization of caretaking" (including the prosecution of water protectors under counterterrorism laws).[29] They did so by discursively claiming and physically embodying in their very presence a struggle *between* sovereigns over the terms of territory, jurisdiction, and ownership. Those practices affirm the prior and equal status of Indigenous societies to exercise sovereignty over their lands and resources. Through this affirmation, they countered ideologies of state and popular sovereignty that naturalize the successive rounds of colonial invasion on behalf of which, and through which, the settler state claims its own sovereignty over Indigenous nations.

By contrast, to interpret this as a struggle over the *conceptual logics* of sovereignty is to apprehend an altogether different source of conflict at stake in the same material practices of mobilization. Here, there is a contest over something more intangible but no less crucial: the very *idea* of sovereignty as a political form. Along these lines, the key questions are, Should political authority be organized around the moral and political grammar of territorialized sovereignty in the first place? If not, what alternative vistas of political community and planetary order do these struggles embody and prefigure in its stead?

To only begin to explain this axis of critique and the alternative horizon of anticolonial normativity it seeks to actualize, consider that the notion of Indigenous sovereignty (hereafter self-determination) *as a relation of care for land* stands in direct antagonism to the notion of sovereignty as a theoretically unlimited form of domination over the subdued and inert nonsovereignty of nature. In protecting Mní Oyate, water protectors articulated their goals as the enactment of self-rule through practices of kinship and care *with and for* water, which bluntly clashes with a logic of asserting their own sovereign rule or ultimate authority *over* water to do what they will. In sum, the conflict as interpreted along this axis is over the *very meaning and validity of sovereignty itself* as a colonial conceptual frame for political community, not just a disavowed dispute *between* sovereigns locked in a colonial relation of domination.

In laying out these two senses of institutional form and conceptual logics of sovereignty, I seek to account for and historically trace the ways that

Indigenous anticolonialisms bind structural critique to constructive projects of self-government. In the first of these senses, the framework of remapping sovereignty tracks those efforts to contest the unilateral authority and consolidation of the political powers vested in the sovereign state, by exposing how its coercive foundations are naturalized through the mythologies and narratives of—or made the site of racially violent attachments to[30]—state, citizenship, territory, and property.[31]

As a mode of critique and agency enacted in constructive political projects, remapping sovereignty poses the task of radically dismantling and redistributing those powers of self-government—and powers of social and ecological reproduction—that the colonial process seizes from Indigenous societies in effecting territorial dispossession. In this sense, remapping sovereignty means remaking social relations and stripping away powers from the state and its tributaries as the self-designated *locus* of authority, so as to forge alternative arrangements that (re)instate the powers of Indigenous societies to govern themselves.

The political problem that this approach casts into sharp relief is the profoundly hierarchical, racialized, and gendered *allocation* of sovereignty—not always the *concept* of sovereignty itself. Here, the alternative models in question focus on institutional and structural transformation aimed at securing collective and individual relations of nondomination to the sovereign state and practices of freedom collectively authored on Indigenous societies' own terms.

Normatively, this account suggests that what it means to disentangle collective self-determination from the sovereign state is to rethink self-determination as a project of *freedom from* the colonial domination of the sovereign state. Liberation and decolonization entail a right of self-determination that can be construed on analogy to the neorepublican model as freedom from the arbitrary power (domination) of the settler state.[32] Nondomination is necessary but not sufficient. What is called for are an array of structural and institutional transformations of the state and of the basic principles underlying a colonial and statist world order.

In turn, this also depends on overturning external practices of international recognition, which structurally reproduce and effectively "cosign" the state's sovereign powers as part of an international order of sovereign states that has been underwritten since World War II by US imperial hegemony. More positively articulated, remapping strategies propose an anticolonial reinterpretation of the international principle of the equality of peoples (or "sovereign equality"). In this paradigm of the criteria for Indigenous decolonization, the equality of peoples must be disambiguated from the notion of equality among sovereign states. This normative aspiration necessarily chips away at or even fully revokes the often-sacrosanct status attributed to territorialized sovereignty for nation-states (especially the most wealthy and powerful ones).

In this way, the territorially bounded sovereign state and the global order that authorizes de facto colonial states as the legitimate vessels of structurally arbitrary power *over* Indigenous societies is significantly disempowered—if not unseated—as the locus of collective democratic self-determination. The theoretical upshot here is that the colonial global order constructed out of states should be utterly remade to encompass far more pluralistic sub- and poststate systems of self-determination.

A second meaning of "remapping sovereignty" points instead to the idea of reconceiving the basic *philosophical* premises of self-determination. The political aim here is to organize sociality and political life so as to move beyond the *concept* of sovereignty. Put otherwise, the goal is to disentangle the notion of collective self-determination from some of the features that are internal to the actual *concept* of sovereignty. Whereas the first meaning of remapping focuses primarily on how sovereignty functions as a persistent rationale for domination effected through state institutions and their proxies, this paradigm brings into much sharper relief sovereignty's systemic erasure of alternative models of social organization. In this respect, this critique concerns the deep assumptions—at once normative, epistemological, and ontological—that are entangled with the functioning of modern political rule.

This focus on conceptual logics also extends such a critique beyond the realm of political institutions narrowly understood to the very idea of sovereignty as a discursive and in some ways always metaphorical grid through which to understand the subject as a self-willing, self-subsistent entity (the "sovereign subject")[33]—whether in the state or the modern notion of the individual. This latter conceptual insight should be related back to the first, more sociological and institutional framework, since it is precisely the status of citizens and the white social body as deputized agents of sovereign violence (i.e., petty sovereigns) and proprietorship that has been core to settler expansionism. While analytically separable, the circulation of meanings of sovereignty between dominant (self-)deputized white subject-citizens and the state is typically connected to circulations of the material apparatus and an imaginary right to violence. In this sense, when I refer to the very idea of sovereignty, it is important to insist that this abstract philosophical register has profound material effects in constituting the wider political culture of settler-colonial societies.

For Indigenous anticolonialisms as explored in this book, it is necessary to think through how their critiques targeted a material context that realizes the conceptual antirelationality of "sovereign subjects" in these specific forms. That is, even when not explicitly framed in the language of sovereignty, these articulations of domineering selfhood against Indigenous societies come to be named and analyzed for anticolonial purposes as problems of sovereignty.

Accordingly, it is no surprise that Indigenous anticolonial struggles waged against sovereignty are often suffused with political-ethical grammars that embody deeply relational notions of self-determination, which eschew or clash with efforts to reproduce or internalize sovereignty at any scale of social, ecological, and political power. Importantly, this kind of remapping practice is present—as is at stake in the NODAPL movement—in the very deep grammars *of the meanings of self-determination* articulated *through* Indigenous anticolonial critique and praxis.

For example, in chapter 2, I interpret Ella Deloria's writings to show how the worldview that is foundational to both popular and state sovereignty entails a deeply *antirelational* notion of self-determination. My interpretation of Ella Deloria's model of treaty as kinship-constituting practice of forging relational interdependence, by contrast, counters this antirelationality of colonial sovereignty. Namely, I try to show how Deloria's philosophical reconstruction of Dakota kinship relations makes the very building blocks of intra- and intercommunal relations—including those between humans and the earth—into *relations* among kin with reciprocal responsibilities.

The political-theoretic upshot of this claim is that anticolonial transformation enacts this resolutely relational grammar of kinship and aims to institutionalize its alternative normativity, in defiance of or eventually through the abolition of colonial sovereignty. This is a distinctively *anticolonial* construal of what it means to "go beyond" sovereignty.

Earthmaking

Earthmaking is a prominent *mode* of Indigenous anticolonial thought and agency that I theorize throughout this book. I use this framework to bring into relief the distinctiveness of the way that thinkers such as George Manuel and Lee Maracle remap the conceptual logics of sovereignty. As a prime illustration of remapping the conceptual logics of sovereignty (that is, the very *idea* of sovereignty), I develop the concept of *earthmaking* as a way of encapsulating core, distinctive dimensions of the constructive political projects of Indigenous anticolonial thought in North America.

Understood as a *response* to the specific form of settler-colonial domination, earthmaking is a project of self-determination articulated in counterpoint to settler-colonial conquest as a mode of *earth-destroying* violence. Namely, settler-colonial conquest operates by constituting colonial states and their social bodies that function as structurally arbitrary forms of political power that not only hierarchically dominate but also live off the parasitic invasion of the entire networks of Indigenous societies' ecological and social reproduction. Though the colonial process has many dimensions, the notion of *earth-destroying* violence specifically points to the ways that colonization necessitates intensely gendered violence both to humans and to the earth itself. In sum, earthmaking as a mode of anticolonial agency arises out of the aspiration to forge alternatives to sovereignty by way of a critique of these practices *as forms of* earth-destroying violence.

More positively framed, projects of earthmaking rest on the central contention that the telos (i.e., the substance and purpose) of anticolonial struggles for self-determination lies in the (re)creation of social and ecological relations of reciprocal care disentangled from the conceptual logics of sovereignty. How so? I derive the term earthmaking from the question in the epigraph posed by Winona LaDuke: "who has the right to make the earth anew, and how is it made so?" The concept of "earth" embodies the notion that human beings are themselves dependent on and enmeshed in an interconnected web of relationships at once ecological, social, spiritual, and political. In this understanding, the earth is made up of beings of diverse kinds endowed with intelligence and moral worth that include yet exceed human endeavors.

By earth*making*, then, I mean the theoretical concept that anticolonial critique and agency is articulated as the defense and fulfillment of both place-based and universal relations of care and responsibility that extend to relations with other-than-human beings. "Making" the earth entails the active pursuit of reciprocal responsibilities of care that mutually sustain both human and other-than-human beings, contrasted to the colonial sovereignty of a self-possessed collective endlessly fabricating its surrounding environmental conditions through extractive domination from subordinated human and other-than-human others. Relations of reciprocal care with the earth are worth struggling for because the "self" of self-determination can become a viable mode of collective agencies only by avowing interdependence on the very web of relations that enables human flourishing. In other world, self-rule is materially enmeshed in and unimaginable without care and interdependence with others with whom the "self" is in relation. In this sense, earthmaking affirms the realization of human freedom as interdependence (or as Marx would have it, "metabolism") with the land itself, which anthropocentric sovereign formations must continually deny in crafting ever-more perfected modes of territorial domination that disavow interdependence with the other-than-human.[34]

I also use the concept of earthmaking to propose an alternative to the model of anticolonialism that is currently prevalent in studies of anticolonial thought and the political theory of empire and imperialism more broadly. Whereas political theorists of empire and imperialism have focused on the relation between Western political ideologies (notably, but not exclusively, liberalism) and imperial practices,[35] my work joins recent scholars who have constructed a canon of anticolonial thought in and across multiple material and intellectual contexts. These discussions provide a reconstructive agenda to conceptualize what Karuna Mantena has described as internationalist "visions of anti-imperialism that explicitly sought ways to build models of solidarity and political modernity beyond the nation-state."[36]

Among these, Adom Getachew has influentially theorized the anticolonialism of the Black Atlantic as a *worldmaking* enterprise. This worldmaking framework counters standard accounts of anticolonial thought as confined to an uncritically statist nationalism and "nation-building" project. According to her narrative, anticolonial state builders fought for the principle of equality among states in concert with efforts to transform international institutions so as to reconfigure global imperial and racial hierarchies. More than simply authorizing postcolonial sovereign states in the sense of replacing colonial "alien rule" with national "native rule," the concept of worldmaking captures these expansive and structurally transformative aspirations to create "democratic, modernizing, and redistributive nation states situated in thick international institutions."[37]

In a productive resonance with and departure from the worldmaking frame, Indigenous earthmaking takes form as an alternative horizon of anticolonial normativity. Specifically, colonized peoples problematize colonial conquest as a form of earth-destroying violence to humans and the entire network of eco-social relations they both steward and depend upon. In so doing, earthmaking calls for the enactment of alternative agencies and normative substance that inhere in the meanings of self-determination and decolonization. In more institutional terms, as my discussions in chapters 2–4 especially show, a range of thinkers and organizations from the International Indian Treaty Council (IITC) to the World Council of Indigenous Peoples (WCIP) have conceptualized these models in direct relation to and in critical appreciation and contrast with the Third World model of the "developmental state" that secures a redistributive politics through sovereignty over its natural resources.

For example, chapter 3's discussion of the notion of a "stewardship world order" focuses on the alternative normative authorization of a nonanthropocentric model of self-determination that requires challenging if not delinking altogether from statist developmentalism. This agenda explicitly dethrones developmental state sovereignty, which functions even in putatively internationalist formations to secure a modernizing, typically monist compulsion toward eliminatory violence exercised against other solidarity-based modes of Indigenous, peasant, and otherwise subaltern sociopolitical and ecological organization. Projects of earthmaking call for a different way of constructing planetary order that is based on efforts to actualize Indigenous self-determination as one of the most promising conceptual frames for eliciting relational human–other-than-human networks of flourishing, alongside the reparative and structurally redistributive politics of Third World internationalism.

Earthmaking affirms the notion that self-determination is a project of fashioning individual and collective "selves" so as to manifest a respectful and mutually sustaining relationship to the other-than-human earth.[38] In this account, *all* modes of self-determination are in fact relational and rely on networks of interdependence with both human and other-than-human others. Built into the concept of sovereignty as the assertion of a self-contained space of political rule is the disavowal of this ultimately irrepressible reality. Earthmaking, then, directly acknowledges this inescapable relationality by incorporating it into the actual grammar of anticolonial struggles and the forms of sociality and institutions they seek to construct.

This notion of the substance of anticolonial struggle as earthmaking lends itself to a nonsovereign[39]—or, perhaps better, antisovereign—frame for political community and for the relations among political communities. Specifically, earthmaking as a decolonizing praxis actually enacts "the nation" or "the people" through the repair and liberation of the earth *itself* from colonial domination. So, to use the language of "national liberation," that is, the liberation of the colonized from the domination of colonial sovereignty, earthmaking enacts the liberation of those human and other-than-human animate beings to whom they owe reciprocal caretaking obligations and who are inescapable partners in social-ecological reproduction.

Understood as creating positive structures of freedom and responsibility *together* through the remaking of social relations and subjectivities, this model of decolonization as earthmaking depends on restoring active avenues of power and participation to colonized subjects. Positively stated, the resurgence of care-based responsibilities to both local and transnational ecological networks becomes a core expression of—and a prerequisite for—

the renewal of collective participatory freedoms, well-being, and the resurgent web of sociality to support it.

The theoretical upshot is that a core part of anticolonial struggles lies in (re)making (relations with) the earth. Understood as earthmaking practices, Indigenous anticolonialisms are political projects that seek to structurally transform domestic and international institutions, to create nonexploitative and reciprocity-oriented relationships between humans and the earth, on terms that sustain and rebuild Indigenous self-determination. That is, decolonization is glimpsed or actualized in efforts to reconstitute and reinvent these networks of freedom, self-defense, and subsistence/survival, whether they take "traditional" or "modern" forms.

Indigenous Internationalism as Transnational Internationalism

Another key through line of "remapping sovereignty" is my interpretation of a variety of projects of Indigenous internationalism under the theoretical rubric of what I call *transnational internationalism*. To be sure, it is not a new observation that Indigenous thinkers and movements have participated in internationalist networks. I place transnational and international together because current approaches seeking to break out of the shell of "methodological nationalism" do not quite grasp the often category-defying political-theoretic features of radical Indigenous internationalist critique.[40] Indigenous internationalism is category defying: it is both the work of distinctive nations meeting and coordinating with one another (internationalism) *and* the crossing of settler-state boundaries (whether internal or external) to do so (transnationalism). In short, understood as practices of internationalism creating new (or renewed) formative kinships and moving across both settler nation-states and dominant international institutions, twentieth-century Indigenous transnational internationalisms remapped sovereignty in aiming to recast the very "boundaries of the international."[41]

My contribution is to interpret these practices as part of remapping sovereignty because they reconfigure the very legitimacy of sovereignty itself as a moral and political grammar that organizes international politics, and, indeed, defines what counts as "international" as such. Sovereignty is a concept that simultaneously grants validity to the "internal" authority of the settler state and secures those "external" structures of representation *of* that colonial state vis-à-vis other sovereigns in international institutions.

Remapping sovereignty aims to reconfigure the structures *defining* self-rule in the global order. In that sense, Indigenous internationalism is a practical *embodied manifestation* and direct political challenge to the very *structures of representation* of those international institutions that co-constitute and secure the antirelational powers of the colonial sovereign state. This is all the more intensified in the case of the US, which as an imperial hegemon still very much has crafted and inherited a world order made in its own image.

My interpretation cuts against a focus among (mainly non-Indigenous) historians that theorizes "Indigenous internationalism" by narrating the participation of Indigenous societies in international institutions, such as the United Nations (UN) and before it the League of Nations. Here, "Indigenous internationalism" is folded into a more general conception of internationalisms as the movement *from* the internal space of the nation-state *to* the external space of international diplomacy.[42] While there is nothing inherently objectionable about this, this frame still misses something fundamental about these efforts, which is that at stake in Indigenous thinkers' theorizations and movements are attempts to refigure the basic, underlying authority relations built into dominant frameworks of internationalism.

When Indigenous projects of remapping sovereignty bring "decolonization" to an arena naturalized as domestic, they necessarily suspend the legitimacy of the settler state as the credited embodiment of collective self-determination in extant international institutions. Indigenous internationalisms sought to challenge sovereign statehood as the fundamental unit of recognizable political authority relations in the global order. What is more, these practices struggle for and enact a radical reinterpretation of the equality of peoples as entailing a right of self-determination for colonized peoples who do not normatively want, or are not in a position to institutionally claim, a state. As a result, my concern is that assimilating these practices to standard accounts of internationalism may reify the very authority relations, borders, and so on that Indigenous internationalisms *call into question* in their critique and enacted practices of self-determination—including challenges to what entities and relations even make up "the international" as such.[43]

In making this argument, I build especially on work in Indigenous studies on internationalisms, by identifying how such internationalisms reconfigure sovereignty. Specifically, Indigenous studies scholars Joseph Bauerkemper and Heidi Kiiwetinepinesiik Stark, Nick Estes, Leanne Betasamosake Simpson, Glen Coulthard, and Mishuna Goeman have produced a more robust and compelling engagement with the generative relations between place-based political formations and the international and transnational mobility and expressivity of Indigenous anticolonial agencies and solidarities within and between different communities.[44]

Especially in my interpretations of projects of "Fourth Worldism" through the writings of George Manuel (chapter 3) and revolutionary solidarities between Indigenous societies and other national liberation movements through Lee Maracle and Howard Adams (chapter 4), I build on and contribute to these more recent interventions—and to the study of "colonial internationalisms" more broadly[45]—by focusing on two ways that twentieth-century Indigenous transnational internationalisms defied sovereign statehood as the fundamental unit of legitimate authority relations in the global order: they *manifest* and *make* Indigenous self-determination in relational networks that disclose disavowed authority relations, and they struggle for the realization of alternative principles that radically decenter sovereignty in the current and future structure of the hegemonic planetary and world order.

The two elements I sketch are nicely captured in distinguished Chickasaw legal scholar James (Sa'ke'j) Youngblood Henderson's account of the impetus behind the international Indigenous rights movements: "The diplomatic network was a manifestation of continued resistance to colonization, and it combined the efforts that had been going on in isolation for generations.... We needed to extend our kinship and relationships."[46]

The first of these elements is crystallized in what Henderson refers to as extended kinship and is signaled, moreover, in his use of the language of "manifestation." In essence, Indigenous internationalisms actually *manifest* other-than-sovereign forms of authoritative social coordination in the actual practice of establishing these diplomatic connections, here via the frames of kinship and relationships. In slightly different terms, they *generate* those other authority relations in their often criminalized or otherwise socially unexpected movement and cooperation across space.[47] These enactments bring into being (or bring back) an alternative set of authoritative international spaces, including those nonanthropocentric kinship and covenant-based relations with other-than-human "nations."[48]

By far the bulk of existing literatures in international law focus on the important strategic and legal dimensions of securing a slate of internationally recognized Indigenous rights through what some international relations scholars have called "transnational advocacy networks."[49] What is instead at stake in looking to the theorists I examine is how they interpret these relational networks as themselves a *disclosive disruption to* settler sovereignty, not just political organizing strategies aimed at instrumentally securing recognition of greater rights (though, of course, they are that, too). In brief, it is through these alternative forms of intersocietal relation and coordination that Indigenous self-determination as a relational practice is positively made and extended (and, thus, remade).⁵⁰

The second dimension of transnational internationalism is the positive effort to reconfigure the moral and political grammar of sovereignty, which revokes sovereignty's status as that which *grants* degrees of recognized authority to heretofore nonsovereign populations. That is, in insisting on a history replete with "continued resistance to colonization," Henderson replaces a narrative focusing on the movement from so-called domestic to so-called international with a narrative that, instead, insists upon the continued self-determining authorities of Indigenous societies. Such resistance manifests a consistent refusal of these divisions of sovereignty in the first place. In this sense, the paradigm of internationalism ought to account for the many historical and present-day Indigenous networks—confederacies, migrations, spaces of urban kinship—that have subtended the dominant "international order" as subjugated/erased but lived forms of internationalism. This formulation, then, challenges presumptions about the very scale and meaning of internationalism, which Indigenous societies have pressed since the onset of colonial invasion.

In this way, Indigenous internationalism ought not to be conceptualized as the "granting" of recognition to Indigenous societies, but rather as the radical transformation of the normative and material foundations of the planetary order so as to allow for the further flourishing of these erased "traditional" and new governing systems and covenant-based accords among polities. As I contend in my reconstruction of Zitkala-Ša's writings in chapter 1, attention to sovereignty as morally arbitrary but structurally pernicious colonial artifice erasing both Indigenous rights and (the potential for) relations among Indigenous peoples and with other colonized and racialized subjects dates back to the Wilsonian counterrevolution against more structurally transformative mobilizations around the politics of self-determination. In sum, by proposing the notion that Indigenous anticolonial internationalism ought to be apprehended as transnational internationalism, I underscore those distinctive practices that reconfigure the legitimacy of the sovereign state as the spatial container for politics and the proper end-goal of and for anticolonial struggles.⁵¹

Chapter Overview

I develop these core theoretical concepts primarily through close readings in which I pair thinkers together in each chapter (with the exception of chapter 3, which focuses solely on George Manuel). Rather than a solely critical-theoretic focus that aims to specify the workings of settler-colonial power relations, I instead adopt an approach that focuses on the back and forth in these thinkers between their philosophical practice of "critique" of those structured patterns of domination that take hold in colonial sovereignty and alternative sources of constructive politics and normative imagination. As such, my approach necessitates a rich engagement with the actual historical nuances of political vocabularies, deeply constitutive contexts, social policies and law, and other material practices.

More specific to my archive, any conceptual historical approach to "Indigenous" thought must be sufficiently alive to its irreducible pluralism as a field that is actually composed of a multinational multiplicity of ideas, ideologies, and expressive forms. Indigenous studies already offers a plethora of examples and "decolonizing methodologies" for engaging deeply and ethically with many strands of Indigenous thought across geographies, including those that are transmitted (less textually) in the context of embodied and land-based knowledge production.[52] By contrast, especially non-Indigenous political theorists' way of studying Indigenous politics has often taken the limiting (and at the extreme, objectifying) form of casting Indigenous peoples as a kind of "test case" through which to evaluate concepts such as "recognition," "Indigenous rights," and so on.[53]

I take issue with the general tendency to represent Indigenous societies or thinkers in wooden form as "cases" rather than full-fledged human beings negotiating the *doing* of decolonizing praxis. So, my aim is to reconstruct these intellectual-historical threads with the kind of depth and nuance that befits an irreducibly plural field of intergenerational thought. To pursue this aim, I build out in my analysis layers of context through which to interpret key thinkers and conceptual frameworks. The result is that I attend to different scales and sites of Indigenous theorizing (tribal-national, regional, pan-Indigenous), as well as efforts to comparatively incorporate and reshape other political-ideological frameworks (e.g., US liberalism, the Black radical tradition, etc.) as these engagements shift across thinkers.

In building out these layers of context, one of my aims is more straightforwardly historical: namely, to reconstruct some of the key (e.g., Vine Deloria Jr.) and lesser-known (e.g., Ella Deloria) thinkers, intellectual frameworks, and formative political experiences from Indigenous societies in North America as the sources of independently valuable strands of anticolonial political thought that braid together a plural fabric of approaches to political modernity. My methodological focus nevertheless also seeks to produce insights into the histories of concepts that have since become core to contemporary Indigenous critique and mobilization, including self-determination, decolonization, resurgence, and kinship.

Interweaving the primary theoretical interventions (remapping colonial sovereignty, earthmaking, and transnational internationalism), each chapter discusses a core concept that is implicated in the overarching "metaproblem" of sovereignty: citizenship, treaty, land, and capitalism.

Chapter 1, "Indigenous Self-Determination against Political Slavery," draws on the writings of Zitkala-Ša (Yankton Dakota) and the prominent scholar-activist Vine Deloria Jr. (Yankton Dakota) to show how they fashioned constructive visions of anticolonial self-determination, against the colonialism of US sovereignty and "civic inclusion." I interpret their conception of self-determination as the realization of collective structures of freedom *from* the settler state's recursive iterations of colonial violence. Specifically, I illustrate how the politics of Indigenous self-determination countered US civic practices of incorporation that have served historically as instruments of further colonization and racial hierarchy. By tracing Zitkala-Ša's analysis of colonial wardship, I reconstruct her and other Progressive Era Indigenous thinkers' account of "political slavery," or colonial domination through war, territorial dispossession, collective punishment, and reserve-based incarceration of Indigenous societies. Turning then to Vine Deloria Jr.'s part in the struggle against the "termination" of tribes in the 1950s and 1960s, I show how he contested the colonial weaponization of the "civic" in line with newer conceptions of civil rights and integration that continued to facilitate territorial dispossession.

By starting with the moment when "self-determination" gained traction after World War I as an organizing frame for US and global politics, I argue that these two thinkers offer an anticolonial conception of self-determination and the equality of peoples against an imperial and (settler-)statist world order. Whereas both thinkers figured incorporation into US citizenship as irreparably colonial, they nevertheless treated it as a kind of pragmatic constitutional tool that could prevent extreme forms of domination ("citizenship without civilization"). In opposing these dominant discourses and governance practices, they negated the colonial denial of the equality of peoples as a structure of domination that functioned through the very artifice of colonial sovereignty and its internal/external borders. To advance a critical-normative reading of dominant models of sovereignty and citizenship in US and international political thought, I also illustrate the deep contexts of how these Yankton Dakota thinkers reworked predominant liberal and republican US political-ideological frameworks in an anticolonial key, such as abolitionism and, of course, citizenship itself.

Whereas chapter 1 lays out a negative conception of self-determination as freedom *from* settler domination, chapter 2 advances a positive account of self-determination as the creation of self-other (including collective international) relations against and beyond sovereignty. Entitled "The Struggle for Treaty," this chapter turns to the ethnographic writings of Ella Deloria (Vine's brilliant aunt) and, again, to Vine Deloria Jr. By attending to the historically variable meanings of the concept of "treaty" in settler-colonial formations, I interpret these thinkers as constructing from Lakota-Dakota lineages an anticolonial conception of treaty. Treaties represent a political struggle to establish interdependent relations among peoples as "relatives." As such, I read Ella Deloria as a theorist of the treaty as an earth-making practice that binds together human and other-than-human groups in networks of reciprocal responsibility. This struggle points toward a non-sovereign universalism, one that construes "self-determination" as the establishment of reciprocal relations with kin ("becoming a good relative")—kin rendered integral to and interdependent with the collective self.

If Ella Deloria's model envisions an alternative social ordering practice that eschews the *conceptual logics* of sovereignty, Vine Deloria Jr. re-internationalized state-Indigenous treaties as a counter to the domesticating *ideologies and institutions* of colonial sovereignty. For Vine Deloria Jr., treaties were political and juridical instruments to claw back limited rights and self-determination from a settler state. Altogether, these Lakota-Dakota treaty-making imaginaries transfigure the canonical Western basis of social order and disorder, by displacing the Hobbesian problem of (in)security generated by the absence of sovereignty for the dystopic consequences that result from a colonial modernity unmade of kinship. As intellectual history, this chapter also demonstrates the frequently overlooked significance of treaties in Indigenous transnational internationalisms.

Chapter 3, "'The Land Is Our Culture,'" reconstructs the roots of the notion of Indigenous *resurgence*, through a contextual analysis of the writings and activism of George Manuel (Secwépmec). I explicate land as a political concept countering Canadian "White Paper multiculturalism" in Manuel's organizing with the National Indian Brotherhood (NIB; later, Assembly of First Nations) and for a transnational project of a "Fourth World" of Indigenous societies around the globe. In doing so, I interpret Indigenous resurgence as a way of generating political-philosophical alternatives to the connected notions of territorialized sovereignty and property as institutionalized expressions of human mastery over land as an inert bundle of natural resources.

My analysis in this chapter draws from Manuel to theorize the colonial expropriation of land as *abduction*, or the structural erasure of the collective participatory capacities of the colonized to (re)engage in earthmaking practices between human and other-than-human relatives. Projects of Indigenous resurgence counter abduction with the aim to institutionalize nonexploitative relations with land and among humans. Moreover, I characterize Manuel's "Fourth World" as a project of transnational internationalism calling for a "stewardship world order," an order that normatively authorizes plural forms of nonanthropocentric self-determination. Fourth Worldism de-authorizes territorial sovereignty, through dialogue with and divergence from "Third Worldism" (African socialism specifically). This chapter also moves from an account of colonialism in US political thought to colonialism in Canadian political thought.

Shifting gears to another form of transnational internationalism, chapter 4 explores how Indigenous Marxists have pursued anticolonial critique by attending to the complex intersections between colonialism and capitalism. In "Indigenous Marxisms," I turn to the writings and radical organizing of scholar Howard Adams (Métis) and award-winning fiction writer and poet Lee Maracle (Stó:lō) to illustrate their structural analyses of *heteropatriarchal colonial-racial capitalism*—accounts animated through deep commitments to revolutionary anticolonial (inter)national liberation. Together, they elicit a praxis of solidarity dedicated to kinship across borders between national liberation struggles, against the antirelational counterinsurgency logics of colonial sovereignty.

Though they developed such frameworks in a shared ideological milieu, I argue that the critical and normative foundations of their accounts of remapping sovereignty diverge. Adams's Marxism focuses on the progressive democratic possibilities of Indigenous self-determination within struggles against capitalism, settler colonialism, and white supremacy. By contrast, at the center of Maracle's account are projects of *gendering decolonization and self-determination*, which hinge on an analysis of the *patriarchal settler state* and enjoin a transnational commitment to the liberation of Indigenous women alongside global feminist anticolonial struggles. For Maracle, anticolonial Marxisms helped to analyze capitalism's role in materializing colonial dispossession, which ought to be struggled against by asserting a permanent mode of Indigenous self-determination based on the recovery of what I call *subjugated responsibilities* to land and community.

[CHAPTER ONE]

Indigenous Self-Determination against Political Slavery

Zitkala-Ša and Vine Deloria Jr. on the Colonialism of US Sovereignty and Citizenship

> Someone should write an *Uncle Tom's Cabin* for the Aborigine. Every Indian Agent is a "Legre" the slave killer. The task would be too difficult for an Indian. The perspective entirely too close. I can hardly write a few pages of a report on conditions in one agency, without being nearly consumed with indignation and holy wrath.
>
> Zitkala-Ša[1]

> The Indian is legally bound and gagged.
>
> Zitkala-Ša[2]

In an address delivered before the US Senate Committee on Indian Affairs on September 9, 1919, Crow lawyer Robert Yellowtail declared that the "American Indian" is "still held in bondage as a political slave."[3] Yellowtail glossed US president Woodrow Wilson's refrain in his League of Nations promotional tour that "the right of self-determination not be denied to any people, no matter where they live."[4] Yellowtail then provocatively imagined a proviso for the league charter more accurately capturing Wilson's position:

> That in no case shall this be construed to mean that the Indians of the United States shall be entitled to the rights and privileges herein, or the right of self-determination . . . but that their freedom and future shall be left subject to such rules and regulations as the Secretary of the Interior may in his discretion prescribe.[5]

Wilson interpreted the principle of self-determination to shore up global racial hierarchies resulting from the imperial expansionism of Western nations.⁶ The League of Nations mandate system followed Wilson in embracing this tutelary model. Such a model deferred collective self-rule for colonized peoples, by claiming they needed further guidance from their imperial rulers to prepare for self-government under Article 22. As part of this white supremacist package, Wilson portrayed Indigenous societies as vanishing primitives. Indigenous peoples were not deferred subjects of collective self-determination but, rather, wards of the state. As such, they remained subordinated to the discretionary supervision of the US Department of the Interior, until assimilated as *individual* citizens into American society.⁷ In the meantime, evaluations that pegged the citizenship and property rights of Indigenous men to "competence" were justified as a temporary way station on the road to their assimilation as citizens into the US nation-state.⁸

Yellowtail's address provides a window into two central arguments this chapter sets out in greater depth. First, I highlight the central role that republican frameworks of slavery, abolition, and domination played in Indigenous intellectuals' efforts to critique and create alternatives to US colonial practices of sovereignty, dispossession, and predatory civic inclusion. Second, I show how Indigenous intellectuals translated the principle of the equality of peoples into self-determination as freedom *from* the sovereign state, through constructive visions of nondomination, reparation, and international recognition of and for Indigenous societies.

Progressive Era Indigenous intellectuals did so through engagement with the rise of international self-determination talk with World War I and in reshaping the idioms and institutional practices of US republicanism and constitutional law. In the course of doing so, I argue that they laid the groundwork for a concept of anticolonial self-determination as freedom from the colonial sovereign state, which meant remapping institutional and structural orders both inside and outside the state. This work to forge an alternative to Wilson's counterrevolutionary project of colonial white supremacist self-determination set the stage for the more well-known post-1968 era identified with the Red Power movement and the globalization of Indigenous movements.

To develop these arguments, this chapter connects the writings of two Ihanktonwan (Yankton Dakota) activist-thinkers, Zitkala-Ša (1876–1938) and Vine Deloria Jr. (1933–2005). Each thinker understood Indigenous collective and individual freedoms from the sovereign state as territorially specific and historically situated, as they imagined the meaning of freedom against domination arising from entrenched axes of colonial violence and racial hierarchy that the settler state imposed on Indigenous societies.

At different moments, they challenged dominant US settler narratives of progress and citizenship, predicated on the erasure and/or incorporation of Indigenous polities into the nation-state as colonized, dispossessed, and racially subordinated populations. Against standard liberal narratives of the expansion of US citizenship in linear time, what I call the civic inclusion narrative, I historicize the tensions between projects of Indigenous self-determination and US colonial citizenship so as to denaturalize and remap colonial sovereignty.

The argument of the chapter proceeds as follows: First, I outline the civic inclusion narrative, a dominant narrative of US nation-building framing the incorporation of Indigenous peoples into the settler state *as* emancipatory. Second, I interpret Zitkala-Ša as a key critic of this narrative, by placing her in the context of a range of Indigenous intellectuals who analyzed the gendered colonial violence of wardship and hierarchical incorporation into US citizenship as "political slavery." She eventually turned more decisively to languages of self-determination and sovereignty drawn both from earlier Indigenous histories and the ongoing mobilization of "small and subject peoples" at the League of Nations. The second half of the chapter moves ahead in time, turning to Vine Deloria Jr. and his interlocutors of the 1950s and 1960s to argue that these same idioms of slavery and emancipation took on an important but opposite valence in the politics of Indigenous *termination* of the 1950s and 1960s. Deloria contested the symbolically ingrained political-cultural sensibilities that fed into the civic inclusion narrative, long after the moment of actual legal debate about formal Indian citizenship. Deloria tied this project in contested ways to anti-imperialism, in defense of specific rights of tribal sovereignty and self-determination. In sum, these thinkers compose part of a relatively occluded axis of political theories of Indigenous decolonization that recast the meaning and scope of self-determination as remedial action, rights, and protection against the expansionary settler state, which calls for transforming international and domestic law and politics together.

Settler Colonialism and US Citizenship

In the American liberal tradition, inclusion into citizenship has long been associated with the expansion of a package of rights and legitimate duties. Typically, this dominant tradition bears witness to the gradual extension of civic ideals, even when attending specifically to contexts of colonial and racial domination. To contextualize Zitkala-Ša and her Progressive Era interlocutors, it is necessary to first begin by reconstructing the dominant settler ideologies and juridical structures that they sought to transform, and then to connect these to the lasting disavowal of the colonial implications of progress and citizenship talk across the spectrum of US-based political theory.

In the late nineteenth century, American statesmen like Theodore Roosevelt regarded the United States as part of an "imperial family of settler-societies" (including Canada, Australia, New Zealand, and South Africa) whose basic goals were twofold: to furnish white settlers with "self-government and economic independence" and to "extract much-needed land and labor from native and non-settler groups."[9] Citizenship had been briefly extended to the formerly enslaved under the Fourteenth Amendment and the Civil Rights Act of 1866—which excluded "Indians not taxed"—then pushed back with the lynch mob and Jim Crow.[10] The US waged Indian wars that intensified after the Civil War and incarcerated Indigenous peoples on reservations. With the US bringing a unilateral end to the treaty system in 1872, Indigenous peoples constituted a captive and confined population whose remaining lands were slowly "allotted" (i.e., privatized, with "surplus" land sold off to settlers) under the Dawes Severalty Act of 1887 and subsequent amendments—a process that facilitated the dispossession of ninety million acres of land.[11]

Excluding Indigenous peoples from the model of birthright citizenship by classifying them as domesticated-yet-foreign nations in *Elk v. Wilkins* (1884) and *United States v. Wong Kim Ark* (1898), the US crafted a juridical philosophy of "wardship" in cases such as *Ex Parte Crow Dog* (1883), *US v. Kagama* (1886), and *Lone Wolf v. Hitchcock* (1903). The system of wardship subjected Indigenous peoples to a mode of unilateral rule mediated by the Indian agent as a discretionary authority over those confined to reservation life.[12] Colonial conquest exercised upon external enemies became internalized through an authoritarian system conceptualized as a benevolent practice of assimilation into citizenship—with the latter construed as "naturalization" of foreigners despite the pre-US histories of Indigenous peoples. As "wards of the state," Indigenous peoples constituted a "dependent" population to be protected until such time as they were eliminated as separate collective entities from the polity by becoming "civilized."

Theodore Roosevelt crystallized dominant understandings of citizenship as they related to Indigenous peoples. For Roosevelt, wardship was a necessary prerequisite *to* citizenship as part of the assimilation process, not a self-evident negation of the egalitarian underpinnings of liberal-democratic citizenship. Concerned with what he perceived to be a rising tide of anti-imperial resistance, Roosevelt insisted that "English-speaking peoples" continue to govern "the world's waste spaces."[13] He embraced the reservation system as a continuation of an assimilation process and the grounds for the eventual elimination of the Indian from the territorial and metaphorical space of sovereignty. But confronted with Indigenous peoples (much like those he qualified as other "lesser" races), Roosevelt maintained a skeptical view of the capacities of Indians to "move forward."[14] Polemically inveighing against the American Anti-Imperialist League in his "Strenuous Life" speech in 1899, Roosevelt insisted on the absurdity of opposition to imperialism in the Philippines when seen from the perspective of the civilizing alchemy of Indian policy. These "doctrines," he argued,

> would make it incumbent upon us to leave the Apaches of Arizona to work out their own salvation, and to decline to interfere in a single Indian reservation. Their doctrines condemn your forefathers and mine for ever having settled in these United States.[15]

Wedded to the possibility of assimilation in the case of Native peoples as the means of the expropriation of collective, tribal lands, such a project was explicitly premised on the "salvation" of inferior wards via their gradual progress to a higher stage of civilization. More than a legal status, "citizenship" was held out as the telos by which subjects took on the attributes of civilization, which included the ownership of private property (thereby forgoing collective lands), heteropatriarchy, and Western-style industrial education.

Here, it is crucial to recognize that citizenship and wardship were not seen as antithetical in this dominant discourse. Instead, for settler elites it was wardship that protected Indigenous rights when properly implemented with the expectation of eventual citizenship. Unlike Roosevelt, prominent white reform groups such as the Indian Rights Association, "friends of the Indian," criticized the reservation system and targeted the widespread corruption of Indian agents as mediators of a massive process of dispossession. Yet they contested the inefficient or corrupt *implementation* of wardship, not the injustice of wardship itself. They criticized greedy Indian agents as an affront to the proper exercise of guardianship and an impediment, therefore, to the advance of Indians as responsible economic holders of fee-simple property.[16] In this way, they typically refrained from attacking the inherently arbitrary power exercised through wardship as a structure of domination core to colonial sovereignty.

The idea that wardship and citizenship could be complementary statuses was reaffirmed in the 1916 Supreme Court case *US v. Nice*. The decision found that "citizenship is not incompatible with tribal existence or continued guardianship, and so may be conferred without completely emancipating the Indians or placing them beyond the reach of congressional regulations adopted for their protection." Note that, here, "tribal existence or continued guardianship" were considered mutually reinforcing statuses, such that tribal existence—especially the holding of land-in-common—was a marker of lack of full personhood in need of continued subjection. To be sure, Indigenous activists at this moment and later insisted that "tribal existence" meant the legitimacy of a differentiated national citizenship on an equally modern plane of political existence to that of any other national citizenship.[17] Yet, the dominant actors portrayed "tribal existence" as civilizational inferiority. Referring to *US v. Nice* in 1924, the white-led Indian Rights Association approvingly summarized the decision in asserting "guardianship" (i.e., wardship) as a *guarantor* of the "rights of any Indian to tribal property." In short, they noted favorably, US citizenship was "not incompatible with wardship."[18]

The Indian Citizenship Act of 1924 (ICA) is often categorized alongside other steps in the country's long march toward greater inclusion and civil rights. This is misleading at best: Unlike, say, the Voting Rights Act, the ICA was passed unilaterally. It was heavily disputed among Indigenous activists from different nations and not much known among the vast majority (nor did it make political suffrage immediately available).[19] Moreover, it was codified in a way that made unilateral American citizenship for the 125,000 covered by the law *compatible* with their treatment as wards of the state.

This dominant set of authoritarian governance practices in the early twentieth century is downplayed across many standard accounts of US citizenship. Canonical American liberal narratives treat citizenship as a gradual struggle for inclusion by disavowing the way that wardship and citizenship were conceptually integrated as stages in a temporal process of uncivilized subjects ascending to the norms of civilization. These narratives thereby reinterpret injustice as solely a matter of exclusion from citizenship. In recent work, Aziz Rana emphasizes the post–World War II emergence of a conception of creedal nationalism reconfiguring American power for a world where conquest by land was viewed as increasingly costly.[20] Whereas the American Creed is an *ontological* claim about the exceptional nature of the American polity as a civic one, the civic inclusion narrative adds a redemptive interpretation of historical temporality. By the civic inclusion narrative, I mean a narrative of US political and constitutional development that comprehends attempts to contest settler colonization and other forms of racial and colonial domination primarily as contributions to an already fixed national democratic project of progressively realized founding ideals.

By positing injustice as a failure of inclusion within the terms of "American universalism," the civic inclusion narrative describes a *telos* of steady progress toward the eventual inclusion of formerly excluded subjects.[21] Instances of such exclusion will emerge redeemed through ultimate adherence to such ideals, promising a steady, linear progress toward this realization. Thus, it frames the source of (former) oppression as *exclusion from* the dominant modes of civic identity, economic opportunity, and fair treatment before the law for which citizenship stands in rather than the domination of colonized and racialized subjects (which might, nevertheless, entail certain specific forms of exclusion) that persists into the present.

To be sure, successive generations of political theorists have rejected complacent progress narratives in favor of analyses attentive to similarly entrenched forms of domination. Yet the civic inclusion narrative continues to haunt American political thought, deflecting critics away from analytic resources and alternative political practices that confront colonial injustice in more direct terms. Though refusing the narrative's teleological impetus and amnesiac qualities, for example, Judith Shklar posits inclusion/exclusion as the central frame through which to interpret the political struggles of marginalized subjects. Shklar interprets citizenship as a form of "social standing" emblematized by two central sociopolitical practices linked to the extension of civil rights: voting and earning.[22] For Shklar, Black chattel slavery defined full citizenship because the value of full citizenship was "derived primarily from its denial to slaves, to some white men, and to all women."[23] While more forthrightly depicting the way the legacies of slavery have haunted US political debates than Gunnar Myrdal's creedal logic would allow, Shklar still interprets the political experiences of marginalized subjects as a quest for inclusion primarily affixed to the language of civil rights.

In his influential account of visions of citizenship in US history, Rogers Smith rejects the civic inclusion narrative's linear account of progress for a more sophisticated narrative that recognizes the possibility of both progress and regress and the ways in which racially emancipatory movements face conservative backlash. Smith retains the focus on inclusion but parses the narrative of American political thought as one of multiple traditions with liberal and democratic-republican threads arrayed against "inegalitarian ascriptive" ones.[24] By casting "egalitarian" and "ascriptive" currents as contradictory threads, Smith implies that the ideological sources of domination reside primarily in this ascriptive track. In other words, Smith's work tends to suggest that it is theories organized around racial hierarchy that promote colonial regimes. When egalitarian currents (democracy, civil rights, etc.) gain the upper hand, Smith then allows that racial domination will emerge transfigured—if only temporarily.[25]

The civic inclusion narrative, therefore, tends to demand that challenges to injustices fall within the terms of inclusion/exclusion. To resolve "past" injustice, the polity must further extend this universal embodied in the achievement of citizenship to excluded others. By obscuring how formative practices of extraction, dispossession, and colonization have been to shaping the US and other settler nation-states—ironically revealed in Roosevelt's own worries about the anticolonial entailments of anti-imperial critique—the civic inclusion narrative makes it peculiarly difficult to formulate a political project that challenges what Vine Deloria Jr. called the "integrationist-individualist" frame underpinning US citizenship.[26]

Moreover, because they come out in the historical wash, histories of injustice emerge less as occasions to doubt the coherence of the narrative than aberrational moments functioning as markers on an upward path of progressive social change. Rather than emerging as a structural dynamic closely wedded to ongoing state formation that doubles for Indigenous peoples as empire formation, practices of dispossession and military conquest become coded as remote, singular, (even) fundamentally alien instances of past misjudgment and/or—in the case of the Bureau of Indian Affairs (BIA)—bureaucratic mismanagement. Rather than a latent universal applied to practices more expansively over time, the concept of citizenship must be thoroughly analyzed against the differentiated paths and purposes to which it has actually been put in settler-colonial contexts to disavow and to crush Indigenous self-determination.

To be sure, Shklar, Smith, and others seeking to refashion accounts of American political thought harshly criticize the triumphalist complacency born of the civic inclusion narrative's Cold War emergence. Yet such a thread continues to tell a story about the incorporation of previously excluded groups into the nation-state by framing those struggles primarily in terms of the harms of exclusion from citizenship. In this chapter, I argue that turning instead to an anticolonial analysis of specific tensions and dilemmas of colonizing citizenship through Zitkala-Ša and Deloria presents a contrary framework aligned with constructive projects of remapping colonial sovereignty. Attuned to the double-edged results of logics of incorporation into citizenship for collective projects of self-determination, Zitkala-Ša sought to create political structures fostering collective Indigenous self-determination, as a counter to the dominant politics comprehending US citizenship as the stadial ascension of the backward "Indian" from (and through) wardship.

Wardship as Political Slavery

Gertrude Simmons Bonnin, who took on the Nakota name Zitkala-Ša (Red Bird), was an astonishingly gifted person. She was a prominent author of stories, prose, and pamphlets; an organizer and activist; lecturer; violinist; opera composer; actor-performer; member of the Society of American Indians (SAI) and editor of its *American Indian Magazine* in 1919; and later founder in 1926 of the National Council of American Indians (distinct from the National *Congress* of American Indians, discussed later). Here, I focus primarily on her writings and advocacy of the 1910s and 1920s, during which time she navigated a near-impossible terrain of representational politics to theorize the rights of Indigenous peoples to self-defense and self-determination.

As a result of her sometimes exuberantly patriotic rhetoric representing Indigenous peoples as loyal Americans during World War I, Zitkala-Ša is sometimes read as acceding to the aims of colonial conquest by embracing "assimilation." Such an interpretive position is also bolstered by her seemingly moderate and pragmatic avowal of US citizenship and her taking the side of opposition to the syncretic pan-Indian religion of Peyotism (along with her fellow Christian convert Charles Eastman).[27] Such a stance, however, misses how she sought to transform the dominant colonial practices of citizenship. Moreover, it conflates her political stagecraft in some of her public lectures—she appeared with countless American flags in the backdrop—with her own deeply considered political views.

As an alternative to this "assimilationist" interpretation, I contend that Zitkala-Ša has to be understood in the context of the then-dominant relationship between wardship and citizenship. To put my argument in compressed fashion, she sought to make US citizenship newly *in*compatible with wardship and newly compatible with collective Indigenous self-determination. Zitkala-Ša's critique and constructive vision lies, then, in her significant efforts to refigure (colonial) citizenship as one among other collective organizational weapons to secure equal constitutional protection, remedial justice, and self-determination for Indigenous societies. As Tsianina Lomawaima and Phillip J. Deloria have argued, Zitkala-Ša and some of her SAI contemporaries sought to realize institutions promoting the "mutuality of [US] citizenship and [Indigenous] sovereignty" to transform the colonial domination of wardship.[28]

In this way, Zitkala-Ša posed citizenship *against* wardship, a stance that actively contested the dominant view of citizenship as a *culmination* of wardship. For Zitkala-Ša and other key Indigenous activists at the turn of twentieth century, the stadial notion that citizenship meant acquiring the trappings of "civilization" served two colonizing purposes: First, the colonialism of US citizenship negated the very possibility of moving an emerging international principle of self-determination across colonial borders to apply to Indigenous peoples. By posing an impossible "choice" between extermination and assimilation (both genocidal), the assimilation process ruled out the possibility of Indigenous peoples publicly negotiating the question of US citizenship *as* collectives. Put more sharply, it made it practically difficult to refuse US citizenship outright as a colonial imposition. Second, the notion of citizenship as a stadial, civilizational achievement made normative a beleaguered citizenship, crafted so as to enforce the prevailing racial hierarchies and continued Indigenous dispossession in US society. On both sides of the coin, these dominant practices inherited the long nineteenth century of US territorial expansionism and Indigenous dispossession.

At the center of the Progressive Era debates Zitkala-Ša intervened in was the question of how to contest the politics of wardship. Before and after the ICA, Zitkala-Ša clearly identified wardship as a mode of domination that placed Indigenous peoples under the arbitrary power of the Indian bureau within the Department of the Interior. She countered wardship and reimagined citizenship as a form of rights-based self-defense and a weapon that could be used in the service of collective, Indigenous self-determination. In order to further consider the differing approaches to citizenship among Indigenous peoples in the 1910s and 1920s, it is important to situate Zitkala-Ša alongside her fellow members of the SAI—the first twentieth-century pan-Indian organization in the United States.[29] When Zitkala-Ša wrote that "the Indian is legally bound and gagged" in 1924, she was theorizing the condition of wardship within a reservation as a legalized form of collective incarceration that enacted a point-by-point negation of individual constitutional freedoms such as those of speech, religion, and movement, sutured to a collective form of oppression. She aimed to recast citizenship, by contrast, as a mechanism of political activity enabling mobilization to ensure collective self-defense and democratic Indigenous self-government *against* collective bondage and punishment "of orderly people kept prisoners"—"prisoners of war"—via the "unlimited autocratic supervision" of the BIA.[30]

She was tarred with the anticommunist label "rankest Bolshevekist" for printing an article in the SAI quarterly journal that demanded the US "break the shackles" of wardship in an article released in December 1917, just after the Russian Revolution.[31] Later in two remarkable posthumously published essays from 1923, "The Sioux Claims" and "Our Sioux People," she explicitly used the term "sovereignty" and asked "by what process has the ownership vested in the United States?" She traced the US state's use of "sharp shooters . . . paid to kill off the buffalo herds in order to starve these freedom loving Sioux into bondage." Unlike the forms of labor extraction enacted upon the formerly enslaved under Jim Crow, the bondage she theorized was the practice of isolating Indigenous peoples under "government control" on "small reservations" by destroying social reproductive capacities for economic self-reliance.[32] The aim of this enforced isolation—which included the use of a military pass system to confine Indigenous peoples that would serve as the archetype for South African apartheid—was primarily to make lands available to settlers and to enforce collective punishment and incarceration.

She argued that the "Indian problem" was not lack of civilization but vulnerability to expropriation, which required responses based in specific legislation aimed at nondomination, that is, structures that would limit the powers of professional guardians, land speculators, and grafters.[33] Her account shifted the source of harm from the excluded "Indian" as a backward figure to be transformed and acculturated onto the collective domination of carceral rightlessness and systemic vulnerability. In her analysis, which borrows from Progressive muckraking critiques of corporate trust power, the bureau functioned as a "greedy octopus" that fed its own existence by psychologically and materially debilitating the subjects it claimed to protect.[34] "Behind the sham protection," Zitkala-Ša observed, "have been at all times great wealth in the form of Indian funds to be subverted."[35] Rather than a form of protection leading to citizenship by working upon uncivilized subjects, she theorized the bureau as a "love-vine strangling the manhood of the Indian race."[36]

In these essays, she further argued that the usual pejorative contrast between "backward" Indians who continued their own cultural and political practices and those "progressive" Indians educated in white institutions (like herself) ought to be inverted. Specifically, she took Indigenous grassroots resistance to assimilation—she referred to treaty councils—as a source of inspiration. A "more liberal [i.e., universal] point of view" would concede that "these Pine Ridge Sioux are the more hopeful because of their reluctance to cast aside our native culture." Such a claim contrasted directly with settler conceptions of progress and civic inclusion that demanded only less corrupt exercises of power over Indigenous communities so as to ensure "competent citizenship": "Would be friends," that is, white reform groups, "know of no other measure of progress than the degree of Caucasian domination over Indians." She argued, by contrast, that the continuance of Indigenous forms of life "need not prevent" them from "acquiring eventually, untethered American citizenship."[37] So, this more universal point of view would *require* the compatibility of "untethered" (i.e., nonwardship) US citizenship for Indians with collective Indigenous self-determination, in accord with what she called the "universal laws of justice."

Zitkala-Ša was one among other activists deploying the idea of collective bondage to analyze and declaim the features of a political-economic and militarized system of enforced incarceration that used political repression and economic dependency on government rations to isolate Indigenous peoples onto smaller and smaller plots of land. She shared the ambition to abolish the bureau with the more radical members of the 1910s and 1920s cohort, sometimes called the "Red Progressives" or "New Indians," who commonly described wardship and the reservation system as a form of slave-like tyranny. For example, in his presentation at the 1911 Universal Congress of the Races in London on a panel alongside W. E. B. Du Bois, fellow (Santee) Dakota and later SAI president Dr. Charles Eastman described the reservation as a "miserable prison existence" with a "pauperizing effect."[38] Later, he characterized Indigenous peoples as existing in a liminal state of subjection as "perpetual inhabitant[s] with diminutive rights."[39] Carlos Montezuma (Yavapai), Zitkala-Ša's fiancé for a brief time, advocated for the complete abolition of the reservation system, describing the reservation similarly as an institution that "imprisoned . . . the Indian . . . in a fixed state of helplessness to resist encroachments upon his rights."[40]

Likewise, one-time SAI member Laura Cornelius Kellogg (Oneida) wrote in her 1920 pamphlet *Our Democracy and the American Indian* that the bureau "substitute[d]" Indigenous self-rule for the unilateral domination of the Indian agent: "As absolute despots over the Reservations, they had the right to seize children away from their parents, to dispose of all questions pertaining to health and education, to interfere in the private lives of their wards and to incarcerate them without trial."[41] For Kellogg, the purpose of this autocratic denial of basic constitutional protections was to dismantle the capacities for collective social reproduction necessary for self-rule. Altogether, these thinkers described an exercise of unfettered sovereign power that subjugated Indigenous *collectivities* in a collective condition of political slavery, that is, enslavement *as peoples*.

As I argued in the introduction, these frameworks resonate with the contemporary neorepublican conception of freedom as nondomination, understood as freedom from the institutionalized exercise of arbitrary power. In this instance, these thinkers specifically invoked sensibilities still alive from the political culture and ideologies of post–Civil War US republicanism in their use of the keystone metaphor of racialized slavery, alongside Progressive Era critiques of domination resulting from bureaucratic and capitalist organizational power. Yet, their notion of "political slavery" captured a distinctive experience of colonial and racial domination, the central feature of which is the structurally authorized arbitrary power of one political community over a subordinated political community subject to the most discretionary, authoritarian faces of sovereign-state power. Indigenous peoples were *political slaves* in the sense that they were both captives *of the (settler) polity* and subordinated *political communities* (i.e., a kind of collective chattel). They situated this experience of "political slavery" in historically specific material practices, including dispossession, reservation confinement, authoritarianism, collective punishment, incarceration, and wardship.

Let me return now to Zitkala-Ša, by zooming in on her analysis of settler domination as a mode of political slavery that she also connected briefly but memorably to gendered systems of power. Under the banner of the (white-led) Indian Rights Association through her (self-created) position as research agent of the "Department of Indian Affairs" of the General Federation of Women's Clubs, she coauthored a scathing, headline-grabbing 1924 report, *Oklahoma's Poor, Rich Indians: An Orgy of Graft and Exploitation of the Five Civilized Tribes, Legalized Robbery, a Report*.[42] The research she did for this report in interviewing Indigenous victims and poring over case records is worthy of closer examination than it has thus far received among scholars. There, she supplements her analysis of wardship by bringing the centrality of patriarchy, gender violence, and heteronormative social structures to settler colonialism into view.

By way of background, the report examines how county judges, lawyers, and "professional guardians" exploited the inherent domination and unaccountability in the system of wardship to plunder Indigenous lands through probate courts. Written the year of the passage of the ICA, the work traces the "orgy of graft, plunder, and exploitation" occasioned by federal legislation in 1921 that allowed state and local courts to disallow "incompetent" Osages and Cherokee, Creek, Chickasaw, Choctaw, and Seminole nations from leasing their lands without the use of (white) guardians. The report details a system of "legalized robbery" by which judges, attorneys, grifters, and other collaborators conspired to steal and otherwise profit off the various administrative fees incurred upon the possession and sale of oil-rich lands through county probate courts—a practice resulting in sixty murders of Osages for their wealth in four years.

Her section of the report relates various cases of how "professional guardians" who got themselves appointed by probate courts established legal control over Indigenous wards. This was a control, she details, that they also sought to maintain at an interpersonal level through sexual assault and physical intimidation (often of minors). In making these connections, she links the gendered dimensions of wardship as an extension of unaccountable sovereign power *and* as a proprietary entitlement over bodies and land in several ways throughout the report. In doing so, she closely ties individual bodily and sexual violence to collective slavery, arguing that the unaccountability of the system enabled both to function as ways to reinforce the other. At the most basic level, those seeking to manipulate the guardianship system disproportionately targeted women and all others who could be viably represented in the courts as less rational and autonomous ("full-bloods," the "insane," "minors"), and, therefore, most likely to be seen as "incompetents."

She captured these links in combining political analysis with a sensationalist literary edge. For example, she evoked the women victims' "smothered cries," a metaphor that brings together forced dispossession and destitution (their cries smothered by guardians) with sexual assault and violence (their cries smothered by rapists).[43] She invited her "decent" audience to imagine a seven-year-old "rich little Choctaw girl," "Little *Ledcie Stechi*," who, though inheriting "rich oil property," "with her feeble grandmother, came to town carrying their clothes, a bundle of faded rags, in a flour sack. Ledcie was dirty, filthy, and covered with vermin. She was emaciated and weighed about 47 pounds." It was "in men's forms" that such "ravenous wolves" had made her into a "sheep for slaughter."[44] In invoking the results of legalized robbery, she sought to convince her readers to bear witness to the systematically enabled moral depravity of wardship's grifters and, in turn, the systemic harms to which Indigenous women were disproportionately subjected.

Most of Zitkala-Ša's analysis does not revolve around how settler colonialism produces and is produced by projects of enforcing normative genders and sexualities, as contemporary Indigenous feminists and queer Indigenous studies scholars have since theorized. Yet there are some examples that suggest her awareness of these dynamics. In the case of one Creek woman, Susanna Butler, she describes how the fact that she went on "motor trips around the country with other Indian girls" was used as a rationale to place her into guardianship. In addition to her disruption of the political experience and cultural expectation of confinement, Susanna Butler also seems to have been targeted because of the way her sexuality challenged patriarchal norms of womanhood. Zitkala-Ša's references to guardianship expose the relation between the violent structural consequences of Indigenous women acting outside expectations of domesticity and confinement within the sphere of patriarchal family formations and of Indigenous societies acting outside the terms of their collective "domestication" within the sphere of the nation-state. Of course, neither of these discourses did much to cover up the functioning of institutions that left plenty of room for thinly veiled violence, corruption, and theft.[45] Her analysis of wardship exposes the links between the ongoing theft of land and gender-based violence under the "competency" based system.

Self-Determination with Citizenship

In decrying collective bondage, Progressive Era Indigenous activists called for the "abolition" of the bureau. Yet, these thinkers diverged on what freedom from settler tyranny really meant. Practices of "abolition" actually encompassed multiple political possibilities, from a more libertarian, individualized politics of self-help within the US Constitution to an avowal of extraconstitutional and collective Indigenous sovereignty.[46] Moreover, these thinkers differed on how they saw the potential of Indigenous peoples gaining US citizenship: was it a purely colonial imposition, a strategic necessity, or potentially a genuine good?

Montezuma is a case in point as to the diverse reasoning behind calls for abolition. In his journal *Wassaja* (Beckoning), Montezuma had advocated for an anticonscription movement in response to the Selective Services Act. He argued that, as noncitizens, Indigenous peoples should not be forced into duties that pertained only to citizens.[47] Montezuma took a more libertarian position that tied Indian individual freedom to the ability to buy and sell property as a full, unhyphenated American citizen. On this basis, he argued for the immediate and unconditional abolition of the reservation system *and* Indigenous societies' collective ownership of lands with it.

Montezuma celebrated Indigenous cultural identity, but he argued that "a law for each nationality in America would be very much un-American."[48] Moreover, as a follower of Richard Henry Pratt's arguments that Indians ought to be de-tribalized and removed from the reservation immediately to learn white social norms, Montezuma often conflated the critique of the reservation as an oppressive institution with the notion that "Indianness" *in itself* constituted a kind of social disability and form of backwardness.[49] Thus, while Montezuma, like Pratt, regarded his own demand to immediately break up reservations into fee-simple properties as a form of egalitarianism in line with American post–Civil War republican norms—one underpinned by the belief that Indians could *become* "civilized"—he did not envision a future for Indigenous peoples as enduring political collectivities. Montezuma's embrace of a singular rule of law and rejection of multinationalism as "un-American" differed from Zitkala-Ša's own vision of what constituted "abolition": the effort to make US citizenship compatible with forms of Indigenous sovereignty, which she understood as local, democratic self-government expressly grounded in the heritage of the people.

By contrast, Laura Cornelius Kellogg focused less on US citizenship than Zitkala-Ša. Instead, she advocated for treaty-based Indigenous sovereignty expressed in the distinctive form of "Indian communism," a cooperative model of industry based on the collective ownership and self-government of the reservation homeland.[50] Kellogg was closer in orientation to activists like Clinton Rickard (Tuscarora), founder of the Indian Defense League of America, who followed a Haudenosaunee tradition of refusing US citizenship as a citizen of a separate confederacy whose consent to serve stemmed from treaty agreements—not from citizenship within the colonial state. As he put it in his autobiography, "By our ancient treaties, we expected the protection of the government.... United States citizenship was just another way of absorbing us and destroying our customs and our government."[51] On his account, the US state conscripting Indigenous peoples into American citizenship was *in itself* a form of domination, because this practice would negate the status of Indigenous peoples as citizens of the different nations of the Haudenosaunee Confederacy (Mohawk, Onondaga, Oneida, Tuscarora, Cayuga, and Seneca).

Zitkala-Ša conceptualized citizenship as a strategic necessity. Like fellow members of the SAI, her writings and activism began to focus most heavily on the citizenship question with the advent of the First World War. During the war, the question of Indigenous service (in particular the debate between segregated and integrated units) was highly contested.[52] She was publicly in favor of integrated units and played upon patriotic images in both her writing and public speaking appearances to insist that the "Red Man, citizen or non-citizen of the United States" had proven through service that he "is a loyal son of America."[53] She contrasted the democratic imaginary of New World sovereignty (i.e., the US) with the "race discrimination" that is "akin to the rule of might of the old-world powers" (i.e., the reactionary Central Powers) and "absolute tyranny."[54] Accordingly, she rejected segregated units publicly because of the discriminatory motives behind them, expressing nationalist fervor in line with US war aims.

Despite her public uses of patriotic themes to emphasize Indigenous loyalty to "the greatest of democracies," her rhetoric was not assimilationist. Evidence of this is that her private writings differ dramatically in tone: she privately feared that Indigenous men (including her husband, Raymond

Bonnin) would be sent to slaughter at the front in yet another continuation of the Indian wars within an intra-Western struggle.[55]

She argued that the Indian soldier's "devotion to America" only recertified the need for full and immediate birthright citizenship ("Americanization") for Indigenous peoples (men and women). Her emphasis on birthright citizenship was important, as it underscored that Indigenous peoples were *not* immigrants needing to be "naturalized" but *already* Americans.[56] "The Red man," she asserted, "asks for a simple thing—citizenship. . . . There never was a time more opportune than now for America to enfranchise the Red man."[57]

In making these demands, Zitkala-Ša sharply distinguished between the option of pragmatically taking up the irreparably compromised meanings of citizenship and the dominant notion of the transformation of Indians from "savage," dependent peoples to "civilization." In short, she specifically focused on citizenship as a tool for Indigenous peoples as political communities. As historian Cathleen Cahill writes: "For Bonnin, citizenship was not individualized, as her [white] allies imagined."[58] Indeed, after the passage of the Nineteenth Amendment in August 1920, she frequently appeared at white women's organizations to advocate for Indigenous women's suffrage. Aside from promoting individual civil and political rights, she argued that enfranchisement and aggressive litigation could serve as a way to bolster the nearly dissolved links between individual and collective freedoms. This was part of a politics of self-defense and remediation of the specific harms of colonization.

To this point, her treatment of citizenship and patriotism frequently connected a rhetoric of love for democracy to the imperative of immediate Indian enfranchisement, which she in turn envisioned as one strategic tool among others in collective, anticolonial struggles. "The Red Man of America," she wrote, "loves democracy and hates mutilated treaties."[59] "Wardship," she argued, "is no substitute for American citizenship, therefore we seek his enfranchisement. The many treaties made in good faith with the Indian by our government we would like to see equitably settled."[60] Of note here is that her politics not only gave formal citizenship a different practical role in these struggles, but it also rejected the dominant *concept* of citizenship as itself a kind of civilizational status. On her model, citizenship was not the culmination of conquest—of assimilationist incorporation of Indigenous peoples into US sovereignty. Instead, Indigenous people could leverage citizenship status to set the US polity on a course of paying off the debts for "despoliation" of their lands and unilateral treaty abrogation.

This was a demand, she underscored, which "can only materialize in a democratic government," by which she implied the kind of democratic system the US had not yet been.⁶¹ As a case in point, she was active with the Black Hills Council, a grassroots organization of Očhéthi Šakówiŋ (Lakota, Dakota, and Nakota) elders aimed at enforcing or gaining remedial justice for the treaties broken when the US government seized the Black Hills from the Očhéthi Šakówiŋ. Debarred from pursuing land claims by explicit statute as to the jurisdiction of the US Court of Claims—access that "was comparatively easy" for other Americans—and disallowed under bureau supervision from selecting their own legal representation, "they must first obtain the consent of Congress of which they are non-constituents."⁶² Citizenship, by contrast, might foster the "protection of law under our constitution."

Against the notion that US citizenship completed an acculturation process that turned the savage into the civilized, she represented struggles for citizenship as entirely *political* practices that could aid in mobilization to rectify intertwined individual and collective domination. She theorized US citizenship as part of enabling the continuing, collective dimension of Indigenous peoples' quest for remedial justice—"like other Indian claims, the progeny of broken treaties."⁶³ In this sense, constitutional protection went beyond individual civil and political rights, since the "fact remains that the Sioux have an intangible right none the less real and just for the postponed settlement."⁶⁴ That the settlement had been "postponed" signaled that the ICA, having declared Indigenous peoples US citizens by fiat, did nothing to supersede the specifically collective harm of "mutilated treaties" of specific peoples.⁶⁵ Collective negotiation among the representatives of "nations" demanded hearings in accord with the "democratic doctrine of justice."

During her time as editor of the SAI's *American Indian Magazine* from late 1917 to 1919, Zitkala-Ša began to relate Indigenous freedoms from the sovereign state more directly to a critique of the settler state's international authorization. Closely tracking the debates at the Paris conference on self-determination and the rights of what were then called "national minorities," she unsuccessfully sought Indigenous peoples' presence at the conference and in the League of Nations. Accordingly, she called in 1919 for "little peoples . . . to be granted the right of self-determination" and to "sit beside their great allies at the Peace Table."⁶⁶ She followed the nascent anticolonial organizations fighting against Wilson's imperial interpretation of self-determination. This included the Japanese fight against "race discrimination" in the league, the Irish, African Americans led by Du Bois, and the League of Small and Subject Nationalities, all of whom demanded equal representation as oppressed peoples. She thereby advanced a constructive vision of Indigenous self-determination as freedom from the sovereign state, in clamoring for new international institutions that would translate the equality of peoples into structures of nondomination within and against the settler state.

Tim Rowse has characterized this moment as one of "Indian participation in a new internationalism." He submits that Indigenous advocates in the Anglo-settler world aimed to redeem the exclusions of Wilson's liberal universalism.[67] In fact, however, I contend that Zitkala-Ša actually rejected the very legitimacy of Wilsonian internationalism interpreted as the institutionalization of relations among territorially bounded sovereign states. In particular, she, much like Yellowtail, specifically critiqued the morally arbitrary yet systemically legitimized character of sovereignty enshrining the domestic-international distinction, which had the effect of "dividing human interests into domestic and international affairs."[68] She used the term "human rights" here as well precisely as a way to place Indigenous self-determination in a realm subject neither to the US colonial institutional order nor to the dominant formation of Eurocentric internationalism in the League of Nations that would go on to uphold this order. While she never defined her use of the term "human rights" in this context, it is notable that she appealed to human rights as a way of constraining and delegitimizing the parochialism of the US sovereignty and citizenship regime.[69]

In questioning the very structures of representation of the new internationalism, she was actually engaging in what I have referred to as "transnational internationalism." Namely, she was pushing against Wilson by redefining Indigenous self-determination as freedom from colonial sovereign states, secured through international cooperation with colonized and oppressed peoples within, across, and outside the state. In this way, she rejected precisely the hierarchies *of* internationalism that ensured the continual reproduction of colonial sovereignty. Moreover, she was participating in and seeking to shape pan-Indigenous federations "within" the state and anticolonial movements outside the state that sought to generate these alternative sites of international authority, in addition to pursuing the transformation of dominant national and international institutions.

Even in grasping for this transformative internationalism, Zitkala-Ša paradoxically remained in central respects within the ambit of American political discourse. She melded US radical republican, Progressive, and Marxist anticolonial vocabularies. In an intentional twist on Lincoln, for example, she contended that "government by the people" had been forcibly denied the "small peoples" who resided within "America's own bounds."[70] She was committed to asserting for Indigenous peoples "full American citizenship and the protection of law under our constitution!" Yet, she placed the politics of "enfranchisement" and the "right of self-determination" next to one another as compatible and mutually reinforcing practices that aimed at the further mobilization and organization necessary to secure rights.[71] To this end, she and her husband Raymond founded the ambitious National Council of American Indians as a national advocacy group in 1926.[72] As part of this work, she emphasized democratic tribal self-government and federated political organization among Indigenous nations. Such practices of transnational internationalism aimed to exert pressures on colonial institutions of the settler state from within, by aligning forces with other (inter)nationalist liberation movements.

In the speeches she delivered to various civil society groups, such as "Bureaucracy versus Democracy" and "America's Indian Problem," she outlined the theoretical commitments that would later underlie the Council's organizing vision. She distinguished the impersonal domination of the BIA ("bureaucracy") from Indigenous sovereignty ("democracy"): The image she invoked was a "democracy wheel" with layers of all-Indigenous representation extending from the local level up to the US federal government. She referred to the wheel's "hub" as "an organization of progressive Indian citizens" whose role was to represent "community interests . . . of the Indians themselves."[73] She envisaged cooperative economic models based on collective landholding that would create economic foundations for Indigenous self-government.[74] This proposed structure clearly imagined Indigenous sovereignty on the model of a participatory Progressive organization that is "within" a significantly transformed US state, albeit one constrained to respect the self-government of Indigenous societies in constitutional and international law. Her plans certainly contained elements of "uplift" ideology in ways that paralleled the struggles to define the role of political leadership within Black political thought (e.g., the famous Du Bois–Washington debate). Yet, she never linked this debate to questions of civilizational capacity or deservingness for US citizenship. As part of the cofounded National Council of American Indians, whose motto was "Help Indians Help Themselves in Protecting Their Rights," she traveled ceaselessly, seeking to form local organizations and register voters.[75]

With the implementation of the Indian New Deal or Indian Reorganization Act (IRA) in 1934 under the Wheeler-Howard Act, she lobbied her home reservation of Yankton to reject the significant power still granted under the IRA constitution to the BIA in favor of more democratic local institutions with final veto power over the bureau. She also included in the proposal a provision to allow off-reservation citizens to vote in council elections. Her proposal was rejected by the Yankton agency of the BIA, and anticipated a far more capacious notion of Indigenous self-determination.[76] In this way, Zitkala-Ša fashioned a constructive vision of anticolonial Indigenous self-determination, against the colonialism of the US civic inclusion project.

Termination after Citizenship

Progressive Era Indigenous activists sought to transform the legal status of citizen-wards into a genuine dual or multilayered citizenship, which would encompass citizenship in Indigenous nations and in the US. Nevertheless, the ambiguity of this legal status and the colonial narratives often attached to differentiated or subnational citizenship in US politics did not disappear. In fact, the colonial notion of Indian status as a kind of civic disability and/or racialized backwardness recurred in a different way in the 1950s and 1960s via the politics of termination.

In 1957, Arthur Watkins, then a Republican senator from Utah, wrote about the termination policy, which as chair of the Senate Interior Committee Subcommittee on Indian Affairs he was helping to shepherd through the Senate. Specifically echoing Lincoln's Emancipation Proclamation, Watkins argued that such policies "would assure [Indigenous peoples] of equality in the enjoyment and responsibilities of our national citizenship."[77] To accomplish this putatively emancipatory end of inclusion, Watkins and the other architects of termination pressed the Department of Interior to end federal services to Indian tribes and to eliminate unilaterally the limited rights to self-government and consolidation of collective lands established under the Indian New Deal.

A century before in *Worcester v. Georgia* (1832), Vine Deloria Jr. argued, the Supreme Court established that the United States "had [only] a minimum power to interfere with the self-government of the Cherokee people" and that the "logical meaning of this [sovereign] status is . . . independence and recognition on a world scale."[78] The catchall label "termination" captured a range of policies that recalled earlier eras of removal and allotment by revoking this sovereign status and, in doing so, created tremendous economic suffering and multiple forms of social dislocation for many Indigenous communities: Such policies cut off social services like health care to reservations;[79] gave states control over civil jurisdiction on reservations; and diminished national land bases and constitutionally guaranteed tax exemptions, eroding the economic livelihood of nations such as the Menominee (65–71).[80]

For Indigenous activists of the post-IRA period like Deloria, "termination" came to index both a temporally bounded period of US policy (approximately 1947–72) and the lingering and more diffuse threat of elimination underlying any settler politics.[81] Deloria referred to termination as reflective of an "individualist-integrationist" moment in which elites combined a Lockean emphasis on possessive individualism familiar from allotment with an integrationist emphasis on inclusion into "mainstream" structures of US citizenship as a liberating process that coercively dispersed Indigenous peoples from remaining lands on the reservation.[82] As the executive director of the National Congress of American Indians (NCAI) from 1964 to 1967, Deloria confronted this perilous moment as a matter of everyday organizing.[83]

Let me briefly introduce Deloria before examining his conceptual contributions in more detail: Many in the field of Native American and Indigenous studies regard Deloria (1933–2005) as the most prominent twentieth-century theorist of American Indian politics. Before his academic career, Deloria had a hand in many of the key struggles of American Indian resistance after 1964, when he was elected as the executive director of the NCAI, the first of many roles he took as a leading pan-Indigenous activist, lawyer, and practice-oriented scholar. From this activist background, Deloria's writings recast Indians as colonized peoples actively demanding sovereignty and decolonization rather than passive recipients of civil rights and further incorporation into the nation-state.

By the early 1970s, Deloria had finished law school at the University of Colorado and become a key player in the first cohort of Indian lawyers who would assemble the necessary expertise and materials to challenge the precedents that had defined treaties, land rights, and Native sovereignty as archaic and irrelevant remainders rather than ongoing governing structures of collective life with legal purchase. In a series of works that thematized the conceptual basis for the Indigenous sovereignty movement that exploded into public consciousness with the takeover of Alcatraz (1969) and the occupation of Wounded Knee (1973), Deloria confronted a dense web of colonial epistemology and politics that afflicted Indian country. *Custer Died for Your Sins* (1969) and *We Talk, You Listen: New Tribes, New Turf* (1970) chronicled the burgeoning sovereignty movement, critiqued anthropological and missionary desires to observe and convert, and painted an optimistic picture of a "tribalizing" America growing toward Native conceptions of community and away from its inveterate illusions of a Lockean "radical idealism of the individual." Often taken as a historical document of Indigenous organizing for its galvanizing impact on the Native American sovereignty movement, *Custer* situated the struggles of the NCAI of the previous decade within the longer historical context of US colonialism and looked forward to the issues Deloria would deepen his engagement with in numerous popular and academic writings.[84] Placing *Custer* within the longer arc of Deloria's thought, I argue that his first major work ought to be seen as a theoretically rich contribution that addressed structures of colonial injustice through a combination of cultural criticism, political analysis, and coruscating polemic.

God Is Red: A Native View of Religion (1973) developed an Indigenous philosophy that contrasted Native accounts of the network of mutual relations and responsibility of peoples to land in situated communities with Western emphases on the abstract unfolding of historical time. *Behind the Trail of Broken Treaties: An Indian Declaration of Independence* (1974), which I discuss in the next chapter, was authored through his work with the Institute for the Development of Indian Law. In it, Deloria assessed the foundational erasures of Indigenous peoples within the law of nations and the Westphalian global order and redescribed Indigenous peoples as sovereign nations. Settling into academic life in 1978, Deloria continued to publish an array of works that refined these earlier contributions until his death in 2005.

For Deloria, what made termination so difficult to contest was the way its proponents tapped into a narrative of democratic sovereignty that equated inclusion into citizenship with emancipation. Whereas settler political elites attacked Indigenous collective landholding in the late nineteenth century with explicit reference to ascriptive racial hierarchies and the developmentalist theory common to European colonial rule in Africa, India, the Caribbean, and across the Anglo-settler world, termination proponents like Watkins drew on ideas not dissimilar to the ideals of integration expressed in the early civil rights movement, for example, the National Association for the Advancement of Colored People's fight for equal protection of Blacks under the law and the defeat of the fiction of "separate but equal" schooling for Blacks and whites in *Brown v. Board of Education*.

Casting the policy as the emancipation of Indigenous peoples from what Deloria critiqued as the figure of the helpless "Indian . . . 'imprisoned' on the reservation," Watkins could represent to the US public a policy that resonated with a familiar narrative of progress toward an inclusive ideal of citizenship.[85] Rather than using reservation *isolation* as an instrument of carceral dispossession, Watkins aimed to *disperse* Indigenous peoples so as to gain access to lands still under tribal control. By figuring integration into citizenship as an incomplete project based on the continuing existence of reservations as legally distinct spaces, Watkins could use the figure of the citizen-ward as a sign of racial backwardness to bombastically equate termination practices aimed at dispossession with emancipation, that is, the freeing of slaves.

Of course, Watkins's imagery of wards excluded from the unalloyed good of American citizenship tapped into the civic inclusion narrative. However, the political context of Indigenous societies in the US had changed in key respects by the end of World War II. With the end of allotment in 1934, of the "pass system," and some elements of the doctrine of wardship, the reservation itself was no longer in fact a site of incarceration and bondage. Countering the way that notions of citizenship were operating to buttress termination, Helen Peterson (Oglala) organized an NCAI Emergency Conference in February 1954 to respond to emerging calls for termination under BIA commissioner Dillon Meyer, issuing a Declaration of Indian Rights.[86] Joseph Garry (Coeur d'Alene), the primary author of the declaration, wrote that "some of our fellow Americans think that our reservations are places of confinement. Nothing could be farther from the truth. Reservations do not imprison us. They are ancestral homelands, retained by us for our perpetual use and enjoyment. We feel we must assert our right to maintain ownership in our own way, and to terminate it only by our consent."[87] In other words, Progressive Era Indigenous activists had used the analytic of political slavery, including notions of collective imprisonment, to contest dominant settler-colonial frameworks. After WWII, it was much the same political-cultural imaginary of slavery, abolition, and (un)freedom of movement that *antitribal* forces used as terminationist weapons.

Drawing on this backdrop of work in the NCAI in the 1950s that refigured reservations as homelands, Deloria's early writings and activism first brought in a colonial frame to analyze the stakes of this transformation within American national identity and postwar political thought. Having witnessed the damage the termination policy did to Indigenous communities in his time at the NCAI, the police violence the Lummi, Puyallup, Tulalip, Nisqually, and other Pacific Northwest treaty fishing rights activists encountered, and the US war in Vietnam, Deloria developed a radical critique of the violence of the civic inclusion narrative's "integrationist-individualist" commitments. He connected these "new incidents involving treaty rights" with other currents of US imperialism, such as "the facade of maintaining . . . commitments in Vietnam" (50). Deloria offered a reading of the productive work this nominal inclusivity did to reproduce practices of colonization under the sign of emancipation.

"Indians are like the weather. Everyone knows all about the weather, but none can change it. . . . One of the finest things about being an Indian is that people are always interested in you and your 'plight.' Other groups have difficulties, predicaments, quandaries, problems, or troubles. Traditionally we Indians have a 'plight'" (1). So begins Deloria's *Custer Died for Your Sins*. Deloria's analogy to weather ironically confronted settler societies' perceptions of the changelessness of Indigenous social orders. Whereas "Indians" are often described in the static anthropological language of "tradition," Deloria observed that "dynamic" Indigenous communities undertook massive changes in the 1960s and "ask[ed] only to be freed from cultural oppression" (12). It is, then, non-Indigenous representations of Native peoples that seem to be immoveable. In their static "traditions," settler societies cast Indians as stalled in a backward state of cultural and economic development or of a lack of citizenship rights, thus continually in need of help to be included within the civic identities and values of US settler society. From this perspective, civic inclusion as a way of casting narratives of progress is folded into a kind of paternalistic investment in "unreal" objects of solicitude and charity rather than horizontal solidarity with "dynamic" and contemporary peoples (2). The discourse of "plight" (unlike "difficulties, predicaments...") projects a permanent ontological status of immiseration onto Indigenous peoples, masking the origins and ongoing causes of marginalization in conquest and colonization and reinvesting the desires of the settler state into a project of inclusion

Though more often noted for its critique of anthropology, Deloria's first work theorizes the discourse of termination, which grafted a (widely contested) narrative of the early civil rights movement as solely focused on integration onto Indigenous politics.[88] Deloria's work addressed the redeployment of the language of civil rights to repress colonial injustice just as these ways of displacing claims about specifically colonial inheritances were (re)emerging.[89] If the civil rights movement provided much of the impetus behind the (eventual) reformulation of American political thought to address the racialized legacies of chattel slavery, reading alongside Deloria pulls at an alternative then-contemporary thread. Deloria acknowledged the power of civil rights discourse as a response to racialized injustice yet also insisted on the way inclusionary claims could be marshaled to pursue what he called "conquest-oriented" projects.[90] Read in dialogue with other decolonizing works of the later 1960s such as Martin Luther King's later interrogation of the Vietnam War and Stokely Carmichael (Kwame Ture) and Charles Hamilton's *Black Power*, Deloria's intervention speaks to an alternative tradition of decolonization erased within American political thought because of pervasive attachment to the civic inclusion narrative. Deloria carefully read and insisted on the influence of *Black Power*, which he described as a "godsend" for "allow[ing] the concept of self-determination suddenly to become valid" (180).[91]

Deloria contrasted the political situations of "the red and the black" as distinctive dilemmas because of the dominance of a narrow and dematerialized conception of civil rights as inclusion (168–96).⁹² In a practical sense, his own effort to distinguish between Indigenous sovereignty and much of the civil rights movement was based on his worry "that the distinctive American Indian agenda would be diluted by participation in a broad coalition." This push to emphasize distinction from other racially subjugated populations placed him at odds with a more left-oriented cohort of activists and friends within the National Indian Youth Council (NIYC).⁹³ The NIYC had formed among a younger generation in response to the 1961 American Indian Chicago Conference, which they had felt was not confrontational enough in their defense of Indigenous peoples' rights. Framing their constituency as a "greater Indian America," they were more enthusiastic than Deloria in their willingness to forge multiracial coalitions with others subject to racial oppression in the US.

In a 1965 speech, Clyde Warrior (Ponca), a key figure in the movement and friend of Deloria, expressed more commonality with "other minorities in the great society" in a shared condition of poverty and subordination. While he traced Indigenous powerlessness to the shell of self-government offered in the 1934 IRA, he also saw a common failure of transformative justice in the emerging Great Society programs designed to "better the Indian," a kind of "so-called improvement" that "reinforce[s] the existing condition . . . in the very structure of the society."⁹⁴ Accordingly, Warrior rejected this top-down model in favor of a demand for resources and a social wage whose actual uses would be shaped directly by oppressed peoples themselves.

This vision of Indigenous self-determination thus included a radical vision of shared economic and participatory citizenship, expressed through both broad-based pan-Indigenous coalitions and mass democratic mobilization with other oppressed groups in US society. Accordingly, the NIYC sent Clyde Warrior (Ponca), Hank Adams (Sioux-Assiniboine), and Tillie Walker (Mandan-Hidatsa) to the Poor People's Campaign in 1968. They were successful in introducing treaty rights in the overall platform through negotiations with Ralph Abernathy of the Southern Christian Leadership Conference.⁹⁵ Deloria continued, however, to see the more civil rights–oriented framework as a weapon in the hands of the state to invalidate the specificity of Indigenous collective self-determination, and I think it is fair to say that he de-emphasized this kind of radical coalition building in his practical politics.

At a more textual register, Deloria rejected the logic of inclusion/exclusion as a frame of civic and cultural identity in favor of an analysis attentive to concrete practices of colonial rule and dispossession.[96] He directly confronted the politically productive historical amnesia of the civic inclusion narrative about the "conquest-oriented" formation of the US state in its very territorial composition. In contrast to the way the civic inclusion narrative obscures links between US imperial war and "domestic" colonial rule, Deloria argued that the "betrayal of treaty promises" should be tied directly to America's failure to "fool the rest of the world about her intentions on other continents" (50–51). In a personal letter, Deloria drew parallels between the then-recent My Lai massacre and the Wounded Knee and Sand Creek massacres:

> I feel that when American troops massacre 500 odd Vietnamese, when Green Berets assassinate individuals without due process, then certain historical parallels can be drawn between contemporary America foreign policy and the Sand Creek and Wounded Knee massacres of innocent Indians by US cavalry and the political assassinations of Crazy Horse and Sitting Bull in the last century.[97]

Deloria analyzed imperialism as a set of continuous practices and processes of which the wars of conquest—the original settler-colonial fronts and fields of empire—served in the repressed settler imaginary as a fecund source of symbolic materials and as an original model for later US counterinsurgency practices.[98] "We have more in common," he argued "with the Africans and Vietnamese and all the non-Western people than we do with the Anglo-Saxon culture of the United States."[99] Deloria reminded his audience of the international links between US wars of conquest waged against Indigenous peoples and those of European nations and of the significant continuity in these practices, as the "frontier" is mobilized to determine boundaries past which unlimited war becomes acceptable:

> When the frontier was declared officially closed in 1890 it was only a short time before American imperialist impulses drove the country into the Spanish-American War and the acquisition of America's Pacific island empire began. The tendency to continue imperialist trends remained constant between the two world wars as this nation was involved in numerous banana wars in Central and South America (51).

Deloria argued that the "the Indian wars of the past should rightly be regarded as the first foreign wars of American history" (51). Rejecting the commonplace myth of isolated "settlement" of the continent, Deloria drew parallels among these "wars of foreign conquest just as England and France were doing in India and Africa" (51). In doing so, Deloria spurred critics of US empire to view it neither as a relic of the nineteenth-century moment of territorial annexation and colonial war nor as a more recent aberration of Cold War logics. Rather, it was the consistent logic of a "militantly imperialistic world power eagerly grasping for economic control over weaker nations" (51).

Deloria identified colonization as a process of land expropriation that builds the foundations of settler sovereignty. In effect, such practices "extinguish[ed] treaty rights," yet Deloria added that the discourse of civic inclusion ironically staged such erasure as an extension of citizenship rights, a form of emancipation.[100] Clinically describing the ongoing "uses of Indian lands as pawns," Deloria argued that dispossession continued into the present through the enduring territorial imperative underpinning state formation (51). Territorial sovereignty *itself* continued to function as a key, ongoing expression of US imperial power. These wrongs are foundational to the settler state: They cannot be superseded or rewritten so as to pretend that the constitutional vision was always an implicit universal, as the American Creed implies.

Whereas the civic inclusion narrative predicts the relatively linear extension of civil rights claims, Deloria observed the opposite trend: the increasing dissolution of Indigenous rights, land title, and sovereignty. Deloria turned to the specific ways Indigenous peoples' own efforts to remake the ward-citizenship pairing into dual citizenship had been refashioned into a politics of termination that defined Indigenous peoples yet again as wards in need of protection. By creating conceptual resonances between frontier genocide and the state violence produced through termination, Deloria confronted the ways in which the civic inclusion narrative obscured the *contemporary* reality of such practices. In an editorial for their in-house publication then entitled *American Aborigine*, the NIYC's Mel Thom (Walker River Paiute) referred to termination as a "cold war." Thom noted the slow violence whereby "Indian life is steadily torn apart and Indian integrity downgraded—all within a legal framework."[101] Echoing Thom, Deloria referred to termination as the "great twentieth century Indian war" (62):

> Just the last two decades have seen a more devious but hardly less successful war waged against Indian communities.... In the past they were systematically hunted down and destroyed. Were an individual citizen to do this it would be classified as cold-blooded murder. When it was done by the U.S. Army it was an "Indian war." (54)

Because Indigenous peoples were outside US law and their own legal and political orders were not regarded as sufficiently "civilized" (9), Deloria pointed out that Indigenous peoples were automatically seen as in a Hobbesian state of war. Referring to Watkins and the other senators who pushed the termination policy, he contended, "it was thought that it would provide the elusive 'answer' to the Indian problem" (55). Civic inclusion under these conditions actually made possible the erosion of Indigenous sovereignty, rights, and land title. Indeed, termination was "heavily disguised as a plan to offer the Indian people full citizenship rights"—in other words as continuous with the project of progressively realizing the civil rights of excluded subjects (76). More than a limited frame that needed to be expanded to include forms of cultural "difference," Deloria pointed out that the extension of citizenship could serve the political function of *reproducing* practices of colonization.

Assimilation, Deloria observed, always appeared historically as the handmaiden of dispossession, no less in the guise of this reformulated postwar politics of inclusion. "There was never a time," he wrote, "when the white man said he was trying to help the Indian get into the mainstream of American life that he did not also demand that the Indian give up land" (173).[102] When it became obvious that the policy did not actually encourage integration on the terms of the civic inclusion narrative—when "it proved to be no answer at all"—"Congress continued its policy, having found a new weapon in the ancient battle for Indian land" (55). What struck Deloria about the discourse of termination was that it "was not conceived as a policy of murder," but as one of inclusionary citizenship (54–55). As a political technology, however, it became no less than a "weapon against the Indian people in a modern war of conquest" (76).

Custer's Sins: From Innocence and Redemption to Treaty and Restitution

Given how Deloria invoked the specter of conquest that rendered domestic social policy yet another "weapon" of colonial war, one might expect him to entirely forgo the project of forcing those (re)enacting this war to reckon with the narratives enabling such practices in favor of a Fanonian account of political subjectivity centered around subaltern counterviolence.[103] Yet Deloria's critique of termination as "a combination of the old systematic hunt and the deprivation of services" enabled a biting analysis of contemporary settler colonialism that also implicated non-Indigenous peoples in working toward decolonization (54). He recalled a Hobbesian logic of war as one way of narrating the wrong of termination, but he also referred to newer forms of abandonment. Here, much like Zitkala-Ša's focus on constitutional protections to pursue collective claims and debts based on broken treaties, Deloria argued that the state has accrued certain *responsibilities* to Indigenous peoples that have now been unilaterally relinquished. Deloria focused on how termination annihilated hard-won collective protections such as the consolidation of land bases and, instead, reinterpreted such (limited) structures of collective nondomination as signs of a restricted American citizenship to be overcome.

Deloria's diagnosis of America's mythological innocence and the misguidedly redemptive kernel of civic inclusion brings together structural critique with a cajoling rhetoric aimed at moving his audience from a condescending "interest" in the "plight" of "the mythical Indians of stereotypeland" toward horizontal solidarity with real, sovereign tribal communities in their present configurations across urban, rural, and reserve spaces (2). Deloria took advantage of George Armstrong Custer's resonance in both American political culture and common Indigenous movement jokes to address settler society's investment in the sort of colonial paternalism that would disavow empire as a question of intergenerational justice. Conscious of the role of missionaries as the avant-garde of conquest—those who "preyed," not prayed (101)—Deloria used the Christian idiom of sin to defang this inclusion narrative. The humorous, biting rhetoric of Deloria's manifesto here was aimed at differently investing his audience in the ongoing stakes of colonialism—"the unrealities that face *us* as Indian people"—as a project that bound them to a disavowed past and its remainders, like treaties (2). By using Custer as a pedagogical device, Deloria pushed his readers to reflect on their responsibility for creating "a new policy by Congress acknowledging our right to live in peace," which would require "the public at large to drop the myths in which it has clothed us for so long" (27).

Deloria argued that the redemptive temporality of the civic inclusion narrative enabled settlers to take up dispositions toward colonial violence premised on disavowal. Deloria drew on Christian idioms of sacrifice and redemption more as a form of mockery than as a true moral compass: Deloria addressed himself to an "avowedly *Christian* nation" to tease those whose own focus on sin, guilt, and redemption as a form of escape from the past might give way to a grounded capacity to "make their will known" to oppose "the continual abuse of the American Indian" (53, 77). Pointing out the resonance of this narrative of redemption for whites, Deloria continually reassessed how the nineteenth-century sediments for which Custer serves as the stand-in weigh on and feed into a present in which "more damage is being done to Indian people" (30).

Deloria addressed such disavowal as yet another irony—another "unreality"—for Indigenous peoples (2). The first irony was simply that the United States could not even recognize Custer's violation of the Treaty of Fort Laramie of 1868 as a sin even on its *own* (Christian) terms: To substitute Custer for such an archetypal figure of reconciliation as Jesus recalled how this redemptive logic displaced questions of colonial rule. "Originally," he explained,

> the Custer bumper sticker referred to the Sioux Treaty of 1868 signed at Fort Laramie in which the United States pledged to give free and undisturbed use of the lands claimed by Red Cloud in return for peace. Under the covenants of the Old Testament, breaking a covenant called for a blood sacrifice for atonement. Custer was the blood sacrifice for the United States breaking the Sioux treaty (148).

Deloria observed that the Lakota—the non-Christians, those supposed to be outside of the community of those redeemed of sin—punished the United States for the crime of treaty breaking. Yet such an act could not be acknowledged *as a crime*—and especially one that has ongoing consequences for Lakota people—even in retrospect because of the supposedly redemptive character of civic inclusion. Many in the counterculture and the broader New Left had begun to identify with Indians, Richard Slotkin writes, as a "figurative alternative to a civilization gone wrong."[104] Deloria admonished settler society for this relatively costless, escapist dissociation that placed Indians into the "contagious trap [of] the mythology of white America" rather than offering solidarity on equal terms (27). By bringing Custer back into the present as a figure of atonement for "your sins," Deloria chastised settlers and questioned their right to dis-identify from the counterinsurgency doctrine Custer embodied.

Deloria again reminded his audience recently awakening to the horrors of the Vietnam War that "there has not been a time when the motives of this country were innocent" (51). "When one considers American history in its imperialistic light," Deloria contended, "it becomes apparent that if morality is to be achieved in this country's relations with other nations a return to basic principles is in order" (51). From this vantage point of a "return," an anticolonial practice explicitly rejects the notion that an implicit universalism of constitutional principles need only be "achieved."[105] These "basic principles" are not located in a redemption of the constitutional order but in its potential reconstruction on different terms, since "America got sick when the first Indian treaty was broken" and it "has never recovered" (76). This demand is less a return to any previous or original condition of an impossible "innocence" in a mythical past than an imagined possibility of what could have been had the United States not "abruptly change[d] from treaties to a program of cultural destruction"—a reference to the 1819 Civilization Bill (49).[106] He argued that relinquishing "cultural and economic imperialism" and respect for treaties are the indispensable starting points of coexistence but ones to which there is no untainted past to return because treaties everywhere have been an irreducibly colonial instrument of power and possession in the United States (53).

Acknowledging the paradoxical character of treaties as both instruments of dispossession and of lasting association, Deloria argued that "in looking back at the centuries of broken treaties, it is clear that the United States never intended to keep any of its promises" (48). Still, in acknowledging the "promises" embedded in those treaties that established an ongoing relation between nations, Deloria argued that present-day disavowal of treaty promises caused Indians to "burn with resentment" (35). Consonant with this insistence on balancing a desire for separation and still confronting settler people with the terms of disavowal they had accepted, Deloria traced the ways in which the civic inclusion narrative configures these colonial dynamics as past aberrations. Deloria pointed out that "people often feel guilty about their ancestors killing all those Indian years ago," which motivated a sympathy that figured Indians entirely in the past tense or as passive rights recipients with a "plight." Non-Indigenous peoples, Deloria argued, "shouldn't feel guilty about the distant past" with termination ongoing (54). As police, the judiciary, wardens, and state officials violated treaty rights, "the general public has sat back, shed tears over the treatment of Indians a century ago, and bemoaned the plight of the Indian" (41). By displacing colonial war onto distant ancestors—or, even claiming Indian ancestry oneself (3-5)—the settler audience could be brought to "tears" in "feel[ing] sorry for us without taking responsibility for present arbitrary harassment" (27). Such tearful responses acknowledged past violence of a mythic past made "unreal" (2). Yet by directing this guilt at "Custer's sins" toward the past and "turn[ing] a deaf ear" to colonial violence in the present, such reactions conveyed a willful confusion at the Native view that situated distinct peoples in a fraught, contemporary struggle in relation to lands (41).

Countering these responses to the desire to start over unmarked by the past, Deloria reversed this temporal script of disappeared/passive Indians and fatedly broken treaties: "the tragedy of the past is that it sets precedents for land theft today" (30). In this vein, the title—"Custer Died for *Your* Sins"—provocatively raised this tendency to make past episodes of "exclusion" aberrational to the progressive expansion of rights, and thus to encourage dispositions that substitute guilt for the acknowledgment of ongoing colonial injustice that might conjure political action based not on misplaced sympathy but on the real solidarity of a "cultural leave-us-alone agreement, in spirit and fact" (27). Deloria thus turned to the language of sin to lampoon the structure of narratives of redemption, including the civic inclusion narrative. By inserting Custer—whom he mockingly labeled the "'Adolph Eichmann' of the nineteenth century"—for Christ (24), Deloria reframed the Christian moment of redemption *from* the past as a comically inadequate response to practices of colonization and erasure. Deloria equated two figures who both represented the pitiful banality of differently constituted genocides. That Custer could at once be Eichmann and Jesus—both functionary and Messiah—alerted readers to the impossibility of narrating settler political development on redemptive terms and called them to reflect on the everyday violence of ongoing colonization.

Deloria's upbraiding of this dominant narrative form spoke to the role of redemption, then, as an idiom that both seems to promise the reconstitution of political community and yet is itself driven by nationalist concerns. Prophecy did play a role in critical languages specific to different Indigenous communities: Deloria cites the Hopi prophet Thomas Banyacya (114). But prophecy was not deployed in an ambivalent relation to the narrative of a "redeemer nation," in George Shulman's terms.[107] Rather, Deloria pointed out that the very narrative form inherent in prophecy tended to privilege time as a redemptive force moving away from a past from which there is no true escape because "the country was founded in violence" (255). Custer enjoined its readers to take up their "real" connections to this foundational violence that is sedimented in and lived out through the current terms of struggles over land.

For Deloria, decolonization required balancing the collective autonomy requisite to "tribal sovereignty" and "self-determination" with the equal demand for a "general policy of restitution for the past." The latter included "definite commitments to fulfill extant treaty obligations," land restitution, and recognition of nonrecognized tribes (52). Deloria thus planted the seeds not of a redemptive politics of "equality" or "inclusion" insofar as these were understood within the terms of civic inclusion but one focused on situated acts of restitution aimed at undoing a colonial war compounded by the "additional moral claims" raised by contemporary abandonment (52).[108] Treaties might function as a "pledge of faith between groups" embedded in ongoing entanglements, but only by shifting away from a politics premised on disavowal.¹⁰⁹ Decolonization would function both through practices of remedial justice and through the creation of ongoing structures of self-determination aimed at securing existing lands as the territorial bases and homelands of modern Indigenous nations. Those "removed" to urban spaces like Minneapolis and Los Angeles with termination would continue to exercise this distinct and differentiated citizenship by retaining access to federal services earmarked for Indigenous peoples via treaties and other mechanisms. Collective self-determination and multilayered citizenships would thus be contoured to the routes of colonial practices themselves. This kind of project was made possible because of the way that Indigenous peoples remade spaces both of confinement and dispersion, in resisting colonial domination.

Conclusion

In this chapter, I contextualized and connected Zitkala-Ša's and Vine Deloria Jr.'s efforts to theorize and enact Indigenous self-determination in relation to changing regimes and discourses of US colonial sovereignty. In particular, I argued that attending to the material contexts of settler-colonial conquest in the twentieth century allows for an analysis of the inherently contradictory character of discourses of citizenship and civil rights in settler-colonial societies. Dominant narratives that shape the political and cultural meanings of the civic in a settler-colonial society, that is, the civic inclusion narrative, are systematically weaponized so as to represent Indigenous forms of social solidarity and political community as civic disability, or, paradoxically, as a kind of prima facie instance of political exclusion. Whereas it is commonly assumed in US political thought that civil and political rights are either sufficiently or insufficiently implemented, this construct portraying barriers to a commonsense normative ideal fails to grapple with the role of civic discourses as *colonial* devices. These have played a central role in actively displacing other prospects of collective self-government and remedial justice.

Settler claims to the civic as a practice of civilizing function to solidify the boundaries between domestic and international, in effect, by pitting full citizenship in the settler society *against* Indigenous peoples' projects of self-government. When the meanings of citizenship are imprinted on the polity as implicitly hierarchical *statuses* relating directly to whiteness as a form of sovereign entitlement over others' lands, bodies, and life chances, citizenship discourse functions as a weapon of domination that can be deployed so as to grab land from Indigenous societies. In this way, the past and current absorption of Indigenous societies within the internal space of sovereignty naturalizes future colonization, under the thinly veiled guise of an emancipatory or even compensatory/humanitarian gesture.

In opposing these dominant discourses and governance practices, Zitkala-Ša and Deloria advanced constructive visions that sought to establish alternatives prioritizing self-determination of Indigenous societies over their lands, bodies, and cultural and political communities. These alternatives radically recontextualized the very links between individual and collective freedoms to account for structures of colonial violence birthed with the nation-state.

Zitkala-Ša and Deloria both theorized the criteria of Indigenous self-determination as integrally connected to the task of historicizing and transforming entrenched practices of domination of the sovereign state. They staged this confrontation especially in relation to constitutional law and administrative practices, which give their writings a structural focus on domination that mainly centers on institutions. As early as the run-up to World War I, North American Indigenous political thinkers offered a conception of freedom as freedom from the sovereign state as a symbol and enforcer of a regime of political slavery. Such ideas radicalized and transformed ambivalent republican inheritances, because they fundamentally reinterpret the background political contexts that typically write the colonialism of sovereignty out of the picture. Bringing this problematic to international discourses, this renovation negated the colonial denial of the equality of peoples by way of their containment within empire states and settler-colonial states. It offered instead an anticolonial conception of the equality of peoples against an imperial and (settler-)statist world order. In this way, Zitkala-Ša and Deloria conceived of self-determination as structures of freedom *from* the complex of changing colonial violence of the state.

Zitkala-Ša and Deloria did not outright reject US citizenship, as some of their interlocutors did on the quite legitimate grounds of holding to memberships in their own political communities. Yet, they still figured US citizenship in quite strategic and critically conscious terms that denied the colonial state both a right to determine belonging on colonized lands and to distribute the life chances that follow from such determinations. To this end, they treated US citizenship as a pragmatic necessity that prevented extreme forms of domination and provided some, albeit precarious and often retractable, avenues of political mobilization for colonized communities. They sought to enact a form of citizenship without civilization, that is, a citizenship shed of its pervasive functionality and signifying force as a way to secure colonial domination. As participants in the long-standing grassroots treaty councils of Lakota and Dakota communities, both emphasized treaties as the grounds for a renewed political imaginary of more horizontal social relations among diverse peoples.

In this chapter, I have primarily sketched elements of Indigenous self-determination defined as a capacious form of nondomination, which requires contesting and reshaping structures of colonial violence. This is a negative definition. Chapter 2 provides a more positive account of Indigenous self-determination as the creation of self-other relations beyond the model of sovereignty. To do so, I further develop the notion of "treaty" briefly touched upon here as a concept framing Indigenous decolonization struggles, both in strategic and more deeply normative terms. In coming back again to Vine Deloria Jr. and examining the writings of his brilliant aunt, the Dakota ethnographer Ella Deloria, I theorize treaties as earth-making practices—expressions of anticolonial agency aiming to realize nonexploitative and care-based relations between human and other-than-human communities, made kin to one another.

[CHAPTER TWO]

The Struggle for Treaty

*Ella Cara Deloria and Vine Deloria Jr.
on Anticolonial Relations*

The ultimate aim of a Dakota life, stripped of its accessories, was quite simple. One must obey kinship rules; one must be a good relative. . . . Without that aim and the constant struggle to attain it, the people would no longer be Dakota in truth. They would no longer even be human. To be a good Dakota, then, was to be humanized, civilized.

Ella Deloria, *Speaking of Indians*[1]

Cession of territory made to a member of the family of nations by a State as yet outside that family is real cession and a concern of the Law of Nations, since such State becomes through the treaty of cession in some respects a member of that family.

Lassa Oppenheim, *International Law: A Treatise*[2]

In its June 1974 "Declaration of Continuing Independence of the Sovereign Native American Indian Nations," the IITC issued what became a landmark agenda for Indigenous decolonization, eventually presenting it as part of a broader platform document to the UN in Geneva in 1977. In the declaration, delegates from Indigenous societies across North America asserted that settler states had "denied all Native people their international Treaty rights, Treaty lands and basic human rights of freedom and sovereignty."[3] The IITC demanded "that the human and treaty rights of all Native Nations will be honored" and sought "United States recognition of treaties signed with Native Nations." The delegates also called "upon the people of the world to support this struggle for our sovereign rights and treaty rights," and extended solidarity by expressing kinship with international "brothers and sisters," that is, colonized peoples around the world.[4]

In the "Declaration of Continuing Independence," the distinctive call to honor treaties—a call that is absent (or negligible) in other anticolonial struggles—sits alongside notions of sovereignty and human rights widely circulated in 1970s global politics. In a document that is otherwise similar to demands for decolonization of other national liberation movements, then, IITC's appeal to treaties stands out. What is the significance of treaties in the IITC's recasting of the terms of decolonization? Why treaties? In brief, IITC's appeal stems from Indigenous conceptions of the concept of treaty and practices of treaty making that have both been central to anticolonial struggles over *the terms* of sovereignty and in struggles for self-determination *beyond* sovereignty.

The account of treaties that follows here both builds upon and takes a different tack from the previous chapter's characterization of Indigenous self-determination in negative terms as a radicalized account of nondomination against colonial sovereignty. I build upon the previous chapter by tracking how Indigenous anticolonial thinkers have rejected structures of settler domination that are shaped through treaties as instruments of colonial dispossession and subordination, both in the making and violation of unequal treaties. Along this negative axis, honoring treaties and treaty rights ought to be understood as one among the many imperatives to redress structures of domination that function through settler-colonial societies' treaty-based colonial practices

More original as a point of departure for the analysis in this chapter are Indigenous accounts of treaties as constructive models for crafting collective self-other relations. Political struggles waged and everyday practices habituated through these models create relationships of political authority that resist and manifest alternatives to colonial sovereignty. Specifically, I construe this notion of treaty as a "scaling up" of the idiom and practice of kinship to the macroregister of international diplomacy. Along this positive axis, honoring treaties and treaty rights ought to be understood as an imperative to create ongoing relations of interdependent and relational self-determination (to "be a good relative"), as the proper *form* of just relations among peoples. This notion of treaty making is one key example of earth-making and transnational internationalism as anticolonial praxes that enact and pursue alternative visions of social order beyond the conceptual logics of sovereignty.

In doing this conceptual work, I aim to reorient existing discussions of the political meanings of treaties, which often focus on a relatively idealized form of egalitarian treaty-based relations as a foil to dominant colonial hierarchies. As a case in point, the eminent Canadian political theorist James Tully has posited a sharp antithesis between, on the one hand, the normative ideal of the "treaty relation" between Indigenous peoples and settlers in Canada and, on the other, the "colonial relation." By contrast, I think Tully overlooks the way that *competing* meanings of treaty in context can support both colonial and anticolonial projects and power relations. Downplaying the contention over what treaty entails as a concept and practice obscures the political force of Indigenous political struggles "to be a good relative" by creating specific *forms* of treaty relation with interdependent others.

Accordingly, a starting methodological premise here for me is to focus on the history of contestation over the *meanings internal to the very idea of treaty*. This premise is distinct from the more widely studied judicial debates over how to interpret the specific terms and clauses of particular treaties. Indeed, I begin with the idea that competing and historically variable *visions of treaties* have been contested throughout the twentieth century. My approach brings into focus more basic registers of conflict about how different conceptions of treaty entail philosophically divergent accounts of the composition of self-determination and self-other relations, with and beyond sovereignty. To mount this argument, I turn back to Vine Deloria Jr. and newly turn to the writings of Ella Cara Deloria (1889–1971), Vine Deloria Jr.'s aunt.

The argument of the chapter proceeds as follows: First, I argue that what the concept of treaty means is an inherent site of conflict in settler-colonial social formations. Altogether, treaties can be (a) unequal, violable contracts that serve settler-colonial societies as colonizing instruments of Indigenous dispossession and subordination, which aim to establish settler sovereignty and extinguish or significantly qualify prior Indigenous sovereignty; (b) contracts subject to an internal critique and made equal, enduring diplomatic accords by Indigenous resistance, which aims at clawing back self-determination *from* those same treaties; and (c) a substantive normative alternative that figures the treaty as a scaled-up kinship relation that establishes terms of mutual aid and interdependence by making collective self and other into relatives.

Second, I then delve into Ella Deloria and Vine Deloria Jr.'s respective accounts of treaty. I interpret Ella Deloria's writings as a response to the colonial form of "self-determination" imposed upon many Indigenous societies in the United States under the 1934 IRA. I conceptualize this as part of a wider Anglo-American (re)turn to indirect rule that influenced John Collier, the key architect of the act. Focusing on her *Speaking of Indians* (1944) and *Waterlily* (posthumously published in 1988), I then contend that Ella Deloria's work articulates a counter to this imposed "self-determination," by formulating kinship as an anticolonial Dakota-Lakota way of establishing ordered relations among citizens and groups as relatives to one another. Her writings manifest an alternative to colonial treaty making by offering a nonanthropocentric account of treaties as scaled-up ways of making kinship-like interdependencies (concept c). Her conception of treaties as anticolonial earthmaking practices that make human and other-than-human communities into interdependent relatives challenges the centrality of sovereignty to the imaginary of self-determination and intersocietal coordination within the international order.

Finally, I turn to Vine Deloria Jr.'s classic *Behind the Trail of Broken Treaties: An Indian Declaration of Independence* (1974), authored in the context of the American Indian Movement's (AIM's) 1972 Trail of Broken Treaties caravan to the White House. I argue that, though sometimes invoking treaty as kinship (what he called the "treaty-covenant" relation), Vine Deloria Jr.'s writing was primarily a strategic effort to recast state-Indigenous treaties as the equal contracts they could never be within the settler imaginary (concept b) by recovering them as international relations among sovereigns. Focused on generating institutional structures of nondomination, this position countered a settler structure of domination that operates through the discrediting and violation of treaties. These two understandings—treaty as anticolonial kinship praxis (concept c) and treaty as an internal critique of unequal colonial contracts (concept b)—coalesce in the IITC's declaration. In conclusion, I contend that treaties create self-determination on distinct terms that center nonanthropocentric relationality and care as the instrument and normative purpose *of* decolonization.

Treaty as Relation versus Treaty as (Subordinating) Contract

What constitutes the prevailing meaning of the treaty as a social form has shifted significantly over time. When Europeans first arrived on the east coast of Turtle Island (i.e., North America), they came into an existing world of diplomacy among Indigenous societies that included agreements to care for the earth itself.[5] Europeans made agreements with Indigenous societies by following specific Indigenous protocols and understandings of diplomacy already in widespread circulation. While evidently diverse in character, these protocols generally aimed at creating material and metaphorical bonds between peoples, that is, kinship. Such protocols included practices like ceremony, the exchange of gifts, intermarriage, and storytelling, which were integral to creating lasting political agreements. One prominent example is when the Haudenosaunee welcomed the Dutch through treaties of peace and friendship beginning in the early seventeenth century, the most famous of which is the Two Row Wampum (Kaswesntha).[6] These diplomatic relations coalesced into the Covenant Chain, a chain of alliance into which the Haudenosaunee enfolded later European powers on the continent.

These relations began to shift as European colonization focused increasingly on permanent land acquisition from Indigenous societies, a change further intensified by the founding of the United States as a settler empire. With them, so did the centrality of this conception of what a treaty is. As colonial state power facilitating markets in land subordinated Indigenous political and legal orders to settler law, the residues of this kinship-oriented understanding of treaty (e.g., gift giving) became subsumed within an empty, formalistic, and coercive logic of expropriation and genocidal pacification. These macrologics functioned in tandem with microlevel practices to facilitate the largest (highly coercive and contested) process of land and population transfer in the history of the modern world.[7] Contractual, eliminatory aspirations characterized much of the respective American and British/Canadian treaty systems.

By the second quarter of the nineteenth century, treaty-making practices in the settler colonies of the United States and the "Canadas" paradigmatically drew upon republican idioms of honor, legality, and consensual exchange between independent and equal collective wills in an attempt to square the increasingly omnipresent coercion of Indigenous peoples with liberal-democratic ideologies of consent-based governance and market exchange.[8] The US and Canadian states conceived of their treaty-making systems as forms of eliminatory inclusion, which freed up land through the forcible removal and/or concentration of Indigenous peoples to "reserved" lands. Such practices drew upon hierarchical categories of self-government arrayed according to the purported capacities of peoples for civilization. In this respect, colonial practices of *recognition by treaty* attributed only so much "sovereign agency" or "legal personality" to colonized peoples as would allow them to constitute the kinds of collective entities capable of consenting to their own destruction.[9]

In the case of settler-colonial practices, this colonial mode of negation issued not only in subordinate (collective) membership—such as exclusion from regimes of collective security and, later, human rights—but also a temporal limitation on the very *future existence* of Indigenous peoples as collectivities. Dividing time into before and after treaties, the state could unilaterally decide when even the annuities given on treaty terms to symbolize an equal "exchange" were no longer politically expedient technologies of dependency, assimilation, and domination. The asymmetrical recognition embedded in the treaty system as a contractual technology of subordination set up the later extinguishment of the very collective "self" of Indigenous peoples' self-rule. As Indigenous powers to make nationhood-based claims upon even these highly asymmetrical terms waned (with the US officially ending its treaty system on March 3, 1871, and Canada in 1923), settler-colonial dominions and full-fledged states could unilaterally revise or abrogate treaty terms.

Oppenheim's 1912 positivist legal analysis from the epigraph sharply reflects how self-government and inclusion on these terms into a colonial international order (a "family of nations") was paradoxically made real from the perspective of colonial powers through the negation of the full sovereignty of the colonized. The colonized, he argues, become "*in some respects* a member of that family" (my emphasis). Oppenheim's formulation here captures hierarchical, subordinate, and patriarchal terms of membership, which entails that in *other unstated respects* the colonized are not (and are never intended to be) full members of the family of nations. The legal scholar Antony Anghie's work broadens out to show how this notion of colonial recognition by treaty was normative to Eurocentric international law, or, more precisely, how imperial and colonial powers retroactively interpreted the law of nations by the second half of the nineteenth century. As Anghie puts it, Eurocentric international law dictated that colonized peoples "enter into the international realm by being conquered. That is, they come into existence as a result of the very act which nullified their sovereignty."[10]

Some contemporary accounts of treaties have responded to this history of colonial nullification by inclusion by seeking to identify intercultural norms (a "hidden constitution") shared between Indigenous and non-Indigenous peoples that underlie colonial treaty-making practices. The aim is to bring these to the surface to inform present-day constitutional debates. Most notably, James Tully has influentially distinguished between the "colonial relation" and the "treaty relation" as two distinct normative logics, an argument he has derived mainly from the "numbered treaties" in Canada based upon his work in the 1990s with Canada's Royal Commission on Aboriginal Peoples.[11] What Tully calls the "treaty relation" has been forged through contextually situated norms of reciprocal recognition between distinct peoples. These norms have been created and are continually remade, he argues, out of a set of embedded intercultural practices over centuries of dialogue between Indigenous and non-Indigenous peoples. This tradition of negotiation amid diversity arises out of six hundred or so treaties signed between the Crown or US state and Indigenous peoples, a tradition that in Canada typically refers back to the foundation of the Royal Proclamation of 1763.

The "colonial relation" is just the opposite. It is instead based on the subordination of the colonized through the unilateral imposition of settler-state systems of sovereignty and property. In brief, the two logics here, the treaty relation and the colonial relation, are framed as antithetical normative commitments.

I contend that a key limitation of this account is that Tully frames treaties as actual historical contexts of political speech and social formation, but only up to a point. Indeed, Tully's framework downplays the socioeconomic, political, and military context of actually existing treaties between Indigenous peoples and colonial powers. This selective contextualization that drives his recovery of what he considers the more genuine tradition of treaty relation then is what allows him to drive a conceptual wedge between a (recovered) treaty relation and the colonial relation.

Against my contention, Tully might offer a similar rebuttal to the one he makes in his refutation of Hume's classic critique of contract theory. That is, "just because a particular practice of consent, such as a treaty with a non-European authority, is surrounded by force and fraud, it does not follow that the practice of treaty making loses its authority."[12] Tully's assessment may be correct from a purely normative point of view. Yet, it still fails to take into account the hegemony of the Euro-American tradition of "the practice of treaty making" itself as a form of subjection that works by eliciting/inventing consent. This, of course, is not to endorse that hegemony but to understand how it operates and what this means for alternatives. This aspect of the real politics of how the treaty form has functioned is not something that theorists can simply rule out as *external* to the treaty-based tradition of interaction between the British Crown/US government and Indigenous peoples.

In contrast to Tully, I argue that paying heed to the contested meanings *internal* to the concept and practice of "treaty" actually helps to elucidate what has been distinctive to the (re)interpretation of treaties in particular strands of Indigenous anticolonial thought as challenges to basic structural antagonisms and structural drives of settler-colonial societies: In the first place, a mountain of historical writing has shown how Euro-American treaty practices have been *instruments* of settler-colonial dispossession, and this has created the actual *purposes and form* of the treaty in such contexts (concept a). In settler-colonial contexts where Indigenous peoples' modes of governance, land tenure, and mere presence posed significant, long-standing obstacles to land acquisition from the perspective of colonial and state administrators, land speculators, and ordinary settlers, treaties have functioned instrumentally to effect various means of eliminating such obstacles to expansionist ends. For example, treaties served as a momentary pause of hostilities in an otherwise continual state of colonial war making. They also functioned to facilitate territorial empire by other—often less costly—means, such as the predatory use of debt,[13] starvation,[14] and kidnapping[15] to coerce land sales and quiescence at the negotiating table.

To be sure, settler states record treaties in accordance with a logic of contract, as nominally free agreements between sovereigns absent unilateral coercion. Yet, treaties ultimately subjected and eclipsed Native self-determination to a subordinate—even eliminable—position *within* settler law and state power. In settler-colonial societies in which colonial powers *produced* state sovereignty in part *through* treaties with Indigenous peoples (e.g., Canada and the United States) rather than via pure terra nullius logics (e.g., Australia), settlers sought to use treaties to fix boundary lines, extract land cessions, and secure the spatial removal of Indigenous peoples as obstacles to desired lands. To neglect those real historical meanings of treaties as contractual instruments of colonization that both create *and* negate the full package of features normally associated with "sovereignty" obscures the significance of the treaty form itself in legitimizing colonial dispossession.

This tendency to shy away from this hegemonic functioning of the colonial treaty system also unintentionally downplays the political force of the anticolonial challenge that Indigenous accounts of treaty making propose. In short, these express and argue on behalf of alternative ways of conceiving of self-determination and social order as such. Many Indigenous scholars have reconstructed conceptions of treaty that offer substantially different accounts of what it means to forge a relation among peoples. For example, Heidi Kiiwetinepinesiik Stark, Gina Starblanket, and James (Sa'ke'j) Youngblood Henderson have theorized how a treaty expresses and generates an "ongoing relationship," a "political agreement," or a form of "international kinship" based in a "permanent living relationship."[16] As Robert Williams Jr. puts it, kinship is a "way of imagining a world of human solidarity where we regard others as relatives."[17] One acts *as if* one is related to another so as to create and maintain bonds of solidarity. Such an imaginative regard enables a commitment to provide certain forms of support and assistance to others and the expectation of a "right to the social labor of others in the group." In this sense, Williams writes, "To be related to another in a system of kinship is to expect assistance from that other person and to expect to be asked for and be ready to render assistance as well."[18]

As was the case with the Indigenous diplomatic worlds that Europeans first stumbled into, the concept of treaty here is not just (or even primarily) the contractual document signed at the end of the negotiation specifying the terms of agreement and/or exchange. The treaty is also the relation itself, that is, the expressive act of negotiating and understanding generated through oral statements. These acts are more than that moment, too. They transform and bind each party into what is assumed to persist as an enduring social, moral, and ecological position of relatedness to one another. Relatedness is taken as a condition of possibility of negotiating terms of "exchange" in the narrower, contractual sense. In this manner, treaties establish self-determination in creating a nexus of relations with kin. The theoretical upshot is that self-determination *and* other-determination are actually forged together as part of the resulting kinship network, as are ways of repairing these connections in cases of violence and various other forms of disrepair.

Many Indigenous counternarratives of treaty in this mode operate as an intergenerational tradition of the continuance and rebuilding of social and cultural worlds, an anticolonial critique of the hegemonic narrative of colonial treaty making, and a continual reassertion of how Indigenous peoples' political and legal orders as jurisdictional authorities approach actually existing treaties with colonial powers. I now turn to one set of Indigenous genealogies of the struggle for treaty in this anticolonial key.

Indirect Rule and the Politics of Self-Determination

Ella Deloria composed the bulk of her writings in the wake of the 1934 Indian New Deal (the Wheeler-Howard Act or IRA), which brought a legal end to allotment and reorganized tribes to adopt constitutions. I interpret her 1944 classic, *Speaking of Indians*, as a critique of and effort to decenter this top-down institutional reorganization as a genuine form and primary site of Indigenous self-determination. Indeed, she describes the IRA in this work as a source of "perpetual guardianship," that is, a continued source of colonial domination.[19] This directly contrasts with some representations of the IRA as a suitable, even self-evident, institutionalization of an Indigenous right to self-government. Her critique comes from the perspective of her account of kinship within Lakota and Dakota communities, as an alternative way of constructing social order and the very "self" of self-determination that the IRA contained and disavowed. In short, this is an anticolonial praxis of kinship, scaled up to treaties, that reaffirms the equality of peoples against colonial sovereignty's (re)definitions of self-determination.

Before focusing on Ella Deloria, it is imperative to provide a sense of the IRA to achieve a wider perspective on her analysis of it as "perpetual guardianship." As discussed in chapter 1, Progressive Indigenous abolitionist intellectuals such as Zitkala-Ša, Carlos Montezuma, and Laura Cornelius Kellogg articulated bureau abolition as an emancipatory project that challenged the collective bondage of reservation life. These kinds of radical challenges emanating from Indigenous circles are rarely placed at the center of research on federal Indian policy. Yet, they are crucial to comprehending why John Collier, Progressive reformer and commissioner of Indian Affairs under FDR from 1933 to 1945, promoted the Indian New Deal as a reform effort that incorporated aspects of their critique of "collective bondage" without abolishing the bureau itself. Indeed, Collier used the same idiom of slavery just as the SAI critics did when he wrote of an "American Congo," a comparison between infamous Belgian atrocities in the Congo and US tyranny over Indigenous peoples.[20] In doing so, however, Collier deflected the politics the bureau abolitionists had in mind by invoking this analogy to chattel slavery: the demand for immediate, unconditional self-determination.

Collier's explicit effort to counter the radical implications of Progressive Indigenous critique appears in his addresses to Indigenous audiences. For example, in a speech at a regional congress with the Plains tribes aimed at convincing them to ratify IRA constitutions, Collier argued:

> Many people and some Indians have risen up and said that the only hope for the Indian is to put an end to the guardianship of the Government so that they may stand a chance in living. Some people have said that the guardianship of the Government is injuring the Indian, is robbing the Indian, is keeping them in a condition of slavery. Therefore, the responsibility must be brought to an end. . . . But that is not the answer. The cure for the evils done by the Government is *not to abolish but to reform it* and make it do good things instead of evil things, and that is true of the guardianship over Indians.[21]

Collier countered the Indigenous abolitionists' structural critiques by refuting the inherent authoritarianism they attributed to bureau domination. In September 1934, he further argued before the Iroquois that "federal guardianship does not have to be an absolution working through an unreviewable bureaucracy."[22] Unlike the directly assimilationist aims of moving individuals from tribalism to civilization, Collier proposed a "partnership" between the bureau and tribes.[23]

What is key to point out here is that Collier objected only to *direct rule* aimed at the coercive assimilation of Indian *individuals* into the polity. He had no objection to *indirect rule* that would enable US (colonial) supremacy while integrating Indigenous societies as *collectives* into the polity. In his autobiography, Collier recalled that the Indian New Deal borrowed from both the progressive "*ejidal* achievements of Mexico's agrarian revolution" and "Britain's system of indirect administration in Fiji, in the country that is now Ghana, and in some other places."[24] Collier specifically admired Julian Huxley's 1931 *Africa View*, which framed British indirect rule as a compromise position between the preservation of timeless "local tradition" of "tribes" considered to be on the verge of disintegration and continued imperial order in a more accountable form.[25]

My interpretation here cuts against typical accounts of Collier's significance. Indeed, Collier has gained a reputation as a cultural pluralist. He often spoke of Indigenous cultures as a romanticized communal solution to the anomie of US industrial society.[26] But this is a retrospective misreading of some of the key *political functions* of avowing "difference" in the wider Anglo-American imperial context. Once this broader context is taken into account, Collier's political vocabulary is better seen as an effort to Americanize indirect rule in the service of neutralizing the abolitionist politics of Indigenous Progressives.

In fact, Collier's claims about cultural difference without the alteration of fundamental asymmetries of power facilitated what purported to be more culturally resonant and self-directed forms of colonial domination. Ella Deloria keenly pointed this out about the IRA, and I will argue later that her political and social framing of culture refutes this mode of legitimation. Indeed, Collier legitimized the IRA on anthropological grounds as a project of harmonizing the cultural personality of Native peoples (the "ancient Sioux communities") with a constitutional government that would fit as a municipality in US federalism. He argued that this strategy would replace the assimilationist logic of allotment by encouraging a "fit" between community "tradition" and the formal institutions of self-government.

To map arenas of Native culture to be preserved within the political container of the IRA, Collier funded an Applied Anthropology Unit in the bureau that sought to establish this basic framework. Scudder Mekeel, a Boasian and head of the unit from 1935 to 1937, dryly stated that the IRA followed British indirect rule's "technique for carrying out administrative objectives": "the technique of working through native organization" so as to "provide the opportunity for necessary and inevitable changes to take place in gradual and orderly fashion."[27] The IRA presumed that the political container for self-government was a priori and would then "organize" and serve as a vehicle for protecting the cultural features of tribal life.

Mekeel and Collier's framing of harmonization between ancient culture and modern politics turned on the assumption that there was, in the first instance, a distinct sphere of culture separate from politics. What they meant by "culture" as distinct from "politics" was ideologically unstable. They oscillated between a primitivist avowal of cultural difference and a more developmental model of the (lack of) cultural fitness of colonized subjects for democracy (subject to "necessary and inevitable changes"). The latter resonated with the politics of "trusteeship" in the wider Anglophone imperial world, whereby the imperial powers would govern mandated territories until colonized peoples were ready for self-rule.

In Collier's words, the IRA would enable "Indian tribes or groups" to "develop the kind of self-government that they want, that is fitted to them, and may take on more power or less power as they prefer."[28] It would give "permission to the Indians to work out self-government which is appropriate to their traditions, to their history and to their social organization."[29] For Collier, this was a preferable way of harnessing "the ruling power of native institutions and energies to secure an improvement of a type harmonious with native capacity."[30] There is significant conceptual slippage here between the directed will and preference of communities shaping their conditions of self-rule and the "fit" or "capacity" of communities for self-rule expressed in forms dictated from above. My reading suggests that this was an uneasy meeting place between (what many see positively as) cultural pluralism and an evolutionary, Burkean politics that sought to mold institutions to the imputed developmental fitness of a collective self, and vice versa.

In its actual implementation, the IRA was marked by two notable features of this new regime of Indian self-government: First, the bureau explicitly retained the legal and administrative capacity to intervene were this collective self not to conform to the dictates of the partnership, so the label "guardianship" was appropriate in the sense of authoritarian institutions with veto power over tribes as well. Second, the new governance entity, the tribal council, would become a federal "instrumentality," a kind of quasi-municipality.[31] According to Chris Pexa, the IRA aimed to found "tribal business and governance in bourgeois and representational democratic molds."[32] What is important here is that, in doing so, the IRA created new tribal councils that *displaced* the authority of previous, albeit evolving, modalities of self-rule for some Indigenous peoples.[33]

Kinship and treaties are historically key here as a response to the IRA's containment and production of a delimited model of self-determination. Specifically, the division between politics and culture that legitimized the terms of indirect rule simultaneously *de*legitimized kinship and treaty relations as politicized forms central to practices of self-rule in the Lakota-Dakota context. In particular, pre-IRA Teton Lakota treaty councils such as those of the Oglala Sioux at Pine Ridge formed in relation to upholding the violated terms of the 1868 Treaty of Fort Laramie.[34] These evolved *out of* kinship relations, in the form of the thióšpaye, or camp fire circle, the social structure that Ella Deloria reconstructs as the "Dakota way of life."

In effect, treaty councils at Pine Ridge evolved earlier "cultural" forms of familial-social structure into a governing body for the purposes of enforcing the terms of treaties signed with the United States in 1851 and 1868, the respective Treaties of Fort Laramie. In this way, Collier's efforts to organize tribes as municipalities within US federalism superseded the very modes of resistant political authority *rooted in treaty relation themselves*. Acknowledging those relations, however, required an acknowledgment of communities articulating politics, sociality, and culture altogether in different forms, because the treaty councils cut across distinctions embedded in the IRA between a "private sphere" of culture and a "public sphere" associated with institutionalized authority relations vis-à-vis the settler state. As Mark Rifkin has argued, the IRA superseded "native-driven processes of self-definition—new traditions—that had emerged as a result of participation in the treaty system. Positioning the IRA as if it were completely separate from the legacy of treaties allowed federal officials to disregard the forms of native governance that had developed in relation to the structures and history of treaty-making."[35] Kinship and treaties are/were central instances of how Lakota-Dakota peoples *made* their own institutions of self-determination, by creating terms of political order and international relations beyond settler-state domination.

Ella Deloria and the Struggle for Kinship

Before elaborating on Ella Deloria's conceptual engagement with kinship in the 1930s and 1940s, a brief intellectual biography is necessary to situate her work. A collaborator of Franz Boas, Ella Deloria was an ethnographer, linguist, teacher, community researcher, and novelist whose work is now hailed as a predecessor of contemporary tribal revitalization movements. Deloria was born in 1889 at the White Swan (Yankton) reservation just two years after allotment and one year before the Wounded Knee massacre; she was raised at Standing Rock, among Hunkpapa and Sihasapa (Teton) Lakota.[36] After a peripatetic educational and career path that led her to Oberlin College and Columbia University teacher's college, and teaching jobs from 1915 to 1927, Deloria worked as a consultant—a translator, collaborator, and research assistant—for Boas from the summer of 1927 until his death in 1942, then for his replacement, Ruth Benedict. Janet Finn has argued that Deloria's work, which depended on "managing from contract to contract," was the "anthropological equivalent of piecework."[37] In spite of her often precarious working life as an informant with significant family responsibilities, Deloria gathered and contributed classic works of Dakota ethnography and stories (*Dakota Texts*, *The Dakota Way of Life*) and linguistics (*Dakota Grammar*).

Ella Deloria was aware of the IRA, and she was present at Pine Ridge when deliberation and voting on it was undertaken. According to Phillip J. Deloria, her research took her to several reservations all over Indian country from 1934 to 1936 while debates on the IRA were raging among tribal communities.[38] In the context, she used her skills to work for the grass roots. She reported in a letter to Franz Boas that she had helped to translate a petition of three Oglala citizens, "which those three Indians made who went to Washington on their own initiative, to kick against the Indian 'New Deal.' They are the 'Illegal Committee,' so called because they are the opposition faction on the Pine Ridge, and their Leader, Ben American Horse was arrested and fined fifty dollars for opposing Mr. Collier's program."[39] This appeal was among the efforts of the grassroots treaty councils to uphold the 1851 and 1868 Treaties of Fort Laramie.

Scholars of Deloria such as Maria Cotera and Chris Pexa have long identified the consistent emphasis in her work on Dakota and Lakota women as the bearers of culture and governance, and as the central figures in teaching proper kinship behavior to the next generation.[40] In another letter to Boas, she recounts how she sat in on a meeting of women at Pine Ridge with "Lucy Cramer, Felix Cohen, and Mr. Derker of the Indian Office" (key figures in the Indian New Deal). In Deloria's translation of their concerns, she recalls: "Now, if you let *us* manage it, they said in effect, we can talk it out, and agree on it because we shall be thinking what is best for our children, instead of how pleasant to meet and eat the government's food; and we can persuade our men to see it that way. We are the boss in our homes anyway, what power have the men?" In other words, Deloria emphasizes that the women—"more concerned over the bill than the men"—were demanding that they be the ones to come to a consensus on which elements of the IRA benefited the next generations.[41] With respect to treaties, Deloria's focus is significant because US and Canadian treaty negotiators elevated male leaders as their counterparts, imposing masculinist governing structures through international diplomacy. The struggle against this restructuring of Lakota diplomacy itself continued into the politics surrounding the IRA.

My interpretation of Ella Deloria aims to deal more systematically with her account of kinship at a philosophical register. Deloria is best known as an ethnographer and linguist of the Lakota and Dakota. I emphasize the pedagogical dimensions of her writings, at the center of which is the effort to teach Lakota-Dakota and non-Indigenous readers about the powerful reach of kinship as a form of life and an idiom of social and political struggle.[42] In other words, in centering her discussion on kinship, she does more than describe culturally particular forms. Rather, she places readers into a "Dakota point of view" on how political communities ought to be organized, and theorizes the enduring value of this political ethic. In short, she theorizes kinship as a way of ordering and imagining politics, and relations among polities, ones grounded in anticolonial, Indigenous-defined practices of self-determination.[43]

In *Speaking of Indians*, Deloria's efforts to rethink familiar categories of political life is easy to miss. Geared toward a dominant white Christian audience, her writing practically chats with the reader, seeks to appease Christian sensibilities, and gives a friendly, "popular science" gloss on the objective expertise typical of an ethnographic lens during her time.[44] Indeed, Deloria presents the thióšpaye, or campfire circle, the core collective unit of Lakota and Dakota social arrangement, in the anodyne language of ethnography and sentimental literature (not the political manifesto).

A careful reading, however, shows how she asserts an alternative account of the philosophical premises that informed Lakota and Dakota prereservation life and that had since developed in relation to treaty-making practices. In other words, her conversational writing smuggles in the powerful and critical notion that kinship is an imaginative and quite flexible solution to the universal problem of how to maintain social order and decency in a political community, not an idiosyncratic or even particular feature of Dakota life. Kinship functions as such a solution, she argues, by creating a complex system for (a) establishing how people are related and (b) creating requirements for the performance of those relations through role-specific "reciprocal obligations" and comportments.[45] In short, by making everyone related to one another in some way, all become aware of what their obligations are with respect to everyone else.

In part 2 of *Speaking of Indians*, "A Scheme of Life That Worked," Deloria outlines Dakota kinship in the thióšpaye. In brief, a thióšpaye is the camp fire circle that traveled together in a seasonal round. She reiterates this description in her novel *Waterlily*: composed of "a larger family, constituted of related households," the thióšpaye is governed according to strict social customs that established the specific roles and responsibilities of each person in the network.[46] At the level of both the basic functioning of the society and the ethics of being Dakota, Deloria stresses how kinship "was the very essence of Dakota communal life." Kinship orchestrates interdependence and belonging by creating relationships. Those relationships all come with role-specific etiquettes within the context of an extended, nonnuclear form of sociality.[47]

Kinship functioned within the thióšpaye to dignify each of its members, by creating a "never-ending interplay of honorings one to another, young and old" (*SI*, 48). Such "honorings" facilitated deeply ingrained practical expectations of reciprocity and assistance, based on assumptions about the inherent interdependence and need for continual care and regard of all beings to which one had made a relation. She describes an endless cycle of gift giving (and receiving) as the central expression of this system of relationship making. The resulting orientations were formative of the self, too, in the sense that becoming a good relative meant internalizing as one's own these kinds of etiquettes and then embodying them in actual practices of relating to others. Kinship meant a discipline of self-fashioning in relation to community norms that draw one into civilization in Dakota terms.

In this way, kinship establishes a system of social solidarity that makes civil life possible. Accordingly, Deloria bluntly rejected what we might now think of as functionalist interpretations of this sociality. Instead, she argued that the "giving system" constituted a "scheme of life," far more than a strategic "bartering game." In a key passage, she writes: "I can safely say that the ultimate aim of Dakota life, stripped of accessories, was quite simple: One must obey kinship rules; one must be a good relative" (*SI*, 25). Being trained into and struggling to be a good relative was at the core of what it meant *to be* Dakota, such that "no Dakota who has participated in that life will dispute that" (*SI*, 25).

Of significance here is the way that Deloria diverges from her mentor Boas, in plainly arguing that an engagement with Dakota principles generates much more than an appreciation for the (usually waning) alterity of the practices of a cultural group.[48] Instead, Deloria argues that being a good relative is a way of humanizing ethical and political conduct *as such*; it is not simply what it means to understand oneself from within this worldview as a "good Dakota." The struggle to be a good relative is cast here as a fragile practice of making inhuman—unordered or disordered—relations *into* ordered and human relations. Deloria avers:

> Without that aim and the constant struggle to attain it, the people would no longer be Dakotas in truth. They would no longer even be human. To be a good Dakota, then, was to be humanized, civilized. And to be civilized was to keep the rules imposed by kinship for achieving civility, good manners, and a sense of responsibility towards every individual dealt with. (*SI*, 25)

This claim cuts against depictions of kinship as prepolitical, which would place the Dakota closer to a "state of nature" than Western state formations.

She undermines the division between culture and politics that informed the IRA's system of indirect rule. In Deloria's formulation here, kinship is explicitly an *institution*: it is a way that a collective "self" is created, represented, and regenerated over time. In fact, Deloria insists upon the notion that it is an institution the explicit aim of which is to humanize and civilize conduct by making oneself and making others into relatives.

In the most basic sense, Deloria argues here that what it means to realize the promise of one's humanity and to create a genuinely civil society is to engage in this struggle for kinship. One struggles to act as kin oneself and make others into kin in turn. What is being rendered here is the "constant struggle" to become civilized, which implies an ethical ideal toward which individuals have to actively orient their conduct in order to meet the demands of the institution. She explains the aim of obedience and responsibility to relations as an injunction toward acting in civilized ways toward human and other-than-human relatives. Though undoubtedly demanding, she deems that "its rewards were pleasant" for its capacity to socialize individuals through such a vast network of support (*SI*, 31).

Conversely, it is the absence of *kinship*—not the absence of *sovereignty*—that threatens to bring the kind of disorder and inhumanity that is associated with the deterioration of conduct that is "humanized, civilized." The colonial onslaught against this system, she implies, meant a loss of humanity. Seeing things from a Dakota and Lakota perspective meant witnessing a disordered world in the sense of a world unmade of kin.

Deloria's emphasis on kinship as a practice of civility and peacemaking within and outside the thióšpaye is reflected, as well, in her peculiar choice to use the umbrella term "Dakota" almost exclusively. She drew her ethnographic materials from *Lakota* informants, so we know that her choice to use the term "Dakota" in her writing was intentional. She comments that "peace is implied by the very name of the people, Odakota, a state or condition of peace; the 'O' is a locative prefix" (*SI*, 22).[49] This choice is additional evidence that she was seeking to represent kinship as a consciously pursued civilizing practice to bring others into a web of roles and responsibilities as relatives.

Throughout this account, she connects kinship as a social system to kinship as a way of ordering political community. In the first instance, she argues that kinship *was* politics in the sense that it was "practically all the government there was. It was what men lived by" (*SI*, 31). More subtly, she argued that "by kinship, all Dakota people were held together in a great relationship that was theoretically all-inclusive and co-extensive with the Dakota domain" (*SI*, 24). By using the term "domain" here, Deloria signals how those relations created a political order. There is also a territorial dimension to "domain": domain indicates a conception of territory premised on negotiation and use through the connections that are mediated by kinship relations, not colonial boundaries. This latter meaning clashes with domain understand as *dominium* in the sense of absolute private ownership determined through a right of exclusion and the state's exercise of a monopoly of violence over land rung by clearly delimited borders.

In the more specific context of the IRA's containment of self-government to the reservation, the "all-inclusive" nature of these connections represents a much more extensive vision of a collective self that spans across a "great relationship" that allowed for mobility *across* territory. Simply, this is a rejection of the boundaries of reservation life as the locus of self-determination. In the chapter entitled "Picture of Reservation Life," she likewise underscores that "kinship continued strong, in spite of the dispersion of reservation life" and "enforced dormancy" (*SI*, 96, 98).[50]

Deloria also argues that the practice of kinship is political in the further sense that it is itself a practice of citizenship. Indeed, what makes someone a good relative coincides with the duties and virtues of good citizenship, since "to be as good relatives was also to act as good citizens of society, meaning persons of integrity and reliability" (*SI*, 31). "The dictates of citizenship," she observes, "demanded of relatives that they do not harm each other" (*SI*, 29). Her conflation here between the citizen and the relative is not a mistake, since it suggests that kinship is essential both to public, civilized conduct and to a specific way of ordering and imagining the polity itself. Moreover, the entire notion of Indigenous societies composed of "citizen-relatives" brings with it a schema that implodes the premise on which the IRA was based, with presumptive borders drawn between the privatized domain of family, a narrow arena of fossilized "native culture," and politics as the institutionalization of self-government within US federalism. In this way, kinship is also political as an anticolonial praxis that makes the collective self *across* these imposed colonial spheres, through patterned practices manifesting reciprocal relatedness to others.

Treaty as Kinship

Let me to now turn to treaties, which I depict as a scaling up of kinship to relations *between* political communities. In doing so, it is first necessary to clarify that one of the primary reasons this notion of kinship as multiscalar is plausible at all is that kinship is *not* strictly familial in any narrow sense. Indeed, Deloria labors throughout her writings to rebut this common misunderstanding, which functions to make kinship seem apolitical, natural, and culturally particular. She directly states that under "social kinship" practices, "even real outsiders became relatives" (*SI*, 27). The task of kinship, in this sense, was not to "be" a relative but to "make relatives" (*SI*, 29).

This emphasis upon kinship as a practice is further illustrated in *Waterlily* in the rearing of children, as parents, grandparents, and other relatives are continually engaged in teaching children how to craft themselves in these commitments to become a good relative. Composed between 1938 and 1942, *Waterlily* uses narrative to exemplify these structures of kinship.[51] Set in the 1830s and 1840s, it is based, Deloria wrote, on "what the many old women informants have told me as being their own or their mothers' or other relatives experiences" and the oral stories collected in her *Dakota Texts*.[52] The novel tells an intergenerational story of thióšpaye life: it begins with Blue Bird, and traces the life of Blue Bird's daughter, Waterlily. The novel is pedagogical in several respects, as Deloria translates oral histories into plot structure and numerous asides to explore the values, forms, and psychological pull (and tension) of kinship relations in the thióšpaye. Though often represented anthropologically as customary and unreflective, the constant training of kinship in the novel shows how making kin is an ongoing, reflective action of creating relations with strangers.

Yet, turning others from strangers into relatives is not just a theoretical possibility. As Lakota scholar Nick Estes (Kul Wicasa Oyate) observes, interpretations of the term *WoLakota* itself include "treaty" and "peace," stemming from the original Lakota treaty with the buffalo (discussed below).[53] It is not surprising, then, that Deloria actually frames kinship-qua-treaty as a political-ethical and even existential imperative that is, nevertheless, a rather flexible and open-ended paradigm through which to establish relations with other communities and beings. Indeed, she notes that it was crucial to make relatives to create a sense of trust and shared expectations about social obligations: "of relatives only you might be sure, because they and you both knew what your reciprocal obligations were as such" (*SI*, 29). Such demands first necessitated making relatives in order to sustain good relations with others: "it was first necessary to make relatives out of erstwhile strangers, thus putting them 'on the spot,' and then deal with them on that basis" (*SI*, 29). Deloria quotes the maxim to children to "be related, somehow, to everyone you know" (*SI*, 49). The demands of kinship compelled those brought inside the "ring" of relations to act as relatives—that is, to act to sustain the specific symbolic and material practices of connectedness required of relatives.

Treaty-making practices constitute an effort to extend the social kinship model further outward to relations with peoples who are understood to be distinct from the Dakota, yet nevertheless capable of performing reciprocal aid. In *Waterlily*, Deloria describes the Sun Dance in just these terms: "The ceremonial give-away was fundamental to all plains life. For the Dakotas, it was their particular pride and glory. And now here it was to be elevated to its sublime height, in one concerned act. Not from person to person, as usual, but from tribe to tribe." "The result of this mass generosity back and forth [between the Lakota and the Omaha]," she concludes, "was an increasing sense of friendship and camaraderie."[54]

In essence, Deloria traces a preexisting way of understanding relationship making based upon kinship protocols, which consequently frame the kind of agreements that can be genuinely called treaties. In doing so, she represents treaty making as a struggle aimed at creating a state of peace "from tribe to tribe," by making relatives out of outsiders.[55] Here, the problem with outsiders to the family is not "difference" subject to eliminatory violence but, rather, uncertainty, which calls for default wariness: strangers could "so easily turn out to be the incarnation of Iktomi, the legendary spirit of deceit, ready to play a trick on you" (*SI*, 29). The aim is to extend relations in such a way as to create a "condition of peace" where before none existed, which does not pretend to rule out the possibility of disruptions in the relationship (*SI*, 22).

For example, in response to a cycle of tit-for-tat violence, Deloria has one elder in *Waterlily* intervene to reconcile by stating that "it ought never to happen among men of the universal kinship of humans. Let us have peace once more."[56] Treaty making understood as a kinship-making practice is an ongoing labor that requires the active fostering, maintenance, and—when necessary—repair of relationships.

By theorizing the struggle for kinship as a paradigm of "civilized" activity that can scale down or up to different tasks of establishing good relations, Deloria offers a set of open-ended earthmaking practices that replace self-other relations with kin-kin relations. In doing so, the model aims to resist and move beyond the disavowal of interdependence core to colonial sovereignty.

She also establishes an external normative perspective from which to critique the colonial form of recognition by treaty (concept a in the introduction to this chapter) as a kind of distorted failure of kinship. In brief: On the one hand, Deloria's account of treaty recovers and prefigures these nonstate oriented meanings and practices of treaty making, and therefore of relations that lend meaning to "self-determination." On the other hand, she provides an external critique from the kinship perspective of the settler state's colonial treaty-making practices.

The practices of treaty that Deloria tracks have little to do with establishing pacific relations with an untrustworthy state and land-hungry settlers.

Instead, the primary models of treaty making aside from the Sun Dance are those with *other-than-human* communities. In these latter interactions, Dakota people learn through stories to treat other-than-human beings as distinct nations who demand care and reciprocity, and, in turn, provide support to the human communities who depend on them. Two examples from her writing illustrate this contention.

In the first of these, Blue Bird remembers her grandmother taking her and her younger brother out to collect "a large cache of earth beans." The grandmother remarks that "I could easily have . . . brought the beans home. But of course I waited." The aim of waiting and returning the next day is to leave time to make a "return gift for the mice when you take away their food. . . . They have to have something to live on, too." "For each handful" Blue Bird's grandmother collects, "she religiously returned a handful of green cord that had been parboiled for the mice indeed."[57]

The second treaty Deloria describes is the relationship between the Dakota and the buffalo as a "covenant"—a relationship that originates in the charter established when "from the son of the Buffalo-woman . . . we roving Tetons come."[58] In both *Waterlily* and *Speaking of Indians*, Deloria retells the story of how the buffalo save the starving Dakota in a time of famine. In *Speaking of Indians*, she relates how the buffalo offer to become the Dakota's "guardian" because "a Dakota found his way by chance into the underworld where the buffalo nation [*Pte Oyate*] lived, and there, with bow and arrow, was able to rid them of a perpetual menace. In gratitude the buffalo-chiefs promised to follow him and his offspring forever" (*SI*, 61).

Deloria explains that the Dakota, who were "starving," come to regard the buffalo as an "arch-relative" who, in each hunt, renew this agreement: they "kept their vow" and "extended hospitality to us."[59] This covenant is an act of promising that endures "for all time" in and through the material relation between the two peoples: "As long as we live, you too shall live and prosper." "While the buffalo live we shall not die."[60] The structure of the relationship prescribes terms of reciprocity premised on distinctive (not inevitably egalitarian nor symmetrical) duties. The buffalo act as a "host nation," and the Dakota learn to "revere" the buffalo to secure a life of freedom and plenitude by, for example, "kill[ing] no more than we need."[61]

The terms of reciprocity require regarding other-than-human others as kin—much as relatives train children to treat fellow humans in accordance with their specific relations to them, and the obligations that follow therefrom. For example, the camp circle historian Woyaka in *Waterlily* recalls that "symbols of the buffalo's sacrifice, were buried while the people wailed ceremonially, as for dead relatives."[62] Woyaka's invocation of the buffalo as "relatives" or "friends" is a way of figuring a form of interdependence guided by permanent relations of reciprocity, which is exemplified in the practice of not taking more than one needs as the fulfillment of a "vow" made to the buffalo.

What Deloria describes here is a form of treaty making that is also a practice of earthmaking: That self-determination is a mode of *inter*dependence with a variety of beings is built into the story, as Woyaka contends that "thus early [our ancestors] learned that man cannot manage alone."[63] By making treaties with the other-than-human "nations" through origin stories and symbolic and material aid—what she calls becoming "*re*-related" (*SI*, 61)—the Dakota engage in a practice of earthmaking aimed at cocreating the shared conditions of care and flourishing.

Treaty making in this conception becomes an important instance of earthmaking, by establishing reciprocal norms and expectations based on nonexploitative and nonextractive obligations to generate permanent relations of mutual interdependence. In the context of a colonial *dis*ordered world of broken relations, earthmaking is of necessity a form of anticolonial agency that (re)creates institutions and reciprocity-informed networks of care that take as primary the struggle to become a good relative.

Moreover, this model challenges the very form taken by the relations between collective self and other that prevails in colonial sovereignty. By enacting collective responsibilities in a relational fashion with animal, plant, and human communities, the collective self is actually made as a product of both internal and external relations with relatives. Conversely, what is the "other" on the model of colonial sovereignty actually becomes a relative; they are no longer an "other" in the sense of an identity that stands as a symbolic opposition or material boundary on the capacities of a collective self to have autonomy over their decisions. Instead, relatives are made integral and interdependent *to* the political decision-making and participatory channels of this collective self.

Deloria does not, however, suggest that this conception of treaty entails that the actual treaties with colonial states could ever follow this model. Rather, struggles framed through this grammar of political resistance provide a lens through which to critique settler domination as a form of domination that is exercised in *both* the practice of making *and* the practice of violating treaties. When we turn soon to Ella's nephew, Vine Deloria Jr., we will see that one way he critiques colonial states is by pointing to their constant failure to uphold the very treaty terms that they claim as expressions of their own constitutional orders. By contrast, Ella Deloria's is a more external critique. She evaluates the structurally induced failure of the subordinating colonial treaty form as an expression of the disordered, dystopic relations from which kin both human and other-than-human must be liberated.

It is worth recalling here Oppenheim's reference in the epigraph to the metaphor of the "family of nations" in colonial international law, which invokes a quintessentially patriarchal and highly coercive model of family formation. While it is rarely interpreted in these terms, the metaphor of the family he invokes can be seen with new eyes from the kinship-based perspective. The colonial treaty system realizes an extended family—brings those outside to the inside—primarily by materially subordinating the colonized to a hierarchically differentiated order of dominant and subordinated (or expiring) sovereigns. On this model, peace is a temporary cessation of structurally reoccurring colonial warfare until such time as the terms of any current relation can be superseded to the advantage of the dominant party.

In this light, it becomes possible to think of Deloria's model as an alternative potential universalism that refuses the colonial treaty system, a "family of [human and other-than-human] nations" created by making relations among nations into an extended kinship group. Universality is not precluded on this model of treaty, but it is also not presumed in advance. Instead, universality can only be created through making others into relatives, and becoming a relative in turn. Such a model aims at peace by (re)orienting the respective parties in ways that allow them to become related, not by securing a "perpetual peace" earned through a coercive civilizing process. The representation and material renewal of the relationship establishes some basis for repair between them when violation of the terms of interdependence does occur.

However, it is not the case that all social formations can be trained into kinship, so struggles to establish certain primary forms of interdependence through protection of all relatives also serve as insurgent self-defense against colonial war making. It is not a surprise, then, that when Deloria rehearses the terms of the original covenant with the buffalo in *Speaking of Indians*, she uses language resembling Article 11 of the 1868 Treaty of Fort Laramie. Article 11 of that treaty guaranteed the Dakota hunting grounds north and to the west of the Black Hills "so long as the buffalo may range" (much like "as long as we live"). As she explains, "when the buffalo were killed off wantonly, within a few years' time after the white men came, the Dakotas almost lost their lives, too" (*SI*, 62). Here, she counterposes treaty violation as colonial war making with the Dakota philosophical substance of treaty, but she does so in the guise of a straightforward explanation of Dakota "culture." Here again, I submit that she trains her audience into the pedagogical and moral force of kinship. Indeed, after describing the "arch-relative" relationship with the buffalo, her account turns immediately to kinship-based ethics to *critique* the contractual strategy of recognition by treaty.

One interpretation of Deloria's use of the term "wantonly" is its strategic resonance with her audience's Christian norms of respectability and restraint. Yet, Deloria also seems to use the term "wantonly" from the more normatively substantive perspective of kinship laws, so as to critique the colonial logic of treaty as it functioned as a violable, subordinating contract. In this sense, such a logic is an uncivilized excess that ought to be treated as an illicit failure to humanize one's conduct through trustworthy action befitting kin. The systematic slaughter of the buffalo violated the sustained reciprocity of earthmaking acts that kinship makes possible. It was wanton in the sense that US treaty-making practices continually failed to respond properly to Lakota-Dakota efforts to make treaties as exercises that extended kinship structures into the terms of self-determination. In the context of settler practices that justified dispossession by appeal to self-defense against "savage" and uncivilized peoples, this critique inverted such familiar terms by reference to an alternative horizon of normative and international order. In this way, she generated a powerful rejoinder beyond the conceptual structure of sovereignty and to "a nation proclaiming the Four Freedoms to the world—for the liberation of all conquered people, except the one it itself had conquered!" (*SI*, 162).

Vine Deloria Jr.'s Political Reading of Treaties

Vine Deloria Jr.'s account of treaty took form in the context of the late 1960s protest movements that made the protection of treaty rights and the demand for the repair of "broken treaties" into key grounds of political claims making and litigation. After the destruction wrought with termination and relocation in the 1950s, Indigenous peoples around the United States began increasingly to organize militant protests to protect treaty-based hunting and fishing rights.[64] The Pacific Northwest "fish-ins" at Frank's Landing served as a central catalyst for subsequent treaty rights–based struggles and litigation in Idaho and the upper Midwest. At the Indians of All Tribes' 1969 occupation of Alcatraz Island, the 1972 Trail of Broken Treaties caravan, and AIM's spring 1973 siege of Wounded Knee, South Dakota, protestors made the repair of treaty violations a central dimension of their platforms.

In this context, Deloria's primary focus was on reinterpreting the meaning of state-Indigenous treaties as political and juridical instruments through to which to secure Indigenous peoples' rights of self-determination and, by extension, rights guaranteed in state-Indigenous treaties. Recall from the beginning of this chapter the three concepts of treaty. For Deloria, at stake in dealing with treaties is the hegemony of concept a, which is premised on the notion that the US had the exclusive right to interpret treaties because "Indian treaties" are domestic, not international. In this conception of treaties as violable unequal contracts, the US could nullify treaties based on "expediency grounded only in the political considerations of the moment."[65]

In this hegemonic view, "Indian treaties" are mechanisms of domination through which Indigenous peoples are coerced into entering unequal and dependent relationships. Then, their terms can be unilaterally superseded ("abrogated"). As Deloria put it: "As the treaty process was allowed to deteriorate from a sacred pledge of faith between nations to a series of quasi-fraudulent real-estate transactions, the United States evidenced by its conduct that it did not view the treaties as binding upon it" (*BT*, 110). In light of Deloria's account of the paradoxical *structure* of settler colonialism as one that operated by positing treaties as violable contracts, Deloria developed a primarily internal and instrumental critique of treaties as constitutional weapons of Indigenous self-determination.

The argument Deloria proposed about treaties differed from that of newly postcolonial states for contextual reasons relating to the specificities of settler colonialism. Postcolonial states mainly rejected the unequal treaties their former colonizers imposed upon them. They argued that enforcing nonconsensual colonial treaties violated the anticolonial aspiration that political communities ought to be able to consent to and shape the international law to which they are subject.[66] In the context of containment *within* the settler state, however, Deloria highlighted how the violation of treaties was integral to an ongoing structure of domination the United States exercised over Indigenous peoples. Such a form of domination operated both *through* (some) treaties and, now, through the attack upon and attempt to extinguish rights promised *in* treaties.[67]

Deloria himself only began to consider a more robust internationalization of Indigenous peoples' struggles under the radicalizing pressures placed on leadership in Indian country (which included him!) by AIM.[68] For a brief moment in the late 1960s, Deloria proposed what he called the "treaty-covenant relationship" as a way of imagining new, permanently constitutionalized guarantees for all racially oppressed populations in the US, not just Indigenous peoples.[69] Deloria's notion of a treaty-covenant relationship borrowed from the Lakota-Dakota conception of the treaty but placed a greater focus than Ella Deloria on the notion that it is an enduring, even sacred, diplomatic accord.

Despite these sweeping *theoretical* efforts to posit new constitutional forms, Deloria's own *practical* commitment to "reinstituting the treaty process" in the context of American Indian politics only emerged decisively in mid-1972 as the Red Power movement developed a more insurgent form of politics. Indeed, in a presentation at the landmark Convocation of American Indian Scholars at Princeton University in 1970, Deloria actually rejected efforts to "reopen" treaty negotiations with the United States. He cautioned that proposals for new treaty negotiations with the federal government with the aim of transforming Indigenous peoples' relationship to the US (back) into an international one would likely worsen Indigenous peoples' condition, by virtue of the ability of the US Congress—which claims "plenary power" over Indigenous peoples—to roll back even the limited protections contained in existing treaty rights.[70] As AIM shifted what seemed possible, however, Deloria began to think that Indigenous peoples could find ways to escape the subordinate domestic status assigned to them by settler states (*BT*, x).

In *Behind the Trail of Broken Treaties* (1974), written as part of the Institute for the Development of Indian Law that he cofounded, Deloria aimed to offer a political and legal reconceptualization of treaties as one of the foundations of an Indigenous peoples' decolonization movement. The book's title stems from the Trail of Broken Treaties caravan, a pan-Indigenous caravan organized by AIM that took place from November 3 to 9, 1972, with the aim of demanding that the Nixon White House reopen the treaty-making process.[71] As part of organizing the caravan, the Sioux-Assiniboine activist Hank Adams authored the groundbreaking "Twenty Points Proposal," which was subtitled "For Renewal of Contracts—Reconstruction of Indian Communities & Securing an Indian Future in America!" In the document, Adams wrote that "all Indian people in the United States shall be considered to be in treaty relations with the Federal Government and governed by doctrines of such relationship."[72] Adams's proposal took as its interpretive starting point the notion that treaties constituted active diplomatic accords between peoples. Treaties *remained* international agreements—"contracts between sovereigns"—in which each people had the right to negotiate and interpret the terms of the contract.

On that basis, the Twenty Points posited treaties as an important aspect of the (re)internationalization of Indigenous peoples as self-determining polities. The movement demanded to "review the treaty violations of the past and present" and the "restoration of constitutional treaty-making authority," so that "all Indians be governed by treaty relations." In addition to the repair and protection of existing treaty rights, the latter would involve the creation of "a new treaty commission . . . which could contract a new treaty relationship with the American Indian community" (*BT*, 48).

The Nixon administration met such proposals to "renew" treaty relations by rejecting the notion that state-Indigenous treaties ought to be characterized as relations between peoples in an international sense at all. The administration argued that Indians had been American citizens since the 1924 ICA. Because of this, Indian tribes could not renegotiate treaties with the United States in the same fashion as other, independent nations outside US territorial boundaries: "the citizenship relationship and the treaty relationship are mutually exclusive; a government makes treaties with foreign nations, not its own citizens. If renunciation of citizenship is implied here, or secession, these are wholly backward steps, inappropriate for a nation which is a Union."[73] To be sure, the administration acknowledged that treaties ratified by Congress included "treaty rights" to Indigenous peoples as reserved *supplements* to US citizenship, but those rights—like those of other US citizens—ought to be litigated through the US courts. As instruments of conquest that enabled the assertion of US sovereignty over wards-turned-citizens, treaties intrinsically negated Indigenous peoples' existence as distinctive peoples in an international sense. According to this view, since Congress refused to issue further appropriations for subsequent treaty making in the Indian Appropriations Act passed on March 3, 1871, treaties functioned as relics signifying an archaic set of practices of mainly historical interest. Indian tribes are solely to be understood as a "domestic creature of the United States" (*BT*, 132).

The Nixon administration's response drew upon the Doctrine of Discovery, which stated that a "discovering" European power generated an exclusive right to the purchase of Indigenous peoples' land (*BT*, 85–112).[74] The US state could thereby regard treaties in retrospect as one of the defunct vehicles of land acquisition—as "archaic remnants" that promised Indigenous peoples only "eventual extinction in a political sense" (*BT*, 151). This interpretation construed the rights contained in treaties—such as hunting and fishing rights—as time-limited "usufruct rights" (e.g., *until* the extinction of the buffalo). As a lesser form of property right slated to be superseded by the full private property rights of settlers, treaty rights were understood on this model as rights that could lapse if overridden de jure or de facto. In the narrative underpinning the Nixon White House's response, treaty rights—as with other "aboriginal rights" subject to the discretion of the sovereign state—had come to signify lesser, quasi-conditional rights subject to eventual expiration for "domestic subjects" (*BT*, 111).

Drawing on the Twenty Points, Deloria responded by seeking "to demonstrate that the proposal to reopen the treaty-making procedure is far from a stupid or ill-considered proposal" and to "force a reconsideration of the treaties in light of the political implications which they might have today" (*BT*, x, 114).[75] The Twenty Points challenged the notion that state-Indigenous treaties constituted violable, domestic contracts whose terms had been or could be superseded. Instead, they posited that existing treaties ought to be respected, since "there is no possible way that either the federal government or an Indian tribe can withdraw from its relationship."[76] The Twenty Points also included the proposal that treaty *making* between Indigenous peoples and the US federal government ought to be revived, so as to reflect the more fundamental question of the continuing interpolity character of these relationships. Because Indigenous peoples remained peoples in the international sense of the term, they required agreements with the United States that reflected that status and institutional forums to adjudicate more egalitarian future terms of political association.

Deloria contended that the dominant interpretation construed state-Indigenous treaties as "documents recording political surrender in return for annuities and reservations on their traditional homelands" (*BT*, 118). However, Deloria argued, treaties are "signed with tribes, not individuals," and, therefore, do not violate any relation between state and citizen. In this way, treaties are not relics of past "political surrender" but ongoing diplomatic accords between distinct political peoples: Treaty rights, then, are collective rights that stem from the fact that Indigenous peoples were and are polities.[77] Treaties "could not conceivably be considered as taking away from the tribes their national recognition or their residual rights as nations" (*BT* 110).

Deloria based his interpretation on what he called a "political reading of treaties," which he contrasted with "a reading of the treaties as symbolic real-estate documents" (*BT*, 137). Understood as enduring contracts between peoples, treaties signified Indigenous peoples' past and ongoing "sovereign manifestation because they were exercised under the independent wills of the respective contracting parties" (*BT*, 108–9). In this way, treaties ought to be considered "equal to the legal status accorded foreign treaties ... the treaties would have stood in a superior position to the laws of several states, as promised by the United States" (*BT*, 53). In the case of ratified treaties (or the "self-operating" clauses of treaties yet to be ratified), treaties are defined in the US Constitution under Article VI, Section II, Clause 2 as the "supreme law of the land" (*BT*, 155–56).

Such an interpretation drew upon treaties as tools to remediate domination by US domestic institutions. Reclaiming the international nature of treaties vis-à-vis the settler state aimed explicitly to "limit ... the powers of the United States over the lives and rights of Indian people" (*BT*, 157). While the reframing of treaties as markers of an extraconstitutional and international self-determination constituted a radical departure from the terms of settler-colonial rule, the very constitutionality of treaties took advantage of a conservative, even originalist appeal. As Deloria put it, the goal was to make the US "live by its own avowed laws, through which it purported to have power to govern them" (*BT*, 28, 245). Yet, more than claims about wrongs buried in an irreversible, tragic past or "internal" (i.e., domestic) agreements subject to the unilateral interpretive monopoly of the state, treaties represented one marker of an international *diplomatic and constitutional* relationship among peoples.

The contemporary denial of a "treaty relationship" functioned by backdating US sovereignty into earlier moments as a way of anachronistically reinterpreting the meaning of earlier treaties to conform to later unilateral bureaucratic power: "To pretend today that the United States was all-powerful during the years when the treaty was being negotiated is simply to read present conditions back into the past and rewrite, falsely, American history."[78] Cases such as *United States v. Kagama* (1886) and *Lone Wolf v. Hitchcock* (1903), which cemented the United States' almost unlimited power over tribes, interpretively conjured the doctrine of wardship and congressional "plenary power" by claiming that Congress had already exercised this authority "from the beginning" (*BT*, 134, 144–45). Such ideological ex post facto reasoning projected absolute US sovereignty into the past so as to legitimize the contemporary exercise of administrative power in the present.

To resist this backdating, Deloria provincialized those arguments focused on the solely coercive character of the removal and mid-nineteenth-century treaties by pointing to the longer history of intra-Indigenous treaty making, colonial-era treaty making with Spain and England, Cherokee treaties with the Confederacy (*BT*, 132), and the early "peace and friendship" treaties between Indigenous peoples and the United States that date to the 1778 treaty between the US and the Delaware (Lenape) people.[79] The 1778 treaty between the US and the Lenape, for example, was not a land cession treaty but one of peace and friendship: during this period, the nascent US "was forced to deal with the Indians on a just and moral basis" because of the continued threat from the British (*BT*, 136). Despite his realist analysis of the ideological and practical foundations of settler-expansionist aspirations of the US from the founding years of the republic (e.g., the Northwest Ordinance of 1787), Deloria pointed to the transformation in the meaning of treaties as a way to contest the retrospective projection of US sovereign power into the past.

Because of the use of past treaty violations to legitimize present ones—or, to entirely reimagine and project backward the basic structural features of the relationship—it was not sufficient simply to insist upon the moral wrong of violated treaties. This is why Deloria cautioned against what he saw as the widespread rhetorical overemphasis on coercion and fraud in "one-sided real estate transactions." Though many treaties were facilitated precisely through fraud and coercion, "even in the removal treaties the political independence of the tribes was recognized" (*BT*, 130). The focus on irreparable harm alone could serve as a political tactic by which to delegitimize Indigenous political agency and contemporary claims grounded in treaty rights (*BT*, 134). Beyond the more institutionally rooted forms of conflict, Deloria observed that such sensibilities gained traction in the more diffuse cultural and historical narratives about the "tragedy" of Indian history then circulated, emblematized in texts such as Dee Brown's best-selling *Bury My Heart at Wounded Knee*.[80]

Despite the centrality of treaties to Deloria's contention about the historical and ongoing endurance of Indigenous sovereignty, treaties neither *created* nor *vindicated* Indigenous peoples' status as sovereign peoples nor their rights to self-determination. Indigenous peoples did not "come into existence" as international entities by virtue of engaging in diplomacy, in the way that the colonial recognition-by-treaty framework suggests. Rather, the act of signing treaties manifested their "pre-American" existence as inherently sovereign peoples within the multiple branches of the family of nations whose own traditions of diplomacy predated the US and its European imperial predecessors (*BT*, 24). The (re)internationalization of treaties was just one tool to recover structures of self-determination. Accordingly, Deloria pressed for national and international recognition for all Indigenous peoples in the United States, including those who had never signed treaties and for the ratification of the 20 percent of negotiated treaties with the US that went unratified in the Senate (*BT*, 49).[81]

In this way, Indigenous peoples remained peoples whose decolonization demanded the realization of their international right of self-determination. Deloria contended that the "logical meaning of this status" of Indigenous peoples as nations "is not eventual extinction in a political sense, but independence and recognition on a world scale" (*BT*, 151). Understanding treaties specifically as international agreements was key here because it shifted the interpretive burden for proving the validity of treaty violations back onto the US. Deloria hoped instead to force the settler state to do more than "justify what passed for legality" by effectively using the fact of past treaty violations to argue for the validity of present, continuing treaty violations (*BT*, x). The fact of past violations of treaties, Deloria argued, ought not to be used as the grounds for further violations of treaties. Indeed, the "tendency of the federal and state governments" was to "pretend that the mere passage of time and changing of conditions is sufficient to invalidate" treaties. (*BT*, 159). To invalidate promises made in those treaties actually deepened present-day structures of domination.

For Deloria, the nature of this unilateral violation *as colonial* emerged with particular clarity once treaties were regarded as international: "Had the tribes been able to maintain a semblance of international status, a violation of their treaty would have been an act of war" (*BT*, 51). This interpretation brought to light that administrative power to abrogate treaties enshrined in ideas like "wardship" constituted a bureaucratized act of war and genocide. Interpreting treaty violation as genocidal in a hemispheric context of mass murder of Indigenous peoples of the Amazon under military dictatorship in Brazil would also intensify pressure on the United States in ways that resembled other Cold War efforts to leverage the "increasingly bad image of the United States overseas" (*BT*, 237–46).

Deloria's aim here was, at minimum, to enable Indian tribes to access the weapons of constitutional and international law to protect against domination. As it stood, Deloria argued, "tribes suffered greatly from the arbitrary actions of state governments, which continually violated their treaties with impunity" (*BT*, 51). The practical goal of this theory was to generate a set of institutionally routinized responsibilities and restraints at several levels of governmental authority—including the international arena—that would prevent the continual violation of treaty-guaranteed rights. For example, the seventh point in the Twenty Points Proposal had included "mandatory relief from treaty violations by state governments," which would give federal district courts "power to issue immediate injunctions against state agencies which would remain in effect until the court satisfied itself that an Indian treaty had not been violated." The idea transferred "the burden of proof upon complaint of treaty violation from themselves to the states" (*BT*, 51). Through strategies like this one, the reframing of the jurisdiction of treaties as international diplomatic accords became one of the important grounds for a right of self-determination that needed to exist both in relation to the United States and outside of it. Treaties could function, then, as political tools to aid in securing relations of nondomination from the US settler state.

In short, settler political domination also rested upon the notion that states could violate treaty rights because the US retained an exclusive right to interpret treaties in the present. Indeed, Deloria invoked even unequal treaties as instances in which Indigenous societies had clearly exercised international diplomacy as sovereign peoples—as "nations with an inherent right to political and cultural existence comparable to any other nation" (*BT*, 262). If treaties were and continue to be political agreements between nations with "rights to national existence," then the very assertion of an interpretive monopoly of one nation constituted a violation of the equality of peoples (*BT*, 20).[82] As such, Indigenous societies ought to have the "right to interpret treaty provisions," as an extension of the placement of "Indian treaties on the same basis as foreign treaties with regard to their enforcement" (*BT*, 52). Though this argument in some sense affirmed the viability of state-Indigenous treaties that themselves had been instruments of colonial violence (e.g., removal treaties), the insistence on enforcing treaties aimed to constrain the state's interpretive power over them and to hold the US to obligations that it had (or should have) constitutionalized. The United States could not act as both party and judge to treaties, and, in that sense, the courts in which they were litigated were "the courts of the conqueror," colonial venues that ought to be replaced with joint practices of co-authorization and co-jurisdiction.

Treaty as Violated Covenant

Vine Deloria Jr. does address more of the Lakota and Dakota philosophical conception of treaty on which Ella Deloria focuses, but he does so for different purposes and emphasizes some very specific aspects of this notion of treaty. In particular, Deloria draws on the idea that treaties constitute "violated covenants," that is, permanent, sacred political agreements between peoples that have been unjustly and recurrently broken. He draws upon this Lakota-Dakota perspective in a different way from Ella Deloria, in that his aim is to bring this alternative philosophical conception to bear as an aspect of his *internal* critique of the colonial treaty form. Namely, Indigenous societies' right of self-determination entailed that they had shared jurisdictional authority over the treaty's present-day interpretation and enforcement. This meant including their own self-understandings of its philosophical underpinnings, the context of the treaty, and the oral history of the negotiations—not just the written document—as a key source in determining the meaning of the original agreement.[83]

This played out in the trials over AIM's occupation of Wounded Knee, in which the defense hinged their strategy on very expansive questions about the legitimacy of US sovereignty (and thus the jurisdiction of the court) itself. The Oglala Lakota elders who testified in Lakota at the eventual consolidated Wounded Knee trials in Lincoln, Nebraska, consistently described the 1868 Treaty of Fort Laramie as a sacred covenant.[84] Deloria's efforts to use treaties as instruments of nondomination recognized that these Lakota "traditionalists" (his term) closely aligned their own understanding of the 1868 treaty with the conception of treaty as a "treaty-covenant." As Ella had written thirty years prior, Vine Deloria Jr. explains that the "treaty-covenant" relationship dating back to Lakota charters with human and other-than-human became the lens through which the Lakota understood subsequent forms of international diplomacy.[85] Vine Deloria Jr. places more emphasis on the enduring and sacred moral character of treaties: "the spiritual faith of the two peoples was pledged so that the agreement called for the best efforts of the two groups to fulfill the terms of agreement."[86] In this sense, the treaty constitutes a practice of entering into a permanent relationship framework with others, which hinged upon the recognition of "the spiritual nature of treaty promises." This conception of treaty as a binding covenant underscored how the original "moral quality" of the violation of the 1868 treaty—when Ulysses S. Grant licensed incursions into the Black Hills on reserved lands of the "Great Sioux Reservation" in 1877—had compounded over time up until the present. In insisting upon this point, Lakota elders recounted their understanding in oral history that treaties created a permanent framework for "political agreements" that endured throughout time.[87]

As this account makes clear, Deloria rejects the normative perspective that there is a hidden and shared form of the treaty relation. As such, he crafted an explicitly political and counterhegemonic alternative to the hegemony of the view of treaties as violable, unequal contracts that serve merely as temporally expired, past instruments of dispossession. Deloria contended that the "history of the treaty relationship . . . contains a strong tradition denying that tribes are wards of the government and describing them as expectant nations with eventual status as nations in the family of nations of the world" (*BT*, 137). Recovering this as *one* angle of interpretation meant returning to meanings available in treaty councils, treaty documents, and US constitutional law predating the later nineteenth century's backdated "full-blown theory of wardship." This is a conscious and strategic internal critique of the contested lineages of argument that affirmed treaties as enduring contracts, to constrain the US state and to recover stolen lands. This strategy aimed to place those stolen lands back into structures of specific Indigenous peoples' authority that combined economic self-reliance and care-based stewardship.

The juridical (re)internationalization of treaties was one key vehicle that connected nondomination—structures of protection against arbitrary interference—to more positive visions of economic and cultural self-determination and self-reliance (*BT*, 134). In this way, the emphasis on treaties constituted an effort to limit US state power and hold the state to a modernized version of its promised obligations (e.g., to provide treaty-based economic resources and health care), which converged with notions of Indigenous sovereignty based on a more positive vision of collective care and flourishing: For example, the Lummi Nation (Lhaq'temish), near where Deloria briefly taught at Western Washington University, had fought throughout the twentieth century to maintain "the integrity of its ancient fishing culture" by securing collective stewardship of tideland flats.[88] On this basis, the Lummi developed a modern aquaculture system designed to foster economic independence, development, and redistribution. The rights to these fishing grounds dispersed outside of the reservation in US and international law came out of treaties signed between 1854 and 1859, which "forbade state control of their livelihood" (*BT*, 14). There is no doubt that, from the US perspective, the treaties themselves emerged from the desire to "clear the land of Indians as quickly as possible," so as to create the Washington Territory, and colonize it unburdened by "Indian title." Despite the colonial aims of these treaties from the US side, Deloria argued that protection of treaty rights by (re)making these as living practices subject to Indigenous jurisdiction could serve as key instruments to suture freedom from the domination of the US state to the substantive aim of self-determination understood as "continued communal and cultural integrity."[89]

Indigenous peoples tied modes of survival and ecological reciprocity to the aims of modern economic self-reliance. In such cases, the defense of treaty rights functioned as an earthmaking practice that entailed a radical rupture with the terms of US sovereignty, yet, paradoxically, also functioned through a conservative insistence that the US uphold its own laws. Moreover, though based on tribal units wedded to federal recognition, the reactivation of those clauses also facilitated an exercise of self-determination that functioned outside of the imposed boundaries of the reservation—in relation to territories that those peoples had historically stewarded, and to which they maintained cultural and material connections. In negotiating to preserve and create specific relations with other-than-human relatives, Indigenous negotiators of treaties had encoded lasting possibilities of earthmaking that envisioned human and other-than-human well-being as invariably interdependent. The protection of these clauses in the present sought to make good on that promise by facilitating interrelated political-economic, cultural, and ecological self-reliance.

Given Vine Deloria Jr.'s oft-stated focus on pragmatically navigating institutional arrangements, his work in treaties influenced yet quickly fell behind some of the more radical currents of the movement. In the 1974 edition of *Behind the Trail of Broken Treaties*, he translated AIM's 1972 demands for the renewal of the "treaty relationship" into a theory of Indigenous peoples as a US "protectorate." Deloria argued that Indigenous peoples constituted nations in an international sense, yet he also believed that Indigenous peoples could transform, to their advantage, certain elements of the US "trust responsibility" that had facilitated colonial dispossession under the guise of wardship (*BT*, 154, 253). In contrast to conceiving of the "trust" on the model of civilizational superiority based on bringing "primitive" Indigenous peoples up to a level of maturation, Deloria instead argued that institutionalizing this trust responsibility was yet another way of making good on an institutional principle that could be turned against colonial logics. Deloria grounded this conception on Justice Johnson's concurring opinion in *Cherokee Nation v. Georgia* (1831), who argued—following Vattel—that accepting US "protection" as a "feudatory" state did not entail any loss for the weaker party of the characteristics of statehood under the law of nations. He argued that Indigenous peoples could translate this structure of argument into what he called "contractual sovereignty," in which they could "contract . . . for the transfer of certain governmental functions without prejudice to its status"—that is, a kind of noncolonial dependency that did not entail "surrendering" their international right of self-determination (*BT*, 177).

AIM's IITC quickly moved past this account of the outer limits of Indigenous decolonization already by 1974. The rapid development of the movement in this direction is reflected in the afterword to the second edition of *Behind the Trail of Broken Treaties* in 1985, which traces AIM's international organizing subsequent to the occupation of Wounded Knee in 1973.[90] AIM and the IITC rejected the protectorate concept as colonial at its core, arguing that Indigenous peoples constituted sovereign nations who had been excluded from the "right of self-determination" articulated in the December 1960 UN General Assembly Resolution 1514 (xv), "The Declaration on the Granting of Independence to Colonial Countries and Peoples."[91] They conceived of the recovery of the protection of their treaty rights and unceded treaty lands as integral to expressing and securing their self-determination against colonial sovereignty. More than an identity-based claim, this demand expressed the effort to reinterpret and fully universalize the anticolonial notion of the equality of peoples in a nonstatist or antistatist form.[92]

Recall that in the June 1974 "Declaration of Continuing Independence of the Sovereign Native American Indian Nations," the IITC asserted that the US had "denied all Native people their international Treaty rights, Treaty lands and basic human rights of freedom and sovereignty."[93] The interpretive argument of this chapter is that the declaration brings together two critical meanings of treaty: On the one hand, the IITC's invocation of an international kinship of the colonized is indebted to the idea that the struggle to live *in* treaty is an anticolonial struggle and extension of kinship. It is a political-ethical orientation by which to figure relations and conduct beyond the limits imposed by colonial sovereignty. On the other hand, the IITC also builds upon Vine Deloria Jr.'s counterhegemonic interpretation that treaties bind "each party to an inviolate international relationship."[94] In both of these registers of external and internal critique, the IITC brought arguments originating from the Lakota and Dakota philosophical conception of the treaty form and long-standing defense of the 1868 treaty into a pan-Indigenous space of anticolonial organizing.

In doing so, the IITC made the treaty council itself into an alternative space of transnational internationalism. They brought Indigenous societies together to pursue a right of self-determination against and beyond sovereignty in the emerging machinery of the UN. Specifically, though denied entry to the UN as peoples, the IITC successfully lobbied to gain consultative status as a nongovernmental organization (NGO) with the UN Economic and Social Council in 1977. At the subsequent September 1977 International NGO Conference on Discrimination against Indigenous Populations in the Americas, held in Geneva at the Palais des Nations, representatives from the Očhéthi Šakówiŋ and the Dene, Hopi, Tuscarora, Onondaga, Northern Cheyenne, the Mapuche Confederation (who had also concluded treaties, *parlamentos*, with the Spanish empire), and the Asociación Indígena de la República Argentina made similar arguments. In the subsequent "Declaration of Principles for the Defense of the Indigenous Nations and Peoples of the Western Hemisphere," the IITC argued that Indigenous treaties and agreements should conform to the "same international laws and principles as other treaties and agreements." Delegates there linked the violation of treaties to a wide-ranging set of genocidal policies that ranged from strip-mining in the Black Hills to the forced sterilization of Indigenous women.

Yet IITC delegates also added a supplement that sought to *bind* settler states to treaties, arguing, "Nor shall any state refuse to recognize and adhere to treaties or other agreements due to changed circumstances where the change in circumstances has been substantially caused by the state asserting that such change has occurred."[95] That is, intensified colonial invasion that *causes* the historical supersession of particular treaty terms as a result of changes in material contexts (e.g., the colonial slaughter of the buffalo) cannot then be used to justify states' frequent refusals to further enforce and relent in their unilateral jurisdiction to interpret a treaty. The latter argument builds in an anticolonial addendum geared specifically to the context of settler-colonial situations. This aimed to counter the structure of domination through treaty *violation* central to twentieth-century settler colonialism, by arguing that settler states ought to be bound by treaty provisions. This notion of preventing the colonialism of sovereign treaty violation is absent under the 1969 Vienna Convention on the Law of Treaties, which does not apply ex post facto.

Conclusion

By examining struggles over the meaning of treaty, I have elucidated how projects of Indigenous decolonization created a distinctive normative and contextual interplay between anticolonial thought and practice. In doing so, I expand on the radicalized critique of colonial domination in chapter 1, which primarily focuses on the construal of a negative sense of self-determination as structural and institutional nondomination. This also meant addressing the reality of a long history of state-Indigenous treaties, in which the colonial form of the treaty is deeply embedded in the entirety of existing settler institutional and ideological arrangements framing Indigenous nationhood as contingent and lapsed. In challenging this notion that treaties are violable, unequal contracts with a built-in expiration date (concept a in the introduction to this chapter), Vine Deloria Jr. provides an internal critique of the treaty form, which ultimately aims to press forward the international character of treaty making to recover and realize the equality of peoples as a claim against colonial sovereignty.

Specifically, Deloria re-internationalized treaties as binding agreements among self-determining nations (concept b in the introduction to this chapter) by pointing out the incoherence and hegemonic functioning of the contention that treaties both elicit and nullify Indigenous self-government. This counterhegemonic reading called for shared jurisdictional authority among peoples over those relations that had been improperly and coercively naturalized as the purview of the unilateral institutional and interpretive powers of settler sovereignty.

More original to this chapter, a more positive alternative praxis of self-determination and decolonization signifies an effort to move beyond the *conceptual structure* of sovereignty. Here as a key praxis of earthmaking, the treaty represents a nonanthropocentric mode of relationship making with others that establishes care-based reciprocal obligations (concept c at the start of this chapter). In this way, Ella Deloria's account of political order as dependent on a care-based praxis of kinship geared toward the struggle to be a good relative recasts the very conceptual structure of self-determination as a relational form—against the antirelational domination of (colonial) sovereignty. Her alternative displaces the very problematic of sovereignty. It refuses the colonial specter of a sovereignty that is always already under threat in favor of the presence of kin who face the uncertainty of a world made of the not-yet-kinned and (in the case of colonizer states) the unkinnable. The former vision calls for treaty as a practice of subordinating pacification and the latter for treaty as the making and remaking of peace generated in robustly reciprocal kinship relations.

This constructive account of self-other relations as kin-kin relations prevails on (all) human communities to think of self-determination as built upon all sorts of often-unacknowledged relations, both human and other-than-human. This necessitates a different notion of the basic composition and normative force of the social and ecological struggles enabling and defining peace and the terms of international order. In this way, self-determination as freedom from colonial sovereignty entails the liberation of both colonized peoples and the earth together, by establishing profoundly relational structures of stewardship and protection that reject state sovereignty's antirelational drive.

At minimum, this vision is a resource for anticolonial self-defense against a distorted logic of coercive family formation. The position of kinship struggle also generates an external route through which to critique the logic of settler treaty making, and, so too, various subsequent claims to promote institutional transformations of Indigenous "self-determination" that emerge neither from Indigenous political communities themselves nor their philosophical interventions. At maximum, it reconceives the very substance of intersocietal coordination through a more expansively universalistic conception of "order" rejecting the constitutive suppression of relations that is a hallmark of colonial sovereignty's reproduction of the hierarchical family of nations. This anticolonial (re)conception of order is made through relational practices of self-determination and draws from the political-theoretic resources of transnational internationalist pan-Indigenous organizing. Moreover, it provides the further possibility of reimagining the horizon for postcolonial global justice by rooting it in the actuality of these struggles of kinned relations for the antistatist equality of peoples. The book focuses on this last contention about rethinking global order and justice next.

In the following chapter, I examine another lineage of Indigenous anticolonialism, focusing on struggles over concepts and institutions of land. Turning away from the US and toward Canada's version of settler-colonial multiculturalism, I trace the anticolonial project of the Indigenous "Fourth World" in the writings and activism of the Secwépmec leader George Manuel.

[CHAPTER THREE]

"The Land Is Our Culture"

George Manuel on the Fourth World and the Politics of Resurgence

> For a colonized people, the most essential value, because it is the most meaningful (*concrète*), is first and foremost the land.
>
> Frantz Fanon, *The Wretched of the Earth*[1]

Indigenous projects of self-determination have long struggled for "land back," that is, the restoration of occupied lands to the government and jurisdiction of Indigenous societies. Belied by more public transcripts about the litigation of "land claims," such projects entail a profound challenge to the terms of political order: transforming fundamental relations of human societies to, and the basic meaning of, land. At its core, this is the notion that "land" (or "earth") is itself a political concept denoting a set of social, ecological, and spiritual connections based on respectful relationships of interdependence between humans and other-than-human beings. Such a concept of land, and what it consequently means to restore land as a (web of) relationship(s), is central to many articulations of the normative substance of self-determination and decolonization within Indigenous anticolonial struggles. In this regard, Fanon puts his finger on an urgent, even existential conceptual imperative that motivates key anticolonial sensibilities and material practices: that land is "an essential value" for the colonized by virtue of its very concreteness.

What is it that makes such a claim about the concept of land so striking? These frameworks are not only asserting the value of land in the more expected register of remedial justice: that it is stolen property that ought to be transferred back to its rightful owners. Instead, I venture in this chapter that these struggles stand out because they give voice to the meaning and meaningfulness of land *itself*. Such an articulation is distinctive because Western political theory has rarely treated land or the earth itself as a political form, let alone a social or cultural one. Instead, land is much more likely to be depicted as an inert bundle of "natural resources" or pristine nature that human-generated meanings are layered on top of, so to speak. In this dominant view, the land or earth itself is usually no more than a brute empirical fact upon which certain constructed social and political forms are overlaid. The upshot from a wide swath of otherwise utterly divergent approaches in Western political thought is that what is genuinely worthy of reflection as part of "the political" are only those processes of meaning making and institutional inscription involved in the creation of (e.g.) property, territory, and sovereignty—certainly not the land itself.

In the previous chapter, I interpreted struggles over the concept and material histories of the treaty form to examine the constructive vision and critical purchase of Vine Deloria Jr. and Ella Deloria's efforts to (re)fashion Lakota-Dakota anticolonial earthmaking practices. In this chapter, I similarly trace key intellectual genealogies of struggles over the meaning and significance of land itself as a political concept. To do so, I turn to the writings and political advocacy of the Secwépemc (Shuswap) activist and intellectual George Manuel (1921–89). For good reason, Manuel is regarded as one of the founders of the modern First Nations movement in Canada. Indeed, he played a major role in setting the First Nations political agenda of self-determination and aboriginal and treaty rights, both in Canada and on the international stage. It is only in recent years, however—especially with the republication of Manuel's 1974 classic *The Fourth World: An Indian Reality* (coauthored with Canadian non-Native journalist Michael Posluns) in 2018—that his *philosophical* centrality to the formulation of Indigenous decolonization in North America has come to be more widely acknowledged and more systematically explored.[2]

In this chapter, I return to Manuel's original formulations to trace the still relatively occluded intellectual genealogies of concepts core to this vision of anticolonialism. At the heart of this was decolonization as "resurgence." Resurgence is a theoretical paradigm that understands decolonization in positive terms as a turn away from state-based frameworks and a turn toward the restoration and transformative (re)emergence of the core philosophical commitments and material practices of colonized Indigenous societies. In particular, Dene political theorist Glen Coulthard captures the core of this framework in identifying an orientation "grounded in the purposeful revitalization of those relational, land-informed indigenous practices and modes of life that settler-colonization sought to destroy."[3] In other words, resurgence is resistance both *through* and *for* a critical remaking of core values of Indigenous societies in their diversity and commonality, not just resistance *against* colonial power relations.

Integral to Fourth Worldism, the notion of decolonization as resurgence has served as an influential and contested philosophical rubric for Indigenous anticolonial struggles (especially but not exclusively in the Canadian context). One of its pitfalls is that some of the more influential subsequent claims on this political vocabulary such as those of Mohawk scholar Taiaiake Alfred treat "resurgence" and "Fourth World" theory as approaches beholden to a relatively static and inflexible paradigm frequently associated with an emphasis on pure autochthony, or as a stereotypically masculinist model of political struggle. This is often referred to as "Indigenous traditionalism."[4]

In turning back to Manuel, I engage in historical reconstruction that works appreciatively alongside many Indigenous and non-Indigenous critics who have since challenged and interrogated the tendency of this widespread interpretation of resurgence theory to contain indigeneity to historical stasis and a solely backward-looking gaze. What is more, these scholars aptly point out how this interpretation of the resurgence framework reproduces patriarchy, heteronormativity, and a certain insensitivity to the historicity of resurgence *itself* as a conditioned articulation of the politics of decolonization.[5] My aim in assessing Manuel and the wider networks he participated in from this historicizing angle, then, is both to interrogate his initial formulation of these concepts and to demonstrate their hybrid intellectual origins and the political-theoretical flexibility that is nearly effaced in traditionalist accounts.

Manuel's other key concept of the "Fourth World" aimed to engender an anticolonial internationalism of Indigenous societies distinct from the "Third World." Manuel intended these concepts to reshape and rally the commitments of Indigenous societies and non-Indigenous allies to mobilize around an alternative constructive vision of planetary order, one aiming to recast the relationship among land, self-determination, and sovereignty. The dynamism and diverse intellectual influences of Fourth World resurgence become much more visible by interpreting Manuel's project *as a project*, that is, as one among related efforts to organize, engage with, and rethink anticolonial internationalism. I bring the distinctiveness of Fourth World resurgence into relief as a formative political-philosophical current of Indigenous decolonization by tracing Manuel's efforts to carve out an alternative politics of land—a politics he explicitly contrasted to the meaning of land in settler-colonial societies based on liberal capitalism, on the one hand, and to postcolonial societies premised on socialist developmentalism, on the other.

The chapter proceeds by contextualizing two overlapping intellectual and political contexts for Manuel's theorization of "resurgence" and the "Fourth World," focusing, respectively, on his engagements with Canadian politics and political thought and the global and transnational contexts of Third World anticolonial struggles. First, I situate Manuel's account of "resurgence" as a rejoinder to the Canadian discourse of what I call "White Paper multiculturalism," after the 1969 White Paper (Canada's later version of what the US called "termination," the latter of which is discussed in chapter 1). Manuel's account of decolonization as Indigenous resurgence functioned as a critique and constructive reimagining of notions of cultural freedom and confederation that had underpinned the reproduction of settler-colonial sovereignty in Canadian political thought. Second, I trace the philosophical basis of Manuel's positive alternative formulation for the Fourth World that the "the land is our culture." My contribution is to read this proposition dynamically and dialectically as a claim that specifies how cultural meaning making refers back to the philosophical connections between land and individual and collective self-formation. Third, I turn to Manuel's account of the transnational internationalism of the Fourth World by explicating how he also came to the framework of resurgence in dialogue with Third World visions of postcolonial statehood and political economy, specifically the African socialism of Tanzanian president Julius Nyerere and the policy proposals of a group of Third World states for the New International Economic Order. The following section then examines the Fourth World idea as an effort to forge what I call a "stewardship world order," that is, a planetary order with transformative structural aspirations to create plural forms of nonanthropocentric self-determination beyond the sovereign state.

White Paper Multiculturalism

To understand the political dilemmas motivating Manuel's formulation of resurgence, it is important to place him in the context(s) of pan-Indigenous resistance to the specific discourses and material practices of Canadian colonialism. By way of introduction to Manuel himself, he came out of a much longer lineage of political thought and organizing on behalf of Indigenous societies to recover stolen and unceded lands that the province of British Columbia claimed via the colonial legal fiction of terra nullius.[6] In this regional context, Manuel first cut his teeth as an activist on the British Columbian land struggle in the North American Indian Brotherhood (the successor organization to the earlier Allied Tribes of British Columbia) in the 1950s, became chief of his Neskonlith band, and served as the head of the Union of British Columbia Indian Chiefs (UBCIC). Then, in a context of increasing pan-Indigenous national and international mobilization after the 1969 White Paper, he became president of Canada's NIB (1970–76; renamed the Assembly of First Nations in 1985) and helped to cofound and chair the WCIP (1975–81). He aspiringly called the latter the "United Nations of the Fourth World," a term that neatly summarizes his aspiration to institutionalize a separate transnational international forum of Indigenous societies. Finally, Manuel played an important role in helping to organize the Constitution Express, itself both a domestic and transnational movement that rejected the 1982 patriation of Canada's constitution from the UK without specific recognition of aboriginal and treaty rights (what became section 35 of the Canadian Constitution).[7]

A deep history of organizing and resistance that really dates back "from the time that colonial forces became oppressive" (*FW*, 73) set the stage for Manuel and other Indigenous leaders' intense and partially successful assault against the landmark 1969 White Paper—the Canadian equivalent of termination in the US. In policy terms, the Pierre Elliot Trudeau administration released the White Paper, or the "Statement of the Government of Canada on Indian Policy," as an omnibus plan for "Indian policy" in June of 1969. Altogether, the White Paper aimed to privatize reserve lands (i.e., destroy remaining collective land bases); abolish the Indian Act; eliminate Indian status and, therefore, aboriginal and treaty rights; abolish the Department of Indian Affairs; and initiate the transfer of authority for First Nations from the federal to provincial level.

In terms of its discursive framing, the White Paper surprisingly begins with a paean to the "positive recognition . . . Of the unique contribution of Indian culture to Canadian life." At the same time, it portrayed the political and legal difference deriving from Indian status under the Canadian Indian Act system paradoxically as a form of "discrimination" *and* "special treatment" that had "made the Indians a community disadvantaged and apart."[8] By implication, eliminating Indian "special status" constituted a form of emancipation, because it removed a discriminatory set of barriers that impeded access to citizenship, equal rights, and cultural rights and freedom. What is distinctive about this notion of civic belonging is the paradoxical assertion that political assimilation into the Canadian federation is precisely what *enables* the recognition and flourishing of a variety of group-based forms of cultural rights and freedoms.

To capture this attempt to suture up these key tensions in the Canadian colonial state-building project, I interpret the White Paper as ideologically animated by a Canadian colonial discourse of "White Paper multiculturalism." By White Paper multiculturalism, I mean a conception of the ethical good of Canadian citizenship and nationhood as a mode of civic belonging and freedom predicated on subordination to Canadian colonial sovereignty. In this sense, colonial sovereignty is not just compatible with diversity; it becomes diversity's enabling condition as that which properly orients and orders it. In chapter 1, I explicated Vine Deloria Jr.'s analysis of the termination policy through the lens of the US colonial discourse of civic inclusion. Likewise, the original formulation of multiculturalism as official public policy and even a public philosophy of the Canadian state-building project both preconditioned the terms of pan-Indigenous resistance and shaped some of the core conceptual frameworks of Manuel's own constructive articulation of resurgence as an anticolonial response to Canadian settler-colonial domination—especially the explicit citation of "culture" as a good of Canadian sovereignty and citizenship.

In a key intervention, Anishinaabe political philosopher Dale Turner has analyzed the White Paper along similar lines, adopting the term "White Paper liberalism" to describe its political-theoretic thrust. Turner emphasizes how White Paper liberalism always places the individual at the center of a theory of justice. Turner's critique is that this framework can never comprehend the collective and sui generis character of Indigenous peoples' self-determination and sovereignty; thus, White Paper liberalism always implicitly puts Canadian sovereignty in a position of discursive and epistemic authority over Indigenous societies.[9]

My rubric of White Paper multiculturalism is indebted to Turner's but diverges from him in drawing greater attention to a common rhetoric used to justify the White Paper: the frequent recourse Canadian settler elites made to the idiom of "cultural freedom" via the image of a culturally diverse confederation or a "Canadian mosaic" as a model of state-society relations. What is most salient here for the purposes of my argument is how efforts to critically reshape this discourse of cultural freedom form part of Indigenous counternarratives to Canadian settler colonialism, and, in turn, the context of the formulation of the concept of resurgence itself.

The commitment to multiculturalism among liberal settler elites was both strategic and genuine, in the broader context of Canadian politics. Specifically, Trudeau successfully passed multiculturalism into law as an official policy in October 1971, but it had already been prominent in Canadian public life. Indeed, Trudeau was a key figure in promoting a kind of limited difference-conscious integration by moving from bilingualism (French-English) to an avowal of multiculturalism in particular into public institutions. The issue of Quebecois nationalism was initially central here. In his strategic attempt to downplay the more territorial and separatist elements of rising Quebecois nationalism, Trudeau argued that "cultural pluralism is the very essence of Canadian identity. Every ethnic group has the right to preserve and develop its own culture and values within the Canadian context."[10]

When it came to the White Paper, however, the Trudeau government framed colonial practices of assimilation, dispossession, and the elimination of treaty rights as a path to civic *and* "cultural freedom." The elimination of Indian status, it was argued, would "enable the Indian people to be free—free to develop Indian cultures." Here, Indian status itself is framed as a civic and cultural disability to be overcome so as to enable group-based cultural freedom to develop within the framework of the Canadian nation-state. This image of Canada as the model for a multicultural, pluralist, and human rights–respecting state that wed "cultural" diversity to "political" unity became a key legitimating narrative of Canadian nationhood.[11]

Indeed, the prominence of an idiom of cultural freedom considered integral to the ethical value and lived experience of liberal citizenship and equal rights represents a genuine divergence from US political discourse. Subsequent prominent Canadian political philosophers such as Will Kymlicka and Charles Taylor have placed quite different emphases on how to bring these elements together, yet they nonetheless draw from this same basic project.[12] What the US and Canadian discourses do have in common is that they are each framed by the assertion of unilateral settler sovereignty over Indigenous societies.

In this respect, Manuel figured the White Paper as an inheritor of past efforts "to reduce the fundamental constitutional and legal issues [pertaining to the formation of Canadian sovereignty itself] to a list of grievances that could be resolved within the existing framework" (*FW*, 92). More generally, early Indigenous responses directly rejected the assumption that collective cultural rights and freedoms were somehow enhanced, instead of negated, by subordinating the political bases for Indigenous self-determination to Canadian state sovereignty. To refuse the artificial division between politics (i.e., usually meaning sovereignty) and culture (i.e., usually meaning ethnicity) entailed bringing into focus the formation of the Canadian state itself in and through colonial conquest. In turn, this meant foregrounding an entire field of contestation over the meanings of land, territory, jurisdiction, and sovereignty, which could not but be both cultural and political.[13] In particular, Harold Cardinal (Cree), the head of the Indian Association of Alberta (IAA) who worked closely with Manuel, authored an influential response along these lines to Trudeau's claims to usher in a "Just Society," entitled *The Unjust Society*. There, he drew upon the image of a "red title" in the "Canadian mosaic" to figure Canada as a diverse, multicultural federation that had contradicted its own promise.[14]

By invoking this image, Cardinal mounted the argument that Indigenous cultural freedom necessitated the political freedom to maintain and enhance "our status, rights, land and tradition." He went so far as to argue that "we would rather continue to live in bondage under the inequitable Indian Act than surrender our sacred rights," the latter capitulation akin to "cultural suicide."[15] The organizational document Cardinal authored under the auspices of the IAA, "Citizens Plus" (1970; a.k.a. the "Red Paper"), promoted a policy vision that emphasized both the need for massive redistribution to promote substantive political and economic equality and the defense of Indigenous rights and self-government, in the form of the constitutional affirmation of treaty and aboriginal rights (the latter constituting the "plus" of citizens plus). Cardinal contended that in the absence of anticolonial revolution, "the recognition of Indian status is essential for justice."[16]

Likewise, Manuel analyzed the White Paper as picking up where prior rounds of colonial invasion and Indigenous dispossession had left off, as a "sophisticated and all-encompassing program designed to destroy any pretensions of self-determination among the Indian Nations of Canada" (*FW*, 54). In this respect, White Paper multiculturalism captures the notion that discrete group "cultures" come together on putatively egalitarian terms but only within the framework of an overarching Canadian state sovereignty, that is, "the Canadian claim to establish a Dominion with sovereignty from sea to sea" (*FW*, 97).

Accordingly, Manuel theorized how dispossession and assimilation in the Canadian context were mutually reinforcing aspects of colonial invasion and the reproduction of Canadian state sovereignty over Indigenous societies. The only laudable aspect of the White Paper, Manuel argued, was its nominally egalitarian objection to "paternalism," but "the way to bring about equality is not to abolish these [aboriginal] rights but to enhance them" (*FW*, 234). Indeed, "the demand for voting rights [i.e., enfranchisement and nondiscrimination] without loss of aboriginal rights and Indian status reflects . . . the central concern of most Indian people today, as well as the constant nature of our basic goals throughout this century of struggle" (*FW*, 97). By contrast, settler-colonial practices of Indigenous rights abolition had long been encoded in a dominant paradigm under which "Canadian authorities, since confederation, have offered an open hand to an Indian who . . . 'Becomes one of us'—that is, an enfranchised, tax-paying Christian *who brings nothing from his past, unless it is saleable*" (*FW*, 8, 21). This process of enfranchisement hinged the promise of citizenship on wresting away the collective political markers of indigeneity and, of course, the land itself.

In particular, Manuel traced the White Paper's legacy back to this history of the Indian Act legislation that had defined "Indian status" through the "racial myths that were the midwives at [the confederation's] birth." In all, this legislative apparatus aimed to reclassify Indigenous peoples as uncivilized subjects subordinated to unfettered state administrative and police power, including the Act for the Better Protection of the Lands and Property of Indians in Lower Canada (1850), the Gradual Civilization Act (1857), and the Gradual Enfranchisement Act (1869). To summarize this vast arsenal of Indian Act legislation, these laws produced the early frameworks for regulating Indian status and transforming Indigenous peoples' governance structures into the colonial administration of the chief and council system under "bands" subject to the rule of the Department of Indian Affairs. The Gradual Civilization Act created the two-tiered juridical structure whereby those incorporated into this omnibus Indian "status" were conceived of as "wards of the state" lacking legal personhood. With voluntary enfranchisement, Indigenous men would become a civilized "person" if they renounced their Indian status, with the notion of "status" already codified by reconfiguring Indigenous peoples' own self-determining authorities into a unilaterally governed racialized population. Altogether, these laws aimed to fashion intermediate paternalistic and authoritarian control of peoples confined to reserves, with the aim of ultimately dispossessing them of their remaining land (*FW*, 220).

To be sure, the Trudeau administration touted the White Paper as an effort to remedy the explicitly racially discriminatory lineages of the Indian Act, aligning themselves with earlier efforts pushed by Indigenous activists (Manuel among them) to liberalize the Indian Act in 1951. Yet the state regulation of status in the first place and the subsequent "rule that an Indian could only become civilized and enfranchised by ceasing to be an Indian" both aimed to transfigure remaining Indigenous territories into alienable real estate under the Canadian national patrimony and, secondarily, to assimilate select (former) Indians into the body politic as citizens (*FW*, 21).

On the basis of this interpretation of the history of Canadian colonial state formation, Manuel posited that the White Paper newly exacerbated, not negated, the colonial governance strategies of the Indian Act. As Trudeau put it in an infamous statement: it was "inconceivable . . . That in a given society one section of the society [could] have a treaty with the other sections society. We must all be equal under the laws and we must not sign treaties amongst ourselves."[17] That is, the White Paper functioned in an analogous way to the earlier enfranchisement process by premising full personhood, civic equality, and the more recently adduced promise of cultural freedom in Canada on the sovereign state's unilateral demand for the dissolution of Indigenous societies' independent political rights (e.g., treaty rights) and the dispossession of Indigenous lands.

Resurgence as "True Multiculturalism"

Manuel's effort to rethink culture beyond its uses for a liberal mode of colonial governance is one key current that feeds into the political concept of resurgence. To be sure, Manuel delivered a coruscating critique of the White Paper as a thinly veiled effort to reaffirm and restructure colonial domination. In doing so, Manuel both remobilized and looked to sources beyond Canadian hegemonic idioms of cultural pluralism as conceptual resources for anticolonial purposes. In particular, Manuel undertook an effort to reconfigure the meanings of "cultural freedom" and culture itself in more expansive ways that could bolster basic challenges both to what land means and the political authority the Canadian settler state claimed over land. Indeed, Manuel's theorization of resurgence emerges out of this move from a critique of White Paper multiculturalism as an ideology of Canadian state building to the contingent affirmation of a deeply transformed multiculturalism (what he called "true multiculturalism").

Yet another source of Manuel's adaptation of ideas to the situation of Indigenous societies in Canada came out of other sites of anticolonial struggle, observed in his travel on diplomatic mission to Tanzania, Zambia, and Kenya. This was part of his fecund engagement with global anticolonial thought, Manuel's reception of which, I argue later in this chapter, provides an important key to interpret the aspirations of the Fourth World. According to Manuel, his visit to Tanzania, Zambia, and Kenya in December of 1971—arranged through Marie Smallface Marule (Blood Tribe)—helped him to "appreciate the identification between our situation and that of the Third World peoples" that a younger generation of activists, including his own children, had been seeking to demonstrate to him (*FW*, 243–44). After his visit to Tanzania, where he met privately with President Julius Nyerere, Manuel came to regard Tanzania as a "bright beacon of inspiration" for the Fourth World with a "common history of being colonized by the English."[18] Upon returning to Canada from his trip, Manuel read Nyerere's *Uhuru Na Ujamaa* (*Freedom and Socialism*). He quickly saw parallels between the situation facing Tanzania and those of Indigenous peoples in Canada.[19]

So, the other source of resurgence is found in Manuel's striking reception of Tanzanian socialism, which he perceived as aspiring to a more robustly multicultural and egalitarian postcolonial society: "like Tanzania, the nation-state would learn to contain within itself many different cultures and life-ways" (*FW*, 5–6). Here, Manuel's template of the postcolonial nation-state embraced a far more pluralistic vision that could encompass fundamentally diverse forms of life ("life-ways"). This (contestable) reading of Tanzania provided Manuel with another model aimed at rejecting a de facto homogenizing nation-building process in Canada, one that herded these multiple forms of life into a singular normative, top-down, and centralized state fitted to this uniformity.

To understand the political dilemmas that turned Manuel toward Nyerere, it is helpful to understand first, however, how he came to resurgence via a critique of multiculturalism in Canada. Namely, Manuel uses the concept of self-determination to reconceive an idiom of "cultural freedom" in Canadian state-building efforts that had been used to further de facto assimilationist ends. In early taped interviews with his coauthor Michael Posluns that formed the materials for *The Fourth World*, Manuel exclaimed to Posluns: "I think that [multiculturalism] is . . . bullshit, until all ethnic groups are given a right of participation." Manuel argued that "true multiculturalism" (his term) entailed that Indigenous societies could themselves set the *terms* of their participation with the larger society "in their own way and through their own value systems." For Manuel, the prospect that social and political forms themselves might be generated through the continuance and/or restoration of cultural value systems necessarily made any talk of multiculturalism a clear matter of political self-determination for Indigenous societies.[20] It "requires first, the degree of sovereignty and self-determination that will make it possible to control our land base" (*FW*, 260). Cultural practices could not truly be separated from political, spiritual, and socioecological practices and beliefs that themselves are mediated through cultural formation. Moreover, political self-determination and the return of a land base that could support vibrant and self-reliant Indigenous political economies are as much connected to—or form part of the substance of—culture as they are politics.

Manuel's insistence on the dynamic interplay between cultural formation and practices of political deliberation had little place in the dominant vision of Canada at the time as a multicultural federation. Instead, a more hegemonic, superficial set of invocations of culture prevailed. As Manuel and Posluns wrote in the original manuscript draft of *The Fourth World*, "certain concessions are made to us under the banner of multiculturalism, a programme that recognizes and sometimes even subsidizes Indian crafts and technology but separates those activities from the culture from which they sprang."[21] That is, various dominant institutions promoted what would count as authentic "Indian culture" under the aegis of multiculturalism. This dominant use of culture amounted to what Manuel called "arts-and-crafts type culture" (*FW*, 51), by which he meant the public presentation of disembodied and dematerialized cultural artifacts as quintessentially and inalterably "Indian."

Such displays ideologically froze Indigenous societies into the past, drawing from and reproducing a "mythical structure": "a belief that an Indian way of life meant something barbaric and savage, frozen in time and incapable of meeting the test of changing social conditions brought about by new technology" (*FW*, 2). Manuel rejected these reified and highly selective state efforts to depict culture as a sum of "cultural artifacts" frozen in time. For Manuel, the political function of recognizing some quite limited aspects of cultural rights was, in fact, to tamp down those potential conflicts over more politically (and culturally) fundamental questions of sovereignty and land. The alternative was initiating land return and self-determination as simultaneously remedial and constructive projects forming the basis of Indigenous futures: "progress—substantial change—can come about only when we again achieve that degree of security and control of our destinies" (*FW*, 4).

Manuel was quick to point out that there were alternatives available to the colonial model of culture. Indeed, the idea of "culture" might instead encompass *all* practices of human meaning making, including political, social, and ecological norms and institutions. This is the capacious model of culture Manuel makes use of in reframing Canada as composed of "two main cultures," "the Indian and the European" (*FW*, 8). On the one hand, this rejection of a narrative of Canada as two founding peoples—English and French—reframed the primary axis of political and cultural conflict in Canada as a colonial situation. On the other hand, it meant that Indigenous societies are dynamic, living peoples whose cultural practices themselves change by appropriating and transforming what is new in ways (that ought to be) freely chosen, against the dictates of one-way colonial assimilation.

With his rejection of the colonial depiction of culture as static, dematerialized, and prepolitical in view, it becomes easier to see that Manuel reframed Indigenous resurgence as a continual rebirth and resistance of interconnected practices that were at once cultural, spiritual, ecological, and political-economic. Resurgence as a philosophical rubric for decolonization, then, entails the strengthening and rebuilding of Indigenous societies' capacities to govern themselves in relation to other political formations and to inherit their past. In general, resurgence as a distinctive paradigm of decolonization is premised on the idea that the invigoration of values and commitments integral to (diverse) Indigenous modes of knowledge, law, and politics ought to both guide choices of the means of struggle and inform the substance of what is to be permanently realized and institutionalized through anticolonial struggle. This is an emphasis that is significantly refined with reference to today's context(s), in contemporary theories of resurgence by Leanne Betasamosake Simpson, Glen Coulthard, and others.[22]

Yet in spite of these crucial interventions, resurgence is still very often framed as teleological in the sense of a backward-looking commitment to tradition (i.e., a kind of static reanimation of the past), a depiction that is actually at cross-purposes to Manuel's original formulation. To the contrary, Manuel captured how the very practice of inheritance necessitates continual reflective affirmation and reinvention of that past to generate new practices of "emergence" themselves forged in novel networks of anticolonial struggle. His often overlooked emphasis was consistently on enfolding the new (e.g., new technologies) in ways that would secure and enhance Indigenous societies' own collective continuance, especially to (newly and once again) resist and fortify relations with land against "the thrust of government policy ... to separate the people from their land" (*FW*, 34).

This emphasis led Manuel to outright reject a picture of political and cultural autonomy as nationalist conservative control over a bounded, unchanging national culture. The latter was more akin to the colonial viewpoint. Indeed, he argued that the mistake central to settler-colonial apprehensions of Indigenous political and cultural practices lay in "confusing the particular forms in use at one time with the values and beliefs they helped to realize" (*FW*, 3). By contrast, this formulation of resurgence instead aimed at the radical and historically situated task of (re)making cultural and political forms in the wake of irreparable loss in the service of a core set of political-philosophical values and commitments. Resurgence did not mean a rejection of and protection from the outside *as such*; instead, Manuel embraced a highly optimistic and global vision of "wedding our own tradition and values with the methods, knowledge, and technology of global civilization throughout our lifetime" (*FW*, 98).

Such a project is founded in a commitment to blending intergenerational continuity with receptivity to the appropriation of the "new" *as itself necessary for* the continued revitalization of the "old." Resurgence hinges on (re)seizing the capacities to determine the noncolonial and nonassimilationist conditions of that reception, not the conservative embrace of a pure return to the inside. Thus, the historical posture Manuel adopts in theorizing the concept of resurgence pushes against interpretations often imputed to contemporary practices of Indigenous resurgence, cast only as a movement inward to a prefigured notion of collective self and toward the past in which that self once flourished.

Moreover, Manuel's longer historical narrative depicts resurgence as *already* a long-standing expression of Indigenous history, culture, and struggles for self-determination, not a single moment of "Indian renaissance." Previous generations had already resurged in response to changing material conditions in ways that "strengthened rather than weakened the existing social and economic systems." For example, Coast Salish peoples had used the vastly expanded networks and the wealth of the fur trade to extend confederal and kinship ties, which itself widened and diversified the ceremonial form that became identified with the Potlatch (*FW*, 24, 52). Manuel traces how the fur trade initially transformed these giving practices into this wider network where "even the dancing symbolizes the invisible bonds of mutual support between each individual and the community" (*FW*, 45).

In this understanding, resurgence had long been practiced in multigenerational inventiveness and "passive resistance" pursued "beneath the surface" to (re)connect past, present, and future—not as pure return (*FW*, 70). Indigenous societies resurged in long-standing and dynamic movement(s). Across these, they consistently aimed at incorporating new forms of cultural adaptation and self-transformation in order to strengthen their own wounded structures of self-determination and structurally negate the implementation of colonial sovereignty.

This formulation of resurgence entailed the "self-conscious" embrace of a mix of revitalized and newly invented cultural, social, and political forms, as core to the praxis of anticolonial struggle itself. Thus, Manuel insisted:

> We do not need to re-create the exact forms by which our grandfathers lived their lives—the clothes, the houses, the political systems, or the means of travel. We do need to create new forms that will allow the future generations to inherit the values, the strengths, and the basic spiritual beliefs—the way of understanding the world—that is the fruit of 1000 generations' cultivation of North American soil by Indian people. (*FW*, 4)

This contention underscores how the capacity to remain rooted in past "values" against colonial subjugation actually *required* the creation of "new forms." Understood in these terms, resurgence was dependent on dynamically (re)interpreting those modes of knowledge that had been attenuated or nearly obliterated under the dominant ideological apparatuses of the colonial state, such as the church and residential schools.

The dynamism I underscore in Manuel's original conception of resurgence hits important limits when it comes to the politics of gender. Specifically, the overarching metaphor of intergenerational renewal in *The Fourth World* is reconstructing a "future history" that will connect us to "our grandfathers." Here, where Manuel casts grandfathers in a position of political leadership essential to the future, grandmothers and mothers are connected more readily to subsistence and the land. Thus, while the land itself is metaphorically cast as a gendered body ("Mother Earth) deserving of reverential regard ("honor"), structures of political leadership and the vital agencies necessary to create new forms appear to be scripted as near-exclusively masculine. Leanne Betasamosake Simpson's more recent efforts to interpret resurgence for Two Spirit and queer and feminist Indigenous politics extend this dynamism beyond the more rigid gendered metaphorical grid and reflexive heteropatriarchy apparent in Manuel.[23]

To conclude this section, Manuel affirmed resurgence as a struggle for self-determination that must include Indigenous rights and freedom to reconfigure the basic institutions of the sovereign state that had been imposed upon them. This also meant the power to remap the institutions of the state by deliberating the terms of constitutional affiliation with (or against) Canada as part and parcel of any actualized vision of "cultural freedom."

Manuel captured this aspiration in the utopian image of a confederation composed of relatively independent political communities related on horizontal terms: "An integration of free communities and the free exchange of people between communities according to their talents and temperaments is the only kind of Confederation that is not an imperial domination" (*FW*, 12). Manuel's vision of confederation as an alternative to "imperial domination" borrowed from a federal imaginary strongly entrenched in the Canadian settler-colonial and British imperial context, but it inverted these terms to offer a utopian depiction of deeply diverse political communities who rejected Canadian colonial sovereignty's hierarchical mediation of their connections, rootedness, and mobility.

"The Land *Is* Our Culture"

In spite of the utopian note sounded in this ideal of confederation, Manuel grounded anticolonial resurgence in quite concrete material struggles for Indigenous self-determination against the colonial state. As I ventured at the outset of this chapter, politics waged as a struggle for land is an effort to disclose and reconfigure what land *means* for all human societies, as embodied in Indigenous self-determination—not just who rightfully owns land subject to colonial occupation. By extension, this articulation of the struggle for land offers a distinctive account of colonial violence as not only the theft of land as a valuable object, but also the theft of land as a relative or web of relationships (Mother Earth).

A philosophical underpinning of the demand for land back can be found in a slogan of the WCIP, which Manuel cofounded: "the land is our culture." The WCIP shortened the statement, originally found in the text of *The Fourth World*, that "our culture is every inch of the land" to "the land is our culture" in its subsequent statements and declarations. By the mid-1980s, the WCIP had shifted its center of gravity to Latin America and adopted the language of "earth." The notion of earth expanded beyond the narrower referent of land alongside what Indigenous societies' also regarded as the many other-than-human reciprocal sites of relation and obligation (such as water, mountains, wild rice, etc.). Nevertheless, the original formulation inspired the latter one, so returning to the text of *The Fourth World* and surrounding political projects reveals key insights into the political-theoretic articulation of land in these resurgent struggles.

In the text of *The Fourth World*, Manuel frames the situation of Indigenous societies as a colonial one marked by a structural antagonism between two antithetical visions of political economy, a "struggle of the past four centuries between . . . two ideas of land" (*FW*, 6). On this basis, he stages a critical contrast between "European cultures" and "Indigenous cultures" as two competing material and metaphysical systems by which land becomes imbued with meaning. In the first place, Manuel avers that "European cultures" conceptualize land as private property. Land is an object that only takes on meaning when it becomes property that can be individually owned and exchanged (*dominium*) and subject to the political-territorial control of sovereignty (*imperium*). From this perspective, land is to be treated as just another commodity that "can be speculated, bought, sold, mortgaged, claimed by one state, surrendered or counter-claimed by another" (*FW*, 6).

By extension, land only becomes salient to the cultural self-understanding of a society when it is translated into the property form, in tandem with the advent of markets in land. In essence, the concept of property-in-land is a way of lumping together and dividing natural bundles of resources ("land" as inert nature) into a single proprietary form, which includes exclusive ownership (i.e., it is accompanied by a right to exclude others), divisibility, and alienability. Of course, Manuel's account of private property as "cultural" is yet another way of saying that these practices are not natural but constructed, and, therefore, that they can be altered. This requires bringing them to light as the historically contingent projects of a particular form of life; pointing to the disavowal(s) inherent in attempts at their universalization; and critiquing a multiculturalism that presumes these as the foundational and uncontestably neutral backdrops to "culture."

In contrast to a system of land as commodity, Manuel observes that Indigenous societies have experienced *the medium of land itself* as integral to practices of collective self-making and self-determination. This framework conceives of land itself as an active force in generating a meaningful (set of) relationship(s). More than just an abstract set of philosophical commitments, such a conception of land as a (source of) relation is itself created, disclosed, and reproduced in practices that generate the material life and normative substance of social, cultural, and political communities.

By way of context, Manuel's account of the politics of land here was really only crystallized in dialogue with other Indigenous communities, first throughout Canada, then internationally, in a visit to Australia and Aotearoa (New Zealand) from March 26 to April 7, 1971, and a visit in June 1972 to the Sámi people as part of the UN Conference on the Environment in Stockholm. Through these initial exchanges, Manuel began to recognize the commonalities of experience among Indigenous societies subject to colonial occupation (*FW*, 238), of "Dark people in a White-Ruled Commonwealth" who have the "additional burden of a European power succeeded by a local administration."[24] Furthermore, these international travels laid the groundwork for an even more geographically capacious notion of an Indigenous "Fourth World," which came together institutionally in the preliminary meetings of the WCIP in April 1974 in Georgetown, Guyana, and 1975 in Port Alberni, British Columbia, on the lands of the Tseshaht First Nation.

Acknowledging the otherwise "wide variations" among Indigenous peoples, Manuel nevertheless observes that all share the notion that conceptualizing land (or water or air) as a relation is a core precondition of (any) just and equal political community, and of relations among political communities. As he puts it, "when I met with the Maori people, on my first trip beyond the shores of North America, if I had said, 'our culture is every inch of the land,' the meaning would've been obvious to them. Wherever I've traveled in the Aboriginal world, there has been a common attachment to the land" (*FW*, 6). Alongside the negative unifying bond of resistance to colonial domination, Manuel contended that the positive "common soil of social and political experience" stems from the fact that "all of our structures and values have developed out of a spiritual relationship with the land on which we have lived" (*FW*, 7).

I propose to interpret the claim that "the land is [every inch of] our culture" dialectically. In short, it is a spatial formulation that specifies the positive ethical content aspired to in orienting Indigenous struggles for self-determination and decolonization. In the manuscript version of *The Fourth World*, Manuel and Posluns invoke the much-debated model of base and superstructure from Marx's "'Preface' to *A Contribution to the Critique of Political Economy*."[25] There, Manuel and Posluns describe land as a "material base" or "economic base" in which "spiritual values" must be "firmly rooted" in order to flourish and survive (*FW*, 67).[26] The unidirectional base-superstructure language is less central in the published version of the *Fourth World*, where the notion that "the land is our culture" clearly encapsulates a more open-ended and reciprocal dialectic.

In what I will call the land-culture dialectic, "land" preconditions and gives rise to "culture." In turn, "culture" shapes the land. That is, there is a continual back-and-forth interaction between each term of the proposition—culture and land. While Manuel continually refers to Indigenous societies' shared spiritual relationship to the land, he also underscores that no reference to the spiritual is ultimately separable from a naturalistic, historically conditioned set of material capacities, systems, and relations that have taken "root" (his term) over time. This relationship, he argued, has grown "over the centuries out of the relationship between the people and the environment" (*FW*, 55).[27]

As part of resurgence, this is an actively inherited mode of anticolonial agency aimed at making the earth by actualizing reciprocal duties to the land—not a natural inheritance. In this way, the concept and practice of self-determination is linked to the project of the continued (re)making of nonexploitative relations with the earth. Manuel contends

> the land from which our culture springs is like the water and the air, one and indivisible. Land is our Mother Earth. The animals that grow on the land are our spiritual brothers [sic]. We are a part of that creation that the Mother Earth brought forth. More complicated, more sophisticated than the other creatures, but no nearer to the Creator who infused us with life. (*FW*, 6)

In this schema, humans derive their responsibilities from their place as "part of that creation that Mother Earth brought forth," not as a result of their capacities for ownership or "dominion" (*FW*, 6). This conception of land as the normative and material force orienting human social relations frames a distinct "worldview" premised on a set of responsibility-based relations to land.[28] In turn, responsibility-based frameworks exercised by Indigenous societies as stewards of the land allow it to preserve and regenerate its culture-bestowing potential.

Manuel argued that "land" ought to be understood as material relationships with other-than-human relatives and "culture" as the normative framework of respect and reciprocity among human beings. What is crucial here is that these are inseparable from one another, as each side of the dialectic sustains the healthy expression of the other side. As such, "the land is our culture" expresses a dynamic and interactive relationship between peoples and land. Together, land and culture form a dynamic totality in which each of these terms actively shapes the other; accordingly, they can only be expressed via processes of mutual co-constitution out of which they emerge. This co-constitution aspect is also reflected in the formulation of "culture" or "spirituality" themselves as thoroughly material products and projects that take shape in relation to the materiality of land. As Manuel observed, "as in most natural or traditional religions, the spiritual has not been separated from the material world" (*FW*, 222). Accordingly, lands only became regarded as spiritually central, that is, "sacred," because they are the "source of all life.... Their sanctity is recognized because of their importance to our survival" (*FW*, 256).

Manuel refers to this dialectic as a system of "natural economy." It is significant here that, by natural economy, he does *not* mean an economy that is the result of a society being somehow "closer" to nature, by virtue of lacking commodity production, complex divisions of labor, and/or material progress. Instead, Manuel uses the term "natural economy" in a looser historicist vein to mean any mode of political economy in which human societies actively cultivate nonexploitative relations with land, which then dialectically shape the character of relations among human beings. For example, prior to the government ban on the Potlatch ceremony, "giving" provided "the whole foundation of our society" (*FW*, 40–44) and pervaded "our daily material life" (*FW*, 40). This relational conception of land was inseparable from consideration for other human beings: "The concern for a life related to the land, the water, and the air cannot be separated from a life related to other human beings" (*FW*, 257). In other words, those nonexploitative relations with land mutually inform—and run in principled alignment to— nonexploitative and egalitarian relations between human beings. In this sense, resurgence meant actualizing these parallel and mutually supporting forms of sociality in and through the building of modern political economies sustaining Indigenous self-determination.

Manuel and Posluns contrast this ideal of a "natural economy" or "giving society" with a political economy based on private property, common to "European culture." In the latter, relations among humans and with land also run "parallel to" and mutually reinforce one another, yet the very form those relations take promote the disavowal of the land-culture dialectic by denying anything more than instrumental value to the land (*FW*, 256). Here, in a reference that is likely attributable to Posluns (who was based in Toronto), they cite Canadian political theorist and University of Toronto professor C. B. MacPherson's famous concept of "possessive individualism." Possessive individualism describes how a specific way of relating to the self *as property*, that is, self-ownership, became integral to the rise of "competitive market societies."[29] In the more specific context of Manuel and Posluns borrowing without citation from MacPherson, they contend that the property form by which the self establishes mastery over land generates an analogous mode of sociality—"the nature of man [*sic*] himself" (*FW*, 6)—based on mastery and domination. That is, in relating to land exclusively via the property form, and, thus, construing the land itself as having no other value beyond its conversion into an object of human will and improvement, this purely instrumental relation to land is transferred over, so to speak, into relations among human beings—and vice versa.

More specific to the context of Manuel's work with the NIB in the first half of the 1970s, this conception of resurgence intervened in the material realities of Canadian political economy. During this period, the Canadian state initiated meager federally directed economic development for Indian bands and massive investment in the extraction of fossil fuels on the lands of the Dene Nation and the James Bay Cree. In his capacity as head of the NIB, Manuel called the new programs in a 1972 speech a "whiteman's whitewash," comparing the paucity and top-down administration of programs given to Indian band governments unfavorably to the more generous "equalization payments" the federal government shelled out to resource-poor provinces like Newfoundland. Aside from the severe inequality in federal resource provision, Manuel also rejected all "economic development without full local control" as "only another form of imperial conquest" (*FW*, 151).[30]

Altogether, Manuel argued that these turns intensified the "non-Indian corporate exploitation of our remaining commercial and industrial potential."[31] Proposals "under the guise of economic development . . . in return for ninety-nine-year leases and unpredicted amounts of pollution" created a false choice that was really that between "one kind of stagnating poverty and another" (*FW*, 151). As a consequence, these programs *both* deprived Indigenous societies of a "land base" *and* never delivered (and were never meant to deliver) on promises of economic development and poverty reduction that putatively compensated local communities for submitting to these external imperatives.

This was reflected in the aspiration *both* to sustain and/or (re)actualize relations with and to land *and* to guarantee full political and economic equality to Indigenous societies *as* polities. In this respect, the "need to redefine our relationship with the land cannot be separated from our need to find more effective and far-reaching ways of redistributing wealth across regional and provincial boundaries as a matter of right and without preconditions" (*FW*, 257). Despite the claims of the Canadian government and industry that new development programs and extractive industries on Indigenous lands would lift communities out of poverty, Manuel argued that "this future being planned by others than ourselves . . . is a sentence to stay at the bottom of the socio-economic ladder in our society."[32] As such, it was necessary to "put the initiative for planning and decision-making into the hands of local communities."[33]

By extension, the ethical system orienting this dialectic of nonexploitation between people and land rejected extractive capitalism as an unlivable form of violence and domination. Notably, these practices are violent both to humanity and to the earth itself, as relationally defined persons whose well-being is co-constituted through practices of earthmaking. In particular, Manuel figures land as an "indivisible" relative—as "Mother Earth." This formulation casts land as a (gendered) caring person, or, more specifically, as a person whose foundational provision of care creates the background conditions for other affective and material networks of care to be established, both among humans and between humans and other-than-human beings. Altogether, the very collective and individual selves being authorized and/or shielded from domination through self-determination cohere as part of this wider network of reciprocal relations.

It is important to underscore here that Manuel's contention is not that land is *more* culturally salient to Indigenous societies. Instead, it is that *all* cultural formations are built upon certain very core notions of the meaning of land, but which Indigenous societies—due to their philosophical commitments and historical experiences—have a generally more robust capacity to acknowledge. What is particular about the settler prerogative lies in the disavowal of the structural grip that land itself has in constituting cultural and social forms. In this way, the property form is quite like sovereignty at the deep level of their conceptual structure. Namely, property is a relation that structurally disguises itself as a nonrelation by framing ownership as an extension of the will of an individual self.[34] Like sovereign territoriality, property obscures in its very form the universal reality of human dependence on land.

By contrast, because water and land are "indivisible" and the "sources of life," they should not be treated as commodities, as a bundle of inert "natural resources" to be divided and alienated. Unlike other objects of personal property, land cannot be detached from the relations and responsibilities it generates for human and other-than-human communities. Therefore, the transformation of land into fungible private property—the drive "to claim more of a title to that land than the right to use it while we have need of it"—is "an affront to our Creator as well as our community" (*FW*, 255). Here, Indigenous anticolonialism represents a struggle to make it impossible to "claim more," as part of a politics of earthmaking premised on realizing structures of nonexploitation and duties of reciprocity against the colonial imposition of regimes of sovereignty and private property. The positive account of Indigenous self-determination hinges on the realization of adaptive systems of care with and for repatriated land as core to the self-determination of the body politic.

Abduction

Land is a distinctive kind of entity as a web of relations (not the product of congealed human labor nor technological invention). Manuel reasons that the theft and commodification of land likewise ought to be characterized as a specific form of harm. In short, this is a "diremption" (i.e., deep violation via being sundered) from the relational responsibilities constituted through interdependencies with land. Manuel differentiates this violation from the exploitation of labor, that is, "any number of inequities and means of unfair exploitation in the system of exchange" that have their basis in "the fruit of human labor" (*FW*, 255).

When Manuel declares the very transformation of land into property an "affront," what is the experience of violence he names beyond exploitation (where the latter, as Manuel himself suggests, is usually understood as the coercive and/or unequal transfer of resources)? If the body politic itself is formed and authorized through relations of care with human and other-than-human beings, then it becomes possible to experience and conceptualize colonial violence as a form of structural domination and deprivation that targets both human collectivities and the land or earth itself.

As I explored in chapters 1 and 2, a powerful aspect of Indigenous decolonization struggles emerges through critiques of the systems and the ideological idioms that accompany and sustain the reproduction of the state as a colonial settler state. Indigenous self-determination is far from exhausted by the resulting negative interpretation of freedom as *non*domination against the many axes around which colonial sovereignty and a colonial world order turn. Nevertheless, it is a key feature of Indigenous anticolonial struggles that they radically reshape what *counts* in the first instance *as* structural domination precisely in reorienting the historical and political imaginaries that arise in the course of articulating the terms of those struggles.

Manuel's project generates important insights along these lines when we spell out the theoretical bases underlying his idiosyncratic use of the term "abduction" alongside "domination" to articulate core dimensions of this affront. Manuel never explains the term "abduction" in any detail in the text of *The Fourth World*. Yet, it becomes clear in the text that by appealing to the term "abduction," Manuel portrays a distinct form of colonial violence premised on the negation—or systemic effort at disruption—of "our traditional means of livelihood" and the reproduction of a system of reciprocal responsibilities (*FW*, 1–2). I submit that abduction is both a descriptive and evaluative term that names a type of colonial violence that dismantles the positive cycles of social reproduction and collective self-determination that the land-culture dialectic tracks (*FW*, 7).

Here, consider the etymology of the term "abduction" as a starting point. An ancient usage of abduction is the "theft or confiscation of a person's property; seizure without consent." However, abduction now typically refers to the theft of a human person: "The action of taking someone away by force or deception, or without the consent of his or her legal guardian; kidnapping."[35] Putting together these two meanings of the coercive theft of property and of a person protected under certain relations of stewardship, abduction characterizes a type of theft that is violence to other-than-human relatives, to Mother Earth.

In this way, Manuel argues that abduction constitutes a harm *in itself*— the "rape of [the conquered's] mother." The seizure of land is violence to the bodily integrity of a person, a person that is both materially *part of* the larger body politic and a *synecdoche for* the body politic. Put otherwise, this is earth-destroying colonial violence. It functions through the literal and figurative enforced starvation of agencies core to the enactment of kinship-based socioecological responsibilities carried out in relations to living other-than-human entities. In other words, this is violence to an other-than-human relative that is also destructive of the enabling constitutive institutions of the body politic (*FW*, 59).

In material terms, abductive practices significantly delimit the scope of collective and individual agency by virtue of undermining the social and ecological conditions for (re)making the earth. In particular, Manuel tracks practices of land theft as a form of structured disruption of kinship-based relations to land, with the primary purpose to generate private property and sovereign rule for citizens of the invading settler society. Abduction captures the harm that occurs to this collective earthmaking agency understood as carrying out particular responsibilities and relationships to a relative of inherent value, a relative integral to the very possibility of exercising freedom oneself. In sum, abduction captures the form of colonial violation that occurs through the severing of a constitutive relationship between "spiritual values" and the "material base" (i.e., the land, water, etc.) in which the former are "rooted."[36]

My close reading of Manuel on abduction helps to supplement what has more recently been called "usurpation." In recent years, political theorists have refashioned the neorepublican focus on nondomination to attend to the assault on colonized collective agency integral to colonial violence. At the core of this assault are practices through which the institutional arrangements of the colonized political community are destroyed and/or absorbed into the colonial state. Analyzing the "insufficiency" of the neorepublican emphasis on the exercise of arbitrary power as domination, Patchen Markell describes this as usurpation, or those practices that "displaced active involvement in political life" by negating existing forms and resources for the actual expression—the carrying out, that is—of collective social and political agency.[37] For Markell, imperialism constitutes a "source of usurpation, through which existing uses and forms of social and political activity are displaced by the world-narrowing power of imperial rule."[38] Robert Nichols has further adapted the notion of usurpation to theorize the systemic violence of settler-colonial practices of "compulsory enfranchisement," which are premised on the forcible dismantling of Indigenous polities in the various iterations of the Indian Act.[39]

Manuel's usage of abduction shares usurpation's focus on the denial and displacement of colonized political agency. Yet he also underscores practices of collective participation that extend well beyond a strictly anthropocentric account of a democratic-republican body politic that authorizes itself via shared public institutions. More than simply *world* narrowing, abduction is *earth* narrowing in the wider sense of displacing resources for the expression of collective participatory capacities that extend to authority relations forged in (re)making nonexploitative relations with and to the earth. In this way, Manuel's account of the constitution of agentic possibilities and involvement in collective life that colonization displaces captures a suitably wider set of meanings. In turn, those meanings better relate to the interrelated activities of social reproduction more adequate to a noncapitalist historical context and to a political horizon of resurgence aimed at building a future society in which "the economy is [bound up with] the total environment" (*FW*, 55).

Put otherwise, the concept of abduction elucidates a *nonanthropocentric mode of structural usurpation,* that is, a form of usurpation that severs the socioecological reproduction and affective circuity of both social and political life with and through the other-than-human.[40] This is an axis of "environmental domination" that alienates Indigenous societies from their participatory capacities for collective continuance,[41] by fundamentally transforming (and seizing for the benefit of the colonizer society) the very background socioecological conditions through which those societies make themselves and, in turn, their structures of political rule.

The land-culture dialectic, then, is one philosophical rendering of an anticolonial politics of earthmaking. This is a politics that ought to be understood as arrayed against the colonial practices of abduction and domination that have been central to the realization of settler-colonial sovereignty. By rethinking the "culture" in multiculturalism through an account of relational reciprocity with land as culture's very *source*, Manuel contended that cultural freedom and development on Indigenous peoples' terms entailed the "resurgence" of these relations to land. This contention sets up a refigured account of the preconditions of lived experiences and enactments of freedom by promoting the recognition of aboriginal title, jurisdiction, and self-determination within a renewed interpretation of Canada's confederation—and, ultimately, the global order. Manuel contrasted Indigenous struggles for land as a decommodified relation foundational to Indigenous self-determination with the colonial sovereign state and proprietary model of land that prevailed in Canadian liberalism. This also entailed a rethinking of the universal meaning of land itself, against the dominance of the imaginary of the sovereign state across the broader political spectrum of Cold War struggles for global hegemony.

The Fourth World

I have primarily argued thus far that the resurgence paradigm emerged in critical resistance to the colonialism of Canadian White Paper multiculturalism. Here, I excavate the other source of influence in Manuel's activist-theorization of "Fourth World" self-determination and decolonization, the global anticolonial struggles of the Third World.[42] Manuel's use of resurgence and especially his idea and pursuit of a nonaligned "Fourth World" was crucially informed by his and others' shifting views toward global efforts to construct an independent Third World, specifically the trajectory of (a) the external politics of international solidarity and (b) the internal politics of land that accompanied the modernizing, often ideologically socialist developmental states of the postcolonial regimes of the 1970s. Those were struggles to found nation-states arrayed in transnational solidarity to socialize the *collective exploitation* of land as a bundle of natural resources for broadly redistributive and democratic purposes. By focusing on Manuel's reception of Third Worldism, my analysis here sharpens the conceptual contours and intellectual influences that informed the articulation of resurgence as a Fourth World model of decolonization.

Manuel's discovery of the Third World happened through the fluid networks tying together colonized peoples with a history of British imperial rule in particular. Indeed, Manuel developed the term "Fourth World" itself in collaboration with friends and comrades he met through Marie Smallface Marule, his secretary and then executive director of the NIB and his longtime political adviser and collaborator. Through Smallface Marule, married to exiled African National Congress (ANC) activist Jacob Marule whom she met in Zambia in the Canadian equivalent of the Peace Corps, Manuel met participants in the ANC's struggle against South African apartheid. Manuel first heard the term "Fourth World" from Mbutu Milando, then first secretary of the Tanzanian High Commission in Ottawa.[43]

Manuel reported that it was not until he traveled to Tanzania that he began to more deeply "appreciate the identification between our situation and that of the Third World Peoples" (*FW*, 244). In December 1971, Manuel embarked for Tanzania on the occasion of the tenth anniversary of Tanganyikan national independence with his executive assistant Ron Shackleton. When Jean Chrétien, the minister of Indian affairs, pulled out of the trip, Manuel and Shackleton were unexpectedly left as the only official Canadian delegates. They found themselves accidentally, and to the later regret of the Canadian government, with VIP access to high-level officials, including face-to-face time with Nyerere himself.[44]

This political history is beginning to enjoy a much wider circulation, but it is nevertheless still all too common to hear the Fourth World wrongly invoked as a kind of anthropological *description* of particular societies. In this formulation, the Fourth World is often identified with precapitalist modes of production of the hunter-gatherer or pastoral mode (much as resurgence is wrongly presumed to be a pure return to origins). The denotative use of the Fourth World as characterized by lack and particularity alone is misleading, especially for the way it eschews the place of the Fourth World as a conscious political project that aimed to transform the world order. Much as historian Vijay Prashad has argued of the "Third World," the Fourth World was a political project in motion rather than (just) the name for a place.[45] So, Fourth Worldism composed a *particular strand* of Indigenous political thinking and organizing—a strand that diverged in key respects from articulations of Indigenous anticolonialisms that otherwise shared many political affinities and close personal contacts.

To illustrate this point further, it helps to briefly foreshadow the focus of the next chapter, in which I explore how another related strand of Indigenous anticolonialism in Canada took a different tack vis-à-vis Third Worldism. Namely, I examine this other strand in interpreting the work of two radical organizers, Howard Adams and Lee Maracle. Active beginning in the latter half of the 1960s, Adams and Maracle rejected the need to invent a separate "Fourth World" political subject. In brief, these radical thinkers opted for an even closer identification than Manuel with Third World anticolonial currents of Marxist-Leninism, especially Maoism for its focus on agrarian struggle. "Natives Are Part of the Third World," the headline of a Maracle article from 1976, nicely summarizes this idea.

This is all to say that when Manuel invoked the Fourth World's need for separate institutions and philosophical and political commitments divergent *from* Third Worldism, he and his interlocutors were not presuming an existing prepolitical basis for Indigenous politics. Instead, they aimed to call into being one specific trajectory among other projects of Indigenous transnational internationalism, by creating Indigenous forms of collective subjectivity, solidarity, and transnational affiliation that would transcend the limitations of claiming a limited slate of rights within the settler nation-state.

Manuel's framework, then, aimed both to *constitute and mobilize* the political subject of the Fourth World, especially in configuring land-based knowledge(s) and practices both as locally enacted realities and as points of transnational connection aimed at supervening and/or structurally transforming the sovereign nation-state. The political-theoretical dilemma here is how to "produce that new reality that reconstructs a tradition in which people can hold a common belief" (*FW*, 245). In considering the multiple scales at which this project took place, it is worth recalling that it was a task to craft this sense of a tradition grounded in "common belief" of Indigenous societies even within the boundaries of a single colonial nation-state. My insistence on interpreting the Fourth World as a constructive project helps to direct attention to the rhetorical and institutional organizing aimed at actually *constituting* it, both institutionally and imaginatively. Textually, Manuel and Posluns's appeal in *The Fourth World* to the Two Row Wampum model of treaty making as a staple of Haudenosaunee diplomacy is one among other efforts to relate similar practices so as to establish transnational affiliations, specifically to connect the West Coast land struggles of the UBCIC to those on the East Coast.[46]

Organizationally, Manuel envisaged the NIB itself as a kind of transnational counterpower working within Canada and across international forums to empower the self-determination of the smaller Indigenous societies of which it was composed. The WCIP extended this project even further outward, as it was Manuel's aspiration to create a separate forum for the representation of Indigenous societies and to mobilize to gain leverage in the existing structures of the UN (where the WCIP received consultative status at the Economic and Social Council in 1979). At its 1977 meeting, the WCIP delegates asserted a "right to land and water" and "to recover the land which rightfully . . . belongs to us," as "prerequisites to an indigenous development of their own institutions, culture and language."[47] It is more familiar to study this mode of Indigenous transnational internationalism as a way to expand the repertoire of international human rights as strategic sites of legal and moral appeal for Indigenous societies that supersede the authority of the settler nation-state.[48] This is certainly the case, but, as Emma Feltes and Sharon Venne aptly point out, these mobilizations were more than (just) "a tactic to apply global pressure to Canada. . . . Rather, the interplay was the objective—that is, to establish Indigenous self-determination on both a local and international basis."[49] In other words, Indigenous self-determination emerges in and through the transnational internationalist project of creating supervening relations—whether between Coast Salish polities and the Haudenosaunee on opposite ends of the continent or between Indigenous societies in Canada and those in Australia on near opposite ends of the world.

The transnational dimensions of Third World solidarity found in projects of Pan-Africanism resonated for the NIB as a pan-Indigenous organization whose own success depended on blending transnational solidarity with a flexible internal political structure of "cooperative federalism" (*FW*, 211). Manuel alighted on Kwame Nkrumah and Julius Nyerere's shared emphasis on pan-African unity and the possibilities of an East Africa Federation, which resonated with his own efforts to span the disparate realities among First Nations to form the NIB.

In his meeting with Nyerere at the Presidential Palace in Dar es Salaam, Manuel reportedly declared "that the Indians of Canada subscribe to the 1957 statement of Nkrumah that Ghana's independence is incomplete until all of Africa is free and Nyerere's statement that Africans are not Europeans, cannot be Europeans, and do not want to be Europeans."[50] Manuel likened the Pan-Africanism of Nkrumah and later Nyerere to the politics of "unity" adopted by the UBCIC, which linked aspirations toward a self-generated and nonassimilationist internal solidarity and reconciliation with resistance to externally imposed, hierarchically racialized structures of colonial domination: "unity is at the same time a spiritual state, a demand for significant political power, and a corresponding end to domination by external political forces, and a reconciliation of the many elements of Indian society."[51] Manuel's aim in forming these pan-Indigenous transnational networks was to generate pan-Indigenous institutions that would allow for the flourishing of the very heterogeneity and particularity of localized practices of resurgence and self-determination.[52] Despite the ideology of unity, then, the goal of these forums and confederations was not to generate a kind of internal hegemony even among Indigenous societies by centralizing or assimilating the terms of their own legal and political systems.

Manuel found this vision enlivened by the commitments of the domestic Tanzanian state-building project itself, which "really changed my thinking and showed me what national independence can mean" because "there is a national government that really works for the local people on the village level without trying to make them all the same."[53] Likewise "Indian people," Manuel argued, "must build a vehicle that can confront a federal government and that can provide resources to communities in every part of the country," but key to this is that this counterpower "does not pull against the bond of local or tribal autonomy, on a cultural level."[54] The WCIP spoke of "mutual self-reliance," which expressed a shared commitment to Indigenous "international cooperation" that would reciprocally enliven diverse practices of self-determination—and, eventually, create political communities with relative self-sufficiency vis-à-vis settler-state political economies.

In the weeds of politics, there were nevertheless important conflicts about demands for community control over resources—all structured within an environment of colonial abandonment. As Sarah Nickel has documented, it was during Manuel's time as president of the NIB opposing the authoritarian, meagerly funded, and technocratic orientation of Canadian development initiatives that he sent a telex in 1975 to UBCIC officials encouraging them to resist a program called the "Grants to Bands Program." He likely did not intend to provoke this action, but his message in 1975 about the importance of eventual self-sufficiency from the colonial state was nonetheless (mis)interpreted by many as calling for an immediate, complete break from government funding of any kind. Though technically the product of a misunderstanding of Manuel's more targeted advice, the UBCIC ultimately made the controversial decision to refuse government funding entirely as a gesture of independence and self-sufficiency.

Where some communities such as the Neskonlith band supported the decision and deepened reliance on traditional subsistence activities, others such as the Owikeno (or Wuikinuxv) Nation and the Caribou Tribal Council at Williams Lake sought to preserve the already minimal funding from the Department of Indian Affairs for health, welfare, and education. Moreover, activists in the British Columbia Homemakers Association, a women's organization, such as Ts'ishaa7ath (Tseshaht) member Agnes Dick, pointed out that funds were needed for "thirty-eight foster children on her reserve including seven in her own home." The BCHA took an active role in securing funding for family services in particular, rejecting this particular version of independence as insufficiently attentive to pressing community needs. As such, the site of decision making within these transnational internationalist projects continued to be a crucial question as to which responsibilities ought to be prioritized and who would bear the consequences of choosing particular strategies of resurgence and refusal.[55]

Manuel was among a number of radical intellectuals and activists drawn to Tanzania as a lodestar of pan-Africanist struggle in the early 1970s that had taken on the mantle once held by Nkrumah's Ghana of the mid-1960s.[56] This cohort was attracted to Nyerere's nonaligned state-building project, including his radical internationalist posture and support of ongoing liberation movements in Southern Africa, nonorthodox socialist commitments, and revered popular and egalitarian leadership style. What makes Manuel's response distinctive among these is that he pulled at a strand of Nyerere's project encompassing a vision of resurgence and popular self-reliance. This vision rejected the model of a culturally uniform nation-state in which centralized national policy enforces a monolithic agenda upon diverse political communities with their own rich modes of self-government and lived traditions of citizenship. Contrasting this kind of deep multiculturalism favorably with the superficiality and violence of liberal capitalist multiculturalism for Indigenous societies in Canada, he cited the example of Nyerere's "decision to postpone the development of a national television network ... in order to leave the limited funds available free to develop eight local radio networks that could accommodate all the local languages." "That," Manuel argued, "was multiculturalism" (*FW*, 245). It was not Canada but Tanzania that illustrated the promise of a postcolonial, multinational federation that actually had begun the process of enacting a just society.

Another dimension of Fourth Worldism stemmed from Manuel's appreciative interpretation of Nyerere and others' struggle for an egalitarian, postcolonial political-economic world order. In particular, Manuel began to look for inspiration to Tanzania's 1967 Arusha Declaration and Third World efforts to forge a New International Economic Order (NIEO).[57] The NIEO was a reform-minded effort that sought to institutionalize a global South–based order based on significant global wealth redistribution, which key actors articulated as an alternative to the structurally unequal neocolonial dependency relations persisting by dint of the rules set and enforced by a dominant "core" over a subordinate "periphery."[58]

Refracting these projects through the situation faced by Indigenous societies in Canada, Manuel imagined connected experiences of oppression: "We share a common experience of poverty; our lands and peoples have been exploited for the benefit of others; and like the people of the third world, we are struggling for a new economic order."[59] Manuel's appeal to a pan-Indigenous struggle for a "new economic order" directly echoed the NIEO's aspiration to construct a more egalitarian transnational political economy bolstered by the participatory power and substantive political-economic independence of the societies making up the global majority.

Specifically, Manuel had thrown the support of the NIB behind the Dene Nation and James Bay Cree, both peoples engaged in fighting petroleum companies allied with the state seeking the construction of oil and gas pipelines on their lands. Recounting this struggle, he suggested that "we're actually in the same position because the economic growth of Tanzania/Tanganyika still has to depend on European support from the outside.... And we're in the same situation except it's an internal domestic situation."[60] So, Manuel posited a direct analogy between Tanzania's dependent position in the global political economy and Indigenous societies' efforts to repel Canada's drive to control Indigenous resources (and offer meager redistribution to bands that failed, anyway, to meet basic needs). The difference here was that this ongoing extractive colonial relation was faced by internally peripheral(ized) Indigenous societies made subject to a direct colonial state apparatus.

Here, the idea of Indigenous resurgence emerged in part by refashioning the concept often rendered as "self-reliance" in the Tanzania state-building project (what the WCIP adapted in its notion of "mutual self-reliance"). The notion of "self-reliance" combined the rejection of colonial-capitalist development with a focus on accruing value to the domestic social formation by taking Indigenous modes of production (inseparable, again, from "culture") as the philosophical and institutional foundation of a mixed political economy. A brief examination of Manuel's reception of Nyerere's philosophy of self-reliance and *Ujamaa* (literally, familyhood) shows how the notion of resurgence bears the influence of—and even reworks—Nyerere's project of Tanzanian socialism. Specifically, Nyerere had invoked "tribal socialism" as an effort to "regain our former attitude of mind—our traditional African socialism—and apply it to the new societies we are building today."[61] The signature concept of Nyerere's resulting philosophy of "Tanzanian socialism" was the Swahili notion of *Ujamaa*, first coined in his landmark 1962 essay "*Ujamaa*—The Basis of African Socialism."[62] Nyerere invoked African political-cultural forms as the "starting point, means, and end of independent Tanganyika's development."[63] Nyerere explained that

> by the use of the world "ujamaa," therefore, we state that for us socialism involves building on the foundation of our past, and building also to our own design. We are not importing a foreign ideology into Tanzania and trying to smother our distinct social patterns with it. We have deliberately decided to grow, as a society, out of our own roots.... We are doing this by emphasizing certain characteristics of our traditional organization and extending them ... to meet the challenge of life in the twentieth century world.
>
> This emphasis on growth from traditional patterns of social living means that we shall be trying to create something which is uniquely ours.... This does not invalidate our claim to be building socialism.[64]

A few months after returning from Tanzania, Manuel told Posluns that Indigenous societies in Canada could learn from Nyerere to "use our culture as the foundation for development ... for everybody, not just a select few."[65] The notion of culture as the foundation of the futurity of Indigenous societies as well as the source of a more robustly egalitarian and nonexploitative philosophical basis for society here is key. The idea is that a self-reflective sense of the specificity of "our distinct social patterns" ought to inform societal trajectories as developmental variations on democratic socialism. This is in contrast to perceiving living modes of production as obstacles to be superseded on the path to a more rationalized infrastructure of democratic socialist politics, which was often entailed in the linear, stadial developmental models imported from Eurocentric communism. In this way, resurgence as a concept crystallizes Manuel's effort to refigure self-reliance and *ujamaa*, if resurgence is understood as a dynamic and self-reflective commitment to modes of social and political progress that grow out of and strengthen the dialectic of land and culture as the philosophical foundation of Indigenous societies.

Manuel's selective appropriation of this reimagined anticolonial developmentalism is also reflected in the articulations of Fourth Worldism in Canada bearing Manuel's influence. As Glen Coulthard has shown in his archival research on the Dene Nation, it is likely due in no small part to Manuel that the 1975 Dene Declaration drew upon the Arusha Declaration's idiom of "self-reliance." Self-reliance entailed progressive social and political transformation to liberate the Tanzanian population from colonial-era cultural and political-economic dependency relations. Rather than pure autochthony or the autarkic closing off of an economy, the concept of self-reliance had a significant transnational structural component in that it meant creating enough of a separate space of epistemic, social, and political-economic power ("de-linking"), in solidarity with other colonized peoples, so as to (re)gain the capacity to deliberate and determine more egalitarian conditions of exchange, interdependence, and integration into the global political economy.

Following this, the *Ujamaa* project as Manuel refracted it through the aspirations of Indigenous societies aimed to pursue a socialist society premised on a dynamic and self-conscious turn inward away from Eurocentric models of development. So, the very notion of progressive development here relies on the idea of generating collective power on the basis of learned capacities to inherit and strengthen that "foundation," not a rupture from defunct and premodern "tradition." Here, culture was more than just an instrumental weapon to achieve transformative socialist ends or a tolerated-and-confined space within liberal multicultural capitalism. Manuel cites "our culture" as the foundation of forward-looking efforts to build a progressive, egalitarian society. In analogous terms, Manuel described how "the strength of Indian cultures in the past have been achieved through working on a communal or cooperative basis," and it was this strength that had to be built upon (*FW*, 235).

Manuel reflected in an emotional July 14, 1973, journal entry on the activism of his son Arthur Manuel that future generations would carry on this radical promise of "my ideology for North American Indian socialism" (*FW*, 271). There is nothing like a formal definition available of what Manuel meant by "North American Indian socialism," nor is there direct textual evidence from this particular journal note to interpret it as Manuel simply substituting "North American Indian" for "African." Nevertheless, Marie Smallface Marule—who first introduced Manuel to Nyerere's politics—gives a suggestive depiction of how the basic architecture of Nyerere's project may have informed Manuel's conception of North American Indian socialism:

> [Nyerere] believed that you couldn't bring in Marxism to such nations of people, that you had to base their development on their own language, their own culture, their own heritage. That's where you develop ... from there. To use their natural cooperation tendency to bring about change ... building from the communities upwards as opposed to imposing.[66]

This is an eloquent justification of decolonization as resurgence. Smallface Marule points to how Manuel wagered on the (relative) exteriority of Indigenous societies' own normative emphases ("natural cooperation tendency") against the encircling logic of possessive individualism. For Manuel, these internal cultural resources of Indigenous societies constituted a horizon of shared practices and experiences, attenuated but not entirely erased: "So long as there is a single thread that links us to the ways of our grandfathers, our lives are strong. However thin and delicate that thread may be, it will support the weight of a stronger cord that will tie us securely to the land" (*FW*, 47). In turn, this grounding figures a model of self-determination that resonates with and substantively coheres around a vision that institutionalized the notion that "the land is our culture" in the collective consciousness and orientations of Indigenous anticolonial struggles. Here, language, culture, and heritage are empirically the very medium of collective self-fashioning and meaning making. In this way, resurgence is a praxis of decolonization that begins from a sense of the intersubjective crafting of Indigenous land-based knowledge as the actual materials of forging decolonial self-determination.

This notion of resurgence has both a practical and normative grounding as a distinctive framework adapted for the purposes of Indigenous anticolonial struggles. On the one hand, the argument here is that resurgence is a practical necessity because culture is the primary source of popular resonance, and thus self-understanding *through* culture has to be the starting point of political transformation. Actualizing self-determination, then, is of necessity a practice of working within and through these inheritances to transform the broader structural conditions that enforce domination.

On the other hand, the normativity of this focus on "building from the communities upward" is also indispensable to this vision, in ways not fully captured by pragmatic appeals to cultural resonance. Along this axis, development *through*, *in*, and *as* the invigoration of Indigenous ethical systems is a way to conduct struggles toward not only any egalitarian social formation, but one that colonized Indigenous societies themselves can collectively experience and craft as the product of their histories in a nonalienated and nonimposed fashion. The implication is that the alternative, the top-down model of development from above, will only remake existing patterns of colonial domination—now in the name of "Marxism"—by once again imposing a (parochial) hegemonic vision on these resurgent practices ("trying to smother our distinct social patterns"). Indigenous resurgence in this sense meant progressive social transformation growing out of what Manuel called an "aboriginal value system," whose roots are disclosed and (re)created in generating land as a relation.

Toward a Stewardship World Order

An overwhelming focus of legal and political science scholarship on Indigenous peoples is on the meanings of "Indigenous rights." Yet a sole focus on rights misses the remapping and earthmaking projects central to Fourth Worldism. Fourth Worldism aimed not only to carve out an independent package of rights to cultural survival or even self-determination, but also to refashion some of the basic principles of legitimacy in the global political-economic order.

This idea that Indigenous decolonization means both securing Indigenous rights *and* transforming the structuring principles of world order can be found early on in Manuel's trajectory. In a May 1971 interview, Manuel argued that, more than just defending their own rights, "Aboriginal peoples . . . must unite to prevent the white race from destroying mankind."[67] This is a provocative account of the universal role of Indigenous transnational internationalism as an indispensable source of capacious resistance to the colonial-capitalist subsumption of land. Indigenous self-determination is articulated as key to halting circuits of ceaseless accumulation, so as to keep the wealthy nations (and potentially the "developing" nations) from annihilating the entirety of humanity's relationship with the biosphere.

I call the constructive project that emerges from Fourth World transnational internationalism a "stewardship world order." By stewardship world order, I mean a vision of postcolonial global justice that aims to (1) ensure a structure of intersocietal relations based on the equality and self-determination of peoples beyond the sovereign state and (2) make the legitimacy of those social and political structures contingent on their compatibility with a relational set of responsibilities of care (i.e., stewardship) for and with the other-than-human world. As a way of remapping sovereignty, such a project aims to create an order of pluralistic self-determination beyond territorialized sovereignty, actualized *as stewardship*. To explicate Fourth Worldism as a source of a constructive vision for a stewardship world order, it is important to assess briefly how Fourth Worldism also came to *clash* with Third Worldism. This divergence became more evident in the latter half of the 1970s and 1980s, as incompatible ways of conceiving the relation between the nation-state and land came more sharply into view. Demonstrating this claim requires a closer examination of the models of state formation and political economy central to Third Worldism.

Scholars of Third Worldism such as Adom Getachew have recently pushed back against the narrowing interpretation of decolonization as beholden to a "fortress-like conception of state-sovereignty."[68] This is a necessary corrective. However, it is also the case that projects of anticolonial emancipation featured strongly statist currents. It was Indigenous critics—not just the (many!) Western apologists for colonialism pathologizing nonwhite sovereignty—who were strongly attuned to the risks that statist imaginaries and practices entailed in producing internal violence and oppression toward minority populations.

Manuel was far from alone among Nyerere's radical admirers of the early 1970s when his interpretation downplayed the more centralizing demands of the ultimately disastrous scheme of state-led "villagization" that came out of the *Ujamaa* philosophy[69]—likely, in order to make it useful and amenable to Indigenous projects of self-determination and resurgence. In a key but characteristically elliptical formulation in *The Fourth World* that hints at this disjuncture, Manuel writes that "the bond of colonialism we share with the Third World peoples is the shared values that distinguish the Aboriginal World from the nation-states of the Third World" (*FW*, 5). Here, Manuel posits a broad affinity of popular struggles and positive values (above all, the land) among colonized peoples (as in this chapter's epigraph from Fanon). What is notable, however, is that he quickly distinguishes this positive connection among *peoples* from projects already beholden to elite *nation-state* capture. Manuel's critique accordingly reflects an acute apprehension about the renewed colonial implications of sovereignty for the many societies thrown together within the geographical contours of the (post)colonial nation-state.

Even with the transfer from "foreign" to "native" rule, there is a contingent possibility that colonial governing logics will be replicated as part and parcel of the material practices of the state form. In these processes of nation-state emergence, there was significant potential that the new leaders would "project the temporary failings of a new and young nation on some minority group who can become a convenient scapegoat" (*FW*, 244).[70] Indeed, the new postcolonial "national bourgeoisie" had begun to use "the symbols of power left behind by the conquerors to establish their own status" (*FW*, 245).[71] This can lead to the (re)subordination of "internal" populations regarded as not yet sufficiently modern(ized), even as the postcolonial society as a whole is also dominated by various neocolonial relations. In replicating these worst elements of the sovereign-state form, some postcolonial societies had become, in Manuel's assessment, a "darker imitation of their colonial masters." In a 1973 speech before the US National Congress of American Indians, Manuel contrasted Nyerere's legitimacy to the rule of Jomo Kenyatta in Kenya, "who uses the same bureaucratic system against his own people as the very white race that he defeated."[72] Manuel largely exempted Tanzania from this analysis, arguing that Tanzania's independence was so pluralistic as to not fall into the trap of equating independence with the state's capacities to project power (*FW*, 245).

More specifically political-economic fissures between Third and Fourth Worldism also widened throughout the 1970s. A core aspiration of the countries of the Non-Aligned Movement was to extricate themselves from their subordinate and dependent position in the postwar political economy, which had remade the transnational racialized hierarchies of the imperial world order of the first half of the twentieth century. By 1979 and likely earlier, there was a recognition that those efforts embodied in the NIEO both provided an opening for recasting the global political economy around the "promise" of wealth redistribution *and* the "peril" of a profound assault on the rights of Indigenous peoples in both "industrialized and developing nations."[73] The WCIP recognized that this global South–centered alternative to Western hegemony continued to articulate a vision of development potentially hostile to the basic survival, let alone structural transformation, demanded by many Indigenous peoples.

Why? The NIEO was a form of transnational institutional reform that stood alongside statism, not against it. It was in this sense that various projects of Third Worldism predicated liberation from externally produced neocolonial dependency, domination, and exploitation of Native labor and natural resources upon leveraging a highly centralized postcolonial state to implement development models that helped to buffer or altogether eschew this subordinate positioning in the world order. In turn, political and economic liberation of a kind often entailed a strong commitment to statism. Those top-down dimensions of statism often threatened alternatives within, such as those of Indigenous and peasant subsistence modes of production.

In this sense, Third World states pursued a particular model of decommodification, often encapsulated in vigorous assertion of the international legal principle of "permanent sovereignty over natural resources." Stated as rights in Article 2 of the 1974 UN Charter on Economic Rights and Duties, the nationalization and public ownership of natural resources served as touchstones for the economic reorganization for redistributive purposes that postcolonial states sought to effect.[74] These decommodifying strategies were oriented toward the socialized, collective exploitation of land to bolster a redistributive social democratic welfare politics. Considered as one important ingredient in creating a social formation based on non-exploitative egalitarian social relations, this collective and socialized exploitation of land would enable a more fundamentally redistributive political economy for colonized and postcolonized peoples. Land was "decommodified" in the very specific sense of being socialized so as to maximize the purely anthropocentric benefits for the entire national community.

This model of resource- and capital-intensive growth with expanded "production and consumption" clashed with an alternative vision of a world order grounded in responsibility-based ecological stewardship. In his continued collaboration with the WCIP, Manuel pointed out at a symposium in 1979 that (in the wake of the OPEC [Organization of Petroleum Exporting Countries] crisis): "when the governments now talk about developing new sources of raw materials [e.g., "energy independence"], they are most often making plans for Indigenous peoples and their resources."[75] Though certainly seeking alternatives to growth *alone* as the only metric of socioeconomic progress, the NIEO appeared from the vantage of Indigenous societies mainly to be adopting the "models of industrialization typified by the United States and Canada" and headed toward a "second industrial revolution by ravaging tribal areas." So, Manuel and other Indigenous intellectuals realized throughout the decade that socialist state developmentalism could just as readily invite certain modes of colonial conceptualization and governance of land as did liberal capitalism. Insofar as the decommodifying strategies that became generic to state developmentalism were based on this drive toward industrialization with redistribution *as a way out of external (neo)colonial domination*, those strategies converged on understanding land as just another extractible, instrumental resource.

Writing in *The Fourth World* in 1974, Manuel noted the importance of creating "an economy that bears a relation to the Fourth World" (*FW*, 246). The surrounding context of this claim suggests that he meant a broader political-economic order (including non-Indigenous peoples) that could both incorporate the basic notion that land is a relation and distributive justice aimed against prevailing racial-colonial hierarchies. This basic claim is iterated in a more globalized scope in the symposium speech Manuel delivered in 1979. Clearly refashioning the NIEO project, the WCIP aspired to a "new world economic order" that would defend "'autonomous indigenous areas' secured by aboriginal title," such as those of the Mapuche in Chile, against "exploitation, genocide and ethnocide." This reconstructed system of international law superseding territorialized colonial sovereignty would "protect natural resources from external exploitation and encroachment without the consent of local indigenous populations and international supervision."[76] Here, Manuel places distinct emphasis on peoples having the authority and structures of protection in place against rapacious practices of state formation to manage and adapt to the "distinct ecologies of particular places."[77]

This "new world economic order" concept that Manuel posits in 1979 explicitly endorsed radical changes to the global regime that created authoritative connections among self-determination, the nation-state, and land and ecology. Here, decommodification meant something different: rather than gaining a share or recuperating all control over the exploitation of land for the nation-state (i.e., "resource nationalism"), decommodification meant operationalizing the concept of the land *itself* as a nonexploitable relation. Decommodification along this axis means (re)creating what I earlier theorized as the land-culture dialectic, by reinserting land into networks of care and reciprocity. Land here is neither a commodity in the liberal capitalist relation of individual ownership nor in the socialist project of collective resource exploitation. Rather, land becomes socialized as the ecological *source of* human sociality instead of a *resource for* human sociality. Pragmatically, "respect for Indigenous peoples' rights is essential to the preservation of the world's final resources," and, normatively, it is "an expression of the fundamental right of self-determination." As such, "where tribal people or other Indigenous peoples can be defined as the principal guardians over a resource like fish, they must be recognized as the permanent authorities over the use and management of the resource."[78]

Against a generic commitment to environmental conservation as such, the notion of Indigenous peoples as stewards or "guardians" of relations to the earth calls for the institutionalized recognition of a nonanthropocentric right of Indigenous self-determination that nullifies sovereign-state supremacy. This required the positive recognition of Indigenous polities as responsible guardians of ecology and the biosphere, *through* self-determination. The later advent of the critique of "extractivism" from Latin American Indigenous movements gave a more singular label to this orientation of Indigenous struggles, which was based on an analysis of the colonial violence to land and people inherent to all modes of resource extraction—whether for the collective or individual good. These struggles seek to make a "post-extractivist" future.[79] The realization of a resurgent, pluralistic world order based on stewardship and self-determination against both *settler and postcolonial* sovereignty would have urgent consequences for all humankind and all species-kind in preserving "life's natural supports."[80]

Conclusion

In recent work, James Tully and John Borrows have excoriated what they perceive as the inflexible modes of political analysis resulting from applications of the colonizer/colonized binary derived from global anticolonial thought onto the relation between Indigenous and non-Indigenous peoples in Canadian settler society. Specifically, they caricature the rigid and "binary framing" of "the defenders of colonization/decolonization" and condemn it as a dead end for the political generativity characteristic of Indigenous resurgence movements. As an alternative, they endorse a more open-ended politics that they attribute to "the language of resurgence and reconciliation."[81]

Pushing against this reading, my argument in this chapter shows how Indigenous resurgence against and beyond the confines of colonial sovereignty and colonial land relations was actually enriched through a reflexive and critical engagement with global decolonizing practices. In a misleading two-step, Tully and Borrows, first, treat global anticolonialism as *only* mimicry of the Eurocentric nation-state, and, second, reduce radical Indigenous receptions of it to a misguided internalization of this mimicry. This is a misreading *both* of Third Worldism and global anticolonial thought in their many currents *and* of the agency and selectivity of Fourth World (re)conceptualizations of them. Indeed, the very creativity of the paradigm of resurgence as a response to settler-colonial violence and abduction came out of a deep conviction that the liberation projects of colonized peoples contained the seeds of alternatives to both liberal capitalism and Eurocentric socialism.

In fact, there is no viable historical and conceptual contradiction between "decolonization" and "resurgence" in the first instance. Resurgence emerged precisely *as a framework of decolonization*, as a critical analysis and dynamic political vision of the terms of Indigenous anticolonial struggles that aimed to remap both the contextual location and some of the fundamental political-philosophical aims of decolonization. Resurgence and the vision glossed here as a stewardship world order were really wagers about what future decolonization could create, if struggles for land as a relation could be made foundational to projects of anticolonial social transformation and self-determination.

In this chapter, I have traced George Manuel's political-theoretic conception of Fourth Worldism, so as to draw attention to the multilayered efforts of Indigenous resurgence paradigms to go beyond sovereignty as vertical institutional order mediating among depoliticized "cultures," as territorial container for land as individual and collective property, and as a mode of collective agency expressed as antirelational mastery over others and the earth. This chapter draws a distinction between the Third and Fourth Worlds as kindred but ultimately divergent political projects. The next chapter turns to Howard Adams and Lee Maracle, in an effort to examine Indigenous revolutionary analyses of capitalism that placed themselves on the front lines alongside Third World national liberation struggles.

[CHAPTER FOUR]

Indigenous Marxisms

Howard Adams and Lee Maracle on Colonial-Racial Capitalism

For Indigenous nations to live, capitalism must die.
    Glen Coulthard, "For Our Nations to Live, Capitalism Must Die"[1]

Marxist analysis should always be slightly stretched every time we have to do with the colonial problem.
    Frantz Fanon, *The Wretched of the Earth*[2]

He spoke to something so old inside my body it felt like floating in a sea of forever.
    Lee Maracle, on Mahmoud Darwish's poetry[3]

Indigenous Marxists have enriched and transformed anticolonial critique by attending to the complex intersections between colonialism and capitalism. Though their decolonizing praxis has mainly been neglected, their rethinking of resistance and resurgence against colonial rule through the lenses of critical political economy and revolutionary theory opens up core insights into significant expressions of Indigenous anticolonial struggles: namely, at the center of these interventions is the thesis that creating structures of lasting Indigenous self-determination and decolonization requires abolishing both capitalism and (settler) colonialism as distinct but converging structures of domination. In this respect, they tether the problem of remapping sovereignty—whether how to redistribute it or how to reconfigure its most basic conceptual logics—to the task of radically transforming the forms of domination exercised through colonial-capitalist political economy. Such an approach is an important forerunner to more recent accounts of the colonial politics of state recognition, which pinpoint the structurally delimited and still-colonial forms of recognition that settler states now *call* Indigenous "self-government."[4] More thorough intellectual-historical narratives of these earlier materialist frameworks, however, remain dispersed and limited. This relative occlusion misses the potential of historically reconstructive and critical engagements with Indigenous Marxist thinkers—whose histories are traceable at least as early as the world-spanning influence of the 1917 Bolshevik Revolution.[5]

This chapter addresses this occlusion by exploring one set of genealogies of Indigenous Marxisms. To evaluate this critical (re)stretching of broadly Marxian accounts of capitalism as a key through line in political theories of Indigenous decolonization, I reconstruct the political engagements and writings of two figures in particular: Howard Adams (1921–2001), a Métis activist and scholar, and Lee Maracle (1950–2022), a Stó:lō feminist literary giant, activist, and traditional knowledge keeper. My aim in turning to these thinkers is to reconstruct key conceptual insights they provide into how capitalism *works* (historically and structurally) and *what is wrong with capitalism* (normatively and politically), from the perspectives they forged within Indigenous anticolonial struggles.

What is more, I contend that they advanced these theoretical perspectives not only through Indigenous anticolonial struggles, but also as a particular interpretation of and challenge to the substance and political orientation of Indigenous decolonization projects. To spell this out, I focus specifically on how these Indigenous Marxists' efforts to apprehend the structurally colonial fashioning of capitalism (and the capitalist fashioning of colonialism) shaped their respective conceptions of the very "problem-space" of movements for Indigenous self-determination, decolonization, and internationalism.[6] In taking up Maracle's writings, I also focus on the centrality of (hetero)patriarchy to all of these practices of domination.

My historical examination of these intersections between Indigenous and Marxist political thought joins the recent work of others like Roxanne Dunbar-Ortiz and Glen Coulthard.[7] Dunbar-Ortiz and Coulthard primarily defend the *productivity* of Indigenous activist uses of Marxian lenses *for* Indigenous political movements. My argument in this chapter complicates this focus by way of a comparative reading of Maracle and Adams. That is, reading them together brings into relief the important tensions and disagreements *within* Indigenous Marxisms, and—in conjunction with the previous chapter on Manuel—within Indigenous socialisms more generally.

Certainly, these approaches adopt similar structural analytics committed to apprehending colonialism and capitalism. Yet, I show how their normative and critical foundations nevertheless diverge substantially. In short, Maracle's materialist commitments are the basis for a critical mapping of power as a tool for decolonization. She conceptualizes decolonization as practices of and for the permanent resurgence of *subjugated responsibili-*

ties core to specific Indigenous governance systems. By contrast, Adams theorizes Indigenous self-determination as a more transitional moment in a more singular democratic revolutionary process.

To elucidate the conceptual contributions of these thinkers to and as political theories of Indigenous decolonization, I take an interpretive cue from Fanon's insight reproduced in the epigraph above. Fanon's oft-quoted formulation was that materialist analyses of capitalism must themselves be adaptable, so as to apprehend the changing structural and experiential dynamics of colonial situations. The intellectual production of the two thinkers I focus on here, both indebted to Fanon, enact this stretching and re-stretching theoretical praxis. My contention is that Adams and Maracle both re-crafted "syncretic Marxisms" from Third World national liberation struggles, by refracting those frameworks through the specific challenges and philosophical premises of Indigenous anticolonialisms. Interpreting Indigenous Marxisms, then, means reconstructing this worldly frame for the transnational exchange of ideas and ideologies of anticolonial critique and liberation.

To specify this process of refraction further, however, it is important to begin by refuting a frequent (sometimes unstated) assumption in current work on decolonization: that decolonial thinkers (like Adams and Maracle) categorically presume that materialist dialectics are themselves in need of a kind of epistemic "decolonization." This sort of assertion typically follows from the premise that "Marxism" *just is* a culturally provincial Eurocentric orthodoxy that recounts the static and objective unfolding of a priori universalistic, self-enclosed, deterministic laws of history (as often applied to the mechanical objectivity of the domain of "the economy").[8] Why was this *not* Adams's and Maracle's starting point? As I have already begun to indicate, they were already self-consciously transforming approaches from Fanon, Marx and Engels, Lenin, Oliver Cromwell Cox, Amilcar Cabral, Walter Rodney, and others who had taken up Marxisms as dynamic theories to be refashioned for specific colonial situations.[9] It bears emphasizing, then, that Adams's and Maracle's own formulations reclaimed anticolonial Marxisms' existing open-ended receptivity. In such a context, historically rich accounts of colonial conquest and slavery, racialization, cultural production, and the psychoaffective life of oppression were assumed from the very start to be indispensable to any globally relevant critical analysis of capitalist political economy.

In what follows, I first explicate Howard Adams's analysis of what I call *colonial-racial capitalism*, by which I mean a conceptual frame that tracks the political fabrication of capitalist political economy and colonial-racial conquest together in the making of Canada as a colonial nation-state. Second, I reconstruct Lee Maracle's theory and organizing of active resistance to colonial-racial capitalism in the Vancouver Native Alliance for Red Power (NARP) as a practice of transnational internationalism. NARP articulated the Red Power movement as part of a broader array of popular Third World anticolonial struggles for land, independence, and dignity. Third, I examine how Adams's and Maracle's similar anticolonial materialist analysis nevertheless opens up divergent analyses of the specific *pathologies* of colonial-racial capitalism, in relation to competing assessments of the normative and political orientations core to Indigenous decolonization.

As the further basis for exploring Maracle's account of decolonization, I then reconstruct her turn to an Indigenous feminist theoretical praxis that addresses gendered domination that intersects with and is integral to colonial-racial capitalism. The latter shift in her politics and poetics provided a focused analysis of the *patriarchal settler state* and political projects of *gendering (de)colonization*, namely, an account of the centrality of patriarchal systems of domination to colonial-racial capitalism and their effects in constituting the experiences of Indigenous women, and their *subordinated responsibilities* and agencies in making the earth anew in the wake of colonial violence. Such a lens aimed to modify feminist and anticolonial theory alike: Maracle envisioned decolonization in the form of reconstructive struggles for a "rematriated" politics of self-determination.

Prefiguring many contemporary Indigenous feminist analyses, Maracle's constructive project linked the autonomy and liberation of women (and, more in later work, nonnormatively gendered Indigenous populations) from colonial gender violence to the renewal of care-based practices of earthmaking that constitute the collective "self" of self-determination *through* relational responsibilities. As her articulation of her own embodied resonance with Palestinian poet Mahmoud Darwish's verse suggests, what is distinctive about Maracle's conception of Indigenous decolonization is her focus on actively making relations of solidarity with a capaciously heterogeneous and transnational set of feminist anticolonial struggles.

Howard Adams on Colonial-Racial Capitalism

In the late 1960s and early 1970s, Howard Adams and Lee Maracle each played formative parts in the Canadian Red Power movement, whose organizing and analyses filtered Indigenous societies' experiences through a global orientation toward the decolonizing Third World.[10] Histories of AIM in the US from the occupation of Alcatraz Island to the siege of Wounded Knee have traditionally received far more coverage. A smaller group of scholars have more recently begun to trace the organizing of radicalized urban and rural Indigenous activists across Canada during this period. Within this, the activist-intellectual frameworks Adams and Maracle, respectively, adopted in part *preceded* AIM's incredible launch onto the international scene. This is to say that Indigenous activists in lands now claimed by Canada initially eschewed AIM's influence, and as a result first derived their theoretical praxis by bringing Indigenous frameworks together with various strands of Black radical thought (most importantly, the Black Panther Party), and the wider swath of ideologies of national liberation struggles throughout Africa, Asia, Latin America, and the Caribbean.[11]

Before turning more directly to the conceptual core of Adams's structural analysis, which I refer to as a theory of *colonial-racial capitalism*, it is helpful to take stock of how his critique emerged out of (a) Adams's diagnosis of the limits of liberal reform for Indigenous peoples and (b) the ferment of Third Worldist analyses of capitalism that heavily influenced the political perspectives of the North American New Left. In acknowledgment of Adams's and Maracle's quite kindred social-theoretic insights and shared intellectual genealogies to political theorist Cedric Robinson's widely influential account of "racial capitalism,"[12] I reconstruct Adams's work by calling it a theory of *colonial-racial capitalism* adapted to account for the power relations facing Indigenous societies in North America. My contextualization of this intellectual history as the site of fertile exchanges with these other intellectual frameworks is, in part, intended to unsettle and challenge the efforts to scrupulously wall off the resulting analytic frames relevant to North American settler colonialism to a supposedly isolatable form of (especially Anglo) settler-colonial subjugation, which has become prevalent to work in settler-colonial studies over the last twenty years. As in other chapters of this book, I thereby attend to one instance of Indigenous anticolonialisms' multiple expressions of relationality as a way of thinking about and doing politics. The siloing that results from the analytic drive to isolate the "settler" form of colonization may otherwise obscure or depoliticize these integral connections in both their historical and political-theoretic significance.

Born in 1921 in Saint Louis, Saskatchewan, to subsistence Métis farmers, Howard Adams was the great-grandson of Maxime Lépine, Louis Riel's adjutant general, on his mother's side. Despite a family heritage that tracked pivotal events in Métis history from ethnogenesis to resistance to Canadian expansionism under Louis Riel,[13] Adams had a kind of late awakening, which he attributed to his own "success" and internalized shame about his background as a light-skinned Métis who could "pass" in white Canadian and US society.[14] In Adams's own account, what radicalized him initially was his experience as a PhD student in education studies at Berkeley during the apex of the free speech and African American civil rights movements. It was his rapid identification with the politics of Black liberation that led him to reevaluate his own background and to want to participate in struggling with and for his Métis community of origin. Among these landmark events of protest, he later commented particularly on seeing Malcolm X speak at Berkeley in October 1963 as a turning point in making him understand North American "white supremacy," including the oppression of Indigenous peoples in Canada, as a specific node of global imperialism.[15]

On returning to Canada in 1966 after receiving his doctorate, Adams brought this newfound perspective with him in taking up a position as a community development officer for the University of Saskatchewan Extension Division. It was during this time that Adams became a popular interview for Canadian media curious to hear (often, to sensationalize) the leaders of the new "Red Power" movement.[16] His development position was originally sponsored by the Indian-Métis Board under the Liberal Ross Thatcher administration in Saskatchewan, and it enabled him to straddle activist and academic roles for a time. Ultimately, the practical limits of the position also sharpened the direct foil for his political analysis, due to his specific frustrations with the liberal welfarist orientation of the Thatcher regime and the post itself.[17] Adams's reports and efforts to organize Métis communities in northern Saskatchewan—where "class" subordination overlapped considerably with white supremacist racial hierarchy—track a number of social policy issues that include the theft and placement of children in residential schools, problems of starvation and endemic poverty, employment discrimination and unemployment, mass incarceration and policing, and analyses of internalized oppression and self-loathing (the "colonized inferiority complex," drawing from Memmi, Freire, and Fanon).[18] Subsequently, in his 1975 classic *Prison of Grass: Canada from a Native Point of View*, he further developed this analysis of the internalized degradation of Indigenous peoples and their histories, noting the opposite condition as well: that colonized subjects come to positively identify with what Adams calls the "white ideal" (*PG* 9–11), that is, they seek what Fanon calls "the values secreted by their masters."[19] Adams emphasizes these subjective and internalized effects of settler-colonial oppression as particularly durable and dynamic forces, with logics that both reinforced *and* lived on apart from changes in the objective character of social structures.

Most important to my distillation of Adams's early reports and advocacy is that he aimed to reappraise these social policy issues as systemic, and, therefore, in need of systemic solutions. He harshly juxtaposed this critique to a liberal analysis of labor market segmentation as the result of implicit discrimination, color-blind exclusion, and/or individual prejudice, to be remedied at the province's behest in the form of more generous welfare and job programs and nominal integration. Acting on the basis of this analysis, Adams began to participate in and found some more radical political organizations that emphasized the need for community self-determination in arenas like education, including cofounding the pan-Indigenous militant Saskatchewan Native Action Committee (SNAC) in April 1968. In its manifesto, SNAC articulated a political stance disdainful of the liberal politics of "token" integration as an assimilationist supplement to the hardline racism that Métis communities encountered in rural northern Saskatchewan, the "Mississippi of Canada."[20] They proclaimed, "Integration is not a solution, especially not forced integration. We oppose Whitey's attempts to assimilate our people, our culture, traditions and philosophies into his supreme society."[21] Adams also sought to bring this emphasis to existing organizations, becoming president of the Métis Society of Saskatchewan in April of 1969.[22]

Adams diagnosed the liberal reformism of the era such as increased state funding of more Indigenous community organizations and programs as efforts to suture back together the structural contradictions that these mobilizations were opening up. As he put it retrospectively, the failure of government "schemes for solving the so-called 'Indian Problem'" throughout the 1960s and early 1970s has "forced us to reject many illusions" about the viability of working within "the system" (*PG*, 206, 208). The political program Adams and SNAC pursued aimed to work outside the electoral system, and advanced direct-action strategies aimed at fostering the basic redistribution of power toward Indigenous peoples. The overarching goals in these actions was to create forms of participatory self-government and community control across urban and rural/reserve Indigenous communities that rejected the constraints of the colonial system.

The subjective emphasis of such a politics echoed the politics of Black Power in asserting a renewed sense of positive group identity and aesthetic-affective investments that affirmed pride in and consciousness of Indigenous peoples' histories. Such a posture orienting the individual in the collective was considered a crucial aspect of overcoming the barrage of hegemonic discourses of Indigenous inferiority, discourses that Indigenous peoples "must endure . . . that shames them, destroys their confidence, and causes them to reject their heritage. . . . A fact of imperialism is that it systematically denies native people a dignified history" (*PG*, 43). Pushing back against "inferiorization," the act of recovering dignified histories as an element of the collective self of self-determination instrumentally bolsters and expressively suffuses political demands for and direct grassroots enactments of community controls on this expanded terrain of struggles for self-government.

It was in the context of these challenges to "reformism" that Adams developed a political-theoretic analysis that I call *colonial-racial capitalism*. By colonial-racial capitalism, I mean an analytic that encompasses two basic insights. First, Adams contends that Métis colonization in what is now Canada is "identical ... to colonies of Asia, Africa, and Latin America" and "parallel to that of the Black people of the U.S."[23] Adams points to Indigenous dispossession in North America as one historically variable axis of specific colonial practices and of a larger network of transnational relations essential to the financial, military, and territorial monopolies (and, eventually, neocolonial relations) that constitute capitalist imperialism. He derives this insight in conversation with numerous thinkers who have likewise theorized the co-emergence of global capitalism with white supremacy, colonial dispossession, and slavery and semi-slave labor (e.g., indenture and debt peonage). In this respect, Adams's analysis articulates the specific histories of Canadian settler-colonial capitalism (and the multiple resistances to its rise), but always in connection to the efforts of other anticolonial and antiracist struggles to identify related technologies of racial hierarchy and colonial conquest as constitutive of capitalism.[24]

Second, Adams identifies colonial rule and its attendant racial hierarchies as central to the reproduction and expansion of the capital relation, and vice versa. These structural connections first had to become entrenched as an outcome of indeterminate struggles for hegemony. Adams's historical analysis suggests that the contemporary form (let alone existence) of Canada as a *colonial* nation-state is inexplicable without the political and military conflicts of the nineteenth century that resulted in the repression of political alternatives to Anglo-settler expansionism. In this sense, sovereign domination over Indigenous societies is not just the morally and politically arbitrary result of Indigenous subjugation and dispossession, which ought to be overcome by establishing a multilayered normative and juridico-political order enforcing Indigenous rights of self-determination within and against sovereign states. Instead, the claim here is that sovereignty is the product of a specific nexus of political economy and colonial-racial order created through the contingent victory of political alliances that themselves *produced* whiteness as a cross-class group status with fundamental investments in the colonial conquest and expropriation of Indigenous lands and resources. With whiteness came the complementary ideologies of racial inferiority that justified settler expansionism in the face of Indigenous societies' resistance.

The political-theoretic consequence of this analysis is that the capacity to materialize formally enunciated "rights" of self-determination hinges on mass Indigenous movements that can radically denaturalize and rupture the entrenched power relations won in this historical victory—a victory outliving that moment via the hegemony of the institutions and modes of structural reproduction that ensure the co-constitution of capitalism and settler colonialism.

To substantiate these theoretical claims, it is necessary here to turn to the text of *Prison of Grass*, Adams's signal work. There, he gives a long-term sociological account of the contingent historical constitution of Canadian colonial-racial capitalism. He begins in the seventeenth century with the contention that "racism is the product of economics": "the racism that native people encounter today had its origins in the rise of western imperialism during the 1600s." In this way, ideologies of Indigenous peoples as "mentally and morally inferior" served to "reduce native people to a subhuman level where they could be freely exploited" to "provide . . . potentially cheap labor for trapping furs" (*PG*, 5). Whereas Lenin had identified imperialism as the monopolistic form taken by nineteenth-century finance capitalism searching out new profits with the military aid of imperial-colonial states ("the highest stage of capitalism"),[25] Adams characterized the fur trade era, with its rivalries among competing "Crown corporations," as a far earlier precedent-setting era for imperial militarism and the efflorescence of race-thinking logics.

Transposing his arguments right from Oliver Cromwell Cox's classic work on the transatlantic slave trade, Adams likewise contends that "race relations" took shape as a form of "class relations," but he focuses readers' attention on the specific case of seventeenth-century Canada. "In Canada," Adams argues, "racism originated in the imperialist fur-trade industry" under the Hudson's Bay Company (HBC) monopoly circa 1670, where the initial invention of innate, "natural" racial attributes under more mercantilist monopoly structures abetted early—albeit mostly failed—attempts to exploit the labor of Indigenous trappers: "as long as Indians were isolated as a special group, they were easily exploited as trappers" (*PG*, 8). Adams's contention about the traces of European race thinking in the "imperialist" (but not yet capitalist) fur trade challenges many efforts since to characterize this moment as an era of "mutual dependence" or a "middle ground" that can serve as a model of just coexistence for settler and Native peoples.[26] Instead, Adams notes how the more materially precarious racial ideas of this era—paralleling what Robinson labeled the "racialism" of intra-European politics—contingently informed the categories of social difference that would become essential to dividing a heterogeneous pool of laborers (slaves, the indentured, wage laborers, debt peons, etc.) in constructing modern production relations.[27]

The position of the emerging Métis society at Red River and of other Indigenous peoples, however, would shift quite dramatically over the course of the nineteenth century. Adams points out that it is during this period from about 1860 to 1914 that there is a macrostructural shift from the mercantilist order of the fur trade toward an agrarian and industrial capitalist order impelling a rising Anglo-settler elite toward more direct control of a territorial base (*PG*, 52). The eventual consequence of this long-term shift is that from the vantage point of these elites, Indigenous peoples and the emerging Métis nation became obstacles to the territorial expansion newly envisaged as key to the building of a modern commercial state.

A brief recounting of Adams's narrative of the "Riel Rebellion" of 1869–70 and his later return in the 1885 struggle against the early Canadian state indicates the formative moments of Canadian capitalism *as* colonial-racial capitalism. In brief, Métis and Cree resistance to the surveying and colonization of their lands threatened the building of the transcontinental Canadian Pacific Railway (CPR) and the confederation of Canada, and, accordingly, those promoting the CPR began to represent Indigenous societies as "savage" external threats to emerging regimes of private property—not the naturally inclined labor force sought under the HBC monopoly (*PG*, 49, 82). In response to the Louis Riel–led movement to form an independent Métis nation centered at Red River in 1869 and upon his return after exile in 1885, Canada put down the independence movements and hanged Riel. In brief, Adams argues that colonial-racial capitalism solidified contingently in Canada as a direct product of conquest, and a different order might have emerged if the competing ("rebellious") political coalitions had triumphed.

The longer story here is that, after Canadian confederation in 1867, the Canadian government tried to impose its will westward. Ottawa convinced the HBC to sell its title to Rupert's Land and the Northwest, including what is now Manitoba and most of Saskatchewan and southern Alberta. The Canadian government would purchase the title to Rupert's Land from the HBC in order to build the CPR. As Adams puts it, "The clash of these two [political-economic orders] fueled the hostilities of 1869–70 in the Northwest, which resulted in Rupert's Land being brought under the constitutional authority of the government in Ottawa, the seat of the industrial empire" (*PG*, 52). Ottawa sought and received a transfer of underlying title from the HBC based on anticipated investments in the CPR. When the Canadian government under Prime Minister John A. Macdonald sent surveyors, the Métis of the Red River, in Riel's own words, "found their ancient surveys, land marks, boundaries and muniments of title, set at naught and disregarded, and a government established over their heads."[28]

Neither the Métis nor local farmers and settlers involved in the fur trade were consulted as to the terms of this exchange. Such an exchange both presumed to sell their land out from under them and obliterated the provisional governments the Métis had established at Red River working within and against the HBC. Adams argues that Ottawa believed that this purchase of HBC land would be straightforward and "expected a peaceful subjugation of the Bay empire and a willing surrender of the Northwest Territories" (*PG*, 53). The Métis challenged the legitimacy of the terms of this transfer in both 1869 and again in 1885, culminating in the Canadian state's execution of Riel for treason on November 16, 1885.

Adams argues that the 1870s struggle was a kind of "people's movement," an effort to make a populist alliance that conserved the basis of the fur trade political economy and refused confederation on the terms of the emergent capitalist (agricultural and industrial) order. Subsequently, Adams suggests, it became possible to ground ongoing resistance in the early 1880s in the continuation of these previous populist-type alliances of 1869–70 between farmers, settlers, and Métis. "Farmers and Metis felt a bond of mutual oppression and wanted a redress of their shared grievances" against massive land transfers to the CPR (*PG*, 78). Increasing discontent built up among white settlers, farmers, and Métis over the transfer of land to Canada for the CPR and an economic recession, which fed continuing demands for "responsible government." While Manitoba was subsequently established as a Canadian province in 1870 as a result of the failure of the 1869–70 front against Ottawa, Canada throughout the 1870s nonetheless failed to establish control over the rest of the Northwest Territories, resulting in a "pseudo-federal administration" that "had no connection to local political development" (*PG*, 77). This dynamic left room for some political autonomy, in particular the establishment of local Métis councils such as at Saint Laurent and Batoche, which translated into more permanent institutions for the Métis.

In response to the threat of these alliances, Conservative prime minister John A. Macdonald began a propaganda campaign scapegoating the Métis and warning of "potential Indian and Métis uprisings" (*PG*, 80–81). In effect, by driving a wedge between the Métis and white farmers and settlers, capitalist elites successfully cemented racial difference as the condition of possibility of a new order linking colonial expansionism to the reproduction of capitalism (*PG*, 93). Adams argues that Métis and other Indigenous peoples like the Cree had been subject to similar regimes of labor exploitation during the fur trade (*PG*, 5), but it was the isolation of the Métis from this cross-racial populist alliance that established a sense of shared interest in 1884. "By summer of 1884," Adams writes, "the Métis and Indians were becoming isolated from the white people's organizations and forces" (*PG*, 81):

> The plan constructed by the federal authorities was that they would make certain concessions to the white residents of the Northwest, while at the same time allowing the Métis and Indian situation to aggravate itself to the point of desperation and hostility. In this way, Ottawa could justify troop movements to the Northwest by saying that savages had created an uprising and were massacring innocent settlers. (*PG*, 82)

The North-West Mounted Police, sent to "protect" Indian reserves and Métis communities established in the wake of the 1870 defeat, "proved instead to be a source of oppression and agitation" and "attempted to arrest Gabriel Dumont, chief of the Batoche Halfbreed Council" (*PG*, 86–87). Over the course of 1884 and 1885, the Canadian federal government had been recruiting soldiers and policemen, culminating in the spring of 1885 when "western Canada looked like a military camp" that adumbrated the "imminent" military invasion. Adams then narrates Canadian efforts to provoke the Métis into taking up arms in order to "force the police to act" and "to have the Métis council expand its confrontations so that Ottawa authorities would sincerely believe that a halfbreed uprising was inevitable," as a continuation of efforts to stoke fear among settlers and paint the Métis as savage and violent (*PG*, 97).

After this strategy successfully convinced white settlers to ally with the federal government, the Métis were, in effect, boxed into taking up arms alongside Indigenous peoples. By way of background here, it is important to note that from 1873 to 1884, Indigenous peoples in the Northwest Territories had signed the first seven of the so-called numbered treaties with the Canadian state. These treaties enabled massive land cessions from the perspective of the Canadian state, setting up what Adams describes as the "subjugation" of Native peoples through the policing and administrative control of reserves. After having signed Treaty 6 in 1884, Cree chief Big Bear, in league with Red River Métis, led an uprising in protest of Canada's immediate failure to fulfill the promised treaty obligations. This brief alliance at Duck Lake and several subsequent victories against Canada suggested for Adams an alternative path based upon international Indigenous alliances, but one that ultimately failed due to the spatial constraints already separating Native peoples on reserves and the Métis.[29]

Altogether, the theoretical point of Adams's analysis of these struggles is that racial and colonial oppression "became deeply entrenched in Canadian society" as a political settlement integral to creating the conditions for state formation and capital accumulation (*PG*, 8). Adams emphasizes that colonial-racial capitalism means for both theoretical and political purposes that "it is quite impossible to separate the development of Canadian society from the growth of our colonized conditions" (*PG*, 209). The "success" of colonial conquest depended on the creation of a kind of cross-class alliance among (those who became) "whites." Such an alliance enabled the partial economic incorporation and privileged social standing awarded to the primarily Anglo lower classes by the bourgeoisie. In sum, Adams contends that it is these colonial foundations that allow the creation of a capitalist "socio-economic structure whereby an elite white group appropriates all the resources and industries unto itself."[30] In turn, Adams's historical narrative allows for insight into the *production* of this racialized political alliance as a systemic source of material privileges and, ultimately, a dominant group identity that naturalized and erased the prior anticapitalist and/or anticolonial possibilities presented in Indigenous and popular resistance. Perhaps most importantly, the macropicture of the distribution of material resources and life chances under Canadian capitalism comes into sharper view in accounting for Canada's status as a colonial state founded on—and continuing to require—the violent repression and/or co-optation of Indigenous peoples' rebellions (and mere presences) that have stood in the way of territorial expansionism and land expropriation.

In Adams's account, it is out of this historical settlement that arises two normative pathologies of oppressive incorporation and dependency that coexist alongside one another in a single colonial social formation. Along one axis lie relations of exclusionary domination between Métis and Indigenous peoples as racialized *individuals* vis-à-vis the settler state and markets. Along another axis Adams posits the growth of settler society through structures of domination and expropriation that ensure the enervating underdevelopment of Indigenous societies as independent forms of social life. As he puts it in a formulation encapsulating both pathological relations at once, "Not only were the native people denied their land and economy, but they were also denied the right to participate in the mainstream agricultural and industrial activity of Canada. . . . Instead, cheap 'coolie' labor was imported, while native people by the thousands were confined to rural 'prisons'" (*PG*, 65). The first aspect of underdevelopment lies in the constitutive denial to Indigenous *individuals* of a "right to participate" as full agents in the construction of Canadian society and thereby to share as full political-economic citizens in the uneven distributive benefits of the logics of accumulation undergirded by the continuing expropriation of

Indigenous lands. The second aspect of this process is the destruction of the political-economic and cultural basis of Indigenous *societies* through colonial violence and theft, and the transformation of their lands into white-settler property.

Such a political structure required both violent repression and the production of a juridical apparatus that could ideologically legitimate the terms of these formative hierarchies. For Adams, "the poverty of Métis and Indians is ultimately linked to colonial suppression." On the repressive side of colonial subjugation, Canadian capitalism consistently relies on an array of state and quasi-state institutions to secure and legalize Indigenous dispossession and pacification. In parallel to repression, provisions like the Dominion Lands Act (1872), the Canadian equivalent of the US Homestead Act of 1862, granted land to citizens on the Lockean principle that they validate ownership by adding value to the land (*PG*, 67). The legislation systematically denied such grants to "Indigenous peoples who had aboriginal claims" and Métis, who, "confined on farm colonies and rural ghettos," became "squatters on road allowances" (*PG*, 66). Adams likens this to a juridical way of vindicating the consistent violence needed to seize land and remake it into private property. The state expropriated Indigenous and Métis peoples, claiming in a contractual ruse that they have fairly ceded their lands in exchange for limited rights through treaties—what Adams calls "contracts of oppression"—or scrip payments for Métis. This massive transfer of land both as source of wealth and resources and as the foundation of alternative Indigenous modes of production alike preconditioned the subjection of Indigenous individuals and communities to a present-day form of racial hierarchy whereby "red lives" are systematically subject to unequal and diminished life chances as *individuals* (*PG*, 145).

In sum, Adams shows how capitalism and the sovereign state are produced and productive of the differentiation and subordination of Indigenous peoples both as colonized peoples subject to land theft and spatial removal engaged in a struggle to reestablish their self-determining authority over their own lands *and* as racialized populations subject to a white supremacist society. Adams argues that it is through these settler-colonial and racial dynamics that the very class relations constituting the structure of capitalist political economy take on their contemporary forms. As such, the "economic conditions of the capitalist system" are constituted through dispossession and legally codified structures of racially differentiated systems of personhood, ownership, and citizenship (*PG*, 144–45). Political economy still remains fundamental here: the racialized construction of Indigenous societies and their lands *enables and justifies* the predatory resource extraction that generates the foundational property structures of capitalist accumulation.

Put simply, a core implication of this analysis for political practices of decolonization is that colonial-racial capitalism as a system is contingent. It is not natural but rather the product of political defeat, repressive violence, and hegemony. Moreover, its reproduction relies on the continuous *ideological* erasure of the historically constitutive conditions of this order. The implication here is that transformative political action must intellectually expose and materially disrupt what came to interconnect with one another as the colonial and the capitalist dimensions of such an order: "the oppression of the native people is so deeply rooted in the capitalist system" that "it cannot be completely eliminated without eliminating capitalism itself" (*PG*, 209). In "objective" terms, Adams maps out this historical totality to insist on the character of the structural situation that makes it imperative to conceive of decolonization *as* and *with* the abolition of capitalism itself. The "subjective" element of this historical project is that Adams intends it to explode the very plausibility and arrogant dictate of the dominant liberal and conservative colonial views that reproduce discourses of Indigenous savagery. For the colonized, he aims to undermine the "colonized inferiority complex" by recovering the actual dignified histories of struggles that challenged the Canadian state-building project at its roots. Adams's contention is that Indigenous decolonization depends upon creating a socialist society. In turn, even glimpsing political orders that aim to enact social equality entails remediating and transforming the foundationally colonial and racial logics of Canadian capitalism.

Red Power Internationalism and The Third World

At the time of her sudden death in November 2021, Lee Maracle had garnered widespread recognition and racked up awards as a prolific, dynamic voice in Indigenous literatures in Canada. And with good reason: she is often credited as having released the "first" published novel by an "Aboriginal writer" in Canada, and she has since written an influential mountain of literary works in multiple genres, from fiction to poetry to memoir (including work in collaboration with her daughters). She is also a pathbreaking predecessor of *both* contemporary Indigenous Marxisms and queer Indigenous feminisms as scholarly and activist hermeneutics.

My interpretation focuses on Maracle's writing as part of a radically internationalist anticolonial political-theoretical approach, a project I call (adapting Kiera Ladner's formulation) *"gendering decolonization" and self-determination*.[31] In order first to situate Maracle's project, it is imperative to begin with her roots in an activist context in the late 1960s and 1970s. At that time, she and others in Indigenous revolutionary organizations sought to radicalize Indigenous peoples' struggles for self-determination by developing an analysis of colonial-racial capitalism that runs closely parallel to Adams's. She and her colleagues also waged these struggles by articulating a distinctive mode of Indigenous transnational internationalism through connections to a capaciously global network of Third World anticolonial liberation struggles.

Born in North Vancouver to a Salish father and Cree mother, Lee Maracle cut her teeth in NARP and a related array of organizing groups committed to moving Indigenous political activity onto the terrain of anticolonial revolution. The small group of Indigenous activists that initially formed NARP—which included Maracle, her then-partner Ray Bobb, Henry Jack, and Gerry Amber—got their start in fall 1967. NARP had its origins in direct-action protests of the unprosecuted rape and murder of a Native teenager, Rose Marie Roper, in Williams Lake by three white Canadians. Spreading to several urban centers in British Columbia, NARP played an especially key role in connecting with young Indigenous students to fight against their institutionalization and abuse in residential schools in the region. With its origins a year prior to AIM in Minneapolis, NARP began its own "Beothuk patrol" to monitor police abuses of Indigenous peoples on the north side of Vancouver.[32] Altogether, their radical politics envisaged collective liberation from the violence of settler domination, white supremacy, and capitalist exploitation and expropriation.

NARP developed a relationship with the Black Panther Party for Self-Defense (BPP), and, like many in the New Left from 1968 to 1973, was energized by the BPP's focus on community self-determination and antiracist social revolution. NARP specifically repurposed the BPP's amalgamation of vocabularies of nationalism, internationalism, and socialism, in service of an analysis of the situation and program of revolutionary action for Indigenous societies. Modeled directly on the Ten-Point Program of the BPP, NARP's Eight-Point Program (printed in each of its few newsletter issues) bore these influences. NARP's program included planks such as (1) the abolition of the Indian Act and "destruction of the colonial office (Indian Affairs Branch)"; (4) "an immediate end to the unjust arrests and harassment of our people by racist police"; and (7) an "immediate end to" the "rape" and "exploitation" of Indigenous lands by "large industrial companies," initiation of "programs concerning housing, agriculture and industrial cooperatives," and "foreign aid for the Indian Nation."[33] After its dissolution in 1970, NARP members spawned related organizing efforts such as the Native Women's Liberation Front, the Native Movement, and the Vancouver Native Study Group (1971–77), the latter of whose discussions and writings focused on the then-popular texts of Third World Marxisms, including Fanon's *Wretched of the Earth*, Marx and Engels, Lenin, and Mao. The group ultimately sent a small friendship delegation to China on a visit that included Maracle in 1975, which reported back favorably to sister organizations on China's politics of "self-reliance."[34]

In looking outward to these other movements, Maracle and fellow NARPers were seeking to rethink the main action-guiding theoretical features and the very protagonists of Marxist-Leninist theory. Like the Panthers and a range of other organizations on the North American New Left, NARP adopted especially Maoist formulations for their own purposes. In doing so, they attempted to comprehend the organization of international capitalism as keyed by racial oppression and the construction of a US-based world order. Maracle contends in her classic *Bobbi Lee*, "the revolutionary proletariat today is mainly in the super exploited Third World by Canada and other rich nations."[35] Politically, this meant that the First World/Third World division became *structurally and politically primary* as the central axis of the international "class" struggle, not between a domestic ruling class and the white working class of the wealthy Western industrialized countries. As Glen Coulthard has shown, it was specifically Maoism's ideological positioning of "backward" peasants in colonized peripheries as prime movers of global revolutionary struggle that allowed urban Indigenous radicals to make connections to their own communities of origin and to Indigenous rural struggles for land defense and self-determination in the North (contemporary Northwest Territories, the Yukon, and Nunavut).

NARP's politics were oriented around the pursuit of Indigenous self-determination, the "power to determine the destiny of our reservations and communities." More specifically, they also aimed to shift what genuine Indigenous self-determination *meant and required*. Namely, they reinterpreted Marxian emphases on the socialization of the means of production in an antidevelopmentalist fashion, as the movement toward self-determined mixed economies grounded in "traditional" Indigenous modes of production and oriented toward community democratic control and needs. This account of self-determination asserted the validity of mixed economy models to create institutions of political-economic self-reliance relatively delinked from oppressive dependencies on the settler state and markets.

Furthermore, Maracle in particular took this anticapitalist framework in a specifically anticolonial direction. She insisted upon the permanent and enduring validity of these self-determined Indigenous futurities *even in the course of revolutionary transformation.* She rejected communist visions of nationalization that called for more statist bureaucratic, or even a democratic commons, thereby envisaging a future in which it would be possible to disavow or transcend Indigenous societies' territorialities in decision making over the management of (and desirable qualities of relations to) land and other factors of production. In positing these expansive anticolonial horizons, Maracle and others insisted upon struggles to enforce Indigenous land and treaty rights and self-determination as among the critical starting points for alternatives to state-initiated capitalist resource extraction. So, too, did these commitments seek to parry self-fulfilling colonial prophecies about the inevitable dependency of Indigenous communities on capitalism, in the form of the wage relation and consumer markets.

In positing this vision, it was central that NARP and its successor organizations consciously mobilized in an explicitly global context with other racialized and colonized subjects and popular worker and peasant alliances. They mobilized *against* those whom they cast as the "revisionists" of Marxist-Leninist tradition. Contrary to many subsequent readings of Marxist-Leninism's Eurocentric tendencies, Maracle and the Vancouver Native Study Group interpreted anticolonial internationalism as a heritage that was absolutely integral to the legacies of the 1917 Russian Revolution. As a case in point, they looked to Lenin's statements in his 1913 "Theses on the National Question."[36] In a "revisionist" betrayal of Lenin's support for anticolonial self-determination struggles, the Canadian Communist Party (CPC) practiced "social imperialism" and "national chauvinism" to the detriment of "alliance based on mutual respect for each other's sovereignty." Concretely responding to the CPC's tepid support of the Native People's Caravan of 1974 in comparison to their full-throated support of the Quebec sovereignty movement, Maracle and the Native Study Group argued that "the left in Canada fails to recognize the historic right of internally colonized native people to self-determination." Instead, the CPC sought to manipulate the more radical (inter)national struggle of Indigenous peoples to regain substantive national control over land by insisting upon the "strictly [non-Indigenous] working class character of the Canadian revolution."[37] The implication of Maracle's contention is not only that the "antirevisionist" position is more *ethically* responsive to the independent histories and traditions of Indigenous societies, but also that such a politics flowed from a more accurate, less parochial account of the *extant structural relations* of capitalist exploitation and oppression in and through colonial hierarchies on both a local and world scale.[38]

This focus on the actuality of capitalist imperialism more explicitly draws attention to the systemic co-constitution of the wealthy white-dominated nations of the imperialist core (of which Canada is a part) and the colonized periphery. Maracle cited Marx and Engels in arguing that the wealth accumulated in the imperial core through (internal and external) primitive accumulation via colonial conquest made the "sector of the international proletariat resident in the oppressing nations" actively invest in nationalism, that is, their imperialized *nation's* domination of the world market. The privileges of this group are won from "colonial economic relations" and justified in ideologically fascist and racist hierarchies enforced over those constructed as nonwhite peoples, which make possible white collaboration in sustaining a racially exclusive capitalist welfare state.

This structural account is, in part, an explanation of the nonrevolutionary and even "reactionary" and racist character of many of the sectors of the trade union movement in the wealthy core countries, by appeal to the way that colonial and imperial politics constructed the basic character of international "class" relations as colonial-racial hierarchies.[39] As such, against a narrow construal of the scene of industrial production, this account redirects the impetus of revolutionary "proletarian internationalism" in the era of decolonization by placing it with the "oppressed masses of the Third World" or the "oppressed nations." It is the expropriation of this global majority that makes possible the inception and continuing expansion of capitalism; in turn, their national consciousness and revolutionary subjectivity are the backbone of international antisystemic movements.[40]

How did this revolutionary politics committed to de-parochializing the North American left account for sovereignty and the nation-state? One illuminating way to assess how NARP displaced the centrality of settler sovereignty in theorizing decolonization and revolutionary coalition building is through their use of the idiom of "internal" or "domestic" colonization. The influential idea of "internal colonialism" held widespread appeal among North American revolutionaries of color, especially in the years 1968–73.[41] Such an analytic functioned by reimagining the space of the "domestic" itself as colonial space, likening US-based racism to the global experience of imperial expansionism and colonial subjugation. Practices such as extractive resource theft; predatory debt and finance; segregation in ghettos, barrios, and reserves; and color-line job discrimination were thereby characterized as modes of *colonial* domination of Chicanos, African Americans, and Indigenous peoples alike.[42]

More recently, Chickasaw theorist Jodi Byrd has called this rubric of "internal" or "domestic" colonialism into question. For Byrd, theorizing domination as internal to the nation-state serves to reinscribe settler sovereignty as the site of remediation for colonization (rather than its source).[43] In short, Byrd contends that, in conflating racialization and colonization, such frameworks reify the boundaries of the settler nation-state in ways that materially exacerbate the domination of Indigenous societies. They too often accept the premise that identity and resistance take place firmly *within* the terms of North American constitutional orders, which function through charged symbolic investments in narratives that conflate "freedom" with the ever-expanding ambit of statist hegemony (as I argued via readings of Zitkala-Ša and Vine Deloria Jr. in chapter 1).

In contrast to Byrd's interpretation, I evaluate the import of Maracle and NARP's use of this framework in light of their revolutionary efforts to delegitimize the nation-state by locating it in a capaciously *trans*national imperial context. NARP aimed to organize politically so as to transcend those US and Canadian state hegemonies that claim sovereign, unilateral authority to enforce the very lines between internal and external, domestic and international. Accordingly, I venture instead that their deployment of the idiom of internal colonization actually sought to desanctify the boundaries of the settler nation-state by knitting together a variety of struggles against colonial-racial capitalism in a web of relations with global revolutionary ambitions.

To wit, Maracle and her comrades analyzed colonial sovereignty's self-narrated boundaries as politically constructed artifices designed to justify imperialist domination over Native land and labor. They proposed that claims representing colonized territories as natural extensions of sovereign space concealed imperial efforts to exercise colonial extraction and subordination. This double movement of naturalizing sovereignty as the site of remediation for harm and also ensuring the actual imposition of colonial structures of domination required maintaining the illusion and the lure of (eventual) equal citizenship for colonized subjects. Maracle and Ray Bobb raise these concerns specifically in a 1976 article in *Canadian Revolution*, which they wrote under the auspices of the Native Study Group and prepared for the Third World Peoples' Coalition's celebration of the eleventh anniversary of the Palestinian Revolution. Entitling their statement "Natives Are Part of the Third World" (also published under the title "Palestinians and Native People Are Brothers" in *Seize the Time*), they contended,

> What is the difference between the oppressed peoples of the Third World as a whole and those of the internal colonies? The difference is not qualitative. That is, internal colonies do not constitute an integral part of the imperialist nations. . . . For instance up until very recently the African nations of Mozambique, Angola and Guinea were not considered nations, but overseas provinces of Portugal. The masses of those

oppressed nations then rose up and seized their independence, outside the context of Portuguese law.... The difference, then, between the oppressed peoples of the Third World as a whole and those of the internal colonies is a quantitative matter related to the existence of the internal colony amid the concentrated power of the imperialist State machinery and the white settler populace that was massively aborted from Europe. It is not a matter of different goals, but of different strategies for achieving those goals.[44]

Such a politics challenged colonial sovereignty by imaginatively drawing together in a single analytic frame the arbitrary lines separating the oppression of "internally" and "externally" colonized peoples by a variety of imperialist nation-states. Above all, this account of internal colonization decisively rejected efforts to figuratively or institutionally channel Indigenous peoples' struggles back into the parameters of the nation-state. Indeed, they situate Indigenous societies alongside other colonized peoples fighting liberation struggles "outside the context" of imperial law. As their comparison with the brutal armed struggles in Mozambique, Angola, and Guinea-Bissau against Portuguese colonialism makes clear, the differences here between so-called internal and external colonies are superficial. They are an artifact of colonial juridical hegemony that is at play *as ideology* in contexts of so-called overseas imperialism as in North American settler-colonial states' projections of their own territorial integrity. Contra Byrd's otherwise convincing indictment of US liberalism's frequent ideological conflation of colonization with domestically bound racialization, NARP used the rubric of internal colonization to reject *any* qualitative structural or cultural-political demarcation between Third World struggles for sovereignty and those of Indigenous societies.

What is more, at stake in this articulation of a kinship of insurgent forces facing down transnationally connected forms of imperial power is the need to throw a core aspect of colonial sovereignty into relief. Namely, colonial sovereignty reproduces its own aura of inevitability through antirelational boundary-drawing strategies that drive wedges between anticolonial struggles. The separation of these struggles functions by hailing Indigenous peoples just as (eventually equal) subjects of the nation-state desiring more expansive incorporation. Internal security and foreign policy elites themselves are fully conscious of such transnational relations when they form repressive "counterinsurgency networks" facilitating exchanges of tactical plans and military/policing technologies among colonizer states. Colonial sovereignty isolates and minoritizes Indigenous peoples' struggles by redirecting and/or disavowing their (actual or potential) relations with those of other colonized peoples—whether within or without the borders of the nation-state.

So, it is the mandate of anticolonial movements to *reaffirm* those relations as fundamental to the flourishing of critical consciousness about how colonization works. Maracle and Bobb thus contended that "the extent to which we, as native people, are moved to indignation by the crime historically perpetrated against the Palestinian people and other oppressed peoples of the Third World is the extent to which we have not been 'successfully integrated' into a parasitic and oppressive culture."[45] Indigenous peoples' capacities to be "stirred" to enacting solidarity with other colonized peoples' insurgencies is itself a litmus test of their own emancipatory aspirations. It is the continued strength of such relational imaginaries that testifies in turn to the failures of settler sovereignty to entirely chain Indigenous peoples psychoaffectively and materially to the "conciliatory crumbs" of the "imperialist system." Moreover, the integration of at least a small layer of Indigenous peoples into the privileges or even the more punitive dependencies on the settler state (e.g., welfare) typically implicated them in the North American political economy's dependence on extraction, labor exploitation, and unequal terms of trade with many of those same colonized societies in the global South.[46] In this way, transnational internationalist consciousness is already implicated in the flourishing of national consciousness, and vice versa.

In this way, such a practice of transnational internationalism hinged on asserting a sense of a *shared* oppositional culture and mutually inflected visions of liberation between the array of Indigenous struggles for (de)colonization in North America and the popular anticolonial struggles of the rest of the colonized world. Politically, NARP and its successor organizations embraced an internationalist identification and explicitly revolutionary alliance of the colonized between "Third World people and Aboriginal people."[47] As was the case with the articulations of many African American radical (inter)nationalists, this shared terrain was signified by Maracle and Adams alike in naming Indigenous peoples throughout the Americas *themselves* as "Third World peoples." In practice, these movements pursued active relations of solidarity with a wide range of national liberation struggles from the Palestine Liberation Organization to that of FRELIMO (Frente de Libertação de Moçambique [Liberation Front of Mozambique]) against Portuguese colonial rule. Rather than domestic minorities, Indigenous peoples became part of a global *majority* of expropriated and racialized peasants, workers, and Indigenous subjects that faced various axes of colonial rule naturalized as legitimate sovereignty.

This approach contrasted directly with Manuel's comparative division between Third and Fourth World internationalisms. Indeed, NARP directly argued that the idea of the Fourth World was insufficient. In their telling, Fourth Worldism overemphasized the eventual transformation of settler societies to achieve peaceful coexistence between Indigenous peoples and settlers ("mutual dependence"). The idea of populations with different "worldviews" eventually reconciling with one another concealed *structural* relations of ongoing colonial domination and dependency under the ideological guise that "native people and finance capital can co-exist for their 'mutual benefit.'"[48] Maracle and Bobb, then, interpreted the institutionalization of the Fourth World concept as a capitulatory politics. It avoided the necessity of direct assault on the structural forces of capitalism-imperialism in solidarity with other revolutionary movements of the oppressed.

Radical (Inter)nationalisms, Neocolonialism, and the Question of Culture

The Vancouver Native Study Group's project of anticolonial international solidarity also ventured a radical counterpoint to some actors' novel uses of Indigenous "self-government" in ways that disavowed the connections between colonialism and capitalism. Adams and Maracle each independently observed by the mid-1970s that the forces of organized violence within the Canadian settler state had begun to repress and exhaust the Red Power movement's more radical grassroots mobilizations. Alongside these more repressive arms of the state, the Canadian government had also participated in creating a new above-ground infrastructure of Indigenous politics. This infrastructure channeled the demands of these movements into a more limited set of reforms, which would come to include land claims settlements, the modern treaty process in British Columbia, a new juridical recognition of a limited "aboriginal title" (to be "reconciled" with Canadian sovereignty), and the recognition of aboriginal and treaty rights in section 35 of the Canadian Constitution Act (and this, only *after* massive mobilization via the Constitution Express). In general, both Adams and Maracle interpreted these changes as a turn away from more expansively popular ambitions indexing the aims of Indigenous decolonization. Maracle summarizes the origins of these processes: "In 1969, a growing division in the movement between Red Power activists and orthodox leaders was hastened by the government creation of 'official organizations' replete with employed bureaucrats and heavy injections of money" (*IW*, 97). With the help of a small-but-rising "Red bourgeoisie" (Adams's term), these organizations participated in the creation (from the state's perspective) of a more compliant set of intermediaries functioning as legitimate representatives.

This relatively elite class operated as representatives of state-recognized, highly differentiated Indigenous constituencies in the form of reserve-based band councils (derived from the colonial band council system) and other regional and national state-dependent organizations and funding channels for First Nations, nonstatus, Métis, and Inuit peoples (*IW*, 216–18).[49] What resulted, Maracle argued, was a wholesale narrowing of horizons as to what Indigenous liberation movements sought when they invoked the concept of self-determination: "the politics of self-government was restricted to regional and tribal autonomy and to joint corporate economic development" (*IW*, 98). For Maracle, this redefinition of self-determination directly contradicted more radical possibilities: "For me, the struggle for self-determination will end with the dissolution of this elite and the leveling of the CanAmerican [i.e., North American] class structure or it will continue—for a thousand years if need be" (*IW*, 103).

In *Prison of Grass* and a later essay on this question entitled "Neocolonialism and the Native Struggle" (1980), Adams further theorized these transformations as quintessentially "neocolonial" by drawing from the already-classic works of Frantz Fanon and Kwame Nkrumah.[50] In these latter theorizations working from the context of African decolonization, neocolonialism designated the limitations on the prospects of self-government to a disempowered postcolonial "sovereignty" *after* the withdrawal of formally authoritarian colonial territorial occupation. Nkrumah traced how the postcolonial state is consequently (re)subjected to an ensemble of more indirect relations of power that function through the political-economic hegemony of global North–ruled financial institutions and monopoly capital.[51] Likewise, Nkrumah and Fanon both observed how this international regime was contingent on the far greater production of domestic inequality. This entailed the ascendance of a "native elite" or "national bourgeoisie," which substituted the popular revolutionary internationalist politics of national liberation for elite rule that was at once accommodating to and highly constrained by the externally oriented investment demands of international capital. The theory of neocolonialism thereby put forward an analysis of materially unequal regimes of formal international recognition that structurally interfaced with the creation of new forms of class hierarchy among the (post)colonized.

When they adapted these ideas loosely to the Canadian context, Adams and Maracle did not mean to suggest that neocolonialism displaced or superseded logics of direct territorial occupation constitutive of colonial-racial capitalism.⁵² Rather, these newer forms of colonial rule were *layered on* those prior logics to produce new governing technologies and discourses of legitimation in response to the crisis-inducing antisystemic challenge Red Power represented. Neocolonialism constituted a form of "pseudo-independence," which solicited the participation of this new "Red bourgeoisie" in these more indirect practices of colonial domination named "self-government" without removing the most basic material realities of territorial dispossession, occupation, and state dependency. In sum, neocolonialism designated the incorporation of Indigenous "self-government" initiatives into the imperatives of the settler state and finance capital, with new forms of internal class stratification materially aligning the prerogatives of this "Red bourgeoisie" with those imperatives in ways that fail to fundamentally transform (or can even exacerbate) the colonial relation for the vast majority of Indigenous peoples.

New ideologies emanating from this class and the settler state that recast Indigenous self-reliance as appropriately translated into "Red capitalism" pointed to the reality of competing political-economic *meanings* of the appeal to self-determination among Indigenous societies themselves.⁵³ Maracle points to this as a sharp contradiction between ideologies of self-determination as liberation and the neocolonial politics of Red capitalism: "To the [Indigenous] elite, liberation means that they become our bosses."⁵⁴

Though they agreed in their basic sociological explanation of this historical shift, Maracle and Adams diverged sharply in how they related this analysis to the politics of Indigenous decolonization. A discussion of these key differences unlocks insights into the normative foundations and political orientations framing their respective engagements with the pathologies of colonial-racial capitalism. It also points more broadly to underexamined, productive tensions between Indigenous Marxist theories of decolonization. Both Maracle and Adams offer radical critiques of what they call "cultural nationalism," that is, a form of nationalism that attributes the disempowerment of Indigenous peoples to their lack of recognition as distinct peoples with a right to rule themselves due to a shared national culture. While superficially resembling more radical claims on behalf of Indigenous peoples' rights to self-determination, they note that cultural nationalism (a) lacks a commitment to radical social transformation of the *material conditions* of colonial-racial capitalism that would coincide with the flourishing of mass Indigenous cultural forms and (b) is a strategic discursive weapon in the hands of the newly emerging Indigenous elite (and, so too, for the state), for whom an emphasis on the shared culture of the group masks the material reality of newly significant differences of social mobility, power, wealth, and prestige between elites and masses. In essence, cultural nationalism splits off from revolutionary nationalism with the neocolonial moment. There are now Indigenous elites that can speak in the language of "Red Power" and cultural solidarity so as to advance a political program that either defines cultural consciousness *alone* as the illusory site of radical political transformation *or* uses this language to enact a set of assimilation-oriented reforms that primarily redound to the material and psychological benefit of this (relatively) elite class.

Adams pressed this materialist critique of cultural nationalism even further. In several of his writings over the years, he vehemently criticized the prevalent focus within Indigenous movements on cultural resurgence, by arguing that it was precisely this set of discourses that enabled the new Red bourgeoisie to ideologically mask the growing political-economic chasm between their own interests and those of the masses. Claims to an authentically shared group culture gained traction as a useful fiction for in-group elites in the form of a (merely) *rhetorically* radical anticolonialism. In this way, an identity-based form of politics could be easily weaponized as a top-down class politics (*PG*, 178–206).

For Adams, the normative implication of this contention is that the (neo)colonial system is pathological because of the way it continued to connect authoritarian domination, state abandonment, and social deprivation: Indigenous elites' "authority to administer the indigenous population" is ultimately "derived, not from the will of the people, but from collaboration with the state."[55] This antidemocratic and externally oriented source of legitimacy ensured the long-term disavowal of more widely transformative alternatives, such as Indigenous Marxist emphases on securing permanent, internationally recognized land bases and redistributive noncapitalist mixed economies through the building of robust institutions of Indigenous self-determination. Put otherwise, neocolonialism signified a powerless form of democratic sovereignty that has as its purpose the preemption of both democracy (participatory or otherwise) and sovereignty.

With this in mind, Adams remained concerned over the years that most (if not all) appeals to culture could be subsumed within cultural nationalist ideologies, and that cultural nationalism inexorably led to "bourgeois nationalism." In other words, elite cultural discourses ultimately aimed to smooth over the fact of relative domination of small Indigenous elites by conflating the latter's interests in a kind of "Red capitalism" with the interests of all Indigenous peoples, through the often quite powerful appeal to an overarching shared history and culture with the masses. Moreover, given the extreme attenuation of Indigenous cultural forms and the colonial discursive and institutional production of "ossified" and "caricature[d]" cultural practices in face of colonial genocide (*PG*, 33–35, 195), romanticized appeals to past sources of cultural solidarity at once gained both profound mass psychological appeal *and* diverted attention away from a more realistic and direct grappling with the relations of power that constituted the present-day colonial situation (*PG*, 195–96).

For Adams, it followed from this analysis that the very idea of Indigenous decolonization as the critical reinscription of the noncapitalist normative exteriority of Indigenous cultural forms is either (a) politically insufficient or (b) politically productive of stratified and resource-extractive models of "self-government" with a veneer of cultural legitimacy and no accountability to the basic needs and material desires of the masses. Indigenous and non-Indigenous elites can manipulate the notion of "culture" in ways amenable to alliances with—and dependency upon—capital and the settler state. While there is some uncertain room in Adams's account for the recovery of self as a way of reaffirming the "dignity" of the colonized as a *means* of mobilization, such a project largely takes a backseat in significance to political mobilization more narrowly understood (*PG*, 192). Aside from a one-off reference in his writings to a "native ethic . . . strongly opposed to the capitalist profit ethic" (*PG*, 194), Adams downplays the idea that resurging Indigenous cultural forms ought to *permanently* inform the project and meaning of self-determination. Indeed, they may ultimately disappear as a transitional step in the longer arc of socialist transformation. Altogether, Adams argued that radical nationalists like himself, that is, those invested in self-determination as a medium for the revolutionary transformation of the social order, must sharply differentiate between the contested class basis and political effects of the varieties of Indigenous "nationalisms."

For Maracle, neocolonial rule's veneer of cultural nationalism is pathological for quite divergent reasons. Namely, neocolonial practices extend *colonial* subjectivities, hierarchies, and institutional forms to the relations *internal to* Indigenous societies. The normative issue for her is more the sharp contradiction between those relations and the alternatives that ought to be found in the ethical qualities underpinning a variety of Indigenous systems of governance. In particular, Maracle notes that her opposition "to the very existence of an elite among us" stems from the fact that this kind of unaccountable hierarchy and incorporation into market imperatives directly contradicts the values, subjugated knowledge, and social practices of Indigenous peoples *as Indigenous peoples*. Moreover, it contributes to a profound alienation from the very processes of self-formation that elites and the state now say they are participants in governing. Neocolonization is in this way part of the long-term colonial process of violent "disconnection" from various Indigenous modes of social life that are (or aspire to be, rightly reconstructed) generated through the land upon principles of sharing, egalitarianism, and respect for individual and collective autonomy, alongside a set of both role-specific and more expansively universalist obligations toward the other-than-human world.[56]

What is more, neocolonial rule specifically diminishes popular expectations of overcoming these already-deep, constitutive, forms of domination through further disconnection from particular communal social forms and knowledge, and even fosters disconnection from the very knowledge *that* such relations are susceptible to other benchmarks of transformation at all. Far from a disavowal of "culture" as such, Maracle's critique of neocolonialism is instead aimed at retrieving a vision of "our essential selves" *from* colonial domination. She argues that "we must fundamentally alter the relations of the colonial system; to dress our enslavement in Native garb is useless. We need to reclaim our essential selves, engage ourselves as the cultural, spiritual, emotional and physical beings we were and march forward, laying to rest one hundred years of cultural prohibition and arrest" (*IW*, 89). To be sure, Maracle accepts the Fanonian contention that colonization atrophies ("arrests") the culture of the colonized by the often-implacable force of colonial law and order. Yet, she argues that the notion that this is all that is left of cultural freedom reflects a mistaken acquiescence to this colonial (re)ordering ("enslavement in Native garb").

Instead, Maracle commends the permanent assertion of "our cultural bundles" as part of the content and aim of struggles for Indigenous self-determination. Colonial hegemony never fully subsumes lived reality nor the capacity to remember and imagine otherwise. This is to say that "cultural imperialism . . . does not occur with the degree of thoroughness desired by the imperialists." As a result, "We are and have always been culturally Cree, Salish, Nisga'a and so forth. One does not lose culture. It is not an object . . . it is constantly changing" (*IW*, 110). The problem lies not with the "loss" of culture per se but instead with the dis-alienating task of becoming whole, that is, revitalizing the ethical qualities of the relationships that suffuse "our systems" and material practices of social and ecological production (e.g., food systems, traditional governance, extended longhouse networks) that allow for the substantive reenactment of collective self-government and self-reliance. As she puts it, "We still have our original cultural bundles. We still have our original concepts of authority, but we lack, first, the space to affect them; second, the time to restore the belief and trust among ourselves to accept them; and third, the time to reconstruct our systems" (*MS*, 118–19). Remapping sovereignty means materially reconstructing systems that

Indigenous peoples can understand themselves as actually *authoring* in the process of creating the relative autonomy to interpret and assess the histories of their own values and material practices.

In this sense, Indigenous self-determination means the very *institutional forms* of self-determination must be reflected upon and experienced as an *outgrowth* of (nation-specific) Indigenous histories, values, laws, and jurisdiction. The fracturing of once-extended polities with confederated connections into (officially) isolated reserves/reservations governed by tribal councils is a territorial and political embodiment of settler sovereignty's diminished terms. The reclaiming of individual responsibilities within a collective self (or multiple connected collective selves) means reinforcing shared jurisdictions over those territories. Likewise, becoming "whole" (her term) means refusing the spatially and spiritually diminished terms of settler sovereignty's demands, even in the (counterfactual) hypothetical situation of a more robustly egalitarian (re)distribution of resources and self-government. Instead, Maracle invites and taps into ongoing, wider struggles for the flourishing of these disavowed normative and material systems of Indigenous self-determination and sovereignty.

To be sure, the idea of a recovery of self at issue here is *not* based on an uncritical or wholesale acceptance of an essence or tradition as uncontestable, unmediated, or transhistorical. Frequently citing Fanon and Amilcar Cabral,[57] Maracle is attentive to the deeply *historical* ways that "cling[ing] to the past" is a profoundly mediated and reconstructive act. Rather than a symptom of wounded attachments, however, the very desire to reintegrate individual and collective selves makes reclaiming the past a critical task in service of authoring and imagining institutions of self-determination. This process of recovery requires judgment, not reflexive attachment. Maracle insists that Indigenous societies must critically examine their own histories even before the colonial wound, insofar as colonial domination can sustain or reinforce ideas that legitimate certain forms of sovereign mastery. For example, she cites the fact that "we [i.e., Coast Salish people] once had slaves." Thereby, she argues for the value of "vigilance" in relation to *Indigenous societies'* pasts as well, which means a continuing "commit[ment] to overcoming masterhood, for we know that the attitude that permitted us to enslave others persists long after the slaves have been freed" (*MS*, 45).

The analyses of Adams and Maracle both feature a further consistent point of tension on the meaning of anticolonial internationalism, a point that relates to these divergences on the normative substance and politics of Indigenous self-determination. Namely, each demonstrates the way that the

Canadian political economy is (re)constituted through colonial relations of domination and the color line, which means that Indigenous peoples themselves must take up the task of transforming those basic structures so as to make any kind of genuine and lasting self-determination possible. One of the overarching aims of Adams's work is to show that "it is quite impossible to separate the development of Canadian society from the growth of our colonized conditions" (*PG*, 209). Likewise, Maracle argues, "segregation alone will not change the basic patterns of colonialism. Only decolonization will do that" (*IW*, 89). If there is no such thing as self-determination that can function permanently by separation, that is, practices of *exiting or escaping* such relations, then there is no struggle for decolonization that must not also aim to transform the much wider structural conditions integral to the reproduction of the Canadian settler society.

The question of alliance, then, becomes a key sticking point. As suggested, these analyses of white supremacy strongly imply that even radical modes of white working-class politics are psychologically and materially invested in privileges aligning them with the white ruling class, the sovereignty of the settler nation-state, and the constitutive material expropriation and disposability of Indigenous peoples. Accordingly, such a line of argument implies that the colonial foundations of capitalist political economy displace the centrality of the industrialized (white) working class as the subjects of exploitation and, so, as the main protagonist of revolutionary change.[58] If the white working class is instead understood as an integral *beneficiary* of the basic institutional hierarchies of property and privilege of sovereignty in the service of colonial and imperial nationhood, their social commitments are more likely invested in conserving power. They ought to be comprehended as structurally durable obstacles to the basic redistribution of power and the reclaiming of different relations to land that is revolutionary Indigenous internationalism's impetus. So, one aim of Indigenous Marxisms is to show how decolonization depends on the transformation of those structures of the settler society. Nevertheless, the problem remains that it is those very structures that appear locked into sustaining colonial domination in overdetermined ways.

Lee Maracle on Gendering (De)colonization

In her 2017 book *My Conversations with Canadians*, Maracle looks back on and reemphasizes the obstacle represented by the more subtle ideological attachments even of white "leftists" to the *nation* despite their apparently radical orientation toward capital and the state: "They are not loyal to their government, but they are loyal to the notion of Canada—the current colonizer, their country."⁵⁹ Notwithstanding the apparent implication of Maracle's contention about white-settler power or, at least, deep imaginative investments in the Canadian social formation, Adams still maintained that "social class features will gradually become more prominent and the movement will turn into a class struggle. Indians and Métis will come to see that the different class struggles throughout Canada are not separate and unrelated" (*PG*, 204–5). While Adams is understandably inconsistent on this point given the daunting necessity of transforming the entire social formation and the need for an elusive coalitional politics to accomplish this, he ends up ascribing to Indigenous nationalism a more transitional and momentary role that is at least *ideologically* subsumed by the terms of a more narrowly construed "class" politics. In turn, the core's white working class could eventually reimagine their interests and conception of oppression itself in a more universalistic light and, in doing so, align themselves outside of the Canadian settler state with the global majority, that is, those oppressed nationalities that have served as the internal and external extractive peripheries to the imperial core. In this way, Adams leaves some room for the idea that Indigenous self-determination is more a *temporary way station* on the journey to a socialist polity than a permanent, existential, and structurally transformative reclaiming and/or reconstruction of individual and collective selfhood from colonial domination.

As I have suggested, Maracle proposed a *permanent and enduring* mode of self-determination, which hinged on the critical retrieval and reconstruction of Salish—and more broadly, Indigenous—sociopolitical structures. She also conceived of this as a dis-alienating praxis, part of reconstructing the integral selfhood of the colonized. By contrast, recipes for the alignment of struggles waged under the sign of Indigenous self-determination with an elusive "class"-based movement seemed to fall back precisely on the more mechanical and deterministic Marxisms that anticolonial frameworks had eschewed, "wooden arguments about proletarian unity and revolution."⁶⁰

The notion of merging struggles into a unified coalition oriented toward the same revolutionary project clashed, too, with the analysis Maracle derived from her own direct experiences. In particular, it was her early persistent encounters with the brutality of the *gendered* violence of cross-class white supremacy that "made it impossible for [her] to think about Canadian or American workers liberating Indians and humanizing the system."⁶¹ As she forcefully exclaims to white revolutionaries in a dialogue in *Bobbi Lee*, "look, do you want me to believe that those guys that I had so much trouble with, who went over the reserve looking for Indian women—raping and plundering—are going to make a revolution to free us all from oppression? You gotta be kidding!"[62]

Maracle began to develop a distinctive mode of queer Indigenous feminist politics in relation to decolonization struggles in the 1980s. In a shift culminating in her influential essay collection *I Am Woman: A Native Perspective on Sociology and Feminism* (1988), Maracle reformulated her analysis of colonial-racial capitalism to theorize and figure the heteropatriarchal violence and productive gendering powers central to colonial invasion. Through these lenses, Maracle interrogated both the existing patriarchal investments of Indigenous decolonization movements and the colonial investments of much of the dominant feminist movement in Canada. As an alternative, she offered a critical account of the pathologies of the *patriarchal settler state* and a constructive project of *gendering decolonization*. She commends the critical restoration and rematriation of Indigenous earthmaking as the horizon of Indigenous decolonization, and continues to locate these visions transnationally alongside a range of principally women-led anticolonial struggles of the (post)colonized *against* environmental degradation and dispossession and *for* land and self-determination.

Maracle observed how Native liberation movements themselves failed to reckon with violence against Indigenous women. Self-appointed male leadership among radicals like AIM and the more mainstream lobby organizations pursued self-determination in ways that downplayed the centrality of gendered oppression to the colonization of Indigenous societies in the first instance: "Indigenous women have been asked to put their issues on the back burner as though the rematriation of our governing structures—ending family and domestic abuse—were somehow secondary to the nation-building process" (*MS*, 660–61).[63] Here, Maracle linguistically marks the failure to acknowledge a direct continuum between the task of resurging "governing structures" and that of remediating everyday gender-based and family violence as primary concerns *of and for decolonization*. Indeed, Maracle found in the responses of mostly male-dominated leadership a deep failure to engage in the kind of critical *self*-examination that addressing patriarchy *within* Indigenous communities requires: "I think that men have a vested interest in holding on to the issue of racism, because then the enemy is external."[64] "Yet very often," she contended, "racism operates as sexism in our community and often sexism operates as internalized racism."[65]

By the 1980s, Maracle responded to these political-ideological failures to center those gendered forms of violence and oppression that continue to be emblematized in widespread violence against Indigenous women in Canadian society. Namely, she theorized and poetically figured an analysis of the constitutively *patriarchal* character of colonial-racial capitalism. She developed a constructive political-theoretic project based on this analysis, *gendering* the theory and politics of Indigenous (de)colonization and self-determination.

Through the concept of "gendering decolonization," I draw together core elements of Maracle's political-theoretical vision. Her vision places movements against gender-based oppression at the center of Indigenous struggles against colonialism and capitalism. To do so, Maracle first advances a critical and historical analysis of the systemically gendered and heterosexist *reproduction* of Canadian colonial-racial capitalism. Specifically, Maracle argues that challenging colonial-capitalist dependency relations necessitates a critique of the state as a "patriarchal settler-state" (*MS*, 129). This latter concept encapsulates how settler states reproduce patriarchy (and are produced by patriarchy) by coercively gendering Indigenous societies in unprecedented ways and dismantling Indigenous women's preexisting roles and influence in Indigenous societies' self-determined modes of authority.

Especially indicative of this history in Canada is the Indian Act, which was not only transparently sexist, but also attempted to produce an explicitly heteronormative and patriarchal regime of racialized "Indian" family formation. It was the 1876 amendment to the original 1868 Indian Act that established that "Indian status" passed down through patrilineal descent. Maracle recalls how, before the 1961 liberalization of the Indian Act, "we were 'wards of the government,' children in the eyes of the law." The liberalization of the Indian Act made it possible to mobilize "the Native question— the forerunner of Native self-government, the Native land question, etc." Up to that point, the "Native question" subsumed the "woman question": "The woman question did not exist for us. Not then" (*IW*, 16).

Maracle's account of the historical formation of Canada as a "patriarchal settler state" pushes the roots of these concerns further back to Canada's origins, by showing how the juridical and social basis of the imposition of colonial order has been fabricated in utterly gendered and patriarchal forms (*MS*, 129). As the key legislation defining Indian status (and excluding "nonstatus"), the Indian Act helps to illustrate this because its various iterations redefined and restructured notions of gender, gender roles, and the very institution of "family." Focusing as she often does on how this process was experienced in a Coast Salish context, Maracle diagnoses how the Indian Act aimed to transform extended kinship relations central to clan governance such as "extended longhouse families" sharing "relationships to other extended longhouse families" in a dynamic confederated structure into narrow and immobile bounds of the private, patriarchal "nuclear" family and compulsory heterosexuality confined to the apartheid reserve system.[66] So, this entailed tearing apart these longhouse-based quasi-confederal relations within relations as part of the "stripping of women power."[67] In this way, the Indian Act first *reconstituted* what counted as kinship in the form of a nuclear, patriarchal, and patrilineal unit that was privatized and distinct from public life.

Of course, these measures "gave" Native men relatively more rights and allowed them to take over areas over which Indigenous women had previously held jurisdiction within colonial structures of collective subjugation. Maracle contends that the Indian Act was based upon the bourgeois model of "nuclear family living arrangements" and "male dominance and insistence on a woman moving to the man's village upon marriage" (*MS*, 117). For example, men were given the right to pass on their state-regulated status to their children and the women they married.[68] In an insight since extended by Indigenous feminist scholars such as Sarah Deer (Mvskoke) and Renya Ramirez (Ho-Chunk),[69] Maracle argues that settler violence against Indigenous women *and* intracommunal "lateral violence" are both traceable to the production of settler sovereignty as a historical and ongoing vector of "colonial violence"—"one of the by-products of colonization that rendered our communities impotent."[70] For Maracle, colonization is not simply manifest as external domination—the "external enemy." It has been constituted all at once through external domination, intracommunal or "lateral violence" and disconnection, and inwardly turned psychoaffective (de)valuing of the self. Central to colonialism are processes whereby invasive institutions such as residential schools annihilate the bonds and ethical substance of existing social forms through extreme "alienation and internal violence" that "overtook the original caring and sharing between Indigenous peoples and their families."[71]

What is notable about this account—and what becomes so essential to subsequent Indigenous feminist theory—is that Maracle recurrently tracks the direct structural-causal links between *patriarchal domination* and the colonial assault on the underlying material capacities upon which *collective self-determination* depends. These include colonial theft of direct access to the means of production, the practice of caretaking of land and (future) citizens, and social reproduction. Maracle's central contention, then, is that patriarchal colonial state power works by divesting Indigenous women not only of the universals of basic dignity, security, and bodily autonomy, but also of powers *within their societies* that allow them a more expansive set of rights *to become themselves*. Maracle calls this a "birthright," that is, the capacity to take up responsibilities due by virtue of membership in their own political communities. Those are the responsibilities that, she argues, have been integral to the intergenerational reproduction and dynamic alteration of the collective "self" of self-determination.

Besides her invocation of the systemically oppressive character of these laws, Maracle's point here is also to show that the Indian Act and institutions like residential schools redefined and usurped the *power* of women as among the key agents of self-determination in Indigenous communities. As Mishuana Goeman (Tonawanda Seneca) has since argued, these practices undercut the intergenerational transmission of knowledge of self in relation to land over the flux of time, which Indigenous women have resisted through the dynamic mapping and reproduction of responsible and relational social practices *across* colonial partitions of space.[72] For Maracle, the production of a Western sex-gender system as such and repressive state violence actually undermined those earthmaking practices, which relied on the authority and integral selfhood of women to steward lands and manage the intergenerational transmission of knowledge about how to care properly for those lands (whether urban or rural).

Maracle traces historically how Indigenous women's "loss of access to tribal territory, their loss of their role as caretakers of the nation, and their loss of their right as mothers to determine their villages' wellness, destroyed the social fabric of our world" (*MS*, 147). Indeed, "the loss of women's authority," Maracle writes, "is directly connected to the loss of male jurisdiction and [women's] restriction to the village of their husbands advanced by the reservation system and the Indian Act." Because Indigenous women produce *themselves* as traditional and new caretakers of the land, waters, and salmon in Stó:lō systems of governance, the evisceration of their power also rips away the *material bases* of survival and the kinds of earthmaking practices that allow for the care and renewal of land. Simply, "the loss of access to land bases from which to access food was contingent on the loss of female authority" (*MS*, 148).

To lend more detail to this claim, Maracle traced how Salish social forms gave women jurisdiction of the "economy" that colonial rule eroded materially and ideologically. By this unorthodox use of the term economy, Maracle means practices of care that assure the intergenerational material and intellectual reproduction of the people in relation to the other-than-human world, including land, water, and animals. For example, she writes of sockeye salmon that they "were sent to Salish women to assist us during times of hunger. We were asked to honor sockeye and take care of the waters" (*MS*, 282–83). As caretakers with these specific roles in Salish culture, women have role-specific responsibilities to particular beings regarded as vital to the survival and flourishing of the interconnected human and nonhuman world. The practice of gendering decolonization entails taking back "our birthright as caretakers of the land," including these role-specific responsibilities (*IW*, 38).[73] Reconstructing these materially dismantled laws, relations, and responsibilities serve as guidance for the forward movement of the project of decolonization itself. They constitute both a way of (re)orienting oneself toward a past that is otherwise structured by "alienation" and "disconnection"—"pulling the threads of my past forward"—and a forward-looking normative compass that seeks to materialize their ethical substance in the political, social, and ecological freedoms imagined in the future—to "reweave our lives together."

To be sure, many feminist theoretical perspectives have captured in different ways the injustice and inequality of gender-based systems of oppression that elevate men to power by denying women the capacity to determine their life courses, fulfill their human potential, and participate as full members in the public institutions that comprise political life. This is what Maracle calls the "European rebel's response," that is, the rebellion against dominant gender ideologies that mask and naturalize the patriarchal subordination of women (*IW*, 15). A core implication of these arguments is that women's liberation must partly entail throwing off, that is, negating, the constricted and subordinated social roles associated with traditional femininity and masculinity. These roles typically designate women as the dominated subjects of a patriarchal social order. In other words, what Maracle calls the "European rebel's response" rests on a primarily *negative* account of heteropatriarchy as the conscription of women and gender and sexually nonconforming persons into constrained and subordinated traditionally feminine (or masculine) social roles that naturalize their oppression and domination. Liberation entails transforming those forms of structural inequality and injustice to ensure the material conditions for self-determination and self-realization.

To be sure, Maracle's analysis of colonial invasion and racial hierarchy overlaps with this latter diagnosis insofar as it speaks to the domination of Indigenous women along multiple axes of oppression as "second-class citizens," both *within* their societies and in the Canadian settler society into which their bodies and lands have been conscripted as both in need of assimilation and disposable. More specifically even, such an account gives particular form to the racialized modes of gender discourses that are otherwise presumed to operate along universal lines with whiteness as the unspoken norm. In this way, colonization is a specific form of racialized gender oppression that denies these very notions of "traditional femininity" as such to Indigenous women: "colonization for Native women signifies the absence of beauty, the negation of sexuality. We are the females of the species" (*IW*, 20). Along these lines, it is clear that, for Maracle, Indigenous women are the subjects of an intersectional form of oppression: that is, of multiple, compounding forms of racial, sexual, and gender oppression (a point she makes often by drawing on and modifying the insights of Black interlocutors like Sojourner Truth and Audre Lorde).

Nevertheless, Maracle's more distinctive *anticolonial* feminist intervention is to change the *system of reference* for feminist liberation toward the relation between individual and collective decolonization and self-determination understood as *subjugated responsibilities*. As has become key to many approaches within contemporary Indigenous feminisms, she is concerned "to redefine what feminism means" because "we have very different histories, conditions, and claims than do Canadian women."[74] Namely, colonial invasion and oppression function to fundamentally *deny and dismantle* the selfhood, power, and duties of Indigenous women as active and valued participants in shaping the destinies of their own Indigenous societies. Along with—and indeed through—targeted violence against Indigenous women and the gender nonconforming, colonial invasion is also productive of alienated social forms. At issue is a patriarchy-*constituting* process that has had the transformative effect of replacing and rupturing those *alternative, positive sources of normativity* that sustain the capacities of Indigenous societies for reproduction of their communities and of/with the earth itself. So, Maracle cashes out these "very different histories, conditions, and claims" in tracing the process by which distinct societies with prior histories in which women held significant forms of social power and knowledge have been transformed into subjects of patriarchal colonial-racial capitalism. Maracle reframes feminism as a politics of decolonization that aims to recover these alternative sources of ethical life expressed in the social and ecological reproductive capacities—the *subjugated responsibilities*—of Indigenous women as essential to the flourishing of the body politic of Indigenous societies.

In this formulation, patriarchy is pathological not because it is foreign per se. Rather "patriarchy is a systemic invasion and must be repelled as unjust, not because it is foreign but because it is mean."[75] The subjugation of women and the remaking of family formation along patriarchal lines is oppressive in choking off Indigenous possibilities of self-realization, and it is colonial because it is core to the material implementation and to gendered ideological frameworks of colonial dispossession as a whole. Describing Salish governance structures as the labor of continual efforts to attune social structures to "the rhythms of the earth," Maracle argues that what colonialism destroys is the way that "respect for the earth and respect for women were bound together, and organized women governors wielded power to enforce this" (*MS*, 143). Violence and *dis*respect to the earth's caretakers is violence and disrespect to the earth itself ("earth-pillage" or "earth-rape," in her terms), and violence and disrespect to the earth itself is violence and disrespect to its caretakers.

To bring the *political* force of Maracle's analysis of colonial patriarchy more sharply into relief, it is helpful to situate her intervention in relation to the contests between settler states, Indigenous peoples, and some Indigenous women's organizations throughout the 1970s and 1980s over the gendered terms of Indigenous self-government. Specifically, Maracle's radical critique of the relay between colonialism and patriarchy integral to Canadian state formation stood in tension with Indigenous and non-Indigenous feminist activists who sought to overturn sex discrimination through the courts, and worked from a civil and human rights perspective in doing so. In their successful efforts to table the White Paper in the early 1970s, the NIB and provincial Indigenous organizations fought to conserve status provisions by arguing that changes in Indian Act legislation that potentially led to greater outside interference in matters of "self-government" constituted ipso facto violations of the principle of Indian self-government.

In response, organizations such as Indian Rights for Indian Women and the Native Women's Association of Canada mounted lawsuits—*Lavell v. Canada* (1971) and *Bedard v. Isaac* (1972)—that aimed to test the constitutionality of the Indian Act's provision (12)(1)b. These organizations ultimately succeeded in amending the Indian Act under Bill C-531 in April 1985 to eliminate the most explicit forms of sex discrimination.[76] The NIB and many bands, however, insisted that the antidiscrimination provisions of international human rights (brought into domestic law in the 1982 Canadian Charter) constituted violations of Indigenous sovereignty and "tradition." Many Indigenous men leading the NIB and band councils stood against women's rights by casting these appeals as existential challenges to tribal autonomy—attacking the original plaintiffs Lavell and Bedard as "whitewashed women libbers." Though such a discourse posed this conflict as an antithesis between sovereignty and individual rights, these litigation efforts really aimed to reestablish basic connections between individual and collective freedoms that are core to the value and practice of self-determination.[77]

Notwithstanding these derogatory portrayals, Maracle insisted that there was a basic structural problem with this liberal form of opposition to gender violence and sex discrimination: it rested on an *appeal to the rule of law vested in the colonial state* as the source of legitimate sovereignty over Indigenous societies and individuals. Such an appeal to the state to protect and secure some Indigenous women's rights required a disavowal of that same state's fundamental role in creating the structural contexts enabling patriarchal and colonial domination. Maracle stated bluntly: "those weren't feminist acts."[78] In her classic *Thunder in My Soul*, Mohawk legal theorist Patricia Monture likewise recounted the difficulty of organizing to confront the pervasive but diffuse violence resulting from the colonial and masculinist character of the state. Monture described the Canadian state as "the invisible male perpetrator who unlike Aboriginal men does *not* have a victim face."[79] Maracle's analysis works along similar lines to trace the *constitutive* role patriarchy played in consolidating and reproducing the continued colonial relation between Indigenous peoples and the settler state. As a result of the intractability of this co-constitution process, Maracle argued that it was impossible to adequately address the gender violence inherent to colonization within the framework of the very colonial state whose own authority to *make* law depends on disavowing the coercive roots and reproduction of that authority. Moreover, these strategies ultimately dealt with sex discrimination selectively against some women, and eschewed commitments to collective liberation that worked with and alongside *all* Indigenous women.

Altogether, Maracle's constructive alternative is to articulate Indigenous decolonization and feminism together, as perspectives and struggles that are mutually transformative.[80] In her words, "feminism and decolonization have to come together," and "rematriation and decolonization must be our response."[81] As such, Maracle writes, "I believe [Indigenous] feminism is a response to the Canadian-state orchestrated invasion of our [women's] areas of jurisdiction by Indigenous men" (*MS*, 149). In this way, decolonization makes "returning to how we were before [into] a feminist struggle."[82] This entailed a "commitment to re-building the governing institutions in which Indigenous women held power alongside men" (*MS*, 132, 151). The latter vision seeks to challenge the ongoing constitution of patriarchal social relations as a key feature of settler-colonial state power, which in turn calls into question the legitimacy of the settler state *itself* as the bounds defining the legitimate scope of Indigenous self-government and the rights (and responsibilities) of Indigenous women.[83]

Though as with any artist her literary output is hardly *reducible* to this political project, I briefly submit here that Maracle's fiction and poetry do contribute to gendering decolonization through her extensive tracing of the experiences of Indigenous characters and communities—and those she invites poetic transnational relations of solidarity with, from Palestine to Soweto—in grappling precisely with these multilayered effects of heteropatriarchal colonization. She characterizes colonial invasion as operating to deform community and individual well-being across different scales, in ways often disavowed by dominant recourse to victim-blaming racialized discourses of cultural dysfunction. Through stories that redirect the rage of colonized subjects toward these structures and away from blaming themselves for their conditions, she intervenes (as she describes) to "devictimize their consciousness and push back on colonization."[84]

Her short story "Bertha," with the titular character a Coast Salish elder working on Cannery Row, expresses this aspiration in literary form. As Bertha wallows in the alcohol binge from which she ultimately dies, the "circle of memory . . . crept out at her from the fog." She recalls the intergenerational practice of raising women to assume their places in hereditary governance: "The efforts of village women to nurture her as keeper of her clan, mother of all youth, had gone to naught. . . . Motherhood, the re-creation of ancient stories that would instruct the young in the laws of her people, and encourage good citizenship from even the babies, had eluded her."[85] The aim of this "devictimization" practice is to denaturalize the experience of alienation toward oneself, others, and—Maracle argues—the earth itself. Through tracking this kind of journey in her protagonists in novels such as *Sundogs* (1992) and *Ravensong* (1993), Maracle figures the ways that colonial logics saturate this felt "disconnection" across political scales from the intimate site of the family to the macropolitics of capitalism and state power.[86]

Just as NARP formed internationalist alliances of and in the Third World, Maracle places these practices of gendering decolonization and self-determination within a "global feminist decolonizing perspective." Indigenous "rematriation" practices thrive in connection to the multiplicity of projects that continue the heritages of popular anticolonial mobilization, such as peasant and Indigenous land and community self-defense, landless worker movements, commoning, agroecology, food sovereignty, and so on that prefigure alternatives to the colonial present in the internal peripheries of the global North and the global South.[87] Her aim was to "alter the structure of our communities to make this original position [of women in matriarchal societies] real. That is, to ensure the power and place of women in the active struggle for self-determination, not simply for Aboriginal nations, *but globally. We need to tie ourselves to the global struggle of women for liberation and emancipation.*"[88]

Conclusion

In this chapter, I examined how Adams and Maracle reconceived the material conditions, normative substance, and agencies of decolonization. They did so in seeking to apprehend and critique the intersecting violence of colonialism, white supremacy, capitalism, and heteropatriarchy. These Indigenous Marxist approaches are an important but often downplayed subset of political-ideological frameworks in twentieth-century Indigenous anticolonial struggles. Yet they provide a relentlessly critical analysis of colonial-racial capitalism and, as a result, a distinctive political-theoretic account of the conditions, substance, and agencies of Indigenous decolonization. The implications of this structural analysis were political, in the sense that Adams and Maracle were, respectively, pointing to a need to hitch the practice and meaning of Indigenous self-determination to the transformation of the broader social structures by which capitalism secures and naturalizes the hierarchies within humanity and between humanity and the other-than-human that it creates (and subsequently leverages for its continued reproduction). In turn, Indigenous Marxists demonstrated to the *non*-Indigenous left that one could neither understand nor identify points of instability within—let alone, the sweeping determinate negation of—capitalism without addressing the material reality that Indigenous dispossession and heteropatriarchal violence are among capitalism's historical and ongoing structural a priori conditions. In this vision, Indigenous struggles for self-determination are a challenge to the heart of these structural conditions and are not merely an external moral supplement to anticapitalist movements.

Altogether, these thinkers knitted together an Indigenous politics waged for decolonization that has often been advanced as the critical *re*surgence of Indigenous cultural, social, and political forms *as antiassimilationist normative antitheses to capitalism* and a broadly Marxian *in*surgent revolutionary politics tying together the fates of heterogeneous working peoples' struggles, struggles oriented toward socialist transformation(s). The epigraph at the start of this chapter from Dene political theorist Glen Coulthard aptly encapsulates what this means for conceptualizing decolonization: "For Indigenous nations to live, capitalism must die." I submit that at stake in this claim are two elements core to the Indigenous Marxisms canvassed in this chapter. On the one hand, this formulation prescribes the *material conditions* of lasting Indigenous resurgence, in the sense that profound structural transformations must occur to create a world where those normative antitheses can flourish in actualized earthmaking practices. On the other hand, Coulthard is also making a claim about how *resurgence* contributes to and is defined by a constitutive contradiction between many anticolonial Indigenous practices and capitalism's relentless erasure or management-via-incorporation of any social formation that privileges relational networks of care and does not conduce to the needs of extraction in a given moment. Simply, the abolition of capitalism's relentlessly extractive hold alongside colonialism over Indigenous peoples' most basic rights and collective self-determination is central to *what Indigenous decolonization ought to mean and enact as such.*

These Indigenous Marxist projects also offer a different expression of and theoretical vantage point on the politics of Indigenous transnational internationalism. If Fourth Worldism was premised on mobilizing the *specificities* of Indigenous self-determination and seeking out separate forums and transformative rights regimes for transnational Indigenous movements, the approaches here oriented activists to more unifying rubrics that drew together many struggles both in and outside the nation-state against different nodes of capitalist imperialism. While these solidarities were certainly the product of the ideological zenith of the "era of decolonization" in the early 1970s, Maracle herself molded them into a lasting vision expressed in an embodied solidarity with the experiences of (among others) the Palestinians' struggle for self-determination.

This expansive conception of transnational alliance also challenged the meanings of Indigenous self-government or tribal sovereignty within the settler state, by virtue of pointing to the expanded relations into which global capitalism constantly thrust Indigenous societies along with others. Maracle's contention was as follows: insofar as Indigenous movements within North America seek certain forms of incorporation into settler states in the imperial core, they are also implicated in exploitative and extractive practices upon typically racialized Indigenous peoples, peasants, and workers in the external peripheries of empire. In other words, Maracle's transnationalism is grounded in the insight that projects of "self-government" sustaining themselves through dependency on the colonial settler state are implicitly or explicitly invested in imperial relations elsewhere. Thus, self-government arrangements and state-dependent leadership structures do not just fall short of reconfiguring sovereignty's conceptual logics for Indigenous peoples because they are neocolonial technologies imposed on their own societies in North America. Instead, her contention was that Indigenous societies may also contribute through their own dependency to the hierarchical core-periphery relations that actively sustain the tight relations between the global North's parasitic overdevelopment and the global South's underdevelopment via colonial dispossession and extraction. Here, again, Indigenous decolonization is a relational project all the way down.

Conclusion

This book began with the NODAPL movement, among the latest in a long history of Indigenous articulations of decolonization and self-determination that reveal and confront the constitutively earth-destroying, antirelational violence of colonial sovereignty. Situated at the structural nexus between colonial sovereignty and capitalist resource extraction, the DAPL is one of the numerous pipeline projects the US Department of Homeland Security classifies as "critical infrastructure." Seen in a wider time frame, building the pipeline through treaty lands is another stratum of colonial sovereignty that reinscribes the underlying structural performance of sovereignty as colonial domination. Always tacitly a counterproject, this wave of colonial invasion erases, criminalizes, and contains alternative visions of self-determination on and for the earth.

By opposing colonial invasion and challenging the limits of mainstream environmental justice movements to address this history at its roots, the NODAPL water protectors dramatized the colonialism of the present. Specifically, they pointed to sovereignty's long-standing, recurrent *dis*ordering of entire forms of life. Sovereignty is both the justificatory grounds for colonial state violence and the conceptual frame that conceives a worldview in which politics necessitates creating the antirelational infrastructures of sovereign order. The water protectors mobilized the affinity and support of people around the globe through their efforts to remake local political authorities and even the planetary order on terms that refuse these pathologies. They reclaimed waters and lands for an alternative to colonial sovereignty: an intergenerational care-based politics oriented around relational and resurgent terms of self-determination.

Remapping Sovereignty draws into view some of the frequently overlooked or otherwise severely flattened intellectual lineages that have contributed to the historical, political, and normative depth grammars of this important twenty-first-century mobilization. By reading Zitkala-Ša (Yankton Dakota), Ella Deloria (Yankton Dakota), Vine Deloria Jr. (Yankton Dakota), George Manuel (Secwépmec), Lee Maracle (Stó:lō), and Howard Adams (Métis) alongside one another as theorists of Indigenous anticolonial struggles, the aim of this book has been to convey how they open up a series of alternative debates about construing the very agencies, philosophical substance, and normative horizons of decolonization in light of the question of sovereignty. By bringing sovereignty into view in its colonial roots and reproduction as an antirelational institution and conceptual logic that is quite compatible with the imperial and statist architecture of twentieth- and twenty-first-century global orders, I have sought to more fully attend to the critical purchase, material practices, and constructive visions of Indigenous approaches to decolonization. Here, decolonization means those political projects that seek to disentangle Indigenous self-determination from sovereignty, and to (re)invigorate relational networks that inform the very making of self-determination on these other terms. Indeed, remapping sovereignty, earthmaking, and transnational internationalism are all frameworks that draw out the interplay between anticolonial thought and agency. These conceptual rubrics help to conceive of "politics" as a task of reclaiming power from sovereignty and struggling for good relations all the way down. They throw into relief the many violent fantasies of suppressing relation that are the conceptual hallmark and political-cultural imprint of colonial and white supremacist sovereignty.

In this respect, the lineages of Indigenous decolonization reconstructed here are not just distinct from other anticolonial intellectual lineages by dint of their contextual location as a response to the "settler" axis of colonial power or because they have gone under the rubric of indigeneity, as is often tacitly presumed. Rather, they also propose *theoretically* rich ways of (re)thinking and enacting decolonization, so as to engender the institutional and imaginative architectures for survivable and emancipatory futures beyond colonialism. What follows from this are insights into the political-theoretic fashioning of anticolonial and decolonial futures. Very summarily, I point to several provisional findings that result for the practice of academic political theory. Of more general interest, I then consider the relation between (de)colonization and sovereignty in present-day North American and global politics.

The starting observation that there is still a notable lack of engagement in (especially) US-based political theory with the historical depth and specificity of Indigenous thinkers motivated me to adopt an interpretive approach that bridges close readings of these figures in context with detailed analysis of the conceptual import of their contributions for global anticolonial thought. This methodological point of departure enables a more productive reconstruction of the specific terms of these theoretical and political projects, as they have been debated and struggled over in the actual material contexts of anticolonial struggles. In doing so, I more broadly commend an approach to "decolonizing political theory" that focuses on the work of political theorizing that is situated in close proximity to the dilemmas of worldly and earthly anticolonialisms.[1] One of the main goals of this methodological orientation is to attend to the independently valuable insights that these lineages make available about core concepts, especially in view of their potential use in imagining a decolonial popular politics that puts front and center the task of dismantling the structural hierarchies that stem from colonialism and empire.

By addressing these thinkers in the context of anticolonial struggles, my aim is also to construct a more robust alternative to the plentiful array of work in political, social, and cultural theory that has tended to paradoxically benchmark these contributions simply for their divergence from and critique of the "West." Instead, I elucidate these pivotal yet overlooked thinkers as authors of independently valuable and capaciously transformative theories of sovereignty, self-determination, land, citizenship, capitalism, and decolonization. What follows from this is a conception of anticolonial critique that remains committed to examining the dilemmas that arise in navigating the layered materiality of political situations of colonial domination. I focus centrally (but not exclusively) on colonial sovereignty as a key concept and often a way of shorthanding in these lineages the overarching "meta-problem" of colonial rule.

One of the primary goals here has been to crystallize the political visions articulated in these interrelated projects as distinctive modes of anticolonial thought. These visions specifically make available an analysis of power and domination that is inseparable from those animating normative aspirations that are continually disrupted and displaced through colonial violence. My conception of earthmaking, for example, underscores how these activities are *political projects* of self-determination premised on reconceiving the substance, agencies, and normative horizons of decolonization. In this sense, earthmaking is neither derived from stereotyped attributes of Indigenous societies as intrinsically ecologically attuned nor is it solely to be framed as a response following mechanically from the specific form of settler-colonial domination. More simply put, earthmaking captures Indigenous decolonization practices as forged through the active *making* of alternatives through inheritance and reconceptualization. So, too, concepts like abduction and kinship provide a critique of the sovereign anthropocentrism of colonial violence that is rooted in constructive alternative imaginaries. More than "claims," these are ways of restructuring the underlying legitimacy principles of the planetary order, on offer by reconceiving, in light of these historically situated theoretical insights, the necessary practices of nondomination and pluralistic self-determination beyond sovereignty. In short, such reformulations would make for a politics oriented toward a far more egalitarian, free, and just planetary order. Those imaginaries that animate these terms of critique are suffused from the outset with a more capacious normativity informing the kinds of practices that might organize (or already do organize) collective life to allow for human and other-than-human flourishing. These can scale from local ecologies up to the planetary order.

What is more, my emphasis on the activist-intellectuals in this book as full-fledged social actors navigating the strategic spaces of politics, policy, and law and the long-term ideological underpinnings of each of these domains also carves out room for more productive ways for academic political theorists to take up the contributions of Indigenous studies. Specifically, I commend a more contextualized engagement than has been prominent in rather pro forma gestures among academic political theorists to the complex histories of Indigenous struggles. To take these intellectual histories themselves as the *source* of political theorizing contributes to a more direct understanding of the diverse and complex lineages of political and social thought that inform contemporary Indigenous anticolonial struggles.

What results is an approach that contributes to but also goes beyond recent efforts to integrate the useful but otherwise generic framework of "settler colonialism" into political theory's accounts of how colonialism, slavery, capitalism, and empire fundamentally shape modern political ideas and ideologies. This book has pursued a genealogically organized set of theoretical perspectives that draws into relief the significant available resources for rethinking political concepts within and alongside Indigenous thought, such as how the resurgent grammar of kinship transfigures the basic meaning and conceptual structures of (struggles for) treaty and self-determination (chapter 2). As a result, this approach also suggests fertile avenues to more systematically work with and adapt the already fruitful theoretical and methodological contributions of Indigenous studies (for example, the notion of remapping that I rethink from Mishuana Goeman), while still bringing to these Indigenous studies frames the traditional strengths of political theory in the critical analysis of political concepts. In short, adding settler colonialism as a "keyword" for political theory is not sufficient; this book suggests one path beyond it.

As an exercise in the history of political thought, the intellectual genealogies in this book thereby model an engagement with Indigenous political thought that insists on the philosophical integrity of the wide-ranging lineages that stem from different Indigenous societies. In pursuing this, however, I also reject the (often tacit) siloing of these lineages from the multiple bodies of theorizing with which they have been in dialogue throughout the twentieth century. From Zitkala-Ša's direct reflections on "small and subject peoples" at the Versailles Conference in 1919 (chapter 1) to Lee Maracle's poetics of decolonizing feminist transnationalism (chapter 4), Indigenous political thinkers have pursued diverse routes of intellectual adaptation and material solidarity that they have brought to bear to debate the political visions of Indigenous societies. What emerges here is the way that these thinkers triangulated the contentious frames of Indigenous nationhood (e.g., Yankton Dakota or Standing Rock Sioux or Ojibwe), pan-Indigenous solidarity (e.g., the Fourth World), settler sovereignty (e.g., US or Canadian thought), and many other transnational linkages (e.g., among them, Palestinian [trans]national liberation, the Non-Aligned Movement, Black Power, and African socialism). As political theorists and intellectual historians have increasingly deployed more transnational and comparative frames, the histories I trace suggest how concepts like George Manuel's Fourth World and resurgence are multilayered and multidirectional. They are (a) Indigenous concepts, (b) concepts of and as interventions into global anticolonial thought, and (c) they also bear the interpretive sediments of the multiple interpretive frames and political situations they sought to navigate (in this case, the sovereignty of Canadian multiculturalism, the land and law relations of Secwépmec peoplehood, Juilius Nyerere's attempts to indigenize socialism and developmentalism, and reflections on the common commitments of Indigenous peoples). Future work should and will trace other ways that Indigenous thinkers triangulated these and other frames and situations, and will show how taking up other thinkers or contexts shifts the terms of the integrity, circulation, and cross-fertilization of Indigenous anticolonialisms.

The effort to appreciate the multilayered and multidirectional character of twentieth century Indigenous political thinking without losing track of its integrity is also more than a methodological intervention into intellectual history. Such a focus more readily presents the substance of these interventions as universally affirmative projects. By virtue of their account of the problem of sovereignty in colonial modernity, these visions are able to fundamentally remake central political concepts by (for example) recasting self-determination and the equality of peoples as demanding liberation from (colonial and settler-colonial) states.[2]

More concretely for today's dilemmas, these lineages pose suggestive possibilities for the task of reorganizing collective life beyond sovereignty, in ways that specifically attend to the enduring reproduction of colonial structures of rule and domination in and through sovereignty. Recall that colonial sovereignty is shaped by, yet consistently must disavow (or perversely embrace), its unavoidable parasitic relation to anticolonial projects that seize the right to remake the earth on different terms.[3] One of the central concerns of this book is the urgent need to address the enduring and intractable conceptual logics of sovereignty that carry out the colonial domination of the earth itself as a bundle of natural resources, that is, territory and property. Among the problems with colonial sovereignty is that it entails the disavowal, spatial partitioning, and evisceration of more expansive responsibility-centered logics, which are and must be central to liberating both the earth itself and acutely racialized and gendered subjects whom colonial projects recurrently depict as the most denigrated and disposable in their proximity to "nature." At stake here is the material and existential way that earth-destroying violence in conjunction with racialized domination, deprivation, and underdevelopment pervade human and other-than-human life in all their deep and constitutive interrelations. In this respect, fully comprehending even the hierarchies within humanity stemming from colonialism's creation of the modern world through the world-obliterating expropriation and control of non-Western land and labor requires an account of the depth of these intersections between ecological and sociopolitical domination.

Here, these perspectives call for a profound change in the overarching relationship between sovereignty and decolonization, not only in North America but the world over. Politically, sovereignty and the state form have functioned as both a vessel for and the resulting edifice of settler-colonial domination. What this analysis further suggests is the need to radically disrupt and rethink the very notion of territorialized sovereignty—which includes democratic sovereignty—in favor of conceptions of local and globe-spanning plural and relational modes of self-determination against colonization. Put bluntly, there is no pluralizing (colonial) sovereignty; there is only countering and forging alternatives to it. Because sovereignty is a core element of this broader planetary order fashioned to make and enforce colonial hierarchies of race, class, and gender, it becomes necessary to rethink the transnational decolonization project in ways that open up alternatives to sovereignty. This is especially the case in relation to contemporary challenges like massive decarbonization.

It is a grave mistake to think that such an argument is exclusively about the ills of colonialism as visited on Indigenous peoples, whether in the global North or global South. Indigenous jurisdiction, knowledge, and co-authorized governance has long been at the front line of struggles for the rights of nature, land back, treaty rights, land trusts, food sovereignty, and protecting sacred sites.[4] Though mainstream Western environmental movements are only now catching up, these practices and more are pivotal to *any* suitably structurally capacious and rapidly pragmatic response to climate change understood as deeply rooted in the dependence of *our* form of life on colonial domination. Such practices take as their point of departure what Kyle Pows Whyte has theorized as the deep roots of ecological disaster in the prior, still-unfolding dystopia of settler colonialism for many Indigenous societies.[5] Justice and planetary flourishing (let alone survival) require adopting this longer view.

To be sure, paradigmatic entrenchments of sovereignty in racial hierarchy and colonial occupation press against hopes for moving toward this horizon. Existing trends in North American politics (e.g., climate denialism) nurture sovereignty in the sense of a fantasy of self-sufficient independence, specifically by materially embedding it in all-too-familiar psychic and political investments of the whiteness of the sovereign people and the inevitable violence (and abandonment) sanctioned by the colonial state. Though certainly not limited to the right, such investments operate even more intensely in the case of right-wing nominally antistatist politics, which claim to represent the true sovereign inheritances of the (violent) freedoms of the settler-colonial project.[6]

These attachments to domination only intensify the zero-sum logic of colonial sovereignty, even in the face of their all-but-suicidal implications for everyone except the wealthiest and most resourced in the global North.[7] This continues, despite (or perhaps because of) the seeming implosion of the idea of an expansionist frontier in North America that once resolved (or was imagined symbolically to have resolved) other kinds of social contradictions for settler-colonial societies (e.g., those of class). And, as always, it of course contributes to the stranglehold of white supremacy on control over racialized others' territories and bodies.[8] Yet if there are already signs of white colonial sovereignty's crumbling or "waning" status, it is striking that it is still desperately protected and expanded upon in the doubling down on and braiding together of xenophobic nationalism and fossil fuel politics amid the global authoritarian turn.[9] All this comes as the result more proximately of Western imperial decline and catastrophic climate change, but colonial sovereignty as concept and logic continues to animate many of these forces.

Notwithstanding these dire investments in colonial sovereignty, Indigenous decolonization projects continue to build upon the lineages examined in this book to enact and imagine an alternative politics. It is therefore urgent to attend to those philosophical and political practices of self-determination that remap sovereignty, remake the earth, and pursue transnational international solidarities so as to care for life in and as connection to other life.

Acknowledgments

The inspiration for this book came about at the University of Minnesota, Twin Cities, what now feels like a lifetime ago, around 2013. There, I benefited and continue to benefit from excellent mentorship under Joan Tronto, Bud Duvall, Nancy Luxon, Robert Nichols, and Jeani O'Brien.

I am deeply grateful to the network of supportive colleagues and friends who have read my writing with a critical and discerning eye since we finished graduate school at Minnesota. Fortunately for me, coauthorship and friendship with Adam Dahl has allowed us an excuse to share endless discussions that frequently spurred key advances in my thinking on the book. I am also grateful to Chris Stone, Chase Hobbs-Morgan, Charmaine Chua, and Bryan Nakayama for their intellectual comradeship in and since graduate school.

I arrived at the University of Michigan–Ann Arbor in the fall of 2017. Thank-you to my political science colleagues at Michigan for welcoming me to Ann Arbor and creating a wonderful environment for junior faculty to bring projects such as this one to fruition. Thanks to Liz Wingrove especially for her tireless mentorship and support of every conceivable effort to provide me with the time and space to realize the book's potential. Along the way, I also benefited from advice, feedback (often, several rounds), and encouragement from many colleagues. For that and more at various critical moments in my journey with the book, I am thankful to my political theory and theory-adjacent colleagues in particular: Liz Wingrove, Lisa Disch, Arlene Saxonhouse, Mika Lavaque-Manty, Mariah Zeisberg, Don Herzog, Pam Brandwein, Rob Mickey, and Anne Manuel. I am also grateful to my newest colleagues, Murad Idris and Annie Heffernan, who have offered equal parts humor and equanimity as we navigated the dark and weird realities of the COVID-19 pandemic together.

My colleagues in the Native American Studies Program at the University of Michigan also invited me into a rich community of scholars that has been invaluable to this book's development. Joe Gone, Greg Dowd, Phil Deloria,

Robin Beck, Michael Witgen, Alphonse Pitawanakwat, Arland Thornton, and Kayla Gonyon all helped to welcome me into the NAS community. More recently, I have been very lucky to benefit from steadfast collegiality and feedback from Barb Meek, Bethany Hughes, Amy Stillman, Kyle Whyte, and Matt Fletcher.

I really began to figure out what this book was actually going to do as a result of the extensive (and good-humored!) feedback I received from the participants in my January 2019 manuscript workshop in Ann Arbor: Audra Simpson, Glen Coulthard, Greg Dowd, and Liz Wingrove. I thank Audra and Glen for flying all the way to Ann Arbor that winter, and for their incredible mentorship, collegiality, and support of the book in those earlier stages (and since).

I presented work from this book in several venues: the American Political Science Association, the Association for Political Theory, the Western Political Science Association, the American Anthropology Association, the Native American and Indigenous Studies Association, the Caribbean Philosophical Association, the Society for Historians of American Foreign Relations, the Newberry Library American Indian Studies Speaker Series, and the University of Toledo Political Science and Public Policy Speaker Series. At the University of Michigan, I also benefited from presenting at the Political Theory Workshop and the Native American Studies Faculty Workshop and participated in the inspiring roundtable "Radical Futures through Indigenous Political Thought" at the Eisenberg Institute for Historical Studies thanks to an invitation from Minnie Sinha.

For research and editing support on chapters 3 and 4 in particular, I am grateful to the careful reading provided by David Suell. I also benefited from research assistance and, even more so, enthusiastic conversations with a number of graduate students pursuing their own brilliant projects, including Merisa Sahin, Janice Feng, Maria Lovetere, Tom Klemm, Lucy Peterson, Amir Fleischmann, Charlotte Boucher, and Max Lykins.

Finishing this book would not have been possible without generous support from the Institute for the Humanities at the University of Michigan in 2021–22, during which time I undertook the bulk of final revisions. I benefited immensely from time at the IH and from the weekly seminar of faculty and graduate student fellows, at which I received pivotal feedback on the introduction to the book from Chandan Reddy, Lisa Nakamura, Hanah Stiverson, Samer Ali, Victor Mendoza, Ian Shin, Ellen Muehlenberger, Emily Lamond, Chis Molnar, Marisol Fila, Liz McNeil, and Raquel Vieira Parrine Sant'Ana. The IH gave me back the sense of an intellectual community I had lost during the long haul of the COVID-19 pandemic, which was indispensable for the morale necessary to finish the book. I am grateful to Peggy McCracken, Gretchen O'Hair, and the entire cohort of fellows.

While authors are obliged to streamline books into one or a few strands of argumentation, a book often feels much more to this author like walking through a labyrinth of conversations with many brilliant and generous scholars—on panels and roundtables, in the halls of conferences, getting drinks and food, and now more on Zoom calls. For conversations throughout the years, I thank Burke Hendrix, Angélica Bernal, Hagar Kotef, Jakeet Singh, Jane Anna Gordon, Inder Marwah, Cristina Beltrán, Alex Livingston, Yasmeen Daifallah, Anuja Bose, Heidi Kiiwetinepinesiik Stark, Uahikea Maile, Leigh Jenco, Roxanne Euben, Ben McKean, Inés Valdez, Renee Heberle, Corey Snelgrove, Elena Gambino, Arturo Chang, Tim Waligore, Yann-Allard Tremblay, Jeanne Morefield, Peggy Kohn, Keally McBride, Sam Chambers, PJ Brendese, Josh Simon, Eli Meyerhoff, Andrew Dilts, Alex Hirsch, Alyosha Goldstein, Jodi Melamed, Heather Pool, Aziz Rana, Andrew Valls, Yves Winter, Helen Kinsella, Ali Aslam, Fred Lee, Kevin Olson, Shuk Ying Chan, Nazmul Sultan, Lorna Bracewell, Lucie Kyrova, Erin Pineda, Çiğdem Çidam, Kennan Ferguson, Nick Estes, Joan Cocks, Charles Lee, Kevin Bruyneel, David Williams, Paul Gutierrez, Tacuma Peters, Nev Köker, Antonio Vazquez-Arroyo, Kathy Ferguson, Tom Dumm, Toby Rollo, Joe Soss, Lester Spence, Rose Miron, Fred Hoxie, Michael Asch, and Emma Feltes. I have forgotten someone—likely more than one someone—with whom I've had valuable conversations relating to this project, so my apologies to anyone who does not appear on this list but should.

I have been very lucky to benefit from conversations with family members of some the thinkers that are the focus of this book. I thank them for this and their affordance to access materials. I thank Doreen Manuel for allowing me to listen to the taped interviews between George Manuel and Michael Posluns that formed the foundation of *The Fourth World*. Thanks to Anne St. Orange and other archivists at York University for processing those tapes. Thank-you to Ska-Hiish Manuel for his generation's continued activism and for sharing chance time talking with me. And thank you Michael Posluns (z"l) and Marilyn Eisenstadt for your time and generosity during my visit to work through Michael's archive at York University in Toronto. And of course thanks are due again to Phil Deloria.

Thank-you to Chuck Myers for his enthusiasm right at the start for the book, to Sara Doskow at the University of Chicago Press for shepherding the book to print, and to Mark Reschke for excellent copyediting. Three anonymous reviewers offered incredibly valuable constructive feedback and commentary, and the book's arguments are far sharper as a result.

I would like to thank my extended family, who provided me with so much support as I was attempting to balance writing, teaching, and child care during the grueling course of the COVID-19 pandemic. Thanks especially to my parents, Hilda Rosenberg and Andy Temin, and to my brother Josh Temin.

None of this would have been possible without Grace Christiansen. There are not enough words of gratitude I could conjure up to do justice to what her partnership, friendship, love, and co-parenting wizardry mean to me. And thank-you to Lev, our heart, for his love and support for his Dada.

Notes

INTRODUCTION

1. Winona LaDuke, *All Our Relations: Native Struggles for Land and Life* (Cambridge: South End Press, 1999), 50.

2. Edward Valandra, "We Are Blood Relatives: No to the DAPL," *Hot Spots, Fieldsites*, December 22, 2016, https://culanth.org/fieldsights/we-are-blood-relatives-no-to-the-dapl.

3. The pipeline has been built, but it is not supposed to be in operation after a July 2020 district court ruling that further environmental review is still required. Nevertheless, Energy Transfer Partners continues to send oil through the pipeline and expand the number of pump stations, despite the lack of a federal permit to cross the Missouri River. See "The NODAPL Movement," special issue, *Indian Country Today*, Fall 2016; Nick Estes, *Our History Is the Future: Standing Rock versus the Dakota Access Pipeline, and the Long Tradition of Indigenous Resistance* (New York: Verso, 2019).

4. Mishuana Goeman, *Mark My Words: Native Women Mapping Our Nations* (Minneapolis: University of Minnesota Press, 2013), 2.

5. On treaty constitutionalism, or treaty federalism, see James Tully, *Strange Multiplicity: Constitutionalism in an Age of Diversity* (Cambridge: Cambridge University Press, 1995); John Borrows, "Wampum at Niagara: The Royal Proclamation, Canadian Legal History, and Self-Government," in *Aboriginal and Treaty Rights in Canada: Essays on Law, Equity, and Respect for Difference*, ed. Michael Asch (Vancouver: University of British Columbia Press, 1997), 155–72; Sharon Venne, "Understanding Treaty 6: An Indigenous Perspective," in *Aboriginal and Treaty Rights in Canada: Essays on Law, Equity, and Respect for Difference* (Vancouver: University of British Columbia Press, 1997), 173–207; Robert A. Williams Jr., *Linking Arms Together: American Indian Treaty Visions of Law and Peace, 1600–1800* (New York: Routledge, 1999); Richard Day, "Who Is This We That Gives the Gift? Native American Political Theory and the Western Tradition," *Critical Horizons* 2, no. 2 (February 17, 2001): 173–201; Kiera L. Ladner, "Treaty Federalism: An Indigenous Vision of Canadian Federalisms," in *New Trends in Federalism* (Peterborough, ON: Broadview Press, 2009), 167–96; John Borrows, *Canada's Indigenous Constitution* (Toronto: University of Toronto, 2010); Maggie Blackhawk, "Federal Indian Law as Paradigm within Public Law," *Harvard Law Review* 132, no. 7 (May 2019): 1787–1877.

6. I follow Kohn and McBride's account of a "political theory of decolonization." It explains "imperial subordination, provides a call to arms, establishes the terms of independence, and lays out a blueprint for the future." Margaret Kohn and Keally McBride,

Political Theories of Decolonization: Postcolonialism and the Problem of Foundations (New York: Oxford University Press, 2011), 50.

7. For the "long red power movement," see Doug Kiel, "Competing Visions of Empowerment: Oneida Progressive-Era Politics and Writing Tribal Histories," *Ethnohistory* 61, no. 3 (Summer 2014): 419–44.

8. Iris Marion Young, "Two Concepts of Self-Determination," in *Ethnicity, Nationalism, and Minority Rights*, ed. Stephen May, Tariq Modood, and Judith Squires (New York: Cambridge University Press, 2004), 176–96; Lorenzo Veracini, "Settler Colonialism and Decolonisation," *Borderlands E-Journal* 6, no. 2 (2007); Mahmood Mamdani, *Neither Settler nor Native: The Making and Unmaking of Permanent Minorities* (Cambridge, MA: Harvard University Press, 2020).

9. Hent Kalmo and Quentin Skinner, eds., *Sovereignty in Fragments: The Past, Present and Future of a Contested Concept* (Cambridge: Cambridge University Press, 2010).

10. For accounts of sovereignty that also advance the notion that we ought to think about it in terms of conceptual "logics" that are "worldview-conceiving" or "symbolic forms," see Jonathan Havercroft, *Captives of Sovereignty* (Cambridge: Cambridge University Press, 2011); Jens Bartelson, *Sovereignty as Symbolic Form* (London: Routledge, 2014); Paul Nadasdy, *Sovereignty's Entailments: First Nation State Formation in the Yukon* (Toronto: University of Toronto, 2017); Christian Volk, "The Problem of Sovereignty in Globalized Times," *Law, Culture and the Humanities* 18, no. 3 (October 2022): 716–38.

11. I am indebted here to the excellent discussion of the conceptual features of sovereignty in Don Herzog, *Sovereignty, RIP* (New Haven, CT: Yale University Press, 2020).

12. On "constitutive exclusion," see Sina Kramer, *Excluded Within: The (Un)Intelligibility of Radical Political Actors* (Oxford: Oxford University Press, 2017).

13. Jodi A. Byrd, "Indigenous Futures beyond the Sovereignty Debate," in *The Cambridge History of Native American Literature*, ed. Melanie Benson Taylor (Cambridge: Cambridge University Press, 2020), 501. For some key interventions in the "sovereignty debate," see Gerald Taiaiake Alfred, *Heeding the Voices of Our Ancestors: Kahnawake Mohawk Politics and the Rise of Native Nationalism* (New York: Oxford University Press, 1995); Robert Warrior, *Tribal Secrets: Recovering American Indian Intellectual Traditions* (Minneapolis: University of Minnesota Press, 1994); Joanne Barker, "For Whom Sovereignty Matters," in *For Whom Sovereignty Matters: Locations of Contestation and Possibility in Indigenous Struggles for Self-Determination*, ed. Joanne Barker (Lincoln: University of Nebraska Press, 2005), 1–31; Joanne Barker, ed., *Critically Sovereign: Indigenous Gender, Sexuality, and Feminist Studies* (Durham, NC: Duke University Press, 2017).

14. Cf. David E. Wilkins and Heidi Kiiwetinepinesiik Stark, *American Indian Politics and the American Political System*, 3rd ed. (Lanham, MD: Rowman & Littlefield, 2010).

15. Audra Simpson, *Mohawk Interruptus: Political Life across the Borders of Settler-States* (Durham, NC: Duke University Press, 2014), 105.

16. Amanda J. Cobb, "Understanding Tribal Sovereignty: Definitions, Conceptualizations, and Interpretations," *American Studies* 46, no. 3/4 (2005): 125; Scott Richard Lyons, "Rhetorical Sovereignty: What Do American Indians Want from Writing?," *College Composition and Communication* 51, no. 3 (2000): 42.

17. Put otherwise, in using the term "Indigenous self-determination," I am not in any way aiming to police Indigenous societies' sovereignty or uses of the term "sover-

eignty" as it stems from their own political struggles. Instead, I mark contrasts to the genealogy of sovereignty in Western political thought.

18. The term "settler colonialism" emerged in the 2000s and is widely attributed to the late Patrick Wolfe. It refers to an axis of colonial violence in which the colonizing society ("settlers") steals the land of the original peoples ("Indigenous") to form the territorial basis of a new, independent society, or state. The prerogative of colonization is, therefore, getting Indigenous societies out of the way of land acquisition, not exploiting the labor of the colonized. See Patrick Wolfe, *Settler Colonialism and the Transformation of Anthropology* (London: Cassell, 1999); Patrick Wolfe, "Settler Colonialism and the Elimination of the Native," *Journal of Genocide Research* 8, no. 4 (December 2006): 387–409; Caroline Elkins and Susan Pedersen, eds., *Settler Colonialism in the Twentieth Century: Projects, Practices, Legacies* (New York: Routledge, 2005); Lorenzo Veracini, *Settler Colonialism: A Theoretical Overview* (London: Palgrave Macmillan UK, 2010).

19. Yves Winter, "Conquest," *Political Concepts: A Critical Lexicon* 1 (2011), http://www.politicalconcepts.org/conquest-winter/; Joan Cocks, "Foundational Violence and the Politics of Erasure," *Radical Philosophy Review* 15, no. 1 (2012): 103–26; Kevin Bruyneel, *Settler Memory: The Disavowal of Indigeneity and the Politics of Race in the United States* (Chapel Hill: University of North Carolina Press, 2021).

20. Cf. Robert Nichols, *Theft Is Property! The Recursive Logic of Dispossession* (Durham, NC: Duke University Press, 2020), 35–43.

21. On settler sovereignty as imposition of jurisdiction, see Lisa Ford, *Settler Sovereignty: Jurisdiction and Indigenous People in America and Australia, 1788–1836* (Cambridge, MA: Harvard University Press, 2010).

22. Lorenzo Veracini, *The Settler Colonial Present* (London: Palgrave Macmillan UK, 2015).

23. On a pluralistic "ethos of sovereignty," see William E. Connolly, *Pluralism* (Durham, NC: Duke University Press, 2005), 145.

24. Karena Shaw lays out this Hobbesian lineage of sovereignty in settler societies like Canada. Karena Shaw, *Indigeneity and Political Theory: Sovereignty and the Limits of the Political* (New York: Routledge, 2008).

25. Joel Olson, *The Abolition of White Democracy* (Minneapolis: University of Minnesota Press, 2004); Aziz Rana, *The Two Faces of American Freedom* (Cambridge, MA: Harvard University Press, 2014); Cocks, "Foundational Violence and the Politics of Erasure"; Joan Cocks, *On Sovereignty and Other Political Delusions* (New York: Bloomsbury, 2014); Lisa Lowe, *The Intimacies of Four Continents* (Durham, NC: Duke University Press, 2015); Adam Dahl, *Empire of the People: Settler Colonialism and the Foundations of Modern Democratic Thought* (Lawrence: University Press of Kansas, 2018); Michael G. Hanchard, *The Spectre of Race: How Discrimination Haunts Western Democracy* (Princeton, NJ: Princeton University Press, 2018); Daniel Martinez HoSang and Joseph E. Lowndes, *Producers, Parasites, Patriots: Race and the New Right-Wing Politics of Precarity* (Minneapolis: University of Minnesota Press, 2019); Jakeet Singh, "Decolonizing Radical Democracy," *Contemporary Political Theory* 18, no. 3 (2019): 331–56; Achille Mbembe, *Necropolitics* (Durham, NC: Duke University Press, 2019); Cristina Beltrán, *Cruelty as Citizenship: How Migrant Suffering Sustains White Democracy* (Minneapolis: University of Minnesota Press, 2020); Michael Gorup, "The Strange Fruit of the Tree of Liberty: Lynch Law and Popular Sovereignty in the United States," *Perspectives on Politics* 18, no. 3 (September 2020): 819–34; David Myer

Temin, "Our Democracy: Laura Cornelius Kellogg's Decolonial-Democracy," in "Race and Politics in America," special issue, *Perspectives on Politics* 19, no. 4: (December 2021): 1082–97; Inés Valdez, "Socialism and Empire: Labor Mobility, Racial Capitalism, and the Political Theory of Migration," *Political Theory* 49, no. 6 (December 1, 2021): 902–33; Tyler Stovall, *White Freedom: The Racial History of an Idea* (Princeton, NJ: Princeton University Press, 2021); Elisabeth R. Anker, *Ugly Freedoms* (Durham, NC: Duke University Press, 2022); Yann Allard-Tremblay, "The Two Row Wampum: Decolonizing and Indigenizing Democratic Autonomy," *Polity* 54, no. 2 (April 2022): 225–49; Inés Valdez, "Empire, Popular Sovereignty, and the Problem of Self-and-Other-Determination," *Perspectives on Politics*, February 14, 2022, 1–17, https://doi.org/10.1017/S1537592721003674.

26. Though there are important recent exceptions that use a political development lens, especially Paul Frymer, *Building an American Empire: The Era of Territorial and Political Expansion* (Princeton, NJ: Princeton University Press, 2017).

27. Dahl, *Empire of the People: Settler Colonialism and the Foundations of Modern Democratic Thought*.

28. Lindsay G. Robertson, *Conquest by Law: How the Discovery of America Dispossessed Indigenous Peoples of Their Lands* (New York: Oxford University Press, 2007); Gregory Ablavsky, "The Savage Constitution," *Duke Law Journal* 63, no. 5 (February 1, 2014): 999–1046; Heidi Kiiwetinepinesiik Stark, "Criminal Empire: The Making of the Savage in a Lawless Land," *Theory & Event* 19, no. 4 (2016).

29. The Red Nation, *The Red Deal: Indigenous Action to Save Our Earth* (Brooklyn, NY: Common Notions, 2021), 25.

30. On "violent attachments," see Hagar Kotef, *The Colonizing Self: Or, Home and Homelessness in Israel/Palestine* (Durham, NC: Duke University Press Books, 2020).

31. Aileen Moreton-Robinson, *The White Possessive: Power, Property, and Indigenous Sovereignty* (Minneapolis: University of Minnesota Press, 2015).

32. Quentin Skinner, *Liberty before Liberalism* (New York: Cambridge University Press, 1998), 49; Cécile Laborde, "Republicanism and Global Justice: A Sketch," *European Journal of Political Theory* 9, no. 1 (January 1, 2010): 48–69; Phillip Petit, "The Globalized Republican Ideal," *Global Justice: Theory, Practice, Rhetoric* 9, no. 1 (2016): 47–68. On the amnesia about race and empire in central global justice debates, see the essays in Duncan Bell, ed., *Empire, Race and Global Justice* (Cambridge: Cambridge University Press, 2019).

33. See, e.g., Sharon R. Krause, *Freedom beyond Sovereignty: Reconstructing Liberal Individualism* (Chicago: University of Chicago Press, 2015).

34. On sovereignty as anthropocentric, see Alexander Wendt and Raymond Duvall, "Sovereignty and the UFO," *Political Theory* 36, no. 4 (August 1, 2008): 607–33.

35. Uday Singh Mehta, *Liberalism and Empire: A Study in Nineteenth-Century British Liberal Thought* (Chicago: University of Chicago Press, 1999); Sankar Muthu, *Enlightenment against Empire* (Princeton, NJ: Princeton University Press, 2003); Jeanne Morefield, *Covenants without Swords: Idealist Liberalism and the Spirit of Empire* (Princeton, NJ: Princeton University Press, 2005); Jennifer Pitts, *A Turn to Empire: The Rise of Imperial Liberalism in Britain and France* (Princeton, NJ: University of Princeton, 2006); Jennifer Pitts, "Political Theory of Empire and Imperialism," *Annual Review of Political Science* 13 (2010): 211–35; Jeanne Morefield, *Empires without Imperialism: Anglo-American Decline and the Politics of Deflection* (Oxford: Oxford University Press, 2014); Inder S. Marwah et al., "Empire and Its Afterlives," *Contemporary Political*

Theory 19, no. 2 (June 1, 2020): 274–305. On settler colonialism, see Duncan Bell, *The Idea of Greater Britain: Empire and the Future of World Order, 1860–1900* (Princeton, NJ: Princeton University Press, 2011); Rana, *The Two Faces of American Freedom*; Duncan Bell, *Reordering the World: Essays on Liberalism and Empire* (Princeton, NJ: Princeton University Press, 2016); Dahl, *Empire of the People: Settler Colonialism and the Foundations of Modern Democratic Thought*; Onur Ulas Ince, *Colonial Capitalism and the Dilemmas of Liberalism* (New York: Cambridge University Press, 2018).

36. Karuna Mantena, "Popular Sovereignty and Anti-Colonialism," in *Popular Sovereignty in Historical Perspective*, ed. Richard Bourke and Quentin Skinner (New York: Cambridge University Press, 2016), 301. A nonexhaustive list of these recent interventions in what I would call "global anticolonial thought" include Karuna Mantena, "On Gandhi's Critique of the State: Sources, Contexts, Conjunctures," *Modern Intellectual History* 9, no. 3 (November 2012): 535–63; Frederick Cooper, *Citizenship between Empire and Nation: Remaking France and French Africa, 1945–1960* (Princeton, NJ: Princeton University Press, 2014); Gary Wilder, *Freedom Time: Negritude, Decolonization, and the Future of the World* (Durham, NC: Duke University Press, 2015); Adom Getachew, *Worldmaking after Empire: The Rise and Fall of Self-Determination* (Princeton, NJ: Princeton University Press, 2019); Murad Idris, *War for Peace: Genealogies of a Violent Ideal in Western and Islamic Thought* (New York: Oxford University Press, 2019); Yasmeen Daifallah, "The Politics of Decolonial Interpretation: Tradition and Method in Contemporary Arab Thought," *American Political Science Review* 113, no. 3 (August 2019): 810–23; Inder S. Marwah, "Provincializing Progress: Developmentalism and Anti-Imperialism in Colonial India," *Polity* 51, no. 3 (July 2019): 498–531; Nichols, *Theft Is Property! The Recursive Logic of Dispossession*; Nazmul S. Sultan, "Self-Rule and the Problem of Peoplehood in Colonial India," *American Political Science Review* 114, no. 1 (February 2020): 81–94; Nazmul S. Sultan, "Between the Many and the One: Anticolonial Federalism and Popular Sovereignty," *Political Theory*, June 23, 2021, https://doi.org/10.1177/00905917211018534; Tejas Parasher, "Beyond Parliament: Gandhian Democracy and Postcolonial Founding," *Political Theory*, May 10, 2022, https://doi.org/10.1177/00905917221092821; David Myer Temin, "Development in Decolonization: Walter Rodney, Third World Developmentalism, and 'Decolonizing Political Theory,'" *American Political Science Review*, July 18, 2022, https://doi.org/10.1017/S0003055422000570.

37. Getachew, *Worldmaking after Empire: The Rise and Fall of Self-Determination*, 28.

38. I use the language of *making* so as to emphasize the active agencies, protocols, struggles, etc., required to actually generate co-constitutive relations of flourishing with the earth. I intend my emphasis to be on making as an *activity* to be read in contrast to stereotypes that Indigenous peoples just are naturally ecologically attuned as such. My use of "making," then, is not seeking to re-ascribe a self-positing sovereign subjectivity to Indigenous peoples. Instead, earthmaking aims to encapsulate an actively relational way of creating structures of self-determination and transforming the broader structural and normative contours of the planetary order. Thanks to Chandan Reddy for alerting me to potential resonances of this term.

39. Cocks, *On Sovereignty and Other Political Delusions*; Dahl, *Empire of the People: Settler Colonialism and the Foundations of Modern Democratic Thought*, 184–94.

40. For methodological nationalism's classic reference point, see Andreas Wimmer and Nina Glick Schiller, "Methodological Nationalism and Beyond: Nation-State Building, Migration and the Social Sciences," *Global Networks: A Journal of Transnational*

Affairs 2, no. 4 (October 2002): 301–34. I often refer to "methodological statism" throughout the book because of my focus on state sovereignty, which is not limited to nationalism per se.

41. On the "boundaries of the international," see Jennifer Pitts, *Boundaries of the International: Law and Empire* (Cambridge, MA: Harvard University Press, 2018).

42. On Indigenous internationalism in this vein, see Ronald Niezen, *The Origins of Indigenism: Human Rights and the Politics of Identity* (Berkeley: University of California Press, 2003), 4; Hanne Hagdvet Vik, "Indigenous Internationalism," in *Internationalisms: A Twentieth Century History*, ed. Glenda Sluga and Patricia Clavin (New York: Cambridge University Press, 2017), 315–39; Tim Rowse, "The Indigenous Redemption of Liberal Universalism," in *Colonial Exchanges: Political Theory and the Agency of the Colonized*, ed. Burke A. Hendrix and Deborah Baumgold (Manchester: Manchester University Press, 2017), 133–55.

43. Cf. Sheryl R. Lightfoot, "The Pessimism Traps of Indigenous Resurgence," in *Pessimism in International Relations: Provocations, Possibilities, Politics*, ed. Tim Stevens and Nicholas Michelsen (London: Palgrave, 2019), 155–72.

44. Classic works on the politics of defining Indigenous nationalisms and nationhood/peoplehood include Elizabeth Cook-Lynn, "The American Indian Fiction Writer: 'Cosmopolitanism, Nationalism, the Third World, and First Nation Sovereignty,'" *Wicazo Sa Review* 9, no. 2 (Autumn 1993): 26–36; Alfred, *Heeding the Voices of Our Ancestors: Kahnawake Mohawk Politics and the Rise of Native Nationalism*; Tom Holm, J. Diane Pearson, and Ben Chavis, "Peoplehood: A Model for the Extension of Sovereignty in American Indian Studies," *Wicazo Sa Review* 18, no. 1 (Spring 2003): 7–24; Jace Weaver, Craig S. Womack, and Robert Warrior, *American Indian Literary Nationalism* (Albuquerque: University of New Mexico Press, 2005); Scott Richard Lyons, *X-Marks: Native Signatures of Assent* (Minneapolis: University of Minnesota Press, 2010). For this more recent work on Indigenous internationalisms, see Joseph Baurkemper and Heidi Kiiwetinepinesiik Stark, "The Trans/National Terrain of Anishinaabe Law and Diplomacy," *Journal of Transnational American Studies* 4, no. 1 (2012); Goeman, *Mark My Words: Native Women Mapping Our Nations*; Mishuana R. Goeman, "Disrupting a Settler-Colonial Grammar of Place: The Visual Memoir of Hulleah Tsinhnahjinnie," in *Theorizing Native Studies*, ed. Audra Simpson and Andrea Smith (Durham, NC: Duke University Press, 2014), 235–65; Estes, *Our History Is the Future: Standing Rock versus the Dakota Access Pipeline, and the Long Tradition of Indigenous Resistance*; Leanne Betasamosake Simpson, *As We Have Always Done: Indigenous Freedom through Radical Resistance* (Minneapolis: University of Minnesota Press, 2017); Glen Sean Coulthard, "Once Were Maoists: Third World Currents in Fourth World Anti-Colonialism, Vancouver, 1967–1975," in *Routledge Handbook of Critical Indigenous Studies* (New York: Routledge, 2020), 378–91; Emma Feltes and Sharon Venne, "Decolonization, Not Patriation: The Constitution Express at the Russell Tribunal," *BC Studies* 212 (Winter 2021): 65–100.

45. Manu Goswami, "Imaginary Futures and Colonial Internationalisms," *American Historical Review* 117, no. 5 (December 2012): 1461–85.

46. James (Sa'ke'j) Youngblood Henderson, *Indigenous Diplomacy and the Rights of Peoples: Achieving UN Recognition* (Saskatoon: Purich Publishing Limited, 2008), 35.

47. Phillip J. Deloria, *Indians in Unexpected Places* (Lawrence: University Press of Kansas, 2004).

48. Leanne Simpson, "Looking after Gdoo-Naaganinaa: Precolonial Nishnaabeg

Diplomatic and Treaty Relationships," *Wicazo Sa Review* 23, no. 2 (October 8, 2008): 29–42.

49. Margaret E. Keck and Kathryn Sikkink, *Activists beyond Borders: Advocacy Networks in International Politics* (Ithaca, NY: Cornell University Press, 1998).

50. See also Robbie Shilliam, *The Black Pacific: Anti-Colonial Struggles and Oceanic Connections* (New York: Bloomsbury, 2015); Sheryl Lightfoot, *Global Indigenous Politics: A Subtle Revolution* (New York: Routledge, 2016).

51. Despite my use of transnational internationalism to render the specificity of Indigenous mobilizations, this framework resonates with what Inés Valdez calls "transnational cosmopolitanism" (as well as other modes of radical or subaltern cosmopolitanism). Inés Valdez, *Transnational Cosmopolitanism: Kant, Du Bois, and Justice as a Political Craft* (Cambridge: Cambridge University Press, 2019).

52. Dale Turner, *This Is Not a Peace Pipe: Towards a Critical Indigenous Philosophy* (Toronto: University of Toronto Press, 2006); David Martinez, *The American Indian Intellectual Tradition: An Anthology of Writings from 1772 to 1972* (Ithaca, NY: Cornell University Press, 2011); Robin Kimmerer, "Restoration and Reciprocity: The Contributions of Traditional Ecological Knowledge," in *Human Dimensions of Ecological Restoration: Integrating Science, Nature, and Culture*, ed. Dave Egan, Evan E. Hjerpe, and Jesse Abrams (Washington, DC: Island Press, 2011), 257–76; Linda Tuhiwai Smith, *Decolonizing Methodologies: Research and Indigenous Peoples*, 2nd ed. (London: Zed Books, 2012); Simpson, *As We Have Always Done: Indigenous Freedom through Radical Resistance*; Toby Rollo, "Back to the Rough Ground: Textual, Oral and Enactive Meaning in Comparative Political Theory," *European Journal of Political Theory* 20, no. 3 (2021): 379–97.

53. Duncan Ivison, Paul Patton, and Will Sanders, eds., *Political Theory and the Rights of Indigenous Peoples* (New York: Cambridge University Press, 2000); Simpson, *Mohawk Interruptus: Political Life across the Borders of Settler-States*, 11; Kevin Bruyneel, "Social Science and the Study of Indigenous People's Politics: Contributions, Omissions, and Tensions," in *Oxford Handbook of Indigenous Peoples' Politics*, ed. José Antonio Lucero, Dale Turner, and Donna Lee Vancott (New York: Oxford University Press, 2014), https://www.oxfordhandbooks.com/view/10.1093/oxfordhb/9780195386653.001.0001/oxfordhb-9780195386653-e-008.

CHAPTER ONE

1. Zitkala-Ša, "Letter to Arthur C. Parker (December 21, 1916)," in *Zitkala-Ša: Letters, Speeches, and Unpublished Writings, 1898–1929*, ed. Tadeusz Lewandowski (Leiden: Brill, 2018), 135–37.

2. Gertrude Bonnin (Zitkala-Ša), Charles H. Fabens, and Matthew K. Sniffen, *Oklahoma's Poor Rich Indians: An Orgy of Graft and Exploitation of the Five Civilized Tribes—Legalized Robbery* (Philadelphia: Office of the Indian Rights Association, 1924), 32.

3. This chapter is an extensively revised version of David Myer Temin, "Custer's Sins: Vine Deloria Jr. and the Settler-Colonial Politics of Civic Inclusion," *Political Theory* 46, no. 3 (2018): 357–79.

4. Robert Yellowtail, "An Address: In Defense of the Rights of the Crow Indians and the Indians Generally, before the Senate Committee of Indian Affairs," *American Indian Magazine* 8, no. 3 (September 9, 1919): 133; Frederick E. Hoxie, *Parading through*

History: The Making of the Crow Nation in America, 1805–1935 (New York: Cambridge University Press, 1995), 263–64.

5. Yellowtail, "An Address: In Defense of the Rights of the Crow Indians and the Indians Generally, before the Senate Committee of Indian Affairs": 133.

6. Wilson sought to contain internationalist socialist support for colonial self-determination by interpreting self-determination late in the war as a conservative and gradualist principle compatible with the tutelary rule of Western world powers over non-Western peoples in need of "instruction" for self-government. V. I. Lenin, "The Right of Nations to Self-Determination," in *Collected Works* (Moscow: Progress Publishers, 1972), 393–454, https://www.marxists.org/archive/lenin/works/1914/self-det/; Erez Manela, *The Wilsonian Moment: Self-Determination and the International Origins of Anticolonial Nationalism* (New York: Oxford University Press, 2007), 1–43; Marilyn Lake and Henry Reynolds, *Drawing the Global Colour Line: White Men's Countries and the International Challenge of Racial Equality* (Cambridge: Cambridge University Press, 2008); Getachew, *Worldmaking after Empire: The Rise and Fall of Self-Determination*.

7. Wilson's desire to maintain and extend anti-Black racism is well known. His academic writings likewise supported colonial conquest, the "Anglo-Saxon's" duty of "territorial expansion." Woodrow Wilson, "Democracy and Efficiency (October 1, 1900)," in *The Papers of Woodrow Wilson*, ed. Arthur S. Link, vol. 12 (Princeton, NJ: Princeton University Press, 1972), 11–12.

8. Janet McDowell, "Competency Commissions and Indian Land Policy, 1913–1920," *South Dakota History* 11 (Winter 1980): 21–34.

9. Aziz Rana, "Colonialism and Constitutional Memory," *UC Irvine Law Review* 5, no. 2 (2015): 266.

10. Daniel McCool, Susan M. Olson, and Jennifer L. Robinson, *Native Vote: American Indians, the Voting Rights Act, and the Right to Vote* (New York: Cambridge University Press, 2007), 3.

11. Judith V. Royster, "The Legacy of Allotment," *Arizona State Law Journal* 1 (1995): 1–78.

12. Sidney Harring, *Crow Dog's Case: American Indian Sovereignty, Tribal Law, and United States Law in the Nineteenth Century* (New York: Cambridge University Press, 1994); David E. Wilkins, *American Indian Sovereignty and the U.S. Supreme Court: The Masking of Justice* (Austin: University of Texas Press, 1997).

13. Theodore Roosevelt, *The Winning of the West* (New York: Hastings House, 1963), quoted in Rana, "Colonialism and Constitutional Memory," 266.

14. Theodore Roosevelt, "Indian Citizenship," *American Indian Magazine* 4, no. 4 (December 1916): 326–27; Frederick E. Hoxie, *A Final Promise: The Campaign to Assimilate the Indians, 1880–1920* (Lincoln: University of Nebraska Press, 2001), 107.

15. Theodore Roosevelt, *The Strenuous Life: Essays and Addresses* (New York: Dover, 1889), 9.

16. Fayette Avery McKenzie, "The American Indian of Today and Tomorrow," *Journal of Race Development* 3 (October 1912): 146.

17. Wilkins, *American Indian Sovereignty and the U.S. Supreme Court: The Masking of Justice*, 24–25. On the judicial context, see Carol Nackenoff, "Constitutionalizing Terms of Inclusion: Friends of the Indian and Citizenship for Native Americans, 1880s–1930s," in *The Supreme Court and American Political Development*, ed. Ronald Kahn and Ken I. Kersch (Lawrence: University Press of Kansas, 2006), 366–413.

18. Indian Rights Association, *Annual Report of the Board of Directors of the Indian Rights Association* (Philadelphia: Office of the Indian Rights Association, 1924), 32; Hoxie, *A Final Promise: The Campaign to Assimilate the Indians, 1880–1920*, 236.

19. Kevin Bruyneel, "Challenging American Boundaries: Indigenous People and the 'Gift' of U.S. Citizenship," *Studies in American Political Development* 18 (Spring 2004): 30–43.

20. Rana, "Colonialism and Constitutional Memory," 263–88, 272–73.

21. Drawing from historian John Higham, Nikhil Singh defines "American universalism" as a doctrine in which the "inclusiveness of U.S. nationality and citizenship is said to derive from an egalitarian tradition of civic nationalism that distinguishes the United States from nation-states with ethno-racial conceptions of the polity." Nikhil Pal Singh, *Black Is a Country: Race and the Unfinished Struggle for Democracy* (Cambridge, MA: Harvard University Press, 2004), 18.

22. Judith Shklar, *American Citizenship: The Quest for Inclusion* (Cambridge, MA: Harvard University Press, 1991), 2.

23. Shklar, 16.

24. Rogers Smith, *Civic Ideals: Conflicting Visions of Citizenship in U.S. History* (New Haven, CT: Yale University Press, 1997).

25. On Native Americans, see especially, Smith, 59–63, 106–10, 459–63. Following Frederick E. Hoxie's work, Smith glosses the Progressive Era jurisprudence of allotment and wardship as a "retreat from full and equal citizenship" for Native Americans in relation to earlier post–Civil War reformers' demands for full citizenship. Smith acknowledges that "few" Native Americans "desired" citizenship, yet he still focuses on equal citizenship, which deflects attention from the more constitutive destruction of Native peoples' exercise of citizenship in their own nations. Smith, 460, 462. I argue for attention to the competing meanings of and investments in citizenship, especially by placing it in relation to collective projects of self-rule in this settler-colonial context.

26. Vine Deloria Jr., *We Talk, You Listen: New Tribes, New Turf* (Lincoln, NE: Bison Books, 1970), 143.

27. For an influential gloss on the SAI and Zitkala-Ša specifically as "Christian and secular assimilationist" that has since been widely challenged and nuanced, see Warrior, *Tribal Secrets: Recovering American Indian Intellectual Traditions*, 4–10. See also Scott Richard Lyons, "The Incorporation of the Indian Body: Peyotism and the Pan-Indian Public, 1911–1923," in *Rhetoric, the Polis, and the Global Village*, ed. C. Jan Swearingen and David Pruett (Mahwah, NJ: Lawrence Erlbaum, 1998), 147–54. For interpretations closer to the one defended here, see K. Tsianina Lomawaima, "The Mutuality of Citizenship and Sovereignty: The Society of American Indians and the Battle to Inherit America." In "The Society of American Indians and Its Legacies," special combined issue, *SAIL: Studies in American Indian Literatures* 25, no. 2, and *American Indian Quarterly* 37, no. 3 (Summer 2013): 333–51; Tadeusz Lewandowski, *Red Bird, Red Power: The Life and Legacy of Zitkala-Ša* (Norman: University of Oklahoma Press, 2016); Tadeusz Lewandowski, "Changing Scholarly Interpretations of Gertrude Bonnin (Zitkala-Ša)," *Journal of the Spanish Association of Anglo-American Studies* 41, no. 1 (June 2019): 31–49; Cathleen D. Cahill, "'Our Democracy and the American Indian': Citizenship, Sovereignty, and the Native Vote in the 1920s," *Journal of Women's History* 32, no. 2 (Spring 2020): 41-51.

28. Lomawaima, "The Mutuality of Citizenship and Sovereignty: The Society of American Indians and the Battle to Inherit America," 340; Phillip J. Deloria, "Ameri-

can Master Narratives and the Problem of Indian Citizenship in the Gilded Age and Progressive Era," *Journal of the Gilded Age and Progressive Era* 14, no. 1 (January 2015): 3–12. See also Lucy Maddox, *Citizen Indians: Native American Intellectuals, Race, and Reform* (Ithaca, NY: Cornell University Press, 2005).

29. For the SAI, see Society of American Indians, *Report of the Executive Council on the Proceedings of the First Annual Society of American Indians Conference* (Washington, DC, 1912); Maddox, *Citizen Indians: Native American Intellectuals, Race, and Reform*; Chadwick Allen, "Introduction: Locating the Society of American Indians." In "The Society of American Indians and Its Legacies," special combined issue, *SAIL: Studies in American Indian Literatures* 25, no. 2, and *American Indian Quarterly* 37, no. 3 (Summer 2013): 3–22; K. Tsianina Lomawaima, "Society of American Indians," in *American History: Oxford Research Encyclopedias* (New York: Oxford University Press, 2015).

30. Lewandowski, *Red Bird, Red Power: The Life and Legacy of Zitkala-Ša*, 159, 162.

31. Zitkala-Ša, "Break the Shackles Now—Make Us Free," *American Indian Magazine* 5, no. 4 (December 1917): 213–21; Estes, *Our History Is the Future: Standing Rock versus the Dakota Access Pipeline, and the Long Tradition of Indigenous Resistance*, 217.

32. Zitkala-Ša, "The Sioux Claims (1923)," in *Zitkala-Ša: Letters, Speeches, and Unpublished Writings, 1898–1929*, ed. Tadeusz Lewandowski (Leiden: Brill, 2018), 189.

33. Zitkala-Ša, "Bureaucracy vs. Democracy (1921)," in *American Indian Stories, Legends, and Other Works*, ed. Cathy N. Davidson and Ada Norris (New York: Penguin Classics, 2003), 245.

34. Zitkala-Ša, "Our Sioux People (1923)," in *Zitkala-Ša: Letters, Speeches, and Unpublished Writings, 1898–1929*, ed. Tadeusz Lewandowski (Leiden: Brill, 2018), 216. This is a reference to Progressive critiques of capitalist monopoly and more specifically to a popular 1901 novel: Frank Norris, *The Octopus: A Story of California* (New York: Penguin Classics, 1994).

35. Zitkala-Ša, "America's Indian Problem (December 1928)," in *American Indian Stories, Legends, and Other Works*, ed. Cathy N. Davidson and Ada Norris (New York: Penguin Classics, 2003), 159; Zitkala-Ša, "Our Sioux People (1923)," 203–4.

36. Zitkala-Ša, "Editorial Comment (Spring 1919)," in *American Indian Stories, Legends, and Other Works*, ed. Cathy N. Davidson and Ada Norris (New York: Penguin Classics, 2003), 201.

37. Zitkala-Ša, "Our Sioux People (1923)," 198.

38. Charles Alexander Eastman, "The North American Indian," in *Papers on Inter-Racial Problems, Communicated to the First Universal Races Congress at the University of London, July 26–29* (Boston: World's Peace Foundation, 1911), 367–76.

39. Charles Alexander Eastman, *The Indian To-Day: The Past and Future of the First American* (New York: Doubleday, 1915), 101.

40. Julianne Newmark, "A Prescription for Freedom: Carlos Montezuma, Wassaja, and the Society of American Indians." In "The Society of American Indians and Its Legacies," special combined issue, *SAIL: Studies in American Indian Literatures* 25, no. 2, and *American Indian Quarterly* 37, no. 3 (Summer 2013): 156.

41. Laura Cornelius Kellogg, "Our Democracy and the American Indian (1920)," in *Laura Cornelius Kellogg: Our Democracy and the American Indian and Other Works* (Syracuse, NY: Syracuse University Press, 2015), 82.

42. In a sign of the waning avenues for bureau abolition as a viable possibility, New York congressman Homer P. Snyder dismissed the conclusions of the Indian Rights Association report that Zitkala-Ša had coauthored in 1924. She did not appear at the

hearing in order to evade potential libel charges. However, the report did lead to the eventual 1928 Meriam Report, which provided the rationale for the Indian New Deal and with it the formal end of the allotment of tribal lands. Lewandowski, *Red Bird, Red Power: The Life and Legacy of Zitkala-Ša*, 170.

43. Bonnin (Zitkala-Ša), Fabens, and Sniffen, *Oklahoma's Poor Rich Indians: An Orgy of Graft and Exploitation of the Five Civilized Tribes—Legalized Robbery*, 26.

44. Bonnin (Zitkala-Ša), Fabens, and Sniffen, 26–27.

45. Bonnin (Zitkala-Ša), Fabens, and Sniffen, 18. On the intersection between gendered domestication and the domestication of Indigenous peoples as collective political entities, see Beth Piatote, *Domestic Subjects: Gender, Citizenship, and Law in Native American Literature* (New Haven. CT: Yale University Press, 2017).

46. For more on these different "bureau abolitionist" positions, see Temin, "Our Democracy: Laura Cornelius Kellogg's Decolonial-Democracy." Many Indian and most non-Indian reformers, such as former commissioner of Indian affairs Francis Leupp, countered the radicalism of this abolitionist perspective by arguing that the immediate abolition of the bureau posed "too heavy a risk of damage to a helpless people"—a claim reiterating the protective function of the bureau. Francis E. Leupp, "Abolish the Bureau," *American Indian Magazine* 4, no. 2 (June 30, 1916): 200. I return to this debate in chapter 2, in my account of the antiabolitionist and colonial ideas motivating some of commissioner John Collier's later IRA reforms.

47. Montezuma came under threat from the FBI for being in violation of the Selective Service Act. Carlos Montezuma, "Another Kaiser in America," in *Say We Are Nations: Documents of Politics and Protest in Indigenous America since 1887*, ed. Daniel Cobb (Chapel Hill: University of North Carolina Press, 2015), 32–35; Carlos Montezuma, "Drafting Indians and Justice," *Wassaja* 2, no. 7 (October 1917): 3. Montezuma and Zitkala-Ša exchanged letters during their engagement and after she broke it off. In several letters, she is quite critical of what she viewed as his failure to appreciate the values of Indigenous peoples as peoples. This seems to be one important reason she broke off the engagement. Zitkala-Ša, "Letter to Carlos Montezuma (December 6, 1918)," in *Zitkala-Ša: Letters, Speeches, and Unpublished Writings: 1898–1929*, ed. Tadeusz Lewandowski (Leiden: Brill, 2018), 177–78.

48. Carlos Montezuma, "The Truth Is Coming to Light," *Wassaja* 2, no. 12 (March 1918): 1.

49. Richard Henry Pratt, "The Advantages of Mingling Indians with Whites: Paper Presented at the Nineteenth Annual Conference of Charities and Correction, Denver, Colorado," in *Americanizing the American Indian: Writings by the "Friends of the Indian," 1880–1900*, ed. Francis Paul Prucha (Cambridge, MA: Harvard University Press, 1973), 260–71.

50. For more on Kellogg in the context of these debates in the SAI, Progressive debates, and the Haudenosaunee Confederacy, see Temin, "Our Democracy: Laura Cornelius Kellogg's Decolonial-Democracy"; Kristina Ackley and Cristina Stanciu, "Introduction: Laura Cornelius Kellogg; Haudenosaunee Thinker, Native Activist, American Writer," in *Laura Cornelius Kellogg: Our Democracy and the American Indian and Other Works*, ed. Kristina Ackley and Cristina Stanciu (Syracuse, NY: Syracuse University Press, 2015), 154–66.

51. Clinton Rickard, *Fighting Tuscarora: The Autobiography of Chief Clinton Rickard*, ed. Barbara Graymont (Syracuse, NY: Syracuse University Press, 1984), 53. The latter view was widespread especially among the Six Nations. See Kevin Bruyneel, *The Third*

Space of Sovereignty: The Postcolonial Politics of U.S.-Indigenous Relations (Minneapolis: University of Minnesota Press, 2007), 111–20.

52. Hazel W. Hertzberg, *The Search for an American Indian Identity: Modern Pan-Indian Movements* (Syracuse, NY: Syracuse University Press, 1981), 155–78.

53. Zitkala-Ša, "Indian Gifts to Civilized Man (July–September 1918)," in *American Indian Stories, Legends, and Other Works*, ed. Cathy N. Davidson and Ada Norris (New York: Penguin Classics, 2003), 185. On her complex performance and rhetoric, see especially Kiara M. Vigil, *Indigenous Intellectuals: Sovereignty, Citizenship, and the American Imagination, 1880–1930* (New York: Cambridge University Press, 2015), 165–233.

54. Zitkala-Ša, "Editorial Comment (Spring 1919)," 210; Zitkala-Ša, "Our Sioux People (1923)," 199.

55. See also articles and information in the Autumn 1918 issue she edited: Chauncey Yellow Robe, "Indian Patriotism," *American Indian Magazine* 6, no. 3 (Autumn 1918): 129–30. In the same issue, the text of the proposed citizenship bill for veterans (passed in 1919) is reprinted on pages 131–34, and excerpts from the *Congressional Record* are featured on pages 134–40.

56. Zitkala-Ša, "Indian Gifts to Civilized Man (July–September 1918)," 186; Cristina Stanciu, "Americanization on Native Terms: The Society of American Indians, Citizenship Debates, and Tropes of 'Racial Difference,'" *Native American and Indigenous Studies Journal* 6, no. 1 (2019): 111–48.

57. Zitkala-Ša, "Editorial Comment (Winter 1919)," in *American Indian Stories, Legends, and Other Works*, ed. Cathy N. Davidson and Ada Norris (New York: Penguin Classics, 2003), 191–92.

58. Cahill, "Our Democracy and the American Indian."

59. Zitkala-Ša, "America, Home of the Red Man (Winter 1919)," in *American Indian Stories, Legends, and Other Writings*, ed. Cathy N. Davidson and Ada Norris (New York: Penguin Classics, 2003), 193.

60. Zitkala-Ša, "America's Indian Problem (December 1928)."

61. Zitkala-Ša, "Our Sioux People (1923)," 199; Zitkala-Ša, "Editorial Comment (Spring 1919)," 202.

62. Zitkala-Ša, "Editorial Comment (Spring 1919)," 201; Zitkala-Ša, "The Sioux Claims (1923)," 191–92.

63. Zitkala-Ša, "Editorial Comment (Spring 1919)," 201.

64. Zitkala-Ša, 202; Zitkala-Ša, "Americanize the First American (1921)," in *American Indian Stories, Legends, and Other Works*, ed. Cathy N. Davidson and Ada Norris (New York: Penguin Classics, 2003), 244.

65. Zitkala-Ša, "America, Home of the Red Man (Winter 1919)," 193.

66. Zitkala-Ša, "Editorial Comment (Winter 1919)."

67. Rowse, "The Indigenous Redemption of Liberal Universalism," 147.

68. Zitkala-Ša, "Editorial Comment (Winter 1919)," 191.

69. Zitkala-Ša, "Editorial Comment (Spring 1919)," 202; Zitkala-Ša, "Americanize the First American (1921)," 244.

70. Zitkala-Ša, "Editorial Comment (July–September 2018)," in *American Indian Stories, Legends, and Other Works*, ed. Cathy N. Davidson and Ada Norris (New York: Penguin Classics, 2003), 182.

71. "Letter to Carlos Montezuma (December 6, 1918)," 178.

72. Vigil, *Indigenous Intellectuals: Sovereignty, Citizenship, and the American Imagination, 1880–1930*, 165–233.

73. Zitkala-Ša, "America's Indian Problem (December 1928)."
74. Cahill, "Our Democracy and the American Indian."
75. Hertzberg, *The Search for an American Indian Identity: Modern Pan-Indian Movements*, 187; P. Jane Hafen, "Zitkala Sa," in *Encyclopedia of North American Indians*, ed. Frederick E. Hoxie (Boston: Houghton Mifflin Harcourt, 1996), Gale Academic OneFile; P. Jane Hafen, "'Help Indians Help Themselves': Gertrude Bonnin, the SAI, and the NCAI." In "The Society of American Indians and Its Legacies," special combined issue, *SAIL: Studies in American Indian Literatures* 25, no. 2, and *American Indian Quarterly* 37, no. 3 (Summer 2013): 199–218.
76. Lewandowski, *Red Bird, Red Power: The Life and Legacy of Zitkala-Ša*, 182.
77. Arthur Watkins, "Termination of Federal Supervision: The Removal of Restrictions over Indian Property and Person," *American Academy of Political and Social Science* 311 (May 1957): 47.
78. Vine Deloria Jr., *Behind the Trail of Broken Treaties: An Indian Declaration of Independence* (Austin: University of Texas Press, 1974), 151.
79. Vine Deloria Jr., *Custer Died for Your Sins: An Indian Manifesto* (New York: Macmillan, 1969), 54. Cited in text hereafter.
80. Termination refers to a diverse group of policies including federal withdrawal of recognition (House Concurrent Resolution 108); the granting of state jurisdiction over Indigenous lands in California, Minnesota, Wisconsin, Oregon, and Nebraska (Public Law 280); and "relocation" of Indigenous peoples to urban areas (the Indian Relocation Act of 1956). On termination, I have consulted the following: Donald L. Fixico, *Termination and Relocation: Federal Indian Policy, 1945–1960* (Albuquerque: University of New Mexico Press, 1986); Nicholas Peroff, *Menominee Drums: Tribal Termination and Restoration, 1954–1974* (Norman: University of Oklahoma Press, 2006); Kenneth R. Philp, *Termination Revisited: American Indians on the Trail to Self-Determination, 1933–1953* (Lincoln: University of Nebraska Press, 1999); Christopher K. Riggs, "American Indians, Economic Development, and Self-Determination in the 1960s," *Pacific Historical Review* 69, no. 3 (2000): 431–63.
81. In 1972, the National Congress of American Indians (NCAI) debated whether Nixon's new "self-determination" policy was a new form of termination. "Self-Determination or Disguised Termination: Let's Be Certain, NCAI 29th Convention," October 1972, Box 21, Folder 3, National Museum of the American Indian Archive Center, Smithsonian Institution. The language of termination also appears frequently in reference to efforts to dissolve Indigenous nations. Gabriel S. Galanda, "Back to the Future: The GOP and Tribal Termination," *Indian Country Today*, September 9, 2015, http://indiancountrytodaymedianetwork.com/2015/09/09/back-future-gop-and-tribal-termination.
82. Deloria Jr., *We Talk, You Listen: New Tribes, New Turf*, 143.
83. For studies on Deloria's contributions, see David Myer Temin, "Remapping the World: Vine Deloria, Jr. and the Ends of Settler Sovereignty" (PhD diss., University of Minnesota, 2016); David E. Wilkins, *Red Prophet: The Punishing Intellectualism of Vine Deloria Jr.* (Golden, CO: Fulcrum Publishing, 2018); David Martinez, *Life of the Indigenous Mind: Vine Deloria Jr. and the Birth of the Red Power Movement* (Lincoln: University of Nebraska Press, 2020). During Deloria's tenure at the NCAI, Congress tried to renew earlier efforts to "terminate" Indigenous peoples by proposing a 1966 omnibus bill, with the NCAI convening an emergency meeting in Santa Fe to oppose (97). Just as the NCAI was fighting to block further termination and to help tribes

already terminated, the Great Society programs administered through the Office of Economic Opportunity and the Black Power movement had allowed the NCAI to speak of "self-determination." Daniel Cobb, *Native Activism in Cold War America: The Struggle for Sovereignty* (Lawrence: University Press of Kansas, 2008), 125–46.

84. Indicating *Custer*'s influence, Paul Chaat Smith and Robert Warrior describe how "when that book came out, it became required reading among Indian student radicals." Paul Chaat Smith and Robert Warrior, *Like a Hurricane: The Indian Movement from Alcatraz to Wounded Knee* (New York: New Press, 1997), 122.

85. Vine Deloria Jr., "Letter to James Buswell, April 23, 1965," Box 75 NCAI Correspondence, 1965–67, Folder 2: April 1965, National Museum of the American Indian Archive Center, Smithsonian Institution.

86. Joseph Garry, "A Declaration of Indian Rights," 1954, Box 257, Folder "Emergency Conference Bulletin," National Museum of the American Indian Archive Center, Smithsonian Institution; Thomas W. Cowger, *The National Congress of American Indians: The Founding Years* (Lincoln: University of Nebraska Press, 2001), 99.

87. Vine Deloria Jr., "Testimony of Joseph R. Garry in Support of Resolution No. 3," in *Of Utmost Good Faith* (San Francisco: Straight Arrow Books, 1971), 214–16.

88. Such frameworks graft a *telos* of inclusion questionably attributed to African American civil rights struggles for racial justice onto Indigenous aspirations for self-determination. A significant literature indebted to the revisionist historiography of the "long civil rights movement" has exploded this narrow rendering of civil rights as reducible to inclusion. See, among other works, Jacquelyn Dowd Hall, "The Long Civil Rights Movement and the Political Uses of the Past," *Journal of American History* 91, no. 4 (2005): 1233–63. For Deloria's influence on anthropology, see Thomas Biolsi and Larry Zimmerman, eds., *Indians and Anthropologists: Vine Deloria, Jr. and the Critique of Anthropology* (Tucson: University of Arizona, 1997).

89. As Indigenous studies scholars have more recently argued, grafting this narrative of inclusion onto Indigenous political experience rests on the displacement and erasure of a politics of decolonization. Kānaka Maoli scholar J. Kēhaulani Kauanui warns of the insufficiency of civil rights discourse as such for Indigenous peoples, since the language of "equal rights" has been co-opted and deployed in neoconservative antitreaty and antisovereigntist movements from Hawai'i to Connecticut. J. Kēhaulani Kauanui, "Colonialism in Equality: Hawaiian Sovereignty and the Question of U.S. Civil Rights," *South Atlantic Quarterly* 107, no. 4 (2008): 635–50. Chickasaw theorist Jodi Byrd has argued that when "remediation . . . is framed through discourses of racialization that can be redressed by further inclusion into the nation-state, there is a significant failure to grapple with the fact that such discourses further reinscribe the original colonial injury." Byrd emphasizes the insistent way that inclusion is reactivated, remaking colonial injustice as only a problem of civil rights (and, later, multicultural) inclusion. Jodi A. Byrd, *The Transit of Empire: Indigenous Critiques of Colonialism* (Minneapolis: University of Minnesota Press, 2011), xxiii.

90. Deloria Jr., *We Talk, You Listen: New Tribes, New Turf*, 43.

91. Stokely Carmichael and Charles Hamilton, *Black Power: The Politics of Liberation* (New York: Vintage, 1992). I have not been able to find any evidence that Deloria had personally met Carmichael or Hamilton, but his frequent references to Black Power across a number of writings show that Deloria was heavily influenced by their work. Deloria had a typescript copy of *Black Power* in his papers in Series II: Chronological Correspondences, Box 15, January–March 1970 Correspondence Folder, Vine

Deloria Papers, Yale Collection of Western Americana, Beinecke Rare Book and Manuscript Library.

92. "The tragedy of the early days of the Civil Rights movement is that many people, black, white, red, and yellow, were sold a bill of goods which said that equality was the eventual goal of the movement. But no one had considered the implications of so simple a slogan. Equality means sameness" (179).

93. Robert Warrior, "The Indian Renaissance, 1960–2000: Stumbling to Victory, or Anecdotes of Persistence?," in *The Oxford Handbook of American Indian History*, ed. Frederick Hoxie (New York: Oxford University Press, 2016), 129–48.

94. Clyde Warrior, "Poverty, Community, and Power," *New University Thought* 4 (Summer 1965): 5–6.

95. Cobb, *Native Activism in Cold War America: The Struggle for Sovereignty*.

96. Kevin Bruyneel focuses on the way that Indigenous politics transgresses this inside/outside binary. More than creating a different spatial orientation to political life—what Bruyneel labels a "third space of sovereignty"—Deloria also delivered a powerful critique of these very practices of boundary drawing as an artifice of the civic inclusion project. Bruyneel, *The Third Space of Sovereignty: The Postcolonial Politics of U.S.-Indigenous Relations*, 1–26, 123–70.

97. "Letter to Charles Isaacs," November 25, 1969, 1969 Correspondence Folder, Box 15, Vine Deloria Papers, Yale Collection of Western Americana, Beinecke Rare Book and Manuscript Library.

98. Deloria's point here finds an important contemporary echo in Chickasaw theorist Jodi Byrd's account of Indianness as a "transit of empire." Jodi A. Byrd, *The Transit of Empire: Indigenous Critiques of Colonialism* (Minneapolis: University of Minnesota Press, 2011).

99. Quoted in Stan Steiner, *The New Indians* (New York: Harper & Row, 1968); Bruyneel, *The Third Space of Sovereignty: The Postcolonial Politics of U.S.-Indigenous Relations*, 148.

100. Deloria Jr., *Behind the Trail of Broken Treaties: An Indian Declaration of Independence*, 20.

101. Mel Thom, "Indian War 1963," *American Aborigine* 3, no. 1 (1964): 2; Mel Thom, "Indian War 1964," *American Aborigine* 3, no. 1 (1964): 4–5.

102. Deloria's point here can partly be captured by what Joel Olson referred to as the "ideals/practices" dichotomy: When framed as a gap between egalitarian ideals and inegalitarian practices, one actually misses the ways in which (here) colonial practices have been integral to creating the very subject positions through which such ideal are embodied. Olson, *The Abolition of White Democracy*, xvi. Thus, e.g., when ideas like "integration" are used to justify the expropriation of Indigenous lands, they may shore up the normative status of white settler citizenship and become part of an arsenal of dispossession. The settler self-conception would view these tight connections between assimilation, dispossession, and standing in the polity as self-evident—as requiring no explanation. There was no contradiction between equality of principle and inequality of practice to disentangle on this conception of the nation.

103. In chapter 4 of this book, I focus on "Indigenous Marxisms" influenced by Fanon. Kevin Bruyneel explicitly contrasts Deloria's politics to Fanon's. Bruyneel, *The Third Space of Sovereignty: The Postcolonial Politics of U.S.-Indigenous Relations*, 145.

104. Richard Slotkin, *The Fatal Environment: The Myth of the Frontier in the Age of Industrialization, 1800–1890* (New York: HarperCollins, 1985), 17.

105. See, e.g., Richard Rorty, *Achieving Our Country: Leftist Thought in Twentieth Century America* (Cambridge, MA: Harvard University Press, 1999), 8.

106. The 1819 Civilization Fund Act authorized $10,000 annuities "for the purpose of guarding against the further decline and final extinction of the Indian tribes, adjoining the frontier settlements of the United States" and "for introducing among them the habits and arts of civilization." Francis Paul Prucha, ed., "1819 Civilization Fund Act," in *Documents of United States Indian Policy*, 3rd ed. (Lincoln: University of Nebraska Press, 33).

107. George Shulman, *American Prophecy: Race and Redemption in American Political Culture* (Minneapolis: University of Minnesota Press, 2008).

108. Deloria took a pragmatic view as a strategic operator vis-à-vis the US federal bureaucracy. See Cobb, *Native Activism in Cold War America: The Struggle for Sovereignty*. In this sense, he did not fully embrace a "politics of refusal" that would question all forms of state-centered recognition, such as the analysis Kahnawà:ke Mohawk scholar Audra Simpson has developed. Simpson, *Mohawk Interruptus: Political Life across the Borders of Settler-States*.

109. Deloria Jr., *We Talk, You Listen: New Tribes, New Turf*, 148.

CHAPTER TWO

1. Ella Deloria, *Speaking of Indians* (Lincoln: University of Nebraska Press, 1998), 25.

2. Lassa Oppenheim, *International Law: A Treatise*, ed. Ronald F. Roxburgh, vol. 1 (London: Longmans, Green and Co., 1912), 286, https://www.gutenberg.org/files/41046/41046-h/41046-h.htm.

3. Lightfoot, *Global Indigenous Politics: A Subtle Revolution*; International Indian Treaty Council, "Declaration of Continuing Independence," June 1974, https://www.iitc.org/about-iitc/the-declaration-of-continuing-independence-june-1974/.

4. Emerging from earlier discussions in its first Platform Document, the IITC unsuccessfully lobbied to have other countries file the 1868 Treaty as an international document at the UN. "Platform Document–Treaty Council," n.d., Standing Rock Correspondence Folder, Box 27: Correspondence Folder N-S, Vine Deloria Papers, Yale Collection of Western Americana, Beinecke Rare Book and Manuscript Library.

5. Ladner, "Treaty Federalism: An Indigenous Vision of Canadian Federalisms." For precolonial treaty-making practices, see Lisa Brooks, *The Common Pot: The Recovery of Native Space in the Northeast* (Minneapolis: University of Minnesota Press, 2008); Simpson, "Looking after Gdoo-Naaganinaa"; Robert Alexander Innes, *Elder Brother and the Law of the People: Contemporary Kinship and Cowessess First Nation* (Winnipeg: University of Manitoba Press, 2013). Michael Witgen writes, "The diplomacy of exchange relationships . . . became deeply intertwined with the creation and negotiation of kinship boundaries and obligations." Michael Witgen, "American Indians in World History," in *Oxford Handbook of American Indian History*, ed. Frederick E. Hoxie (New York: Oxford University Press, 2016), 611.

6. Jon Parmenter, "The Meaning of Kaswentha and the Two Row Wampum Belt in Haudenosaunee (Iroquois) History: Can Indigenous Oral Tradition Be Reconciled with the Documentary Record?," *Journal of Early American History* 3 (2013): 82–109.

7. On the transformation of treaty over time, see J. R. Miller, *Compact, Contract, Covenant: Aboriginal Treaty-Making in Canada* (Toronto: University of Toronto Press,

2009); Colin G. Calloway, "Treaties and Treaty Making," in *The Oxford Handbook of American Indian History*, ed. Frederick E. Hoxie (New York: Oxford University Press, 2016), 539–52. On the scale of this massive "land rush," see John C. Weaver, *The Great Land Rush and the Making of the Modern World, 1650–1930* (Quebec: McGill-Queen's University Press, 2003); James Belich, *Replenishing the Earth: The Settler Revolution and the Rise of the Anglo-World* (Oxford: Oxford University Press, 2011).

8. Jeffrey Ostler, "'Just and Lawful War' as Genocidal War in the (United States) Northwest Ordinance and Northwest Territory, 1787–1832," *Journal of Genocide Research* 18, no. 1 (2016): 1–20; Bethel Saler, *The Settlers' Empire: Colonialism and State Formation in America's Old Northwest* (Philadelphia: University of Pennsylvania Press, 2014). See also Cocks, "Foundational Violence and the Politics of Erasure"; Cocks, *On Sovereignty and Other Political Delusions*.

9. Antony Anghie, *Imperialism, Sovereignty, and the Making of International Law* (New York: Cambridge University Press, 2005), 67–82, 105; Audra Simpson, "The Ruse of Consent and the Anatomy of 'Refusal': Cases from Indigenous North America and Australia," *Postcolonial Studies* 20, no. 1 (2017): 26.

10. Anghie, *Imperialism, Sovereignty, and the Making of International Law*, 219. Dorothy V. Jones, *License for Empire: Colonialism by Treaty in Early America* (Chicago: University of Chicago Press, 1982); Saliha Belmessous, ed., *Empire by Treaty: Negotiating European Expansion, 1600–1900* (New York: Oxford University Press, 2014); Nichols, *Theft Is Property! The Recursive Logic of Dispossession*, 103–5. Another classic version of this argument in international law scholarship distinguishes between an earlier era of "equal treaties" and a later era (ca. nineteenth century) of "unequal treaties": C. H. Alexandrowicz, *The European-African Confrontation: A Study in Treaty Making* (Leiden: A. W. Sijthoff, 1973).

11. The opposition appears with some variations across multiple works. See James Tully, "Rediscovering America: The Two Treatises and Aboriginal Rights," in *Locke in Contexts: An Approach to Political Philosophy* (Oxford: Oxford University Press, 1993), 137–78; James Tully, "Aboriginal Property and Western Theory," *Social Philosophy and Policy* 11, no. 2 (1994): 153–80; Tully, *Strange Multiplicity: Constitutionalism in an Age of Diversity*; James Tully, *Public Philosophy in a New Key*, vol. 1, *Democracy and Civic Freedom* (Cambridge: Cambridge University Press, 2008), 223–56; James Tully, "Consent, Hegemony, and Dissent in Treaty Negotiations," in *Between Consenting Peoples*, ed. Jeremy Webber and Colin M. Macloed (Vancouver: University of British Columbia Press, 2010), 223–56. The anthropologist Michael Asch has made similar arguments: Michael Asch, *On Being Here to Stay: Treaties and Aboriginal Rights in Canada* (Toronto: University of Toronto Press, 2014).

12. Tully, "Consent, Hegemony, and Dissent in Treaty Negotiations," 238. To be sure, Tully is aware of the widespread use of treaties for domination, and he has addressed this in other work. Yet the central tendency of his argument is nonetheless to use "treaty" as a shorthand for respectfully negotiated, egalitarian relations among distinct peoples with the aim of peaceful reconciliation between them, and to use "colonial" as a gloss for violent and dominative relations inimical to those expressed in "treaty." For a parallel reading of Tully, see Bonnie Honig, "'[Un]Dazzled by the Ideal?': Tully's Politics and Humanism in Tragic Perspective," *Political Theory* 39, no. 1 (February 2011): 138–44.

13. Michael Witgen, *Seeing Red: Indigenous Land, Black Lives, and the Political*

Economy of Plunder in North America (Williamsburg, VA: Omohundro Institute for the Study of Early American History and Culture, 2022).

14. James O. Daschuk, *Clearing the Plains: Disease, Politics of Starvation, and the Loss of Aboriginal Life* (Regina: University of Regina Press, 2013).

15. Susan Sleeper-Smith, *Indigenous Prosperity and American Conquest: Indian Women of the Ohio River Valley* (Chapel Hill, NC: Omohundro Institute of Early American History and Culture, 2018).

16. James Youngblood Henderson, "Empowering Treaty Federalism," *Saskatchewan Law Review* 58 (1994): 241–329; Heidi Kiiwetinepinesiik Stark, "Changing the Treaty Question: Remedying the Right(s) Relationship," in *The Right Relationship: Reimagining the Implementation of Historical Treaties*, ed. John Borrows and Michael Coyle (Toronto: University of Toronto Press, 2017), 248–76; Gina Starblanket, "The Numbered Treaties and the Politics of Incoherency," *Canadian Journal of Political Science* 52, no. 3 (May 2019): 1–17. See also Suzan Shown Harjo, ed., *Nation to Nation: Treaties between the United States and American Indian Nations* (Washington, DC: Smithsonian, 2014).

17. Williams Jr., *Linking Arms Together: American Indian Treaty Visions of Law and Peace, 1600–1800*, 84.

18. Williams Jr., 63. See also Aaron Mills, "What Is a Treaty? On Contract and Mutual Aid," in *The Right Relationship: Reimagining the Implementation of Historical Treaties*, ed. John Borrows and Michael Coyle (Toronto: University of Toronto Press, 2017), 208–47.

19. Deloria, *Speaking of Indians*, 158.

20. John Collier, "The Red Slaves of Oklahoma," *Sunset* 52 (March 1924): 10; John Collier, "The American Congo," *Survey* 50, no. 9 (August 1923): 467–76.

21. Vine Deloria Jr., ed., "Minutes of the Plains Congress, Rapid City Indian School, Rapid City, South Dakota," in *The Indian Reorganization Act: Congresses and Bills* (Norman: University of Oklahoma Press, 2002), 27 (my emphasis).

22. Laurence M. Hauptman, "Africa View: John Collier, the British Colonial Service and American Indian Policy, 1933–1945," *Historian* 48, no. 3 (May 1986): 361.

23. Deloria Jr., "Minutes of the Plains Congress, Rapid City Indian School, Rapid City, South Dakota," 28. On "guardianship" among IRA officials, see Elmer Rusco, *A Fateful Time: The Background and Legislative History of the Indian Organization Act* (Reno: University of Nevada Press, 2000). Collier later served as the US delegate to the first UN conference on trusteeship of colonial territories. See John Collier, *On the Gleaming Way: Navajos, Eastern Pueblos, Zunis, Hopis, Apaches, and Their Land; and Their Meanings to the World* (Denver: Sage, 1962). My aim here is to contextualize the IRA, not to dismiss it as wholly negative in effect: Collier's IRA ended catastrophic allotment of lands and acknowledged in a deeper way than had previous OIA/BIA administrations how the bureau had functioned as a vehicle of assimilationist violence. He condemned allotment as an effort to "crush Indian life," a commitment that stemmed from his early activism on behalf of Pueblo communities in the Southwest.

24. John Collier, *From Every Zenith: A Memoir* (New York: Sage Books, 1963), 217.

25. John Collier, "Africa View—and Indian," *American Indian Life*, July 1931, 40; Collier, *From Every Zenith: A Memoir*, 123; Hauptman, "Africa View: John Collier, the British Colonial Service and American Indian Policy, 1933–1945." On indirect rule in the British Empire in the work of Henry Maine (whom Collier had also read) and, later, ethnographers of the 1920s such as Bronislaw Malinowski, see Frederick Cooper, "Development, Modernization, and the Social Sciences in the Era of Decolonization:

The Examples of British and French Africa," *Revue d'Histoire Des Sciences Humaines* 10 (2004): 11–14; Karuna Mantena, *Alibis of Empire: Henry Maine and the Ends of Liberal Imperialism* (Princeton, NJ: Princeton University Press, 2010).

26. Dalia Tsuk, "Pluralisms: The Indian New Deal as a Model," *University of Maryland Law Journal of Race, Religion, Gender, and Class* 1, no. 2 (2001): 393–449; Everett Helmut Akam, *Transnational America: Cultural Pluralist Thought in the Twentieth Century* (Lanham, MD: Rowman & Littlefield, 2002). Others likewise emphasize Collier's preference for community over individualism: Graham D. Taylor, *The New Deal and American Indian Tribalism: The Administration of the Indian Reorganization Act, 1934–45* (Lincoln: University of Nebraska Press, 1980); Rusco, *A Fateful Time: The Background and Legislative History of the Indian Organization Act*.

27. Scudder Mekeel, "An Appraisal of the Indian Reorganization Act," *American Anthropologist* 46, no. 2, pt. 1 (June 1944): 209.

28. Deloria Jr., "Minutes of the Plains Congress, Rapid City Indian School, Rapid City, South Dakota," 37.

29. Deloria Jr., 38.

30. Collier, "Africa View—and Indian," 38–39.

31. Mark Rifkin, *When Did Indians Become Straight? Kinship, the History of Sexuality, and Native Sovereignty* (New York: Oxford University Press, 2011), 192.

32. Christopher J. Pexa, *Translated Nation: Rewriting the Dakhóta Oyáte* (Minneapolis: University of Minnesota Press, 2019), 191.

33. Such changes included forming a corporate charter to make tribes into entities capable of holding credit (and debt). The IRA also aimed to protect the private ownership of property via "households" created under the Dawes Severalty Act's allotment procedures. These assigned 160-acre allotments to men as the head of households.

34. The Lakota had won a significant victory in Red Cloud's War, which led to the US suing for peace in the 1868 Treaty, which many Lakota and some other signatory peoples take to be a final treaty defining the terms of relationship with the United States. Representatives from the Brulé, Oglala, Minneconjou, Hunkpapa, Sans Arc, Cuthead, Blackfeet, Yanktonai, Santee, and the Arapaho people were signatories. For the language of the 1868 Treaty, see Charles Kappler, ed., "Fort Laramie Treaty of 1868," in *Indian Affairs: Laws and Treaties*, vol. 2, *1788–1883* (Washington, DC: Government Printing Office, 1904), 999–1007. For a summary of the political and legal context of the 1868 Treaty and the earlier 1851 Treaty, see Jeffrey Ostler and Nick Estes, "'The Supreme Law of the Land': Standing Rock and the Dakota Access Pipeline," *Indian Country Today*, January 16, 2017, https://indiancountrymedianetwork.com/news/opinions/supreme-law-land-standing-rock-dakota-access-pipeline/.

35. Rifkin, *When Did Indians Become Straight? Kinship, the History of Sexuality, and Native Sovereignty*, 130.

36. Maria Eugenia Cotera, *Native Speakers: Ella Deloria, Zora Neale Hurston, Jovita Gonzalez and the Poetics of Culture* (Austin: University of Texas Press, 2008), 45.

37. Janet L. Finn, "Ella Cara Deloria and Mourning Dove: Writing for Cultures, Writing against the Grain," *Critique of Anthropology* 13, no. 4 (1993): 340; Susan Gardner, "Speaking of Ella Deloria: Conversations with Joyzelle Gingway Godfrey, 1998–2000, Lower Brule Community College, South Dakota," *American Indian Quarterly* 24, no. 3 (Summer 2000): 456–81; Phillip J. Deloria, *Becoming Mary Sully: Toward an American Indian Abstract* (Seattle: University of Washington Press, 2019), 231–32.

38. Deloria, *Becoming Mary Sully: Toward an American Indian Abstract*, 247–48.

39. "Ella Deloria to Franz Boas," August 25, 1935, Franz Boas Papers: Inventory D at the American Philosophical Society, Philadelphia, https://search.amphilsoc.org/collections/view?docId=ead/Mss.B.B61.inventory04-ead.xml; "Ella Deloria to Franz Boas," February 12, 1938, Franz Boas Papers: Inventory D at the American Philosophical Society, Philadelphia, https://search.amphilsoc.org/collections/view?docId=ead/Mss.B.B61.inventory04-ead.xml.

40. Chris Pexa argues that central to Ella Deloria's writings is "the renewal of thióšpaye ethics and forms of caretaking through the performance of long-standing gender roles. These appear within a gender binary and emphasize collective forms of care and affection, of anarchic power sharing rather than hierarchy. They observe the sustaining power of Dakota women to remake the Oyate, in part by passing on stories that are theories—of how to be Dakota, of how to treat those who are not Dakota, of how to treat your relatives so all may survive." Pexa, *Translated Nation: Rewriting the Dakhóta Oyáte*, 220; Bea Medicine, *The Native American Woman: A Perspective* (Las Cruces, NM: National Educational Laboratory Publishers, 1978); Bea Medicine, "Ella C. Deloria: The Emic Voice," in "Ethnic Women Writers II: 'Of Dwelling Places,'" *MELUS* 7, no. 4 (Winter 1980): 23–30; Cotera, *Native Speakers: Ella Deloria, Zora Neale Hurston, Jovita Gonzalez and the Poetics of Culture*.

41. "Ella Deloria to Franz Boas," August 25, 1935; Roseanne Hoefel, "'Different by Degree': Ella Cara Deloria, Zora Neale Hurston, and Franz Boas Contend with Race and Ethnicity," *American Indian Quarterly* 25, no. 2 (Spring 2001): 181–202.

42. "The first thing to learn was how to treat other people and how to address them . . . this was the core of all kinship training. But Gloku did not lecture all the time. Instead she stated the rules of behavior toward one another and pointed out examples. When the right opportunity came up she never failed to take advantage of it." Ella Cara Deloria, *Waterlily* (Lincoln, NE: Bison Books, 1988), 34. Penelope Myrtle Kelsey argues that Deloria can be read as Woyaka, the camp circle historian in *Waterlily* who recounts the stories key to Lakota culture. Penelope Myrtle Kelsey, *Tribal Theory in Native American Literature: Dakota and Haudenosaunee Writing and Indigenous Worldviews* (Lincoln: University of Nebraska Press, 2010), 91–92. I tentatively posit that she—an educator, after all—may have written herself into *Waterlily* as Gloku or many other kinship teachers, in that she is teaching kinship protocols to Dakota and Lakota people and—especially in *Speaking of Indians*—very gently educating outsiders into a kind of treaty making understood as an extension of social kinship that rejects missionary, ethnographic, and militaristic invasion. The two positions—camp circle historian and relative-educator—can be read as compatible, since both aimed to "state the rules of behavior toward one another and pointed out examples."

43. Others have interpreted Deloria's work as an intervention into the directly assimilationist model: Susan Gardner, "Subverting the Rhetoric of Assimilation: Ella Cara Deloria (Dakota) in the 1920s," *Hecate* 39, no. 1 (2013): 9–32.

44. Pexa, *Translated Nation: Rewriting the Dakhóta Oyáte*, 187; Deloria, *Becoming Mary Sully: Toward an American Indian Abstract*, 238.

45. Deloria, *Speaking of Indians*, 24. Subsequent citations are given in the text as *SI*.

46. Deloria, *Waterlily*, 20.

47. Kelsey, *Tribal Theory in Native American Literature: Dakota and Haudenosaunee Writing and Indigenous Worldviews*, 81–82.

48. Deloria's emphasis reflects the "cultural relativist" approach Boas had introduced, which rejected developmentalist and biological views of races in favor of an

attention to cultural units of equal status. See Franz Boas, *The Mind of Primitive Man* (New York: Macmillan, 1922). Yet, her approach on projects like "Project 35: Acculturation" with Ruth Benedict differ in two crucial ways from the Boas model, whose terms she was laboring under: First, she uses kinship to signal a capacious—perhaps even universally valid—way of organizing social and political relations, not just a provincial cultural activity. Second, she rejected the salvage model of anthropology. She recorded oral traditions in order to create a modern form of self-determination that continued the intergenerational production of knowledge.

49. Maria Cotera contends that "by employing the descriptive term for 'peace' as the primary identifier of her people, Deloria offers an intervention, at the level of language, against the popular perception that the Sioux were a 'warlike' people." Cotera, *Native Speakers: Ella Deloria, Zora Neale Hurston, Jovita Gonzalez and the Poetics of Culture*, 236n. My claim is that she also theorizes kinship as an alternative practice of *politics itself*.

50. This line of thought is also reflected in the striking cover art of the original 1944 edition of *Speaking*, a design from Deloria's sister Mary Sully: "The cover design is composed of the traditional camp-circle of the Dakotas and within it is as a figure representing the 'altar' or enclosed space used by a man fasting in solitude and seeking a vision. Its elongated points, originally indicating the four winds, form a cross. The artist here had in mind some allusion to the fact that many Indians today hold almost unconsciously to what is good in the old ways, at the same time giving a new significance to it." See Deloria, *Becoming Mary Sully: Toward an American Indian Abstract*, 68.

51. Susan Gardner, "'Though It Broke My Heart to Cut Some Bits I Fancied': Ella Deloria's Original Design for Waterlily," in "Urban American Indian Women's Activism," special issue, *American Indian Quarterly* 27, no. 3/4 (Summer-Autumn 2003): 667–96.

52. Gardner, 667.

53. Estes, *Our History Is the Future: Standing Rock versus the Dakota Access Pipeline, and the Long Tradition of Indigenous Resistance*, 109–10.

54. Deloria, *Waterlily*, 107, 110.

55. As Coyle puts it, treaties mean to "establish a new structure of relationships between the parties that would endure indefinitely." Michael Coyle, "As Long as the Sun Shines: Recognizing That Treaties Were Intended to Last," in *The Right Relationship: Reimagining the Implementation of Historical Treaties*, ed. John Borrows and Michael Coyle (Toronto: University of Toronto Press, 2017), 49.

56. Deloria, *Waterlily*, 190.

57. Deloria, 9.

58. Deloria, 57; Julian Rice, ed., *Ella Deloria's The Buffalo People* (Albuquerque: University of New Mexico Press, 1994), 67–126.

59. Deloria, *Waterlily*, 56.

60. Deloria, 57.

61. Deloria, 56.

62. Deloria, 56.

63. Deloria, 56.

64. Steiner, *The New Indians*; Charles Wilkinson, *Blood Struggle: The Rise of Modern Indian Nations* (New York: W. W. Norton & Company, 2005).

65. Deloria Jr., *Behind the Trail of Broken Treaties: An Indian Declaration of Independence*, x. Subsequent citations are given in the text as *BT*.

66. For the Third World rejection of unequal treaties, see Anna Brunner, "Acquired Rights and State Succession: The Rise and Fall of the Third World in the International Law Commission," in *The Battle for International Law: South-North Perspectives on the Decolonization Era*, ed. Jochen von Bernstorff and Phillip Dann (New York: Oxford University Press, 2019), 124–40.

67. Vine Deloria Jr., *God Is Red* (New York: Grossett & Dunlap, 1973), 23–24.

68. "Vine Deloria Discusses Native American Rights and History," *Studs Terkel Radio Archive*, January 20, 1975, https://studsterkel.wfmt.com/programs/vine-deloria-discusses-native-american-rights-and-history.

69. Deloria Jr., *We Talk, You Listen: New Tribes, New Turf*, 100; Warrior, *Tribal Secrets: Recovering American Indian Intellectual Traditions*, 91.

70. Vine Deloria Jr., "Implications of the 1968 Civil Rights Act on Tribal Autonomy," in *Convocation of American Indian Scholars* (Princeton, NJ: Princeton University Press, 1970), 97.

71. Vine Deloria Jr., "On Wounded Knee 1973," *Akwesasne Notes* 5, no. 2 (Spring 1973): 38; Vine Deloria Jr., "The Most Important Indian," *Race Relations Reporter* 5, no. 21 (November 1974): 26–28.

72. "Trail of Broken Treaties 20-Point Position Paper," October 1972, www.aimmovement.org/archives; David Wilkins, ed., *The Hank Adams Reader: An Exemplary Native Activist and the Unleashing of Indigenous Sovereignty* (Golden, CO: Fulcrum Publishing, 2011).

73. The Nixon response to the Twenty Points is also reproduced in Deloria Jr., *God Is Red*, 325–38; *BT*, viii.

74. Robertson, *Conquest by Law: How the Discovery of America Dispossessed Indigenous Peoples of Their Lands*; Robert J. Miller, "The Doctrine of Discovery: The International Law of Colonialism," *UCLA Indigenous Peoples' Journal of Law, Culture, and Resistance* 5, no. 1 (2019): 35–42.

75. "Behind the Trail of Broken Treaties: Research Materials," 1973, Box 2, Vine Deloria Papers, Yale Collection of Western Americana, Beinecke Rare Book and Manuscript Library.

76. Vine Deloria Jr., "A Different Perspective: Indian Treaties in 1972 (Unpublished MS)," 1972, 1972 Publisher's Correspondence Folder, Box 44, Vine Deloria Papers, Yale Collection of Western Americana, Beinecke Rare Book and Manuscript Library.

77. Deloria Jr., "Implications of the 1968 Civil Rights Act on Tribal Autonomy," 93.

78. Vine Deloria Jr., "The United States Has No Jurisdiction in Sioux Land," in *The Great Sioux Nation: Sitting in Judgment on America*, ed. Roxanne Dunbar-Ortiz (Lincoln, NE: Bison Books, 2013), 143.

79. Vine Deloria Jr., *A Chronological List of Treaties and Agreements Made by Indian Tribes with the United States* (Washington, DC: Institute for the Development of Indian Law, 1973); Vine Deloria Jr. and Raymond J. DeMallie, *Documents of American Indian Diplomacy: Treaties, Agreements and Conventions*, 2 vols. (Norman: University of Oklahoma Press, 1999).

80. Deloria Jr., *God Is Red*, 35, 44. On the use of tragedy in this manner, see David Myer Temin and Adam Dahl, "Narrating Historical Injustice: Political Responsibility and the Politics of Memory," *Political Research Quarterly* 70, no. 4 (December 2017): 905–17.

81. On unratified treaties, see also Deloria Jr., *God Is Red*, 335.

82. Deloria Jr., "A Different Perspective: Indian Treaties in 1972 (Unpublished MS)."

83. Vine Deloria Jr., "A Violated Covenant (1971)," in *For This Land: Writings on Religion in America*, ed. James Treat (New York: Routledge, 1999), 72–76.

84. Dunbar-Ortiz, ed., *The Great Sioux Nation: Sitting in Judgment on America*, 17–18.

85. Vine Deloria Jr., "Native American Spirituality (1977)," in *For This Land: Writings on Religion in America*, ed. James Treat (New York: Routledge, 1999), 130–34; Vine Deloria Jr., "Preface," in *Spirit and Reason* (Golden, CO: Fulcrum Publishing, 1999), xi–xv.

86. Deloria Jr., "A Violated Covenant (1971)." See also an essay by Raymond DeMallie, one of Deloria's longtime collaborators: Raymond J. DeMallie, "American Indian Treaty Making: Motives and Meanings," *American Indian Journal* 3, no. 2 (1977): 2–10.

87. Vine Deloria Jr., "The Significance of the 1868 Treaty," *Medicine Root Magazine* (1974): 14–16.

88. Vine Deloria Jr., "The Lummi Indian Community: The Fishermen of the Pacific Northwest," in *American Indian Economic Development*, ed. Sam Stanley (Berlin: De Gruyter, 1978), 89.

89. Deloria Jr., 97–98; Vine Deloria Jr., "Self-Determination and the Concept of Sovereignty," in *Economic Development in American Indian Reservations*, ed. Roxanne Dunbar-Ortiz (Albuquerque: University of New Mexico Press, 1979), 26.

90. Glen T. Morris, "Vine Deloria Jr., and the Development of a Decolonizing Critique of Indigenous Peoples and International Relations," in *Native Voices: American Indian Identity and Resistance*, ed. Richard A. Grounds, George E. Tinker, and David E. Wilkins (Lawrence: University Press of Kansas, 2003), 97–154.

91. United Nations General Assembly, "Resolution 1514 (XV) Declaration on the Granting of Independence to Colonial Countries and Peoples," 1960.

92. "Decolonization, Liberation, and the International Community," *Treaty Council News*, December 1977.

93. Lightfoot, *Global Indigenous Politics: A Subtle Revolution*; International Indian Treaty Council, "Declaration of Continuing Independence."

94. Emerging from earlier discussions in its first Platform Document, the IITC unsuccessfully lobbied to have other countries file the 1868 Treaty as an international document at the UN. "Platform Document–Treaty Council."

95. "International NGO Conference on Discrimination against Indigenous Populations in the Americas" (International Indian Treaty Council, September 20, 1977).

CHAPTER THREE

1. Frantz Fanon, *The Wretched of the Earth*, trans. Richard Philcox (New York: Grove Press, 2004), 9.

2. George Manuel and Michael Posluns, *The Fourth World: An Indian Reality* (Minneapolis: University of Minnesota Press, 2019). Subsequent citations to *The Fourth World* are to the republished 2019 edition and are given in the text as *FW*. Manuel and Posluns collaboratively coauthored *The Fourth World*, which poses a problem in attributing insights to one author or the other. As part of my archival research, I listened to the taped dialogues Posluns and Manuel recorded beginning in March 1971 that formed the basis of the book. These tapes show that Manuel was the motive force behind articulating the core concepts in the book, but Posluns played a crucial role in expanding on these concepts in the written form. I refer primarily to Manuel as the source of

core insights in the text, but where possible I infer from the evidence Posluns's likely contribution.

3. Glen Sean Coulthard, "Introduction: A Fourth World Resurgent," in *The Fourth World: An Indian Reality*, by George Manuel and Michael Posluns (Minneapolis: University of Minnesota Press, 2019), xi.

4. Alfred, *Heeding the Voices of Our Ancestors: Kahnawake Mohawk Politics and the Rise of Native Nationalism*; Taiaiake Alfred, *Wasáse: Indigenous Pathways of Action and Freedom* (Toronto: University of Toronto Press, 2005); Taiaiake Alfred and Jeff Corntassel, "Being Indigenous Resurgences against Contemporary Colonialism," *Government and Opposition* 40, no. 4 (2005): 597–614; Taiaiake Alfred, *Peace, Power, Righteousness: An Indigenous Manifesto* (New York: Oxford University Press, 2009); Michael Elliott, "Indigenous Resurgence: The Drive for Renewed Engagement and Reciprocity in the Turn Away from the State," *Canadian Journal of Political Science* 51, no. 1 (March 2018): 61–81.

5. Vicki Hsueh, "Cultivating and Challenging the Common: Lockean Property, Indigenous Traditionalisms, and the Problem of Exclusion," *Contemporary Political Theory* 5, no. 2 (May 1, 2006): 193–214; Leanne Betasamosake Simpson, "Indigenous Resurgence and Co-Resistance," *Critical Ethnic Studies* 2, no. 2 (Fall 2016): 9–34; Simpson, *As We Have Always Done: Indigenous Freedom through Radical Resistance*; Gina Starblanket and Heidi Kiiwetinepinesiik Stark, "Toward a Relational Paradigm—Four Points for Consideration: Knowledge, Gender, Land, and Modernity," in *Resurgence and Reconciliation: Indigenous-Settler Relations and Earth Teachings*, ed. Michael Asch, John Borrows, and James Tully (Toronto: University of Toronto Press, 2018), 175–207; Sarah A. Nickel, *Assembling Unity: Indigenous Politics, Gender, and the Union of BC Indian Chiefs* (Vancouver: University of British Columbia Press, 2019).

6. Canada, Parliament, Commons, Special Committees, "Report of the Special Committee of the Senate and House of Commons Meeting in Joint Session to Inquire into the Claims of the Indian Tribes of British Columbia" (Ottawa: King's Printer, 1927); Paul Tennant, *Aboriginal Peoples and Politics: The Indian Land Question in British Columbia, 1849–1989* (Vancouver: University of British Columbia Press, 1990), 111–12; Nickel, *Assembling Unity: Indigenous Politics, Gender, and the Union of BC Indian Chiefs*.

7. Peter McFarlane, *From Brotherhood to Nationhood: George Manuel and the Making of the Modern Indian Movement* (Toronto: Between the Lines, 1993); Rudolph C. Ryser, "The Legacy of Grand Chief George Manuel" (Center for World Indigenous Studies, 1995). On the WCIP, see Douglas Sanders, *The Formation of the World Council of Indigenous Peoples* (Copenhagen: International Working Group for Indigenous Affairs, 1974); Jochen Kemner, "Lobbying for Global Indigenous Rights: The World Council of Indigenous Peoples (1975–1997)," *Forum for Inter-American Research* 4, no. 2 (November 2011); Jonathan Crossen, "Decolonization, Indigenous Internationalism, and the World Council of Indigenous Peoples" (PhD diss., Waterloo, ON, University of Waterloo, 2014); Jonathan Crossen, "Another Wave of Anti-Colonialism: The Origins of Indigenous Internationalism," *Canadian Journal of History* 52, no. 3 (Winter 2017): 533–59; Hagdvet Vik, "Indigenous Internationalism," 326–32; Alyosha Goldstein, "The Anti-Imperialist Horizon," *Critical Ethnic Studies* 7, no. 1 (Spring 2021), https://manifold.umn.edu/read/ces0701-anti-imperialist-horizon/section/fdf4dff9-00d9-4ce9-b893-f05d2b831e4f. On the Constitution Express, see Madeleine Rose Knickerbocker and Sarah Nickel, "Negotiating Sovereignty: Indigenous Perspectives on the Patriation of a Settler Colonial Constitution, 1975–1983," *BC Studies*, no. 190 (Summer

2016): 67–88; Emma Feltes and Glen Coulthard, "The Constitution Express Revisited," *BC Studies* 212 (Winter 2021): 13–32; George Manuel, "Petition and Bill of Particulars on the Political Standing of Indigenous Tribes and Bands under the Protection of the British Government in the Face of Impending Canadian Independence," December 1980, http://constitution.ubcic.bc.ca/sites/constitution.ubcic.bc.ca/files/PetitionTo UNOCR.pdf.

8. "Statement of the Government of Canada on Indian Policy (White Paper)," 1969.

9. Turner, *This Is Not a Peace Pipe: Towards a Critical Indigenous Philosophy*.

10. Hugh Donald Forbes, "Trudeau as the First Theorist of Canadian Multiculturalism," in *Multiculturalism and the Canadian Constitution*, ed. Stephen Tierney (Vancouver: University of British Columbia Press, 2007), 28.

11. See Jeremy Webber, *Reimagining Canada: Language, Culture, Community, and the Canadian Constitution* (Montreal: McGill-Queen's University Press, 1994); Richard J. F. Day, *Multiculturalism and the History of Canadian Diversity* (Toronto: University of Toronto Press, 2000).

12. For those approaches, see Charles Taylor, *Reconciling the Solitudes: Essays on Canadian Federalism and Nationalism* (Montreal: McGill-Queen's University Press, 1993); Will Kymlicka, *Multicultural Citizenship: A Liberal Theory of Minority Rights* (Oxford: Clarendon Press, 1995); Mark Redhead, "Charles Taylor's Deeply Diverse Response to Canadian Fragmentation: A Project Often Commented on but Seldom Explored," *Canadian Journal of Political Science/Revue Canadienne de Science Politique* 36, no. 1 (2003): 61–83. For important critiques of multiculturalism, see Day, *Multiculturalism and the History of Canadian Diversity*; Day, "Who Is This We That Gives the Gift?"

13. As has been widely documented, the White Paper prompted a near-immediate backlash from Indigenous organizations, who—having been consulted during the 1960s, what Manuel called the "decade of consultation"—expressed outrage at the proposed policies (*FW*, 156–80). This mobilization ultimately prompted Trudeau and his minister of Indian affairs, Jean Chrétien, to table the proposed legislation. On the White Paper, see Harold Cardinal, *The Unjust Society* (Vancouver: Douglas & MacIntyre, 1999), 1; Sally M. Weaver, *Making Canadian Indian Policy: The Hidden Agenda, 1968–70* (Toronto: University of Toronto Press, 1981); Marie Smallface Marule, "The Canadian Government's Termination Policy: From 1969 to the Present Day," in *One Century Later: Western Canadian Indian Reserves since Treaty 7*, ed. Ian A. L. Getty and Donald B. Smith (Vancouver: University of British Columbia Press, 1978); Bryan D. Palmer, *Canada's 1960s: The Ironies of Identity in a Rebellious Era* (Toronto: University of Toronto Press, 2008).

14. Cardinal, *The Unjust Society*, 13.

15. Cardinal, 140.

16. Indian Chiefs of Alberta, "Citizens Plus," *Aboriginal Policy Studies* 1, no. 2 (June 2011): 192.

17. Quoted in Alan C. Cairns, *Citizens Plus: Aboriginal Peoples and the Canadian State* (Vancouver: University of British Columbia Press, 2000), 52 (my emphasis).

18. Crossen, "Decolonization, Indigenous Internationalism, and the World Council of Indigenous Peoples," 48.

19. Crossen, 19.

20. George Manuel and Michael Posluns, *GM Interview, March 18, 1972*, York University Special Collections, Michael Posluns Fonds, Box 1989-020/008 (024); George

Manuel and Michael Posluns, *GM Interview, January 22, 1973*, York University Special Collections, Michael Posluns Fonds, Box 1989-020/008 (07).

21. George Manuel and Michael Posluns, "Manuscripts, The Fourth World," 1974, York University Special Collections, Michael Posluns Fonds, Box 1989-20/021, Folder 5.

22. See Glen Sean Coulthard, *Red Skins, White Masks: Rejecting the Colonial Politics of Recognition* (Minneapolis: University of Minnesota Press, 2014); Leanne Betasamosake Simpson, *Dancing on Our Turtle's Back: Stories of Nishnaabeg Re-Creation, Resurgence and a New Emergence* (Manitoba: ARP Books, 2011); Leanne Betasamosake Simpson, "Indigenous Resurgence and Co-Resistance"; Simpson, *As We Have Always Done: Indigenous Freedom through Radical Resistance*; Gina Starblanket, "Being Indigenous Feminists: Resurgences against Contemporary Patriarchy," in *Making Space for Indigenous Feminism*, ed. Joyce Green (Halifax: Fernwood Publishing, 2017), 21–41; Elaine Coburn, ed., *More Will Sing Their Way to Freedom: Indigenous Resistance and Resurgence*, illustrated ed. (Halifax: Winnipeg: Fernwood Publishing, 2015).

23. Simpson, *As We Have Always Done: Indigenous Freedom through Radical Resistance*.

24. George Manuel, "Canadian Indians and Maoris Share Common Problems," *Northian: Magazine of the Society for Indian and Northern Education (Saskatchewan Teachers Federation)* 11, no. 2 (1975): 11.

25. Karl Marx, "Preface to *A Contribution to the Critique of Political Economy*," 1859, https://www.marxists.org/archive/marx/works/1859/critique-pol-economy/preface.htm.

26. Manuel and Posluns, "Manuscripts, The Fourth World," 1–2.

27. On the specific contours of peoplehood, land relations, and law within Manuel's Secwépemc nation, see Marianne Ignace and Ronald E. Ignace, *Secwépemc People, Land, and Laws* (Montreal: McGill-Queen's University Press, 2017).

28. The language of "worldview" is not a move away from structural analysis. Though he identifies this conflict over land as one between "worldviews," Manuel is far from suggesting that settler colonialism ought to be understood as a kind of cultural misunderstanding or question of "ignorance" (*FW*, 78). Instead, Manuel argues that the "insistence on the separation of the people from the land" had characterized the most basic drive of settler-colonial invasion (*FW*, 12).

29. C. B. MacPherson, *The Political Theory of Possessive Individualism: Hobbes to Locke* (New York: Oxford University Press, 2011).

30. George Manuel, *Indian Economic Development: A Whiteman's Whitewash, as Presented to the Union of BC Indian Chiefs Annual Conference* (Ottawa: National Indian Brotherhood, 1972).

31. Manuel.

32. George Manuel, "Letter from George Manuel to Jean Chretien, June 25, 1971," York University Special Collections, Michael Posluns Fonds, Box 1989-20/019 (04).

33. Manuel, *Indian Economic Development: A Whiteman's Whitewash, as Presented to the Union of BC Indian Chiefs Annual Conference*.

34. Cf. Nichols, *Theft Is Property! The Recursive Logic of Dispossession*, 116–43; Brenna Bhandar, *Colonial Lives of Property: Law, Land, and Racial Regimes of Ownership* (Durham, NC: Duke University Press, 2018).

35. "Abduction," in *Oxford English Dictionary*, https://bbcwords.oed.com/view dictionaryentry/Entry/215;jsessionid=264066ED92BAB1E1E7D0D9F514F5B4C3.

36. Manuel and Posluns, "Manuscripts, The Fourth World," 3.

37. Patchen Markell, "The Insufficiency of Non-Domination," *Political Theory* 36, no. 1 (February 2008): 25.

38. Markell, 26.

39. Robert Nichols, "Contract and Usurpation: Enfranchisement and Racial Governance in Settler-Colonial Contexts," in *Theorizing Native Studies*, ed. Audra Simpson and Andrea Smith (Durham, NC: Duke University Press, 2014), 99–121. Manuel also describes the implementation of the colonial system: the "forces of conquest and colonial rule" such as the church, the agent system of the Department of Indian Affairs, and residential schools sought to "displace our traditional leaders" (*FW*, 54).

40. For more recent interventions theorizing environmental injustice in the context of settler colonialism, see Kyle Pows Whyte, "The Dakota Access Pipeline, Environmental Injustice, and U.S. Colonialism," *Red Ink* 19, no. 1 (Spring 2017): 154–69; Kyle Pows Whyte, "Settler Colonialism, Ecology, and Environmental Injustice," *Environment and Society: Advances in Research* 9 (2018): 125–44; J. M. Bacon, "Settler Colonialism as Eco-Social Structure and the Production of Colonial Ecological Violence," *Environmental Sociology* 5, no. 1 (2018): 59–69.

41. Sharon R. Krause, "Environmental Domination," *Political Theory* 48, no. 4 (August 2020): 443–68.

42. Mark T. Berger, "After the Third World? History, Destiny and the Fate of Third Worldism," *Third World Quarterly* 25, no. 1 (2004): 9–39.

43. McFarlane, *From Brotherhood to Nationhood: George Manuel and the Making of the Modern Indian Movement*, 129–60.

44. "Canada Red Indians Seek Ties with Us," *Standard*, December 13, 1971.

45. Vijay Prashad, *The Darker Nations: A People's History of the Third World* (New York and London: New Press, 2007), 34.

46. Posluns, who was working in Six Nations territory at the time with the journal *Akwesasne Notes*, came up with the idea of using the Two Row Wampum from the political repertoire of the Haudenosaunee Confederacy to illustrate the parallels between peoples on the East and West Coasts. Michael Posluns, Author Interview, December 1, 2017.

47. World Council of Indigenous Peoples Second General Assembly, "Declaration of Human Rights" (Center for World Indigenous Studies, September 24, 1977).

48. Miranda Johnson, "Connecting Indigenous Rights to Human Rights in the Anglo Settler States: Another 1970s Story," in *Decolonization, Self-Determination, and the Rise of Global Human Rights Politics*, ed. A. Dirk Moses, Marco Durati, and Roland Burke (New York: Oxford University Press, 2020), 109–31.

49. Feltes and Venne, "Decolonization, Not Patriation: The Constitution Express at the Russell Tribunal," 67.

50. Crossen, "Decolonization, Indigenous Internationalism, and the World Council of Indigenous Peoples," 45.

51. Manuel and Posluns, "Manuscripts, The Fourth World."

52. Karen Engle, *The Elusive Promise of Indigenous Development: Rights, Culture, Strategy* (Durham, NC: Duke University Press, 2010), 49–55.

53. Manuel and Posluns, "Manuscripts, The Fourth World," 11.

54. Manuel and Posluns, "Manuscripts, The Fourth World." See also Michael W. Posluns, *Speaking with Authority: The Emergence of the Vocabulary of First Nations' Self-Government* (New York: Routledge, 2007), 171.

55. This paragraph relies on the detailed account of these events in Nickel,

Assembling Unity: Indigenous Politics, Gender, and the Union of BC Indian Chiefs, 91–110.

56. Seth Markle, *A Motorcycle on Hell Run: Tanzania, Black Power, and the Uncertain Future of Pan-Africanism, 1964–1974* (Lansing: Michigan State University Press, 2017).

57. Julius K. Nyerere, "The Arusha Declaration and TANU's Policy on Socialism and Self-Reliance" (Tanganyika African National Union, February 5, 1967), https://www.marxists.org/subject/africa/nyerere/1967/arusha-declaration.htm.

58. On the NIEO, see Nils Gilman, "The New International Economic Order: A Reintroduction," *Humanity: An International Journal of Human Rights, Humanitarianism, and Development* 6, no. 1 (2015): 1–16; Johanna Bockman, "Socialist Globalization against Capitalist Neocolonialism: The Economic Ideas behind the New International Economic Order," *Humanity: An International Journal of Human Rights, Humanitarianism, and Development* 6, no. 1 (Spring 2015): 109–28; Getachew, *Worldmaking after Empire: The Rise and Fall of Self-Determination*, chapter 5.

59. George Manuel, "Government Making Gross Error If Indian Voice Is Not Heard, as Presented to the MacKenzie Valley Pipeline Inquiry," *Native Perspective* 1, no. 6 (1976): 33.

60. Manuel and Posluns, *GM Interview, March 18, 1972*.

61. Julius K. Nyerere, "Ujamaa—The Basis of African Socialism," in *Freedom and Unity/Uhuru Na Umoja: A Selection from Writings and Speeches, 1952–1965* (Dar es Salaam, Tanzania: Oxford University Press, 1966), 167.

62. Nyerere, "Ujamaa—The Basis of African Socialism."

63. In 1968, Nyerere recounted that the Tanganyikan African National Union had chosen the term *Ujamaa* for reasons that run deeper than "the desire to find a Swahili equivalent to socialism." Instead, they chose the word for two reason, according to Nyerere: "First, it is an African word and thus emphasizes the African-ness of the policies we intend to follow. Second, its literal meaning is 'family-hood,' so that it brings to the mind of our people the idea of mutual involvement in the family as we know it." Julius K. Nyerere, "Introduction," in *Freedom and Socialism/Uhuru Na Ujamaa: A Selection from Writings and Speeches, 1965–1967* (Dar es Salaam, Tanzania: Oxford University Press, 1968), 2. On African socialisms, see M. Anne Pitcher and Kelly M. Askew, "African Socialisms and Postsocialisms," *Africa: The Journal of the International Africa Institute* 76, no. 1 (2006): 1–14; Lal, *African Socialism in Postcolonial Tanzania: Between the Village and the World*, 27.

64. Nyerere, "Introduction," 3.

65. Manuel and Posluns, *GM Interview, March 18, 1972*.

66. Crossen, "Decolonization, Indigenous Internationalism, and the World Council of Indigenous Peoples," 42.

67. Manuel quoted in McFarlane, *From Brotherhood to Nationhood: George Manuel and the Making of the Modern Indian Movement*, 160.

68. Adom Getachew, "The Limits of Sovereignty as Responsibility," *Constellations* 26, no. 2 (June 2019): 225–40.

69. Indeed, the state-initiated forced relocations displaced Tanzania's actual "fourth world" for reasons similar to other developmental state-building projects. Vijay Prashad argues that "Nyerere's consideration for this Canadian Native leader did not extend to the Barabaig, a cattle-herding clan of the Datoga community." Vijay Prashad, *The Poorer Nations: A Possible History of the Global South* (London: Verso, 2012), 124.

For a definitive history of the *Ujamaa* villagization project, see Lal, *African Socialism in Postcolonial Tanzania: Between the Village and the World.*

70. Nickel, *Assembling Unity: Indigenous Politics, Gender, and the Union of BC Indian Chiefs*, 49.

71. Crossen, "Decolonization, Indigenous Internationalism, and the World Council of Indigenous Peoples," 48.

72. George Manuel, "Transcript—George Manuel Speech to the National Congress of American Indians," 1975, Box 24 George Manuel: National Museum of the American Indian Archive Center, Smithsonian Institution.

73. Center for World Indigenous Studies, Chief George Manuel Library and Fourth World Documentation Project World Council of Indigenous Peoples et al., "The New International Economic Order: A Promise or Peril for the Indigenous Peoples of the World" (Northwest Regional Conference on the Emerging International Economic Order—Plenary Session, Seattle, 1979).

74. United Nations General Assembly, "Resolution 3281(Xxix) Charter of Economic Rights and Duties of States," 1974.

75. Center for World Indigenous Studies, Chief George Manuel Library and Fourth World Documentation Project World Council of Indigenous Peoples et al., "The New International Economic Order: A Promise or Peril for the Indigenous Peoples of the World."

76. Center for World Indigenous Studies, Chief George Manuel Library and Fourth World Documentation Project World Council of Indigenous Peoples et al.

77. Anthony J. Hall, *The American Empire and the Fourth World: The Bowl with One Spoon, Part One* (Montreal: McGill-Queen's University Press, 2003), 241.

78. Nyerere and the institutional successors of the NIEO, the South Commission, expressed some awareness of Fourth World organizing against extractive development but did nothing to meet the challenges presented. Moreover, structural adjustment programs and the debt crisis of the 1980s consumed their attention. Prashad, *The Poorer Nations: A Possible History of the Global South*, 123–25.

79. Thea Riofrancos, *Resource Radicals: From Petro-Nationalism to Post-Extractivism in Ecuador* (Durham, NC: Duke University Press, 2020); Angélica María Bernal, "Ecuador's Dual Populisms: Neocolonial Extractivism, Violence and Indigenous Resistance," *Thesis Eleven* 164, no. 1 (June 1, 2021): 9–36.

80. George Manuel, "Indigenous Peoples' Fishing Rights and Responsibilities, Draft Presentation before the International Conference on Fisheries, Sponsored by the Government of Mexico" (Document, December 15, 1979).

81. John Borrows and James Tully, "Introduction," in *Resurgence and Reconciliation: Indigenous-Settler Relations and Earth Teachings*, ed. Michael Asch, John Borrows, and James Tully (Toronto: University of Toronto Press, 2018), 6–8.

CHAPTER FOUR

1. Glen Coulthard, "For Our Nations to Live, Capitalism Must Die," *Unsettling America* (blog), November 5, 2013, https://unsettlingamerica.wordpress.com/2013/11/05/for-our-nations-to-live-capitalism-must-die/.

2. Fanon, *The Wretched of the Earth*, 40.

3. Hadani Ditmars, "Palestinians and Canadian Natives Join Hands to Protest Colonization," *Haaretz*, January 29, 2013, https://www.haaretz.com/2013-01-29/ty-article/.

premium/canadian-natives-palestinians-rally-for-colonized/0000017f-f6d0-ddde-abff-fef5de7a0000.

4. For different critiques of recognition, see Elisabeth Povinelli, *The Cunning of Recognition: Indigenous Alterities and the Making of Australian Multiculturalism* (Durham, NC: Duke University Press, 2002); Joanne Barker, *Native Acts: Law, Recognition, and Cultural Authenticity* (Durham, NC: Duke University Press, 2011); Simpson, *Mohawk Interruptus: Political Life across the Borders of Settler-States*; Coulthard, *Red Skins, White Masks: Rejecting the Colonial Politics of Recognition*; Simpson, *As We Have Always Done: Indigenous Freedom through Radical Resistance*.

5. For exceptions to this occlusion, see Ward Churchill, *Marxism and Native Americans* (Boston: South End Press, 1983); John Mohawk, "Marxism: Perspectives from a Native Movement," in *Thinking in Indian*, ed. Jose Barreiro (Golden, CO: Fulcrum Publishing, 2010), 213–23; Sandy Grande, *Red Pedagogy: Native American Social and Political Thought* (Lanham, MD: Rowman & Littlefield, 2015); Coulthard, *Red Skins, White Masks: Rejecting the Colonial Politics of Recognition*, 35; Coulthard, "Once Were Maoists"; Roxanne Dunbar-Ortiz, *Blood on the Border: A Memoir of the Contra War* (Norman: University of Oklahoma Press, 2005); Roxanne Dunbar-Ortiz, "The Relationship between Marxism and Indigenous Struggles and Implications of the Theoretical Framework for International Indigenous Struggles," *Historical Materialism* 24, no. 3 (2016): 76–91; Benjamin Balthasar, "'Travels of an American Indian into the Hinterlands of Soviet Russia': Rethinking Indigenous Modernity and the Popular Front in the Work of Archie Phinney and D'Arcy McNickle," *American Quarterly* 66, no. 2 (June 2014): 385–416; Molly Suzanne Swain, "Victim of Deceit and Self-Deceit: The Role of the State in Undermining Jim Brady's Métis Socialist Politics" (Alberta, University of Alberta, 2018), https://era.library.ualberta.ca/items/92c80d28-bc1e-4744-88bd-558441a16ec4/view/727ba824-a660-441d-9d5b-fbd0fba93e91/Swain_Molly_S_201809_MA.pdf; György Tóth, "'Red' Nations: Marxists and the Native American Sovereignty Movement of the Late Cold War," *Cold War History* 20, no. 2 (April 2, 2020): 197–221; Scott Rutherford, *Canada's Other Red Scare: Indigenous Protest and Colonial Encounters during the Global Sixties* (Montreal: McGill-Queen's Press, 2020).

6. On the concept of a "problem-space," see David Scott, *Conscripts of Modernity: The Tragedy of Colonial Enlightenment* (Durham, NC: Duke University Press, 2004), 3–5.

7. Dunbar-Ortiz, "The Relationship between Marxism and Indigenous Struggles and Implications of the Theoretical Framework for International Indigenous Struggles"; Coulthard, *Red Skins, White Masks: Rejecting the Colonial Politics of Recognition*; Coulthard, "Once Were Maoists."

8. My approach to an already anticolonial terrain of dialectical inquiry differs in this way from the useful account of "decolonizing dialectics" found in George Ciccariello-Maher, *Decolonizing Dialectics* (Durham, NC: Duke University Press, 2017).

9. For "syncretic Marxism," see Robert J. C. Young, *Postcolonialism: An Historical Introduction* (Malden, MA: Wiley & Sons, 2001), 7. In calling these approaches "syncretic," I am intentionally *not* intervening into the many debates that seek to re-litigate what is or is not central to Marx and Engels' views or to "Marxism" as such. My point of departure is inquiry into the re-stretching of an already dynamically anticolonial vocabulary. For a further account of the critical reevaluation of all kinds of Marxisms (plural) central to many anticolonial thinkers and movements, pursued through an examination of languages of developmentalism and with regard to projects seeking to "decolonize

political theory," see Temin, "Development in Decolonization: Walter Rodney, Third World Developmentalism, and 'Decolonizing Political Theory.'"

10. Coulthard, "Introduction: A Fourth World Resurgent"; Coulthard, "Once Were Maoists"; Rutherford, *Canada's Other Red Scare*.

11. On the debates surrounding "Third World Marxism" in the revolutionary anti-imperialist and antiracist politics of the North American left from 1968 to 1975 especially, see Max Elbaum, *Revolution in the Air: Sixties Radicals Turn to Lenin, Mao and Che* (Brooklyn, NY: Verso, 2002); Robin D. G. Kelley and Betsy Esch, "Black Like Mao: Red China and Black Revolution," *Souls: Critical Journal of Black Politics and Culture* 1, no. 4 (1999): 6–41.

12. As a starting point into the concept of racial capitalism, see Cedric J. Robinson, *Black Marxism: The Making of the Black Radical Tradition* (Chapel Hill: University of North Carolina Press, 2000); Jodi Melamed, "Racial Capitalism," *Critical Ethnic Studies* 1, no. 1 (2015): 76–85; Robin D. G. Kelley, "What Did Cedric Robinson Mean by Racial Capitalism?," *Boston Review*, January 12, 2017, https://bostonreview.net/articles/robin-d-g-kelley-introduction-race-capitalism-justice/; Charisse Burden-Stelly, "Modern U.S. Racial Capitalism: Some Theoretical Insights," *Monthly Review* 72, no. 3 (August 2020), https://monthlyreview.org/2020/07/01/modern-u-s-racial-capitalism/.

13. On Métis peoplehood as a category of indigeneity, see Chris Andersen, *"Métis": Race, Recognition, and the Struggle for Indigenous Peoplehood* (Vancouver: University of British Columbia Press, 2014).

14. Harmut Lutz, Murray Hamilton, and Donna Heimbecker, eds., *Howard Adams: Otapawy! The Life of a Métis Leader in His Own Words and Those of His Contemporaries* (Saskatoon: Gabriel Dumont Institute, 2005), 20, 28; Jesse McLaren, "Indigenous Socialism: The Life and Politics of Howard Adams," *Spring Magazine*, September 6, 2019, https://springmag.ca/.

15. Howard Adams, *Prison of Grass: Canada from the Native Point of View* (Toronto: New Press, 1975), 176. This book will be cited subsequently in text as *PG*. Malcolm X, "America's Gravest Crisis since the Civil War," in *Malcolm X: The Last Speeches* (Atlanta: Pathfinder Press, 1989), 68. Lutz, Hamilton, and Heimbecker, *Howard Adams: Otapawy! The Life of a Métis Leader in His Own Words and Those of His Contemporaries*, 163–65.

16. "MSS Annual Meeting Report," April 26, 1969, Library and Archives Canada, Howard Adams Fonds, Volume 3, Folder 10 Metis Society of Saskatchewan— Correspondence and Related Materials, 1969, reproduction copy number R-10982.

17. Lutz, Hamilton, and Heimbecker, *Howard Adams: Otapawy! The Life of a Métis Leader in His Own Words and Those of His Contemporaries*, 171–75.

18. Howard Adams, "Tourist Industry U of S," 1967, Library and Archives Canada, Howard Adams Fonds, Volume 5, Folder 18—Notes and Manuscripts 1948–95, reproduction copy number R-10982; Howard Adams, "Poverty Report: Metis of Saskatchewan," June 14, 1969, Library and Archives Canada, Howard Adams Fonds, Volume 2, Folder 25—Howard Adams Speeches and/or Articles, 1957–69, reproduction copy number R-10982; Howard Adams, "The Outsiders: An Educational Survey of Metis and Non-Treaty Indians of Saskatchewan," June 1972, Library and Archives Canada, Howard Adams Fonds, Volume 3, Folder 3—Howard Adams Speeches and/or Articles, 1970s (2 of 2), reproduction copy number R-10982.

19. Albert Memmi, *The Colonizer and the Colonized* (Boston: Beacon Press, 1967),

77–89; Frantz Fanon, *Black Skin, White Masks*, trans. Richard Philcox (New York: Grove Press, 1952), 221.

20. Howard Adams, "Saskatchewan: The Mississippi of Canada," December 1969, Library and Archives Canada, Howard Adams Fonds, Volume 2, Folder 25—Howard Adams Speeches and/or Articles, 1957–69, reproduction copy number R-10982.

21. James M. Pitsula, "The Thatcher Government in Saskatchewan and the Revival of Metis Nationalism, 1964–1971," *Great Plains Quarterly* 17 (Summer 1997): 223.

22. Pitsula, 223; "MSS Annual Meeting Report."

23. Howard Adams, "From Colonialism to Liberation, Saskatoon, University of Saskatchewan," March 1968, 3, Library and Archives Canada, Howard Adams Fonds, Volume 2, Folder 25—Howard Adams Speeches and/or Articles, 1957–69, reproduction copy number R-10982. See also Deborah Simmons, "Socialism from Below and Indigenous Resurgence: Reclaiming Traditions," in "Indigenous Resurgence," special issue, *New Socialist: Ideas for Radical Change*, no. 58 (October 2008): 13–15; McLaren, "Indigenous Socialism: The Life and Politics of Howard Adams."

24. To develop this argument, Adams stitches together insights from classics such as the Trinidadian-American Marxist Oliver C. Cox's 1948 neglected masterpiece *Caste, Class, and Race: A Study in Social Dynamics*, Third World theorists of neocolonialism such as Kwame Nkrumah, Latin American dependency theorists, and predecessor Métis Marxist-Leninists like James Brady and Malcolm Norris—the latter of whom had already put forward "a racial analysis of class society" in the 1930s and 1940s. Oliver C. Cox, *Caste, Class and Race: A Study in Social Dynamics* (New York: Monthly Review Press, 1948). Cox was also among Cedric Robinson's key reference points. On Norris and Brady, see Murray Dobbin, *The One-and-a-Half Men: The Story of Jim Brady and Malcolm Norris, Metis Patriots of the 20th Century* (Vancouver: New Star Books, 1981).

25. V. I. Lenin, *Imperialism, the Highest State of Capitalism* (1917) (New York: Penguin Classics, 2010).

26. Richard White, *The Middle Ground: Indians, Empires, and Republics in the Great Lakes Region, 1650–1815*, 2nd ed. (New York: Cambridge University Press, 2010).

27. Robinson, *Black Marxism: The Making of the Black Radical Tradition*; Kelley, "What Did Cedric Robinson Mean by Racial Capitalism?"

28. Louis Riel, "Memorial of the People of Rupert's Land and North-West," in *The Collected Writings of Louis Riel: Les Ecrits Complets de Louis Riel*, vol. 1, ed. Gilles Martel and George F. G. Stanley (Edmonton: University of Alberta Press, 1985), 111.

29. On the distinctive and "awkward" multidirectionality of the Métis' shifting alliances with settlers and Indigenous peoples, see Daniel Voth, "The Devil's Northern Triangle: Howard Adams and Métis Multidimensional Relationships with and within Colonialism" (University of British Columbia, 2015).

30. Howard Adams, "The Cree as Colonial People," *Western Canadian Journal of Anthropology* 1, no. 1 (1969): 122.

31. Kiera L. Ladner, "Gendering Decolonisation, Decolonising Gender," *Australian Indigenous Law Review* 13, no. 1 (2009): 62–77.

32. Lee Carter, "Indigenous Students Lobby for Better Conditions," *Indian Magazine*, 1970, CBC Digital Archives, https://www.cbc.ca/archives/entry/native-students-lobby-for-better-conditions; Henry Jack, "Native Alliance for Red Power," in *The Only Good Indian: Essays by Canadian Indians*, ed. Waubgeshig (Toronto: New Press, 1974), 111–27.

33. "NARP Eight Point Program," *NARP Newsletter*, February 1969.

34. Clem Chartier, "China through a Native Perspective," *New Breed*, October 1975, 5–6; Lee Maracle, *Bobbi Lee: Indian Rebel* (1975) (Toronto: Women's Press, 1990), 217–22; Coulthard, "Once Were Maoists."

35. Maracle, *Bobbi Lee: Indian Rebel* (1975), 196.

36. V. I. Lenin, "The Right of Nations to Self-Determination."

37. "On the National Question: Letter from the Native Study Group," *Liberation Support Movement*, Spring 1975, 19. Some non-Indigenous Marxists echoed exactly these terms of analysis in addressing the racism and sheer ineptitude of other white communists in their relation to Indigenous movements: "Our movement must understand what 'justice' really means for Native people, and what 'genocide' really means as well. It must understand the necessity of educating our own working class in full measure about the Native struggle for national liberation." Two Members of the Bolshevik Tendency, "Nationhood or Genocide: The Struggle of the Native People against Canadian and American Imperialism," *Canadian Revolution* 4 (September 1975), https://www.marxists.org/history/erol/periodicals/canadian-revolution/19760402.htm.

38. "On the National Question: Letter from the Native Study Group," 20.

39. Lee Maracle, *I Am Woman: A Native Perspective on Sociology and Feminism* (Vancouver: Write-on Press, 1988), 109. Subsequent citations are given in the text as *IW*.

40. Lee Carter of the Native Movement, one such successor organization, likewise argued, "the trade union movement and the wage struggle was nothing more than workers fighting for a bigger chunk of the wealth stolen from the colonies." Lee Carter, "Capitalism—The Final Stage of Exploitation," *Native Movement*, 1970.

41. Elbaum, *Revolution in the Air*; Coulthard, "Once Were Maoists."

42. On internal colonialism, see Harold Cruse, *Rebellion or Revolution?* (Minneapolis: University of Minnesota Press, 1968); Robert L Allen, *Black Awakening in Capitalist America: An Analytic History* (Garden City, NY: Doubleday, 1969); Robert Blauner, "Internal Colonialism and Ghetto Revolt," *Social Problems* 16, no. 4 (April 1, 1969): 393–408; Mario Barrera, Carlos Muñoz, and Charles Ornelas, "The Barrio as Internal Colony," *Urban Affairs Annual Review* 6 (1972): 465–98; Carmichael and Hamilton, *Black Power: The Politics of Liberation*, 11; Ramón A. Gutiérrez, "Internal Colonialism: An American Theory of Race," *Du Bois Review: Social Science Research on Race* 1, no. 2 (September 2004): 281–95; Morgan Adamson, "Internal Colony as Political Perspective: Counterinsurgency, Extraction, and Anticolonial Legacies of '68 in the United States," *Cultural Politics* 15, no. 3 (November 1, 2019): 343–57.

43. Byrd, *The Transit of Empire: Indigenous Critiques of Colonialism*, 117–46.

44. Lee Maracle and Ray Bobb, "Natives Are Part of the Third World," *Canadian Revolution* 6 (October 1976), https://www.marxists.org/history/erol/periodicals/canadian-revolution/19760603.html.

45. Maracle and Bobb.

46. Lee Maracle, "Red Power Legacies and Lives: An Interview by Scott Rutherford," in *New World Coming: The Sixties and the Shaping of Global Consciousness*, ed. Karen Dubinsky et al. (Toronto: Between the Lines, 2009), 358–67.

47. Maracle, 362.

48. Maracle and Bobb, "Natives Are Part of the Third World."

49. Howard Adams, "Neocolonialism and the Native Struggle (1980)," Library and Archives Canada, Howard Adams Fonds, Volume 2, Folder 4—Speeches and/or Articles 1980s, reproduction copy number R-10982.

50. Adams's book of twenty years later, *A Tortured People*, expands on the con-

solidation of this class of Native bureaucrats and professionals involved especially in managing resource extraction and economic development as a form of "neocolonialism," whereas what he had in mind in the mid-1970s was (in retrospect) more limited to grants to Native organizations, aid, and efforts to promote Indigenous "small business" so as to head off more radical movements. Howard Adams, "Neocolonialism and the Native Struggle (1980)," Library and Archives Canada, Howard Adams Fonds, Volume 2, Folder 4—Speeches and/or Articles 1980s, reproduction copy number R-10982.

51. Kwame Nkrumah, *Neo-Colonialism: The Last Stage of Imperialism* (New York: International Publishers, 1966).

52. Neocolonialism as a rather loose term had also circulated in Canada mainly to signify the newness of the scramble to extract oil and gas and to establish the requisite territorial control over Canada's so-called Northern frontier. See Douglas Daniels, "The Coming Crisis in the Aboriginal Rights Movement: From Colonialism to Neocolonialism to Renaissance," *Native Studies Review* 2, no. 2 (1986): 97–115; Miranda Johnson, *The Land Is Our History: Indigeneity, Law, and the Settler State* (New York: Oxford University Press, 2016), 102–3.

53. M. O'Mally, "Red Capitalism: Self Sufficiency for Native Peoples," *Canadian Business* 53, no. 4 (April 1980).

54. Maracle, *I Am Woman: A Native Perspective on Sociology and Feminism*, 38.

55. Adams, "Neocolonialism and the Native Struggle (1980)."

56. Lee Maracle, *Memory Serves: Oratories*, ed. Smaro Kamboureli (Edmonton: NeWest Press, 2015), 52–53. Subsequent citations are given in the text as *MS*.

57. Lee Maracle, *My Conversations with Canadians* (Toronto: BookThug, 2017), 62–63.

58. Maracle, *My Conversations with Canadians*, 47.

59. Maracle, 86.

60. Maracle, *Bobbi Lee: Indian Rebel (1975)*, 146.

61. Maracle, 196.

62. Maracle, 146.

63. Maracle, 98–102.

64. Jennifer Kelly, "Coming Out of the House: A Conversation with Lee Maracle," *ARIEL: A Review of International English Literature* 25, no. 1 (January 1994): 80.

65. Kelly, 80.

66. Maracle, *My Conversations with Canadians*, 105–8.

67. Lee Maracle, *Sojourner's Truth and Other Stories* (Vancouver: Press Gang, 1990), 19; Maracle, *My Conversations with Canadians*, 107.

68. For this historical sketch, I have drawn from Bonita Lawrence, "Gender, Race, and the Regulation of Native Identity in Canada and the United States: An Overview," *Hypatia* 18, no. 2 (May 2003): 3–31; Joanne Barker, "Gender, Sovereignty, and the Discourse of Rights in Native Women's Activism," *Meridians* 7, no. 1 (2006): 127–61; Joyce Green, *Making Space for Indigenous Feminism* (London: Zed Books, 2007); Dian Millon, *Therapeutic Nations: Healing in an Age of Indigenous Human Rights* (Tucson: University of Arizona Press, 2013), 58–61.

69. Renya Ramirez, "Race, Tribal Nation, and Gender: A Native Feminist Approach to Belonging," *Meridians* 7, no. 2 (2007): 22–40; Sarah Deer, *The Beginning and End of Rape: Confronting Sexual Violence in Native America* (Minneapolis: University of Minnesota Press, 2015).

70. Maracle, "Red Power Legacies and Lives: An Interview by Scott Rutherford," 362.

71. Maracle, *My Conversations with Canadians*, 105.

72. Mishuana R. Goeman, "Notes toward a Native Feminism's Spatial Practice," *Wicazo Sa Review* 24, no. 2 (2009): 169–87; Goeman, *Mark My Words: Native Women Mapping Our Nations*.

73. M. Gouldhawke, "Land Back: The Matrilineal Descent of Modern Indigenous Land Reclamation," December 29, 2019, https://mgouldhawke.wordpress.com/2019/12/29/land-back-the-matrilineal-descent-of-modern-indigenous-land-reclamation/.

74. Maracle, "Red Power Legacies and Lives: An Interview by Scott Rutherford," 365; Mishuana R. Goeman and Jennifer Nez Denetdale, "Native Feminisms: Legacies, Interventions, and Indigenous Sovereignties," *Wicazo Sa Review* 24, no. 2 (Fall 2009): 9–13; Maile Arvin, Eve Tuck, and Angie Morrill, "Decolonizing Feminism: Challenging Connections between Settler Colonialism and Heteropatriarchy," *Feminist Formations* 25, no. 1 (2013): 8–34; Barker, *Critically Sovereign: Indigenous Gender, Sexuality, and Feminist Studies*.

75. Maracle, *My Conversations with Canadians*, 45.

76. Kathleen Jamieson, "Sex Discrimination and the Indian Act," in *Arduous Journey: Canadian Indians and Decolonization*, ed. J. Ponting (Toronto: McClelland and Stewart, 1989), 112–36.

77. Green, *Making Space for Indigenous Feminism*, 24; Millon, *Therapeutic Nations: Healing in an Age of Indigenous Human Rights*, 58–61.

78. Maracle, "Red Power Legacies and Lives: An Interview by Scott Rutherford," 357.

79. Patricia Monture-Angus, *Thunder in My Soul: A Mohawk Woman Speaks* (Halifax: Fernwood, 1995), 75.

80. It is necessary to emphasize here one of the pitfalls Maracle explicitly addressed. Namely, she rejected other Indigenous and non-Indigenous voices who used the idiom of "tradition" to emphasize the fundamental *continuity* of gender roles over time as a natural, depoliticized feature of Indigenous "cultures." The latter claim, Maracle contended, was often rhetorically weaponized in the form of conservative quiescence about directly confronting contemporary gender-based violence. For Maracle, these claims disavowed contemporary realities: "we weren't violent to aboriginal women before, but we are now." Maracle, "Red Power Legacies and Lives: An Interview by Scott Rutherford," 365.

81. Maracle, 366.

82. Maracle, 365.

83. Lee Maracle, "The Operation Was Successful, but the Patient Died," *BC Studies* 212 (Winter 2021): 7–12.

84. Maracle, "Oratory: Coming to Theory."

85. Maracle, *Sojourner's Truth and Other Stories*, 19–20.

86. Lee Maracle, *Sundogs* (Penticton, BC: Theytus Books, 1992); Lee Maracle, *Ravensong* (Vancouver: Press Gang, 1993); Maracle, *Memory Serves: Oratories*, 120.

87. Maracle, "Red Power Legacies and Lives: An Interview by Scott Rutherford," 366.

88. Chantal Fiola, "Transnational Indigenous Feminism: An Interview with Lee Maracle," in *Transnationalism, Activism, Art*, ed. Aine McGlynn and Kit Dobson (Toronto: University of Toronto Press, 2013), 164.

CONCLUSION

1. Elsewhere I have developed other elements of this account of worldly anticolonialism, as an alternative to the emphasis in political, social, and cultural theory on what I characterize as the inflated role of the epistemic critique of Eurocentrism: Temin, "Development in Decolonization: Walter Rodney, Third World Developmentalism, and 'Decolonizing Political Theory.'" See also Adom Getachew and Karuna Mantena, "Anticolonialism and the Decolonization of Political Theory," *Critical Times: Interventions in Global Critical Theory* 4, no. 3 (2021): 359–88.

2. For one critique of this siloing, see Manu Vimalassery, Juliana Hu Pegues, and Alyosha Goldstein, "Introduction: On Colonial Unknowing," *Theory & Event* 19, no. 4 (2016), http://muse.jhu.edu/article/633283.

3. Manu Karuka, *Empire's Tracks: Indigenous Nations, Chinese Workers, and the Transcontinental Railroad* (Oakland: University of California Press, 2019), chap. 1; Kai Bosworth and Charmaine Chua, "The Countersovereignty of Critical Infrastructure Security: Settler-State Anxiety versus the Pipeline Blockade," *Antipode*, October 27, 2021, https://doi.org/10.1111/anti.12794.

4. For some examples of these many projects, see Beth Rose Middleton, *Trust in the Land: New Directions in Tribal Conservation*, First Peoples: New Directions in Indigenous Studies (Tucson: University of Arizona Press, 2011); Clint Carroll, "Native Enclosures: Tribal National Parks and the Progressive Politics of Environmental Stewardship in Indian Country," *Geoforum* 53 (2014): 31–40; Naomi Klein, *This Changes Everything: Capitalism vs. the Climate* (New York: Simon and Schuster, 2014); Amanda Raster and Christina Gish Hill, "The Dispute over Wild Rice: An Investigation of Treaty Agreements and Ojibwe Food Sovereignty," *Agriculture and Human Values* 34, no. 2 (June 2017): 267–81; Stephen T. Garnett et al., "A Spatial Overview of the Global Importance of Indigenous Lands for Conservation," *Nature Sustainability* 1 (2018): 369–74; Dina Gilio-Whitaker, *As Long as Grass Grows: The Indigenous Fight for Environmental Justice, from Colonization to Standing Rock* (Boston: Beacon Press, 2019).

5. Kyle Pows Whyte, "Indigenous Science (Fiction) for the Anthropocene: Ancestral Dystopias and Fantasies of Climate Change Crises," *Environment and Planning E: Nature and Space* 1, no. 1–2 (2018): 224–42; Alexandra Alter, "'We've Already Survived an Apocalypse': Indigenous Writers Are Changing Sci-Fi," *New York Times*, August 14, 2020.

6. Alyosha Goldstein, "Where the Nation Takes Place: Proprietary Regimes, Antistatism, and U.S. Settler Colonialism," *South Atlantic Quarterly* 107, no. 4 (October 1, 2008): 833–61.

7. For example, see Jonathan M. Metzl, *Dying of Whiteness: How the Politics of Racial Resentment Is Killing America's Heartland*, updated ed. (New York: Basic Books, 2020).

8. Greg Grandin, *The End of the Myth: From the Frontier to the Border Wall in the Mind of America* (New York: Metropolitan Books, 2019).

9. Wendy Brown, *Walled States, Waning Sovereignty* (Cambridge: Zone Books, 2010); Andreas Malm and the Zetkin Collective, *White Skin, Black Fuel: On the Danger of Fossil Fascism* (London New York: Verso, 2021).

Bibliography

Ablavsky, Gregory. "The Savage Constitution." *Duke Law Journal* 63, no. 5 (February 1, 2014): 999–1046.

Ackley, Kristina, and Cristina Stanciu. "Introduction: Laura Cornelius Kellogg; Haudenosaunee Thinker, Native Activist, American Writer." In *Laura Cornelius Kellogg: Our Democracy and the American Indian and Other Works*, edited by Kristina Ackley and Cristina Stanciu, 154–66. Syracuse, NY: Syracuse University Press, 2015.

Adams, Howard. "The Cree as Colonial People." *Western Canadian Journal of Anthropology* 1, no. 1 (1969): 120–24.

Adams, Howard. "From Colonialism to Liberation, Saskatoon, University of Saskatchewan," March 1968. Library and Archives Canada, Howard Adams Fonds, Volume 2, Folder 25—Howard Adams Speeches and/or Articles, 1957–69, reproduction copy number R-10982.

Adams, Howard. "Neocolonialism and the Native Struggle (1980)." Library and Archives Canada, Howard Adams Fonds, Volume 2, Folder 4—Speeches and/or Articles 1980s, reproduction copy number R-10982.

Adams, Howard. "The Outsiders: An Educational Survey of Metis and Non-Treaty Indians of Saskatchewan," June 1972. Library and Archives Canada, Howard Adams Fonds, Volume 3, Folder 3—Howard Adams Speeches and/or Articles, 1970s (2 of 2), reproduction copy number R-10982.

Adams, Howard. "Poverty Report: Metis of Saskatchewan," June 14, 1969. Library and Archives Canada, Howard Adams Fonds, Volume 2, Folder 25—Howard Adams Speeches and/or Articles, 1957–69, reproduction copy number R-10982.

Adams, Howard. *Prison of Grass: Canada from the Native Point of View*. Toronto: New Press, 1975.

Adams, Howard. "Saskatchewan: The Mississippi of Canada," December 1969. Library and Archives Canada, Howard Adams Fonds, Volume 2, Folder 25—Howard Adams Speeches and/or Articles, 1957–69, reproduction copy number R-10982.

Adams, Howard. *A Tortured People: The Politics of Colonization*. Vancouver: Theytus Books, 1995.

Adams, Howard. "Tourist Industry U of S," 1967. Library and Archives Canada, Howard Adams Fonds, Volume 5, Folder 18—Notes and Manuscripts 1948–95, reproduction copy number R-10982.

Adamson, Morgan. "Internal Colony as Political Perspective: Counterinsurgency, Extraction, and Anticolonial Legacies of '68 in the United States." *Cultural Politics* 15, no. 3 (2019): 343–57.

Akam, Everett Helmut. *Transnational America: Cultural Pluralist Thought in the Twentieth Century*. Lanham, MD: Rowman & Littlefield, 2002.
Alexandrowicz, C. H. *The European-African Confrontation: A Study in Treaty Making*. Leiden: A. W. Sijthoff, 1973.
Alfred, Gerald Taiaiake. *Heeding the Voices of Our Ancestors: Kahnawake Mohawk Politics and the Rise of Native Nationalism*. New York: Oxford University Press, 1995.
Alfred, Taiaiake. *Peace, Power, Righteousness: An Indigenous Manifesto*. New York: Oxford University Press, 2009.
Alfred, Taiaiake. *Wasáse: Indigenous Pathways of Action and Freedom*. Toronto: University of Toronto Press, 2005.
Alfred, Taiaiake, and Jeff Corntassel. "Being Indigenous Resurgences against Contemporary Colonialism." *Government and Opposition* 40, no. 4 (2005): 597–614.
Allard-Tremblay, Yann. "The Two Row Wampum: Decolonizing and Indigenizing Democratic Autonomy." *Polity* 54, no. 2 (April 2022): 225–49.
Allen, Chadwick. "Introduction: Locating the Society of American Indians." In "The Society of American Indians and Its Legacies," special combined issue, *SAIL: Studies in American Indian Literatures* 25, no. 2, and *American Indian Quarterly* 37, no. 3 (Summer 2013): 3–22.
Allen, Robert L. *Black Awakening in Capitalist America: An Analytic History*. Garden City, NY: Doubleday, 1969.
Alter, Alexandra. "'We've Already Survived an Apocalypse': Indigenous Writers Are Changing Sci-Fi." *New York Times*, August 14, 2020.
Andersen, Chris. *"Métis": Race, Recognition, and the Struggle for Indigenous Peoplehood*. Vancouver: University of British Columbia Press, 2014.
Anghie, Antony. *Imperialism, Sovereignty, and the Making of International Law*. New York: Cambridge University Press, 2005.
Anker, Elisabeth R. *Ugly Freedoms*. Durham, NC: Duke University Press, 2022.
Arvin, Maile, Eve Tuck, and Angie Morrill. "Decolonizing Feminism: Challenging Connections between Settler Colonialism and Heteropatriarchy." *Feminist Formations* 25, no. 1 (2013): 8–34.
Asch, Michael. *On Being Here to Stay: Treaties and Aboriginal Rights in Canada*. Toronto: University of Toronto Press, 2014.
Bacon, J. M. "Settler Colonialism as Eco-Social Structure and the Production of Colonial Ecological Violence." *Environmental Sociology* 5, no. 1 (2018): 59–69.
Balthasar, Benjamin. "'Travels of an American Indian into the Hinterlands of Soviet Russia': Rethinking Indigenous Modernity and the Popular Front in the Work of Archie Phinney and D'Arcy McNickle." *American Quarterly* 66, no. 2 (June 2014): 385–416.
Barker, Joanne, ed. *Critically Sovereign: Indigenous Gender, Sexuality, and Feminist Studies*. Durham, NC: Duke University Press, 2017.
Barker, Joanne. "For Whom Sovereignty Matters." In *For Whom Sovereignty Matters: Locations of Contestation and Possibility in Indigenous Struggles for Self-Determination*, edited by Joanne Barker, 1–31. Lincoln: University of Nebraska Press, 2005.
Barker, Joanne. "Gender, Sovereignty, and the Discourse of Rights in Native Women's Activism." *Meridians* 7, no. 1 (2006): 127–61.
Barker, Joanne. *Native Acts: Law, Recognition, and Cultural Authenticity*. Durham, NC: Duke University Press, 2011.

Barrera, Mario, Carlos Muñoz, and Charles Ornelas. "The Barrio as Internal Colony." *Urban Affairs Annual Review* 6 (1972): 465–98.
Bartelson, Jens. *Sovereignty as Symbolic Form*. London: Routledge, 2014.
Baurkemper, Joseph, and Heidi Kiiwetinepinesiik Stark. "The Trans/National Terrain of Anishinaabe Law and Diplomacy." *Journal of Transnational American Studies* 4, no. 1 (2012).
Belich, James. *Replenishing the Earth: The Settler Revolution and the Rise of the Anglo-World*. Oxford: Oxford University Press, 2011.
Bell, Duncan, ed. *Empire, Race and Global Justice*. Cambridge: Cambridge University Press, 2019.
Bell, Duncan. *The Idea of Greater Britain: Empire and the Future of World Order, 1860–1900*. Princeton, NJ: Princeton University Press, 2011.
Bell, Duncan. *Reordering the World: Essays on Liberalism and Empire*. Princeton, NJ: Princeton University Press, 2016.
Belmessous, Saliha, ed. *Empire by Treaty: Negotiating European Expansion, 1600–1900*. New York: Oxford University Press, 2014.
Beltrán, Cristina. *Cruelty as Citizenship: How Migrant Suffering Sustains White Democracy*. Minneapolis: University of Minnesota Press, 2020.
Berger, Mark T. "After the Third World? History, Destiny and the Fate of Third Worldism." *Third World Quarterly* 25, no. 1 (2004): 9–39.
Bernal, Angélica María. "Ecuador's Dual Populisms: Neocolonial Extractivism, Violence and Indigenous Resistance." *Thesis Eleven* 164, no. 1 (June 1, 2021): 9–36.
Bhandar, Brenna. *Colonial Lives of Property: Law, Land, and Racial Regimes of Ownership*. Durham, NC: Duke University Press, 2018.
Biolsi, Thomas, and Larry Zimmerman, eds. *Indians and Anthropologists: Vine Deloria, Jr. and the Critique of Anthropology*. Tucson: University of Arizona, 1997.
Blackhawk, Maggie. "Federal Indian Law as Paradigm within Public Law." *Harvard Law Review* 132, no. 7 (May 2019): 1787–1877.
Blauner, Robert. "Internal Colonialism and Ghetto Revolt." *Social Problems* 16, no. 4 (April 1, 1969): 393–408.
Boas, Franz. *The Mind of Primitive Man*. New York: Macmillan, 1922.
Bockman, Johanna. "Socialist Globalization against Capitalist Neocolonialism: The Economic Ideas behind the New International Economic Order." *Humanity: An International Journal of Human Rights, Humanitarianism, and Development* 6, no. 1 (Spring 2015): 109–28.
Bonnin (Zitkala-Ša), Gertrude, Charles H. Fabens, and Matthew K. Sniffen. *Oklahoma's Poor Rich Indians: An Orgy of Graft and Exploitation of the Five Civilized Tribes—Legalized Robbery*. Philadelphia: Office of the Indian Rights Association, 1924.
Borrows, John. *Canada's Indigenous Constitution*. Toronto: University of Toronto, 2010.
Borrows, John. "Wampum at Niagara: The Royal Proclamation, Canadian Legal History, and Self-Government." In *Aboriginal and Treaty Rights in Canada: Essays on Law, Equity, and Respect for Difference*, edited by Michael Asch, 155–72. Vancouver: University of British Columbia Press, 1997.
Borrows, John, and James Tully. "Introduction." In *Resurgence and Reconciliation: Indigenous-Settler Relations and Earth Teachings*, edited by Michael Asch, John Borrows, and James Tully, 3–28. Toronto: University of Toronto Press, 2018.
Bosworth, Kai, and Charmaine Chua. "The Countersovereignty of Critical Infra-

structure Security: Settler-State Anxiety versus the Pipeline Blockade." *Antipode*, October 27, 2021. https://doi.org/10.1111/anti.12794.

Brooks, Lisa. *The Common Pot: The Recovery of Native Space in the Northeast*. Minneapolis: University of Minnesota Press, 2008.

Brown, Wendy. *Walled States, Waning Sovereignty*. Cambridge: Zone Books, 2010.

Brunner, Anna. "Acquired Rights and State Succession: The Rise and Fall of the Third World in the International Law Commission." In *The Battle for International Law: South-North Perspectives on the Decolonization Era*, edited by Jochen von Bernstorff and Phillip Dann, 124–40. New York: Oxford University Press, 2019.

Bruyneel, Kevin. "Challenging American Boundaries: Indigenous People and the 'Gift' of U.S. Citizenship." *Studies in American Political Development* 18 (Spring 2004): 30–43.

Bruyneel, Kevin. *Settler Memory: The Disavowal of Indigeneity and the Politics of Race in the United States*. Chapel Hill: University of North Carolina Press, 2021.

Bruyneel, Kevin. "Social Science and the Study of Indigenous People's Politics: Contributions, Omissions, and Tensions." In *Oxford Handbook of Indigenous Peoples' Politics*, edited by José Antonio Lucero, Dale Turner, and Donna Lee Vancott. New York: Oxford University Press, 2014. https://www.oxfordhandbooks.com/view/10.1093/oxfordhb/9780195386653.001.0001/oxfordhb-9780195386653-e-008.

Bruyneel, Kevin. *The Third Space of Sovereignty: The Postcolonial Politics of U.S.-Indigenous Relations*. Minneapolis: University of Minnesota Press, 2007.

Burden-Stelly, Charisse. "Modern U.S. Racial Capitalism: Some Theoretical Insights." *Monthly Review* 72, no. 3 (August 2020). https://monthlyreview.org/2020/07/01/modern-u-s-racial-capitalism/.

Byrd, Jodi A. "Indigenous Futures beyond the Sovereignty Debate." In *The Cambridge History of Native American Literature*, edited by Melanie Benson Taylor, 501–18. Cambridge: Cambridge University Press, 2020.

Byrd, Jodi A. *The Transit of Empire: Indigenous Critiques of Colonialism*. Minneapolis: University of Minnesota Press, 2011.

Cahill, Cathleen D. "'Our Democracy and the American Indian': Citizenship, Sovereignty, and the Native Vote in the 1920s." *Journal of Women's History* 32, no. 2 (Spring 2020): 41–51.

Cairns, Alan C. *Citizens Plus: Aboriginal Peoples and the Canadian State*. Vancouver: University of British Columbia Press, 2000.

Calloway, Colin G. "Treaties and Treaty Making." In *The Oxford Handbook of American Indian History*, edited by Frederick E. Hoxie, 539–52. New York: Oxford University Press, 2016.

Canada. Parliament. Commons. Special Committees. "Report of the Special Committee of the Senate and House of Commons Meeting in Joint Session to Inquire into the Claims of the Indian Tribes of British Columbia." Ottawa: King's Printer, 1927.

"Canada Red Indians Seek Ties with Us." *Standard*, December 13, 1971.

Cardinal, Harold. *The Unjust Society*. Vancouver: Douglas & MacIntyre, 1999.

Carmichael, Stokely, and Charles Hamilton. *Black Power: The Politics of Liberation*. New York: Vintage, 1992.

Carroll, Clint. "Native Enclosures: Tribal National Parks and the Progressive Politics of Environmental Stewardship in Indian Country." *Geoforum* 53 (2014): 31–40.

Carter, Lee. "Capitalism—The Final Stage of Exploitation." *Native Movement*, 1970.

Carter, Lee. "Indigenous Students Lobby for Better Conditions," *Indian Magazine*,

1970. CBC Digital Archives. https://www.cbc.ca/archives/entry/native-students-lobby-for-better-conditions.
Center for World Indigenous Studies, Chief George Manuel Library and Fourth World Documentation Project World Council of Indigenous Peoples, et al. "The New International Economic Order: A Promise or Peril for the Indigenous Peoples of the World." Seattle, 1979.
Chaat Smith, Paul, and Robert Warrior. *Like a Hurricane: The Indian Movement from Alcatraz to Wounded Knee*. New York: New Press, 1997.
Chartier, Clem. "China through a Native Perspective." *New Breed*, October 1975, 5–6.
Churchill, Ward. *Marxism and Native Americans*. Boston: South End Press, 1983.
Ciccariello-Maher, George. *Decolonizing Dialectics*. Durham, NC: Duke University Press, 2017.
Cobb, Amanda J. "Understanding Tribal Sovereignty: Definitions, Conceptualizations, and Interpretations." *American Studies* 46, no. 3/4 (2005): 115–32.
Cobb, Daniel. *Native Activism in Cold War America: The Struggle for Sovereignty*. Lawrence: University Press of Kansas, 2008.
Coburn, Elaine, ed. *More Will Sing Their Way to Freedom: Indigenous Resistance and Resurgence*. Illustrated edition. Halifax: Winnipeg: Fernwood Publishing, 2015.
Cocks, Joan. "Foundational Violence and the Politics of Erasure." *Radical Philosophy Review* 15, no. 1 (2012): 103–26.
Cocks, Joan. *On Sovereignty and Other Political Delusions*. New York: Bloomsbury, 2014.
Collier, John. "Africa View—and Indian." *American Indian Life*, July 1931, 36–40.
Collier, John. "The American Congo." *Survey* 50, no. 9 (August 1923): 467–76.
Collier, John. *From Every Zenith: A Memoir*. New York: Sage Books, 1963.
Collier, John. *On the Gleaming Way: Navajos, Eastern Pueblos, Zunis, Hopis, Apaches, and Their Land; and Their Meanings to the World*. Denver: Sage, 1962.
Collier, John. "The Red Slaves of Oklahoma." *Sunset* 52 (March 1924): 9–11, 94–100.
Connolly, William E. *Pluralism*. Durham, NC: Duke University Press Books, 2005.
Cook-Lynn, Elizabeth. "The American Indian Fiction Writer: 'Cosmopolitanism, Nationalism, the Third World, and First Nation Sovereignty.'" *Wicazo Sa Review* 9, no. 2 (Autumn 1993): 26–36.
Cooper, Frederick. *Citizenship between Empire and Nation: Remaking France and French Africa, 1945–1960*. Princeton, NJ: Princeton University Press, 2014.
Cooper, Frederick. "Development, Modernization, and the Social Sciences in the Era of Decolonization: The Examples of British and French Africa." *Revue d'Histoire Des Sciences Humaines* 10 (2004): 9–38.
Cotera, Maria Eugenia. *Native Speakers: Ella Deloria, Zora Neale Hurston, Jovita Gonzalez and the Poetics of Culture*. Austin: University of Texas Press, 2008.
Coulthard, Glen. "For Our Nations to Live, Capitalism Must Die." *Unsettling America* (blog), November 5, 2013. https://unsettlingamerica.wordpress.com/2013/11/05/for-our-nations-to-live-capitalism-must-die/.
Coulthard, Glen Sean. "Introduction: A Fourth World Resurgent." In *The Fourth World: An Indian Reality*, by George Manuel and Michael Posluns, ix–xxxiv. Minneapolis: University of Minnesota Press, 2019.
Coulthard, Glen Sean. "Once Were Maoists: Third World Currents in Fourth World Anti-Colonialism, Vancouver, 1967–1975." In *Routledge Handbook of Critical Indigenous Studies*, 378–91. New York: Routledge, 2020.

Coulthard, Glen Sean. *Red Skins, White Masks: Rejecting the Colonial Politics of Recognition.* Minneapolis: University of Minnesota Press, 2014.
Cowger, Thomas W. *The National Congress of American Indians: The Founding Years.* Lincoln: University of Nebraska Press, 2001.
Cox, Oliver C. *Caste, Class and Race: A Study in Social Dynamics.* New York: Monthly Review Press, 1948.
Coyle, Michael. "As Long as the Sun Shines: Recognizing That Treaties Were Intended to Last." In *The Right Relationship: Reimagining the Implementation of Historical Treaties,* edited by John Borrows and Michael Coyle, 39–69. Toronto: University of Toronto Press, 2017.
Crossen, Jonathan. "Another Wave of Anti-Colonialism: The Origins of Indigenous Internationalism." *Canadian Journal of History* 52, no. 3 (Winter 2017): 533–59.
Crossen, Jonathan. "Decolonization, Indigenous Internationalism, and the World Council of Indigenous Peoples." PhD dissertation, University of Waterloo, 2014.
Cruse, Harold. *Rebellion or Revolution?* Minneapolis: University of Minnesota Press, 1968.
Dahl, Adam. *Empire of the People: Settler Colonialism and the Foundations of Modern Democratic Thought.* Lawrence: University Press of Kansas, 2018.
Daifallah, Yasmeen. "The Politics of Decolonial Interpretation: Tradition and Method in Contemporary Arab Thought." *American Political Science Review* 113, no. 3 (August 2019): 810–23.
Daniels, Douglas. "The Coming Crisis in the Aboriginal Rights Movement: From Colonialism to Neocolonialism to Renaissance." *Native Studies Review* 2, no. 2 (1986): 97–115.
Daschuk, James O. *Clearing the Plains: Disease, Politics of Starvation, and the Loss of Aboriginal Life.* Regina: University of Regina Press, 2013.
Day, Richard. *Multiculturalism and the History of Canadian Diversity.* Toronto: University of Toronto Press, 2000.
Day, Richard. "Who Is This We That Gives the Gift? Native American Political Theory and the Western Tradition." *Critical Horizons* 2, no. 2 (2001): 173–201.
"Decolonization, Liberation, and the International Community." *Treaty Council News,* December 1977.
Deer, Sarah. *The Beginning and End of Rape: Confronting Sexual Violence in Native America.* Minneapolis: University of Minnesota Press, 2015.
Deloria, Ella. *Speaking of Indians.* Lincoln: University of Nebraska Press, 1998.
Deloria, Ella. *Waterlily.* Lincoln, NE: Bison Books, 1988.
Deloria, Vine, Jr. *Behind the Trail of Broken Treaties: An Indian Declaration of Independence.* Austin: University of Texas Press, 1974.
Deloria, Vine, Jr. "Behind the Trail of Broken Treaties: Research Materials," 1973. Box 2, Vine Deloria Papers, Yale Collection of Western Americana, Beinecke Rare Book and Manuscript Library.
Deloria, Vine, Jr. *A Chronological List of Treaties and Agreements Made by Indian Tribes with the United States.* Washington, DC: Institute for the Development of Indian Law, 1973.
Deloria, Vine, Jr. *Custer Died for Your Sins: An Indian Manifesto.* New York: Macmillan, 1969.
Deloria, Vine, Jr. "A Different Perspective: Indian Treaties in 1972," unpublished ms.,

1972. 1972 Publisher's Correspondence Folder, Box 44. Vine Deloria Papers. Yale Collection of Western Americana, Beinecke Rare Book and Manuscript Library.

Deloria, Vine, Jr. *God Is Red.* New York: Grossett & Dunlap, 1973.

Deloria, Vine, Jr. "Implications of the 1968 Civil Rights Act on Tribal Autonomy." In *Convocation of American Indian Scholars,* 85–103. Princeton, NJ: Princeton University Press, 1970.

Deloria, Vine, Jr. "Letter to James Buswell, April 23, 1965," n.d. Box 75, Correspondence, 1965–67; Folder 2: April 1965; National Museum of the American Indian Archive Center, Smithsonian Institution.

Deloria, Vine, Jr. "The Lummi Indian Community: The Fishermen of the Pacific Northwest." In *American Indian Economic Development,* edited by Sam Stanley, 87–158. Berlin: De Gruyter, 1978.

Deloria, Vine, Jr., ed. "Minutes of the Plains Congress, Rapid City Indian School, Rapid City, South Dakota." In *The Indian Reorganization Act: Congresses and Bills,* 24–101. Norman: University of Oklahoma Press, 2002.

Deloria, Vine, Jr. "The Most Important Indian." *Race Relations Reporter* 5, no. 21 (November 1974): 26–28.

Deloria, Vine, Jr. "Native American Spirituality (1977)." In *For This Land: Writings on Religion in America,* edited by James Treat, 130–34. New York: Routledge, 1999.

Deloria, Vine, Jr. "On Wounded Knee 1973." *Akwesasne Note* 5, no. 2 (Spring 1973): 38.

Deloria, Vine, Jr. "Preface." In *Spirit and Reason,* xi–xv. Golden, CO: Fulcrum Publishing, 1999.

Deloria, Vine, Jr. "Self-Determination and the Concept of Sovereignty." In *Economic Development in American Indian Reservations,* edited by Roxanne Dunbar-Ortiz, 22–28. Albuquerque: University of New Mexico Press, 1979.

Deloria, Vine, Jr. Series II: Chronological Correspondences, Box 15, January–March 1970 Correspondence Folder. Vine Deloria Papers. Yale Collection of Western Americana. Beinecke Rare Book and Manuscript Library.

Deloria, Vine, Jr. "The Significance of the 1868 Treaty." *Medicine Root Magazine* (1974): 14–16.

Deloria, Vine, Jr. "Testimony of Joseph R. Garry in Support of Resolution No. 3." In *Of Utmost Good Faith,* 214–16. San Francisco: Straight Arrow Books, 1971.

Deloria, Vine, Jr. "The United States Has No Jurisdiction in Sioux Land." In *The Great Sioux Nation: Sitting in Judgment on America,* edited by Roxanne Dunbar-Ortiz, 141–46. Lincoln, NE: Bison Books, 2013.

Deloria, Vine, Jr. "A Violated Covenant (1971)." In *For This Land: Writings on Religion in America,* edited by James Treat, 72–76. New York: Routledge, 1999.

Deloria, Vine, Jr. *We Talk, You Listen: New Tribes, New Turf.* Lincoln, NE: Bison Books, 1970.

Deloria, Vine, Jr., and Raymond J. DeMallie. *Documents of American Indian Diplomacy: Treaties, Agreements and Conventions.* 2 vols. Norman: University of Oklahoma Press, 1999.

Deloria, Phillip J. "American Master Narratives and the Problem of Indian Citizenship in the Gilded Age and Progressive Era." *Journal of the Gilded Age and Progressive Era* 14, no. 1 (January 2015): 3–12.

Deloria, Phillip J. *Becoming Mary Sully: Toward an American Indian Abstract.* Seattle: University of Washington Press, 2019.

Deloria, Phillip J. *Indians in Unexpected Places*. Lawrence: University Press of Kansas, 2004.

DeMallie, Raymond J. "American Indian Treaty Making: Motives and Meanings." *American Indian Journal* 3, no. 2 (1977): 2–10.

Ditmars, Hadani. "Palestinians and Canadian Natives Join Hands to Protest Colonization." *Haaretz*, January 29, 2013. https://www.haaretz.com/2013-01-29/ty-article/.premium/canadian-natives-palestinians-rally-for-colonized/0000017f-f6d0-ddde-abff-fef5de7a0000.

Dobbin, Murray. *The One-and-a-Half Men: The Story of Jim Brady and Malcolm Norris, Metis Patriots of the 20th Century*. Vancouver: New Star Books, 1981.

Dunbar-Ortiz, Roxanne. *Blood on the Border: A Memoir of the Contra War*. Norman: University of Oklahoma Press, 2005.

Dunbar-Ortiz, Roxanne, ed. *The Great Sioux Nation: Sitting in Judgment on America*. Lincoln, NE: Bison Books, 2013.

Dunbar-Ortiz, Roxanne. "The Relationship between Marxism and Indigenous Struggles and Implications of the Theoretical Framework for International Indigenous Struggles." *Historical Materialism* 24, no. 3 (2016): 76–91.

Eastman, Charles Alexander. *The Indian To-Day: The Past and Future of the First American*. New York: Doubleday, 1915.

Eastman, Charles Alexander. "The North American Indian." In *Papers on Inter-Racial Problems, Communicated to the First Universal Races Congress at the University of London, July 26–29*, 367–76. Boston: World's Peace Foundation, 1911.

Elbaum, Max. *Revolution in the Air: Sixties Radicals Turn to Lenin, Mao and Che*. Brooklyn, NY: Verso, 2002.

Elisabeth Povinelli. *The Cunning of Recognition: Indigenous Alterities and the Making of Australian Multiculturalism*. Durham, NC: Duke University Press, 2002.

Elkins, Caroline, and Susan Pedersen, eds. *Settler Colonialism in the Twentieth Century: Projects, Practices, Legacies*. New York: Routledge, 2005.

"Ella Deloria to Franz Boas," August 25, 1935. Franz Boas Papers: Inventory D at the American Philosophical Society, Philadelphia, PA. https://search.amphilsoc.org/collections/view?docId=ead/Mss.B.B61.inventory04-ead.xml.

"Ella Deloria to Franz Boas," February 12, 1938. Franz Boas Papers: Inventory D at the American Philosophical Society, Philadelphia, PA. https://search.amphilsoc.org/collections/view?docId=ead/Mss.B.B61.inventory04-ead.xml.

Elliott, Michael. "Indigenous Resurgence: The Drive for Renewed Engagement and Reciprocity in the Turn Away from the State." *Canadian Journal of Political Science* 51, no. 1 (March 2018): 61–81.

Engle, Karen. *The Elusive Promise of Indigenous Development: Rights, Culture, Strategy*. Durham, NC: Duke University Press, 2010.

Estes, Nick. *Our History Is the Future: Standing Rock versus the Dakota Access Pipeline, and the Long Tradition of Indigenous Resistance*. New York: Verso, 2019.

Fanon, Frantz. *Black Skin, White Masks*. Translated by Richard Philcox. New York: Grove Press, 1952.

Fanon, Frantz. *The Wretched of the Earth*. Translated by Richard Philcox. New York: Grove Press, 2004.

Feltes, Emma, and Glen Coulthard. "The Constitution Express Revisited." *BC Studies* 212 (Winter 2021): 13–32.

Feltes, Emma, and Sharon Venne. "Decolonization, Not Patriation: The Constitution Express at the Russell Tribunal." *BC Studies* 212 (Winter 2021): 65–100.
Finn, Janet L. "Ella Cara Deloria and Mourning Dove: Writing for Cultures, Writing against the Grain." *Critique of Anthropology* 13, no. 4 (1993): 335–49.
Fiola, Chantal. "Transnational Indigenous Feminism: An Interview with Lee Maracle." In *Transnationalism, Activism, Art*, edited by Aine McGlynn and Kit Dobson, 162–70. Toronto: University of Toronto Press, 2013.
Fixico, Donald L. *Termination and Relocation: Federal Indian Policy, 1945–1960*. Albuquerque: University of New Mexico Press, 1986.
Forbes, Hugh Donald. "Trudeau as the First Theorist of Canadian Multiculturalism." In *Multiculturalism and the Canadian Constitution*, edited by Stephen Tierney, 27–42. Vancouver: University of British Columbia Press, 2007.
Ford, Lisa. *Settler Sovereignty: Jurisdiction and Indigenous People in America and Australia, 1788–1836*. Cambridge, MA: Harvard University Press, 2010.
Frymer, Paul. *Building an American Empire: The Era of Territorial and Political Expansion*. Princeton, NJ: Princeton University Press, 2017.
Galanda, Gabriel S. "Back to the Future: The GOP and Tribal Termination." *Indian Country Today*, September 9, 2015. http://indiancountrytodaymedianetwork.com/2015/09/09/back-future-gop-and-tribal-termination.
Gardner, Susan. "Speaking of Ella Deloria: Conversations with Joyzelle Gingway Godfrey, 1998–2000, Lower Brule Community College, South Dakota." *American Indian Quarterly* 24, no. 3 (Summer 2000): 456–81.
Gardner, Susan. "Subverting the Rhetoric of Assimilation: Ella Cara Deloria (Dakota) in the 1920s." *Hecate* 39, no. 1 (2013): 9–32.
Gardner, Susan. "'Though It Broke My Heart to Cut Some Bits I Fancied': Ella Deloria's Original Design for Waterlily." In "Urban American Indian Women's Activism," special issue, *American Indian Quarterly* 27, no. 3/4 (Summer-Autumn 2003): 667–96.
Garnett, Stephen T., Neil D. Burgess, John E. Fa, Álvaro Ferdández-Llamazares, and Zsolt Molnár. "A Spatial Overview of the Global Importance of Indigenous Lands for Conservation." *Nature Sustainability* 1 (2018): 369–74.
Garry, Joseph. "A Declaration of Indian Rights," 1954. Box 257, Folder "Emergency Conference Bulletin," National Museum of the American Indian Archive Center, Smithsonian Institution.
Getachew, Adom. "The Limits of Sovereignty as Responsibility." *Constellations* 26, no. 2 (June 2019): 225–40.
Getachew, Adom. *Worldmaking after Empire: The Rise and Fall of Self-Determination*. Princeton, NJ: Princeton University Press, 2019.
Getachew, Adom, and Karuna Mantena. "Anticolonialism and the Decolonization of Political Theory." *Critical Times: Interventions in Global Critical Theory* 4, no. 3 (2021): 359–88.
Gilio-Whitaker, Dina. *As Long as Grass Grows: The Indigenous Fight for Environmental Justice, from Colonization to Standing Rock*. Boston: Beacon Press, 2019.
Gilman, Nils. "The New International Economic Order: A Reintroduction." *Humanity: An International Journal of Human Rights, Humanitarianism, and Development* 6, no. 1 (2015): 1–16.
Goeman, Mishuana "Disrupting a Settler-Colonial Grammar of Place: The Visual

Memoir of Hulleah Tsinhnahjinnie." In *Theorizing Native Studies*, edited by Audra Simpson and Andrea Smith, 235–65. Durham, NC: Duke University Press, 2014.

Goeman, Mishuana. *Mark My Words: Native Women Mapping Our Nations*. Minneapolis: University of Minnesota Press, 2013.

Goeman, Mishuana. "Notes toward a Native Feminism's Spatial Practice." *Wicazo Sa Review* 24, no. 2 (2009): 169–87.

Goeman, Mishuana R., and Jennifer Nez Denetdale. "Native Feminisms: Legacies, Interventions, and Indigenous Sovereignties." *Wicazo Sa Review* 24, no. 2 (Fall 2009): 9–13.

Goldstein, Alyosha. "The Anti-Imperialist Horizon." *Critical Ethnic Studies* 7, no. 1 (Spring 2021). https://manifold.umn.edu/read/ces0701-anti-imperialist-horizon/section/fdf4dff9-00d9-4ce9-b893-f05d2b831e4f.

Goldstein, Alyosha. "Where the Nation Takes Place: Proprietary Regimes, Antistatism, and U.S. Settler Colonialism." *South Atlantic Quarterly* 107, no. 4 (October 1, 2008): 833–61.

Gorup, Michael. "The Strange Fruit of the Tree of Liberty: Lynch Law and Popular Sovereignty in the United States." *Perspectives on Politics* 18, no. 3 (September 2020): 819–34.

Goswami, Manu. "Imaginary Futures and Colonial Internationalisms." *American Historical Review* 117, no. 5 (December 2012): 1461–85.

Gouldhawke, M. "Land Back: The Matrilineal Descent of Modern Indigenous Land Reclamation," December 29, 2019. https://mgouldhawke.wordpress.com/2019/12/29/land-back-the-matrilineal-descent-of-modern-indigenous-land-reclamation/.

Grande, Sandy. *Red Pedagogy: Native American Social and Political Thought*. Lanham, MD: Rowman & Littlefield, 2015.

Grandin, Greg. *The End of the Myth: From the Frontier to the Border Wall in the Mind of America*. New York: Metropolitan Books, 2019.

Green, Joyce. *Making Space for Indigenous Feminism*. London: Zed Books, 2007.

Gutiérrez, Ramón A. "Internal Colonialism: An American Theory of Race." *Du Bois Review: Social Science Research on Race* 1, no. 2 (September 2004): 281–95.

Hafen, P. Jane. "'Help Indians Help Themselves': Gertrude Bonnin, the SAI, and the NCAI." In "The Society of American Indians and Its Legacies," special combined issue, *SAIL: Studies in American Indian Literatures* 25, no. 2, and *American Indian Quarterly* 37, no. 3 (Summer 2013): 199–218.

Hafen, P. Jane. "Zitkala Sa." In *Encyclopedia of North American Indians*, edited by Frederick E. Hoxie. Gale Academic OneFile. Boston: Houghton Mifflin Harcourt, 1996.

Hagdvet Vik, Hanne. "Indigenous Internationalism." In *Internationalisms: A Twentieth Century History*, edited by Glenda Sluga and Patricia Clavin, 315–39. New York: Cambridge University Press, 2017.

Hall, Anthony J. *The American Empire and the Fourth World: The Bowl with One Spoon, Part One*. Montreal: McGill-Queen's University Press, 2003.

Hall, Jacquelyn Dowd. "The Long Civil Rights Movement and the Political Uses of the Past." *Journal of American History* 91, no. 4 (2005): 1233–63.

Hanchard, Michael G. *The Spectre of Race: How Discrimination Haunts Western Democracy*. Princeton, NJ: Princeton University Press, 2018.

Harjo, Suzan Shown, ed. *Nation to Nation: Treaties between the United States and American Indian Nations*. Washington, DC: Smithsonian, 2014.

Harring, Sidney. *Crow Dog's Case: American Indian Sovereignty, Tribal Law, and United States Law in the Nineteenth Century*. New York: Cambridge University Press, 1994.
Hauptman, Laurence M. "Africa View: John Collier, the British Colonial Service and American Indian Policy, 1933–1945." *Historian* 48, no. 3 (May 1986): 359–74.
Havercroft, Jonathan. *Captives of Sovereignty*. Cambridge: Cambridge University Press, 2011.
Henderson, James (Sa'ke'j) Youngblood. *Indigenous Diplomacy and the Rights of Peoples: Achieving UN Recognition*. Saskatoon: Purich Publishing Limited, 2008.
Hertzberg, Hazel W. *The Search for an American Indian Identity: Modern Pan-Indian Movements*. Syracuse, NY: Syracuse University Press, 1981.
Herzog, Don. *Sovereignty, RIP*. New Haven, CT: Yale University Press, 2020.
Hoefel, Roseanne. "'Different by Degree': Ella Cara Deloria, Zora Neale Hurston, and Franz Boas Contend with Race and Ethnicity." *American Indian Quarterly* 25, no. 2 (Spring 2001): 181–202.
Holm, Tom, J. Diane Pearson, and Ben Chavis. "Peoplehood: A Model for the Extension of Sovereignty in American Indian Studies." *Wicazo Sa Review* 18, no. 1 (Spring 2003): 7–24.
Honig, Bonnie. "'[Un]Dazzled by the Ideal?': Tully's Politics and Humanism in Tragic Perspective." *Political Theory* 39, no. 1 (February 2011): 138–44.
HoSang, Daniel Martinez, and Joseph E. Lowndes. *Producers, Parasites, Patriots: Race and the New Right-Wing Politics of Precarity*. Minneapolis: University of Minnesota Press, 2019.
Hoxie, Frederick E. *A Final Promise: The Campaign to Assimilate the Indians, 1880–1920*. Lincoln: University of Nebraska Press, 2001.
Hoxie, Frederick E. *Parading through History: The Making of the Crow Nation in America, 1805–1935*. New York: Cambridge University Press, 1995.
Hsueh, Vicki. "Cultivating and Challenging the Common: Lockean Property, Indigenous Traditionalisms, and the Problem of Exclusion." *Contemporary Political Theory* 5, no. 2 (May 1, 2006): 193–214.
Idris, Murad. *War for Peace: Genealogies of a Violent Ideal in Western and Islamic Thought*. New York: Oxford University Press, 2019.
Ignace, Marianne, and Ronald E. Ignace. *Secwépemc People, Land, and Laws*. Montreal: McGill-Queen's University Press, 2017.
Indian Chiefs of Alberta. "Citizens Plus." *Aboriginal Policy Studies* 1, no. 2 (June 2011): 188–281.
Indian Rights Association. *Annual Report of the Board of Directors of the Indian Rights Association*. Philadelphia: Office of the Indian Rights Association, 1924.
Innes, Robert Alexander. *Elder Brother and the Law of the People: Contemporary Kinship and Cowessess First Nation*. Winnipeg: University of Manitoba Press, 2013.
International Indian Treaty Council. "Declaration of Continuing Independence," June 1974. https://www.iitc.org/about-iitc/the-declaration-of-continuing-independence-june-1974/.
"International NGO Conference on Discrimination against Indigenous Populations in the Americas." International Indian Treaty Council, September 20, 1977.
Ivison, Duncan, Paul Patton, and Will Sanders, eds. *Political Theory and the Rights of Indigenous Peoples*. New York: Cambridge University Press, 2000.
Jack, Henry. "Native Alliance for Red Power." In *The Only Good Indian: Essays by Canadian Indians*, edited by Waubgeshig, 111–27. Toronto: New Press, 1974.

Jamieson, Kathleen. "Sex Discrimination and the Indian Act." In *Arduous Journey: Canadian Indians and Decolonization*, edited by J. Ponting, 112–36. Toronto: McClelland and Stewart, 1989.

Johnson, Miranda. "Connecting Indigenous Rights to Human Rights in the Anglo Settler States: Another 1970s Story." In *Decolonization, Self-Determination, and the Rise of Global Human Rights Politics*, edited by A. Dirk Moses, Marco Durati, and Roland Burke, 109–31. New York: Oxford University Press, 2020.

Johnson, Miranda. *The Land Is Our History: Indigeneity, Law, and the Settler State*. New York: Oxford University Press, 2016.

Jones, Dorothy V. *License for Empire: Colonialism by Treaty in Early America*. Chicago: University of Chicago Press, 1982.

Kalmo, Hent, and Quentin Skinner, eds. *Sovereignty in Fragments: The Past, Present and Future of a Contested Concept*. Cambridge: Cambridge University Press, 2010.

Kappler, Charles, ed. "Fort Laramie Treaty of 1868." In *Indian Affairs: Laws and Treaties*, vol. 2, *1788–1883*, 999–1007. Washington, DC: Government Printing Office, 1904.

Karuka, Manu. *Empire's Tracks: Indigenous Nations, Chinese Workers, and the Transcontinental Railroad*. Oakland: University of California Press, 2019.

Kauanui, J. Kēhaulani. "Colonialism in Equality: Hawaiian Sovereignty and the Question of U.S. Civil Rights." *South Atlantic Quarterly* 107, no. 4 (2008): 635–50.

Keck, Margaret E., and Kathryn Sikkink. *Activists beyond Borders: Advocacy Networks in International Politics*. Ithaca, NY: Cornell University Press, 1998.

Kelley, Robin D. G. "What Did Cedric Robinson Mean by Racial Capitalism?" *Boston Review*, January 12, 2017. https://bostonreview.net/articles/robin-d-g-kelley-introduction-race-capitalism-justice/.

Kelley, Robin D. G., and Betsy Esch. "Black Like Mao: Red China and Black Revolution." *Souls: Critical Journal of Black Politics and Culture* 1, no. 4 (1999): 6–41.

Kellogg, Laura Cornelius. "Our Democracy and the American Indian (1920)." In *Laura Cornelius Kellogg: Our Democracy and the American Indian and Other Works*, 65–110. Syracuse, NY: Syracuse University Press, 2015.

Kelly, Jennifer. "Coming Out of the House: A Conversation with Lee Maracle." *ARIEL: A Review of International English Literature* 25, no. 1 (January 1994): 73–88.

Kelsey, Penelope Myrtle. *Tribal Theory in Native American Literature: Dakota and Haudenosaunee Writing and Indigenous Worldviews*. Lincoln: University of Nebraska Press, 2010.

Kemner, Jochen. "Lobbying for Global Indigenous Rights: The World Council of Indigenous Peoples (1975–1997)." *Forum for Inter-American Research* 4, no. 2 (November 2011).

Kiel, Doug. "Competing Visions of Empowerment: Oneida Progressive-Era Politics and Writing Tribal Histories." *Ethnohistory* 61, no. 3 (Summer 2014): 419–44.

Kimmerer, Robin. "Restoration and Reciprocity: The Contributions of Traditional Ecological Knowledge." In *Human Dimensions of Ecological Restoration: Integrating Science, Nature, and Culture*, edited by Dave Egan, Evan E. Hjerpe, and Jesse Abrams, 257–76. Washington, DC: Island Press, 2011.

Klein, Naomi. *This Changes Everything: Capitalism vs. the Climate*. New York: Simon and Schuster, 2014.

Knickerbocker, Madeleine Rose, and Sarah Nickel. "Negotiating Sovereignty: Indigenous Perspectives on the Patriation of a Settler Colonial Constitution, 1975–1983." *BC Studies*, no. 190 (Summer 2016): 67–88.

Kohn, Margaret, and Keally McBride. *Political Theories of Decolonization: Postcolonialism and the Problem of Foundations*. New York: Oxford University Press, 2011.

Kotef, Hagar. *The Colonizing Self: Or, Home and Homelessness in Israel/Palestine*. Durham, NC: Duke University Press Books, 2020.

Kramer, Sina. *Excluded Within: The (Un)Intelligibility of Radical Political Actors*. Oxford: Oxford University Press, 2017.

Krause, Sharon R. "Environmental Domination." *Political Theory* 48, no. 4 (August 2020): 443–68.

Kymlicka, Will. *Multicultural Citizenship: A Liberal Theory of Minority Rights*. Oxford: Clarendon Press, 1995.

Laborde, Cécile. "Republicanism and Global Justice: A Sketch." *European Journal of Political Theory* 9, no. 1 (January 1, 2010): 48–69.

Ladner, Kiera L. "Gendering Decolonisation, Decolonising Gender." *Australian Indigenous Law Review* 13, no. 1 (2009): 62–77.

Ladner, Kiera L. "Treaty Federalism: An Indigenous Vision of Canadian Federalisms." In *New Trends in Federalism*, 167–96. Peterborough, ON: Broadview Press, 2009.

LaDuke, Winona. *All Our Relations: Native Struggles for Land and Life*. Cambridge: South End Press, 1999.

Lake, Marilyn, and Henry Reynolds. *Drawing the Global Colour Line: White Men's Countries and the International Challenge of Racial Equality*. Cambridge: Cambridge University Press, 2008.

Lal, Priya. *African Socialism in Postcolonial Tanzania: Between the Village and the World*. New York: Cambridge University Press, 2015.

Lawrence, Bonita. "Gender, Race, and the Regulation of Native Identity in Canada and the United States: An Overview." *Hypatia* 18, no. 2 (May 2003): 3–31.

Lenin, V. I. *Imperialism, the Highest State of Capitalism* (1917). New York: Penguin Classics, 2010.

Lenin, V. I. "The Right of Nations to Self-Determination." In *Collected Works*, 393–454. Moscow: Progress Publishers, 1972. https://www.marxists.org/archive/lenin/works/1914/self-det/.

"Letter to Charles Isaacs," November 25, 1969. 1969 Correspondence Folder, Box 15. Vine Deloria Papers. Yale Collection of Western Americana, Beinecke Rare Book and Manuscript Library.

Leupp, Francis E. "Abolish the Bureau." *American Indian Magazine* 4, no. 2 (June 30, 1916): 200.

Lewandowski, Tadeusz. "Changing Scholarly Interpretations of Gertrude Bonnin (Zitkala-Ša)." *Journal of the Spanish Association of Anglo-American Studies* 41, no. 1 (June 2019): 31–49.

Lewandowski, Tadeusz. *Red Bird, Red Power: The Life and Legacy of Zitkala-Ša*. Norman: University of Oklahoma Press, 2016.

Liberation Support Movement. "On the National Question: Letter from the Native Study Group," Spring 1975.

Lightfoot, Sheryl. *Global Indigenous Politics: A Subtle Revolution*. New York: Routledge, 2016.

Lightfoot, Sheryl. "The Pessimism Traps of Indigenous Resurgence." In *Pessimism in*

International Relations: Provocations, Possibilities, Politics, edited by Tim Stevens and Nicholas Michelsen, 155–72. London: Palgrave, 2019.

Lomawaima, K. Tsianina. "The Mutuality of Citizenship and Sovereignty: The Society of American Indians and the Battle to Inherit America." In "The Society of American Indians and Its Legacies," special combined issue, *SAIL: Studies in American Indian Literatures* 25, no. 2, and *American Indian Quarterly* 37, no. 3 (Summer 2013): 333–51.

Lomawaima, K. Tsianina. "Society of American Indians." In *American History: Oxford Research Encyclopedias*. New York: Oxford University Press, 2015.

Lowe, Lisa. *The Intimacies of Four Continents*. Durham, NC: Duke University Press, 2015.

Lutz, Harmut, Murray Hamilton, and Donna Heimbecker, eds. *Howard Adams: Otapawy! The Life of a Métis Leader in His Own Words and Those of His Contemporaries*. Saskatoon: Gabriel Dumont Institute, 2005.

Lyons, Scott Richard. "The Incorporation of the Indian Body: Peyotism and the Pan-Indian Public, 1911–1923." In *Rhetoric, the Polis, and the Global Village*, edited by C. Jan Swearingen and David Pruett, 147–54. Mahwah, NJ: Lawrence Erlbaum, 1998.

Lyons, Scott Richard. "Rhetorical Sovereignty: What Do American Indians Want from Writing?" *College Composition and Communication* 51, no. 3 (2000): 447–68.

MacPherson, C. B. *The Political Theory of Possessive Individualism: Hobbes to Locke*. New York: Oxford University Press, 2011.

Maddox, Lucy. *Citizen Indians: Native American Intellectuals, Race, and Reform*. Ithaca, NY: Cornell University Press, 2005.

Malm, Andreas, and the Zetkin Collective. *White Skin, Black Fuel: On the Danger of Fossil Fascism*. London New York: Verso, 2021.

Mamdani, Mahmood. *Neither Settler nor Native: The Making and Unmaking of Permanent Minorities*. Cambridge, MA: Harvard University Press, 2020.

Manela, Erez. *The Wilsonian Moment: Self-Determination and the International Origins of Anticolonial Nationalism*. New York: Oxford University Press, 2007.

Mantena, Karuna. *Alibis of Empire: Henry Maine and the Ends of Liberal Imperialism*. Princeton, NJ: Princeton University Press, 2010.

Mantena, Karuna. "On Gandhi's Critique of the State: Sources, Contexts, Conjunctures." *Modern Intellectual History* 9, no. 3 (November 2012): 535–63.

Mantena, Karuna. "Popular Sovereignty and Anti-Colonialism." In *Popular Sovereignty in Historical Perspective*, edited by Richard Bourke and Quentin Skinner, 297–319. New York: Cambridge University Press, 2016.

Manuel, George. "Canadian Indians and Maoris Share Common Problems." *Northian: Magazine of the Society for Indian and Northern Education* (Saskatchewan Teachers Federation) 11, no. 2 (1975): 10–18.

Manuel, George. "Government Making Gross Error If Indian Voice Is Not Heard, as Presented to the MacKenzie Valley Pipeline Inquiry." *Native Perspective* 1, no. 6 (1976): 10–11, 33–34.

Manuel, George. *Indian Economic Development: A Whiteman's Whitewash, as Presented to the Union of BC Indian Chiefs Annual Conference*. Ottawa: National Indian Brotherhood, 1972.

Manuel, George. "Indigenous Peoples' Fishing Rights and Responsibilities, Draft

Presentation before the International Conference on Fisheries, Sponsored by the Government of Mexico." December 15, 1979.
Manuel, George. "Letter from George Manuel to Jean Chretien, June 25, 1971." York University Special Collections, Michael Posluns Fonds, Box 1989-20/019 (04).
Manuel, George. "Petition and Bill of Particulars on the Political Standing of Indigenous Tribes and Bands under the Protection of the British Government in the Face of Impending Canadian Independence," December 1980. http://constitution.ubcic.bc.ca/sites/constitution.ubcic.bc.ca/files/PetitionToUNOCR.pdf.
Manuel, George. "Transcript—George Manuel Speech to the National Congress of American Indians," 1975. Box 24 George Manuel: National Museum of the American Indian Archive Center, Smithsonian Institution.
Manuel, George, and Michael Posluns. *The Fourth World: An Indian Reality*. Minneapolis: University of Minnesota Press, 2019.
Manuel, George, and Michael Posluns. *GM Interview, January 22, 1973*. York University Special Collections, Michael Posluns Fonds, Box 1989-020/008 (07).
Manuel, George, and Michael Posluns. *GM Interview, March 18, 1972*. York University Special Collections, Michael Posluns Fonds, Box 1989-020/008 (024).
Manuel, George, and Michael Posluns. "Manuscripts, The Fourth World," 1974. York University Special Collections, Michael Posluns Fonds, Box 1989-20/021, Folder 5.
Maracle, Lee. *Bobbi Lee: Indian Rebel* (1975). Toronto: Women's Press, 1990.
Maracle, Lee. *I Am Woman: A Native Perspective on Sociology and Feminism*. Vancouver: Write-on Press, 1988.
Maracle, Lee. *Memory Serves: Oratories*. Edited by Smaro Kamboureli. Edmonton: NeWest Press, 2015.
Maracle, Lee. *My Conversations with Canadians*. Toronto: BookThug, 2017.
Maracle, Lee. "The Operation Was Successful, but the Patient Died." *BC Studies* 212 (Winter 2021): 7–12.
Maracle, Lee. "Oratory: Coming to Theory." *Essays on Canadian Writing* 54 (Winter 1994): 7–11.
Maracle, Lee. *Ravensong*. Vancouver: Press Gang, 1993.
Maracle, Lee. "Red Power Legacies and Lives: An Interview by Scott Rutherford." In *New World Coming: The Sixties and the Shaping of Global Consciousness*, edited by Karen Dubinsky, Catherine Krull, Susan Lord, Sean Mills, and Scott Rutherford, 358–67. Toronto: Between the Lines, 2009.
Maracle, Lee. *Sojourner's Truth and Other Stories*. Vancouver: Press Gang, 1990.
Maracle, Lee. *Sundogs*. Penticton, British Columbia: Theytus Books, 1992.
Maracle, Lee, and Ray Bobb. "Natives Are Part of the Third World." *Canadian Revolution* 6 (October 1976). https://www.marxists.org/history/erol/periodicals/canadian-revolution/19760603.html.
Marion Young, Iris. "Two Concepts of Self-Determination." In *Ethnicity, Nationalism, and Minority Rights*, edited by Stephen May, Tariq Modood, and Judith Squires, 176–96. New York: Cambridge University Press, 2004.
Markell, Patchen. "The Insufficiency of Non-Domination." *Political Theory* 36, no. 1 (February 2008): 9–36.
Markle, Seth. *A Motorcycle on Hell Run: Tanzania, Black Power, and the Uncertain Future of Pan-Africanism, 1964–1974*. Lansing: Michigan State University Press, 2017.

Martinez, David. *The American Indian Intellectual Tradition: An Anthology of Writings from 1772 to 1972*. Ithaca, NY: Cornell University Press, 2011.

Martinez, David. *Life of the Indigenous Mind: Vine Deloria Jr. and the Birth of the Red Power Movement*. Lincoln: University of Nebraska Press, 2020.

Marule, Marie Smallface. "The Canadian Government's Termination Policy: From 1969 to the Present Day." In *One Century Later: Western Canadian Indian Reserves since Treaty 7*, edited by Ian A. L. Getty and Donald B. Smith. Vancouver: University of British Columbia Press, 1978.

Marwah, Inder S. "Provincializing Progress: Developmentalism and Anti-Imperialism in Colonial India." *Polity* 51, no. 3 (July 2019): 498–531.

Marwah, Inder S., Jennifer Pitts, Timothy Bowers Vasko, Onur Ulas Ince, and Robert Nichols. "Empire and Its Afterlives." *Contemporary Political Theory* 19, no. 2 (June 1, 2020): 274–305.

Marx, Karl. "Preface to *A Contribution to the Critique of Political Economy*," 1859. https://www.marxists.org/archive/marx/works/1859/critique-pol-economy/preface.htm.

Mbembe, Achille. *Necropolitics*. Durham, NC: Duke University Press, 2019.

McCool, Daniel, Susan M. Olson, and Jennifer L. Robinson. *Native Vote: American Indians, the Voting Rights Act, and the Right to Vote*. New York: Cambridge University Press, 2007.

McDowell, Janet. "Competency Commissions and Indian Land Policy, 1913–1920." *South Dakota History* 11 (Winter 1980): 21–34.

McFarlane, Peter. *From Brotherhood to Nationhood: George Manuel and the Making of the Modern Indian Movement*. Toronto: Between the Lines, 1993.

McKenzie, Fayette Avery. "The American Indian of Today and Tomorrow." *Journal of Race Development* 3 (October 1912): 135–55.

McLaren, Jesse. "Indigenous Socialism: The Life and Politics of Howard Adams." *Spring Magazine*, September 6, 2019. https://springmag.ca/.

Medicine, Bea. "Ella C. Deloria: The Emic Voice." In "Ethnic Women Writers II: 'Of Dwelling Places.'" *MELUS* 7, no. 4 (Winter 1980): 23–30.

Medicine, Bea. *The Native American Woman: A Perspective*. Las Cruces, NM: National Educational Laboratory Publishers, 1978.

Mehta, Uday Singh. *Liberalism and Empire: A Study in Nineteenth-Century British Liberal Thought*. Chicago: University of Chicago Press, 1999.

Mekeel, Scudder. "An Appraisal of the Indian Reorganization Act." *American Anthropologist* 46, no. 2, pt. 1 (June 1944): 209–17.

Melamed, Jodi. "Racial Capitalism." *Critical Ethnic Studies* 1, no. 1 (2015): 76–85.

Memmi, Albert. *The Colonizer and the Colonized*. Boston: Beacon Press, 1967.

Metzl, Jonathan M. *Dying of Whiteness: How the Politics of Racial Resentment Is Killing America's Heartland*. Updated edition. New York: Basic Books, 2020.

Middleton, Beth Rose. *Trust in the Land: New Directions in Tribal Conservation*. First Peoples : New Directions in Indigenous Studies. Tucson: University of Arizona Press, 2011.

Miller, J. R. *Compact, Contract, Covenant: Aboriginal Treaty-Making in Canada*. Toronto: University of Toronto Press, 2009.

Miller, Robert J. "The Doctrine of Discovery: The International Law of Colonialism." *UCLA Indigenous Peoples' Journal of Law, Culture, and Resistance* 5, no. 1 (2019): 35–42.

Millon, Dian. *Therapeutic Nations: Healing in an Age of Indigenous Human Rights*. Tucson: University of Arizona Press, 2013.
Mills, Aaron. "What Is a Treaty? On Contract and Mutual Aid." In *The Right Relationship : Reimagining the Implementation of Historical Treaties*, edited by John Borrows and Michael Coyle, 208–47. Toronto: University of Toronto Press, 2017.
Mohawk, John. "Marxism: Perspectives from a Native Movement." In *Thinking in Indian*, edited by Jose Barreiro, 213–23. Golden, CO: Fulcrum Publishing, 2010.
Montezuma, Carlos. "Another Kaiser in America." In *Say We Are Nations: Documents of Politics and Protest in Indigenous America since 1887*, edited by Daniel Cobb, 32–35. Chapel Hill: University of North Carolina Press, 2015.
Montezuma, Carlos. "Drafting Indians and Justice." *Wassaja* 2, no. 7 (October 1917): 3.
Montezuma, Carlos. "The Truth Is Coming to Light." *Wassaja* 2, no. 12 (March 1918): 1–2.
Monture-Angus, Patricia. *Thunder in My Soul: A Mohawk Woman Speaks*. Halifax: Fernwood, 1995.
Morefield, Jeanne. *Covenants without Swords: Idealist Liberalism and the Spirit of Empire*. Princeton, NJ: Princeton University Press, 2005.
Morefield, Jeanne. *Empires without Imperialism: Anglo-American Decline and the Politics of Deflection*. Oxford: Oxford University Press, 2014.
Moreton-Robinson, Aileen. *The White Possessive: Power, Property, and Indigenous Sovereignty*. Minneapolis: University of Minnesota Press, 2015.
Morris, Glen T. "Vine Deloria Jr., and the Development of a Decolonizing Critique of Indigenous Peoples and International Relations." In *Native Voices: American Indian Identity and Resistance*, edited by Richard A. Grounds, George E. Tinker, and David E. Wilkins, 97–154. Lawrence: University Press of Kansas, 2003.
"MSS Annual Meeting Report," April 26, 1969. Library and Archives Canada, Howard Adams Fonds, Volume 3, Folder 10 Metis Society of Saskatchewan—Correspondence and Related Materials, 1969, reproduction copy number R-10982.
Muthu, Sankar. *Enlightenment against Empire*. Princeton, NJ: Princeton University Press, 2003.
Nackenoff, Carol. "Constitutionalizing Terms of Inclusion: Friends of the Indian and Citizenship for Native Americans, 1880s–1930s." In *The Supreme Court and American Political Development*, edited by Ronald Kahn and Ken I. Kersch, 366–413. Lawrence: University Press of Kansas, 2006.
Nadasdy, Paul. *Sovereignty's Entailments: First Nation State Formation in the Yukon*. Toronto: University of Toronto, 2017.
"NARP Eight Point Program." *NARP Newsletter*, February 1969.
Newmark, Julianne. "A Prescription for Freedom: Carlos Montezuma, Wassaja, and the Society of American Indians." In "The Society of American Indians and Its Legacies," special combined issue, *SAIL: Studies in American Indian Literatures* 25, no. 2, and *American Indian Quarterly* 37, no. 3 (Summer 2013): 139–58.
Nichols, Robert. "Contract and Usurpation: Enfranchisement and Racial Governance in Settler-Colonial Contexts." In *Theorizing Native Studies*, edited by Audra Simpson and Andrea Smith, 99–121. Durham, NC: Duke University Press, 2014.
Nichols, Robert. *Theft Is Property! The Recursive Logic of Dispossession*. Durham, NC: Duke University Press, 2020.
Nickel, Sarah A. *Assembling Unity: Indigenous Politics, Gender, and the Union of BC Indian Chiefs*. Vancouver: University of British Columbia Press, 2019.

Niezen, Ronald. *The Origins of Indigenism: Human Rights and the Politics of Identity.* Berkeley: University of California Press, 2003.

Nkrumah, Kwame. *Neo-Colonialism: The Last Stage of Imperialism.* New York: International Publishers, 1966.

"The NODAPL Movement." Special issue, *Indian Country Today*, Fall 2016.

Norris, Frank. *The Octopus: A Story of California.* New York: Penguin Classics, 1994.

Nyerere, Julius K. "The Arusha Declaration and TANU's Policy on Socialism and Self-Reliance." Tanganyika African National Union, February 5, 1967. https://www.marxists.org/subject/africa/nyerere/1967/arusha-declaration.htm.

Nyerere, Julius K. "Introduction." In *Freedom and Socialism/Uhuru Na Ujamaa: A Selection from Writings and Speeches, 1965–1967*, 1–32. Dar es Salaam, Tanzania: Oxford University Press, 1968.

Nyerere, Julius K. "Ujamaa—The Basis of African Socialism." In *Freedom and Unity/Uhuru Na Umoja: A Selection from Writings and Speeches, 1952–1965*, 162–71. Dar es Salaam, Tanzania: Oxford University Press, 1966.

Olson, Joel. *The Abolition of White Democracy.* Minneapolis: University of Minnesota Press, 2004.

O'Mally, M. "Red Capitalism: Self Sufficiency for Native Peoples." *Canadian Business* 53, no. 4 (April 1980).

Oppenheim, Lassa. *International Law: A Treatise.* Edited by Ronald F. Roxburgh. Vol. 1. London: Longmans, Green and Co., 1912. https://www.gutenberg.org/files/41046/41046-h/41046-h.htm.

Ostler, Jeffrey. "'Just and Lawful War' as Genocidal War in the (United States) Northwest Ordinance and Northwest Territory, 1787–1832." *Journal of Genocide Research* 18, no. 1 (2016): 1–20.

Ostler, Jeffrey, and Nick Estes. "'The Supreme Law of the Land': Standing Rock and the Dakota Access Pipeline." *Indian Country Today*, January 16, 2017. https://indiancountrymedianetwork.com/news/opinions/supreme-law-land-standing-rock-dakota-access-pipeline/.

Palmer, Bryan D. *Canada's 1960s: The Ironies of Identity in a Rebellious Era.* Toronto: University of Toronto Press, 2008.

Parasher, Tejas. "Beyond Parliament: Gandhian Democracy and Postcolonial Founding." *Political Theory*, May 10, 2022. https://doi.org/10.1177/00905917221092821.

Parmenter, Jon. "The Meaning of Kaswentha and the Two Row Wampum Belt in Haudenosaunee (Iroquois) History: Can Indigenous Oral Tradition Be Reconciled with the Documentary Record?" *Journal of Early American History* 3 (2013): 82–109.

Peroff, Nicholas. *Menominee Drums: Tribal Termination and Restoration, 1954–1974.* Norman: University of Oklahoma Press, 2006.

Petit, Phillip. "The Globalized Republican Ideal." *Global Justice: Theory, Practice, Rhetoric* 9, no. 1 (2016): 47–68.

Pexa, Christopher J. *Translated Nation: Rewriting the Dakhóta Oyáte.* Minneapolis: University of Minnesota Press, 2019.

Philp, Kenneth R. *Termination Revisited: American Indians on the Trail to Self-Determination, 1933–1953.* Lincoln: University of Nebraska Press, 1999.

Piatote, Beth. *Domestic Subjects: Gender, Citizenship, and Law in Native American Literature.* New Haven, CT: Yale University Press, 2017.

Pitcher, M. Anne, and Kelly M. Askew. "African Socialisms and Postcsocialisms." *Africa: The Journal of the International Africa Institute* 76, no. 1 (2006): 1–14.

Pitsula, James M. "The Thatcher Government in Saskatchewan and the Revival of Metis Nationalism, 1964–1971." *Great Plains Quarterly* 17 (Summer 1997): 213–35.

Pitts, Jennifer. *Boundaries of the International: Law and Empire.* Cambridge, MA: Harvard University Press, 2018.

Pitts, Jennifer. "Political Theory of Empire and Imperialism." *Annual Review of Political Science* 13 (2010): 211–35.

Pitts, Jennifer. *A Turn to Empire: The Rise of Imperial Liberalism in Britain and France.* Princeton, NJ: University of Princeton, 2006.

"Platform Document–Treaty Council," n.d. Standing Rock Correspondence Folder, Box 27: Correspondence Folder N-S. Vine Deloria Papers, Yale Collection of Western Americana, Beinecke Rare Book and Manuscript Library.

Posluns, Michael W. *Speaking with Authority: The Emergence of the Vocabulary of First Nations' Self-Government.* New York: Routledge, 2007.

Pows Whyte, Kyle. "The Dakota Access Pipeline, Environmental Injustice, and U.S. Colonialism." *Red Ink* 19, no. 1 (Spring 2017): 154–69.

Pows Whyte, Kyle. "Indigenous Science (Fiction) for the Anthropocene: Ancestral Dystopias and Fantasies of Climate Change Crises." *Environment and Planning E: Nature and Space* 1, no. 1–2 (2018): 224–42.

Pows Whyte, Kyle. "Settler Colonialism, Ecology, and Environmental Injustice." *Environment and Society: Advances in Research* 9 (2018): 125–44.

Prashad, Vijay. *The Darker Nations: A People's History of the Third World.* New York and London: New Press, 2007.

Prashad, Vijay. *The Poorer Nations: A Possible History of the Global South.* London: Verso, 2012.

Pratt, Richard Henry. "The Advantages of Mingling Indians with Whites: Paper Presented at the Nineteenth Annual Conference of Charities and Correction, Denver, Colorado." In *Americanizing the American Indian: Writings by the "Friends of the Indian," 1880–1900*, edited by Francis Paul Prucha, 260–71. Cambridge, MA: Harvard University Press, 1973.

Prucha, Francis Paul, ed. "1819 Civilization Fund Act." In *Documents of United States Indian Policy.* 3rd edition. Lincoln: University of Nebraska Press, 33.

Ramirez, Renya. "Race, Tribal Nation, and Gender: A Native Feminist Approach to Belonging." *Meridians* 7, no. 2 (2007): 22–40.

Rana, Aziz. "Colonialism and Constitutional Memory." *UC Irvine Law Review* 5, no. 2 (2015): 263–88.

Rana, Aziz. *The Two Faces of American Freedom.* Cambridge, MA: Harvard University Press, 2014.

Raster, Amanda, and Christina Gish Hill. "The Dispute over Wild Rice: An Investigation of Treaty Agreements and Ojibwe Food Sovereignty." *Agriculture and Human Values* 34, no. 2 (June 2017): 267–81.

Redhead, Mark. "Charles Taylor's Deeply Diverse Response to Canadian Fragmentation: A Project Often Commented on but Seldom Explored." *Canadian Journal of Political Science/Revue Canadienne de Science Politique* 36, no. 1 (2003): 61–83.

The Red Nation. *The Red Deal: Indigenous Action to Save Our Earth.* Brooklyn, NY: Common Notions, 2021.

Rice, Julian, ed. *Ella Deloria's The Buffalo People.* Albuquerque: University of New Mexico Press, 1994.

Richard Lyons, Scott. *X-Marks: Native Signatures of Assent*. Minneapolis: University of Minnesota Press, 2010.

Rickard, Clinton. *Fighting Tuscarora: The Autobiography of Chief Clinton Rickard*. Edited by Barbara Graymont. Syracuse, NY: Syracuse University Press, 1984.

Riel, Louis. "Memorial of the People of Rupert's Land and North-West." In *The Collected Writings of Louis Riel: Les Ecrits Complets de Louis Riel*, vol. 1, edited by Gilles Martel and George F. G. Stanley. Edmonton: University of Alberta Press, 1985.

Rifkin, Mark. *When Did Indians Become Straight? Kinship, the History of Sexuality, and Native Sovereignty*. New York: Oxford University Press, 2011.

Riggs, Christopher K. "American Indians, Economic Development, and Self-Determination in the 1960s." *Pacific Historical Review* 69, no. 3 (2000): 431–63.

Riofrancos, Thea. *Resource Radicals: From Petro-Nationalism to Post-Extractivism in Ecuador*. Durham, NC: Duke University Press, 2020.

Robertson, Lindsay G. *Conquest by Law: How the Discovery of America Dispossessed Indigenous Peoples of Their Lands*. New York: Oxford University Press, 2007.

Robinson, Cedric J. *Black Marxism: The Making of the Black Radical Tradition*. Chapel Hill: University of North Carolina Press, 2000.

Rollo, Toby. "Back to the Rough Ground: Textual, Oral and Enactive Meaning in Comparative Political Theory." *European Journal of Political Theory* 20, no. 3 (2021): 379–97.

Roosevelt, Theodore. "Indian Citizenship." *American Indian Magazine* 4, no. 4 (December 1916): 326–27.

Roosevelt, Theodore. *The Strenuous Life: Essays and Addresses*. New York: Dover, 1889.

Rorty, Richard. *Achieving Our Country: Leftist Thought in Twentieth Century America*. Cambridge, MA: Harvard University Press, 1999.

Rowse, Tim. "The Indigenous Redemption of Liberal Universalism." In *Colonial Exchanges: Political Theory and the Agency of the Colonized*, edited by Burke A. Hendrix and Deborah Baumgold, 133–55. Manchester: Manchester University Press, 2017.

Royster, Judith V. "The Legacy of Allotment." *Arizona State Law Journal* 1 (1995): 1–78.

Rusco, Elmer. *A Fateful Time: The Background and Legislative History of the Indian Organization Act*. Reno: University of Nevada Press, 2000.

Rutherford, Scott. *Canada's Other Red Scare: Indigenous Protest and Colonial Encounters during the Global Sixties*. Montreal: McGill-Queen's Press, 2020.

Ryser, Rudolph C. "The Legacy of Grand Chief George Manuel." Center for World Indigenous Studies, 1995.

Saler, Bethel. *The Settlers' Empire: Colonialism and State Formation in America's Old Northwest*. Philadelphia: University of Pennsylvania Press, 2014.

Sanders, Douglas. *The Formation of the World Council of Indigenous Peoples*. Copenhagen: International Working Group for Indigenous Affairs, 1974.

Scott, David. *Conscripts of Modernity: The Tragedy of Colonial Enlightenment*. Durham, NC: Duke University Press, 2004.

"Self-Determination or Disguised Termination: Let's Be Certain, NCAI 29th Convention," October 1972. Box 21, Folder 3, National Museum of the American Indian Archive Center, Smithsonian Institution.

Sharon R. Krause. *Freedom beyond Sovereignty: Reconstructing Liberal Individualism*. Chicago: University of Chicago Press, 2015.

Shaw, Karena. *Indigeneity and Political Theory: Sovereignty and the Limits of the Political*. New York: Routledge, 2008.
Shilliam, Robbie. *The Black Pacific: Anti-Colonial Struggles and Oceanic Connections*. New York: Bloomsbury, 2015.
Shklar, Judith. *American Citizenship: The Quest for Inclusion*. Cambridge, MA: Harvard University Press, 1991.
Shulman, George. *American Prophecy: Race and Redemption in American Political Culture*. Minneapolis: University of Minnesota Press, 2008.
Simmons, Deborah. "Socialism from Below and Indigenous Resurgence: Reclaiming Traditions." In "Indigenous Resurgence," special issue, *New Socialist: Ideas for Radical Change*, no. 58 (October 2008): 13–15.
Simpson, Audra. *Mohawk Interruptus: Political Life across the Borders of Settler-States*. Durham, NC: Duke University Press, 2014.
Simpson, Audra. "The Ruse of Consent and the Anatomy of 'Refusal': Cases from Indigenous North America and Australia." *Postcolonial Studies* 20, no. 1 (2017): 18–33.
Simpson, Leanne Betasamosake. *As We Have Always Done: Indigenous Freedom through Radical Resistance*. Minneapolis: University of Minnesota Press, 2017.
Simpson, Leanne Betasamosake. *Dancing on Our Turtle's Back: Stories of Nishnaabeg Re-Creation, Resurgence and a New Emergence*. Manitoba: ARP Books, 2011.
Simpson, Leanne Betasamosake. "Indigenous Resurgence and Co-Resistance." *Critical Ethnic Studies* 2, no. 2 (Fall 2016): 9–34.
Simpson, Leanne Betasamosake. "Looking after Gdoo-Naaganinaa: Precolonial Nishnaabeg Diplomatic and Treaty Relationships." *Wicazo Sa Review* 23, no. 2 (October 8, 2008): 29–42.
Singh, Jakeet. "Decolonizing Radical Democracy." *Contemporary Political Theory* 18, no. 3 (2019): 331–56.
Singh, Nikhil Pal. *Black Is a Country: Race and the Unfinished Struggle for Democracy*. Cambridge, MA: Harvard University Press, 2004.
Skinner, Quentin. *Liberty before Liberalism*. New York: Cambridge University Press, 1998.
Sleeper-Smith, Susan. *Indigenous Prosperity and American Conquest: Indian Women of the Ohio River Valley*. Chapel Hill, NC: Omohundro Institute of Early American History and Culture, 2018.
Slotkin, Richard. *The Fatal Environment: The Myth of the Frontier in the Age of Industrialization, 1800–1890*. New York: HarperCollins, 1985.
Smith, Linda Tuhiwai. *Decolonizing Methodologies: Research and Indigenous Peoples*. 2nd edition. London: Zed Books, 2012.
Smith, Rogers. *Civic Ideals: Conflicting Visions of Citizenship in U.S. History*. New Haven, CT: Yale University Press, 1997.
Society of American Indians. *Report of the Executive Council on the Proceedings of the First Annual Society of American Indians Conference*. Washington, DC, 1912.
Stanciu, Cristina. "Americanization on Native Terms: The Society of American Indians, Citizenship Debates, and Tropes of 'Racial Difference.'" *Native American and Indigenous Studies Journal* 6, no. 1 (2019): 111–48.
Starblanket, Gina. "Being Indigenous Feminists: Resurgences against Contemporary Patriarchy." In *Making Space for Indigenous Feminism*, edited by Joyce Green, 21–41. Halifax: Fernwood Publishing, 2017.

Starblanket, Gina. "The Numbered Treaties and the Politics of Incoherency." *Canadian Journal of Political Science* 52, no. 3 (May 2019): 1–17.
Starblanket, Gina, and Heidi Kiiwetinepinesiik Stark. "Toward a Relational Paradigm—Four Points for Consideration: Knowledge, Gender, Land, and Modernity." In *Resurgence and Reconciliation: Indigenous-Settler Relations and Earth Teachings*, edited by Michael Asch, John Borrows, and James Tully, 175–207. Toronto: University of Toronto Press, 2018.
Stark, Heidi Kiiwetinepinesiik. "Changing the Treaty Question: Remedying the Right(s) Relationship." In *The Right Relationship: Reimagining the Implementation of Historical Treaties*, edited by John Borrows and Michael Coyle, 248–76. Toronto: University of Toronto Press, 2017.
Stark, Heidi Kiiwetinepinesiik. "Criminal Empire: The Making of the Savage in a Lawless Land." *Theory & Event* 19, no. 4 (2016).
Steiner, Stan. *The New Indians*. New York: Harper & Row, 1968.
Stovall, Tyler. *White Freedom: The Racial History of an Idea*. Princeton, NJ: Princeton University Press, 2021.
Sultan, Nazmul S. "Between the Many and the One: Anticolonial Federalism and Popular Sovereignty." *Political Theory*, June 23, 2021. https://doi.org/10.1177/00905917211018534.
Sultan, Nazmul S. "Self-Rule and the Problem of Peoplehood in Colonial India." *American Political Science Review* 114, no. 1 (February 2020): 81–94.
Swain, Molly Suzanne. "Victim of Deceit and Self-Deceit: The Role of the State in Undermining Jim Brady's Métis Socialist Politics." University of Alberta, 2018.
Taylor, Charles. *Reconciling the Solitudes: Essays on Canadian Federalism and Nationalism*. Montreal: McGill-Queen's University Press, 1993.
Taylor, Graham D. *The New Deal and American Indian Tribalism: The Administration of the Indian Reorganization Act, 1934–45*. Lincoln: University of Nebraska Press, 1980.
Temin, David Myer. "Development in Decolonization: Walter Rodney, Third World Developmentalism, and 'Decolonizing Political Theory.'" *American Political Science Review*, July 18, 2022, https://doi.org/10.1017/S0003055422000570.
Temin, David Myer. "Our Democracy: Laura Cornelius Kellogg's Decolonial-Democracy." In "Race and Politics in America," special issue, *Perspectives on Politics* 19, no. 4 (December 2021): 1082–97.
Temin, David Myer. "Remapping the World: Vine Deloria, Jr. and the Ends of Settler Sovereignty." PhD dissertation, University of Minnesota, 2016.
Temin, David Myer, and Adam Dahl. "Narrating Historical Injustice: Political Responsibility and the Politics of Memory." *Political Research Quarterly* 70, no. 4 (December 2017): 905–17.
Tennant, Paul. *Aboriginal Peoples and Politics: The Indian Land Question in British Columbia, 1849–1989*. Vancouver: University of British Columbia Press, 1990.
Thom, Mel. "Indian War 1963." *American Aborigine* 3, no. 1 (1964): 2–4.
Thom, Mel "Indian War 1964." *American Aborigine* 3, no. 1 (1964): 4–6.
Tóth, György. "'Red' Nations: Marxists and the Native American Sovereignty Movement of the Late Cold War." *Cold War History* 20, no. 2 (April 2, 2020): 197–221.
"Trail of Broken Treaties 20-Point Position Paper," October 1972. www.aimmovement.org/archives.

Tsuk, Dalia. "Pluralisms: The Indian New Deal as a Model." *University of Maryland Law Journal of Race, Religion, Gender, and Class* 1, no. 2 (2001): 393–449.
Tully, James. "Aboriginal Property and Western Theory." *Social Philosophy and Policy* 11, no. 2 (1994): 153–80.
Tully, James. "Consent, Hegemony, and Dissent in Treaty Negotiations." In *Between Consenting Peoples*, edited by Jeremy Webber and Colin M. Macloed, 223–56. Vancouver: University of British Columbia Press, 2010.
Tully, James. *Public Philosophy in a New Key*, vol. 1, *Democracy and Civic Freedom*. Cambridge: Cambridge University Press, 2008.
Tully, James. "Rediscovering America: The Two Treatises and Aboriginal Rights." In *Locke in Contexts: An Approach to Political Philosophy*, 137–78. Oxford: Oxford University Press, 1993.
Tully, James. *Strange Multiplicity: Constitutionalism in an Age of Diversity*. Cambridge: Cambridge University Press, 1995.
Turner, Dale. *This Is Not a Peace Pipe: Towards a Critical Indigenous Philosophy*. Toronto: University of Toronto Press, 2006.
Two Members of the Bolshevik Tendency. "Nationhood or Genocide: The Struggle of the Native People against Canadian and American Imperialism." *Canadian Revolution* 4 (September 1975). https://www.marxists.org/history/erol/periodicals/canadian-revolution/19760402.htm.
Ulas Ince, Onur. *Colonial Capitalism and the Dilemmas of Liberalism*. New York: Cambridge University Press, 2018.
Valandra, Edward. "We Are Blood Relatives: No to the DAPL." *Hot Spots, Fieldsites*, December 22, 2016. https://culanth.org/fieldsights/we-are-blood-relatives-no-to-the-dapl.
Valdez, Inés. "Empire, Popular Sovereignty, and the Problem of Self-and-Other-Determination." *Perspectives on Politics*, February 14, 2022, 1–17. https://doi.org/10.1017/S1537592721003674.
Valdez, Inés. "Socialism and Empire: Labor Mobility, Racial Capitalism, and the Political Theory of Migration." *Political Theory* 49, no. 6 (December 1, 2021): 902–33.
Valdez, Inés. *Transnational Cosmopolitanism: Kant, Du Bois, and Justice as a Political Craft*. Cambridge: Cambridge University Press, 2019.
Venne, Sharon. "Understanding Treaty 6: An Indigenous Perspective." In *Aboriginal and Treaty Rights in Canada: Essays on Law, Equity, and Respect for Difference*, 173–207. Vancouver: University of British Columbia Press, 1997.
Veracini, Lorenzo. *Settler Colonialism: A Theoretical Overview*. London: Palgrave Macmillan UK, 2010.
Veracini, Lorenzo. "Settler Colonialism and Decolonisation." *Borderlands E-Journal* 6, no. 2 (2007).
Veracini, Lorenzo. *The Settler Colonial Present*. London: Palgrave Macmillan UK, 2015.
Vigil, Kiara M. *Indigenous Intellectuals: Sovereignty, Citizenship, and the American Imagination, 1880–1930*. New York: Cambridge University Press, 2015.
Vimalassery, Manu, Juliana Hu Pegues, and Alyosha Goldstein. "Introduction: On Colonial Unknowing." *Theory & Event* 19, no. 4 (2016). http://muse.jhu.edu/article/633283.
"Vine Deloria Discusses Native American Rights and History." *Studs Terkel Radio*

Archive, January 20, 1975. https://studsterkel.wfmt.com/programs/vine-deloria-discusses-native-american-rights-and-history.

Volk, Christian. "The Problem of Sovereignty in Globalized Times," *Law, Culture and the Humanities* 18, no. 3 (October 2022): 716–38.

Voth, Daniel. "The Devil's Northern Triangle: Howard Adams and Métis Multidimensional Relationships with and within Colonialism." University of British Columbia, 2015.

Warrior, Clyde. "Poverty, Community, and Power." *New University Thought* 4 (Summer 1965): 5–10.

Warrior, Robert. "The Indian Renaissance, 1960–2000: Stumbling to Victory, or Anecdotes of Persistence?" In *The Oxford Handbook of American Indian History*, edited by Frederick Hoxie, 129–48. New York: Oxford University Press, 2016.

Warrior, Robert. *Tribal Secrets: Recovering American Indian Intellectual Traditions*. Minneapolis: University of Minnesota Press, 1994.

Watkins, Arthur. "Termination of Federal Supervision: The Removal of Restrictions over Indian Property and Person." *American Academy of Political and Social Science* 311 (May 1957): 47–55.

Weaver, Jace, Craig S. Womack, and Robert Warrior. *American Indian Literary Nationalism*. Albuquerque: University of New Mexico Press, 2005.

Weaver, John C. *The Great Land Rush and the Making of the Modern World, 1650–1930*. Quebec: McGill-Queen's University Press, 2003.

Weaver, Sally M. *Making Canadian Indian Policy: The Hidden Agenda, 1968–70*. Toronto: University of Toronto Press, 1981.

Webber, Jeremy. *Reimagining Canada: Language, Culture, Community, and the Canadian Constitution*. Montreal: McGill-Queen's University Press, 1994.

Wendt, Alexander, and Raymond Duvall. "Sovereignty and the UFO." *Political Theory* 36, no. 4 (August 1, 2008): 607–33.

White, Richard. *The Middle Ground: Indians, Empires, and Republics in the Great Lakes Region, 1650–1815*. 2nd edition. New York: Cambridge University Press, 2010.

Wilder, Gary. *Freedom Time: Negritude, Decolonization, and the Future of the World*. Durham, NC: Duke University Press, 2015.

Wilkins, David E. *American Indian Sovereignty and the U.S. Supreme Court: The Masking of Justice*. Austin: University of Texas Press, 1997.

Wilkins, David, ed. *The Hank Adams Reader: An Exemplary Native Activist and the Unleashing of Indigenous Sovereignty*. Golden, CO: Fulcrum Publishing, 2011.

Wilkins, David E. *Red Prophet: The Punishing Intellectualism of Vine Deloria Jr*. Golden, CO: Fulcrum Publishing, 2018.

Wilkins, David E., and Heidi Kiiwetinepinesiik Stark. *American Indian Politics and the American Political System*. 3rd edition. Lanham, MD: Rowman & Littlefield, 2010.

Wilkinson, Charles. *Blood Struggle: The Rise of Modern Indian Nations*. New York: W. W. Norton & Company, 2005.

Williams, Robert A., Jr. *Linking Arms Together: American Indian Treaty Visions of Law and Peace, 1600–1800*. New York: Routledge, 1999.

Wilson, Woodrow. "Democracy and Efficiency (October 1, 1900)." In *The Papers of Woodrow Wilson*, edited by Arthur S. Link, 12:6–20. Princeton, NJ: Princeton University Press, 1972.

Wimmer, Andreas, and Nina Glick Schiller. "Methodological Nationalism and Beyond:

Nation-State Building, Migration and the Social Sciences." *Global Networks: A Journal of Transnational Affairs* 2, no. 4 (October 2002): 301–34.

Winter, Yves. "Conquest." *Political Concepts: A Critical Lexicon* 1 (2011). http://www.politicalconcepts.org/conquest-winter/.

Witgen, Michael. "American Indians in World History." In *Oxford Handbook of American Indian History*, edited by Frederick E. Hoxie, 591–614. New York: Oxford University Press, 2016.

Witgen, Michael. *Seeing Red: Indigenous Land, Black Lives, and the Political Economy of Plunder in North America*. Williamsburg, VA: Omohundro Institute for the Study of Early American History and Culture, 2022.

Wolfe, Patrick. "Settler Colonialism and the Elimination of the Native." *Journal of Genocide Research* 8, no. 4 (December 2006): 387–409.

Wolfe, Patrick. *Settler Colonialism and the Transformation of Anthropology*. London: Cassell, 1999.

World Council of Indigenous Peoples Second General Assembly. "Declaration of Human Rights." Center for World Indigenous Studies, September 24, 1977.

X, Malcolm. "America's Gravest Crisis since the Civil War." In *Malcolm X: The Last Speeches*, 60–79. Atlanta: Pathfinder Press, 1989.

Yellow Robe, Chauncey. "Indian Patriotism." *American Indian Magazine* 6, no. 3 (Autumn 1918): 129–30.

Yellowtail, Robert. "An Address: In Defense of the Rights of the Crow Indians and the Indians Generally, before the Senate Committee of Indian Affairs." *American Indian Magazine* 8, no. 3 (September 9, 1919): 130–37.

Young, Robert J. C. *Postcolonialism: An Historical Introduction*. Malden, MA: Wiley & Sons, 2001.

Youngblood Henderson, James. "Empowering Treaty Federalism." *Saskatchewan Law Review* 58 (1994): 241–329.

Zitkala-Ša. *American Indian Stories, Legends, and Other Works*. Edited by Cathy N. Davidson and Ada Norris, 184–90. New York: Penguin Classics, 2003.

Zitkala-Ša. "Break the Shackles Now—Make Us Free." *American Indian Magazine* 5, no. 4 (December 1917): 213–21.

Zitkala-Ša. *Zitkala-Ša: Letters, Speeches, and Unpublished Writings, 1898–1929*. Edited by Tadeusz Lewandowski. Leiden: Brill, 2018.

Index

abduction, 122–25, 185
Abernathy, Ralph, 52
abolition, 41
Adams, Hank, 88
Adams, Howard, 127; anticolonial internationalism and, 169–70; biography of, 145–46; class and, 171; colonial internationalisms and, 21; colonial-racial capitalism and, 143–44, 148–52; cultural nationalism and, 165–66; decolonization and, 142–43; Fourth Worldism and, 163; Marxism and, 143; neocolonialism and, 163–66; self-determination and, 166–67. See also *Prison of Grass* (Adams)
Africa View (Huxley), 73
Alfred, Taiaiake, 103
American Indian Magazine. See Society of American Indians (SAI)
American Indian Movement (AIM), 66, 87–88, 94, 96–97, 144–45
Anghie, Antony, 68
anticolonial internationalism, 169–70
anticolonialism: earthmaking and, 17; internationalism and, 158, 169–70; Maracle and, 157–62; NODAPL and, 1–2, 6, 11; self-determination and, 28. See also colonialism; decolonization; earthmaking
arts-and-crafts type culture, 111–12. See also culture
assimilation: Canada and, 105, 107–8, 112; citizenship and, 28, 30–31, 35–37; coercive, 72; dispossession and, 55

Banyacya, Thomas, 59
Behind the Trail of Broken Treaties (Deloria), 49, 66, 88, 96–97
"Bertha" (Maracle), 180
Big Bear, 152
Black Hills Council, 44
Black Panther Party, 156
Black radical thought, 145–47, 208n91
Blue Bird, 83
Bobb, Ray, 160–63
Bobbi Lee (Maracle), 171–72
bondage, 38
Bonnin, Gertrude Simmons. See Zitkala-Ša
Borrows, John, 139–40
bourgeois nationalism, 166
British Columbia Homemakers Association, 130
Brown, Dee, 92
Brown v. Board of Education, 49
Bruyneel, Kevin, 209n96
Bureau of Indian Affairs (BIA), 34, 36, 46, 73
Bury My Heart at Wounded Knee, 92
Butler, Susanna, 40–41
Byrd, Jodi A., 7–8, 159–60, 207n89

Cabral, Amilcar, 169
Cahill, Cathleen, 43
Canada: British Columbian land struggle and, 104; culture and, 111–12; Indian Act legislation and, 109, 173–75, 178; Indigenous activists and, 144–45; multiculturalism and, 111–15;

Canada (*continued*)
  neocolonialism and, 163–68; 1969 White Paper and, 104–10; patriarchy and, 178; race and, 170–71; racial and colonial oppression and, 150–55; Riel Rebellion and, 150–52; treaty-making practices and, 67; Trudeau administration and, 105–7, 109. *See also* colonial-racial capitalism; Red Power Movement; treaties (specific); treaty (concept)
Canadian Communist Party (CPC), 158
Canadian Pacific Railway (CPR), 150
Canadian Revolution, 160
capitalism: colonialism and, 141; colonial-racial, 148–52; Marxism and, 142, 157
Cardinal, Harold, 107–8
Cherokee Nation v. Georgia (1831), 97
Christianity, 59
citizenship: birthright, 43; as a form of social standing, 33; White Paper multiculturalism and, 105–6
citizenship (Indigenous): birthright, 43; Indian Citizenship Act of 1924 (ICA) and, 32; as a necessity, 42; Selective Services Act and, 41; self-determination and, 41–47; self-government and, 60; termination and, 47–55; United States and, 28–35; wardship and, 30–32, 35–41, 43, 49–50. *See also* wardship
civic inclusion narrative: American universalism and, 32–33; critique of, 29; Deloria and, 50–56; injustice and, 34; Rogers Smith and, 33–34
Civilization Bill (1819), 58
Civilization Fund Act (1819), 210n106
Civil Rights Act of 1866, 30
civil rights movement, 49, 51–52, 208nn88–89
Collier, John, 65, 72–73
colonialism: capitalism and, 141; civic inclusion narrative and, 56–57; dispossession and, 55, 148, 154; Doctrine of Discovery and, 89; earthmaking and, 15–16; gender and, 171–76; Indigenous rights abolition and, 108; modern world order and, 2–3; recognition by treaty and, 67–68; self-determination and, 45; settler, 197n18; sovereignty and, 5–11, 14, 148; treaties as instruments of settler-colonial dispossession and, 69–70; violence and, 173–74. *See also* settler domination
colonial-racial capitalism: Adams on, 148–52; analysis of, 143–44, 180–82; Maracle and, 172–73
colonial-racial hierarchies, 159
Congo, 72
Constitution Express, 105, 163
contract theory, 69
Contribution to the Critique of Political Economy, A (Marx), 118
Cotera, Maria, 76
Coulthard, Glen, 102, 132, 142, 157, 181
creedal nationalism, 32
Cromwell, Oliver, 149
cultural nationalism, 165–66
culture, 73–74, 85–86; land and, 115–22; natural economy and, 119; resurgence and, 111–12, 132–33
Custer Died for Your Sins (Deloria), 48–49, 51, 55–60

Dakota Access Pipeline (DAPL), 1–2
Dakota Texts (Deloria), 81
Dawes Severalty Act of 1887, 30
Declaration of Indian Rights, 50
decolonization: Adams and, 167; capitalism and, 142–44; class and, 171; cultural nationalism and, 165–66; definition of, 3; Deloria and, 55–60; direct-action strategies and, 147; feminism and, 171–80; gender and, 171–80; patriarchy and, 172–76; political theories of Indigenous, 4–5, 195n6; Red Power Movement and, 144; resurgence and, 102–3, 133–34, 140; sovereignty and, 2–11, 183–84, 188–90; treaty rights and, 63–64, 97. *See also* colonial-racial capitalism; Fourth Worldism; self-determination (Indigenous)
Deloria, Ella: analysis of the IRA and, 71–

75; intellectual biography of, 75–76; kinship and, 76–80; treaty as kinship and, 15. *See also Speaking of Indians* (Deloria); *Waterlily* (Deloria)
Deloria, Phillip J., 35, 76
Deloria, Vine, Jr.: assimilation and, 55; background of, 48–49; civic inclusion narrative and, 29, 34, 50, 52–54, 56; civil rights movement and, 49, 51–52; freedom and, 28; political reading of treaty and, 86–94; self-determination and, 60–62; termination and, 47–51, 55–56; treaty-covenant relationship and, 94–99; US imperialism and, 53–54; *Worcester v. Georgia* and, 48
Dene Nation, 132
Dick, Agnes, 130
"diremption," 122
dispossession, 55, 148, 153
Doctrine of Discovery, 89
domain, 79–80
Dominion Lands Act (1872), 154
Dumont, Gabriel, 152
Dunbar-Ortiz, Roxanne, 142

earthmaking: anticolonialism and, 17; definition of, 5; kinship and, 82–84, 185; making and, 199n38; responsibilities of care and, 16; self-determination and, 15–16, 18–19, 185; stewardship world order and, 135–39; treaties and, 66, 83–84
Eastman, Charles, 38
Elk v. Wilkins (1884), 30
Estes, Nick, 81
exclusion, 33–34, 52, 59–60, 80
expansionism, 9
Ex Parte Crow Dog (1883), 30

Fanon, Frantz, 143, 146, 164, 169
Feltes, Emma, 128
feminism, 172–79
Finn, Janet, 75
Fourth World, The (Manuel and Posluns), 102, 111, 116, 118, 123, 127, 138, 217n2
Fourth Worldism: Manuel and, 125–34, 140, 187; NARP and, 163; resurgence and, 102–4; stewardship world order and, 135–39; Third Worldism and, 135–38
freedom, 10, 13, 28, 38

Garry, Joseph, 50
gender: colonialism and, 40–41; colonial-racial capitalism and, 144, 172–73; decolonization and, 171–80; Indian Act (Canada) and, 173–75, 178; kinship and, 76; politics of, 114–15
General Federation of Women's Clubs, 39
Getachew, Adom, 17, 135
God Is Red (Deloria), 49
Goeman, Mishuana, 4, 175
Grant, Ulysses S., 95
"Grants to Bands Program," 129
guardianship. *See* wardship

Henderson, James (Sa'ke'j) Youngblood, 21, 70
Hudson's Bay Company (HBC), 149–51

I Am Woman (Maracle), 172
imperialism: capitalist, 148, 158–59, 182; internal colonization and, 160–61; nationalism and, 159; transnational, 160
Indian Act legislation (Canada), 109, 173–75, 178
Indian Citizenship Act of 1924 (ICA), 32, 44, 89
Indian communism, 42
Indian Defense League of America, 42
Indianness, 41
Indian New Deal. *See* Indian Reorganization Act (IRA)
Indian Reorganization Act (IRA), 46, 52, 71–75, 204n42
Indian Rights Association, 31–32, 39, 204n42
Indian wars, 30, 53
Indigenous citizenship. *See* citizenship (Indigenous)
Indigenous decolonization. *See* decolonization
Indigenous internationalism, 19–22
Indigenous studies, 7–8
Indigenous traditionalism, 103

interdependence, 15–18, 65, 77–78, 82–85, 101
International Indian Treaty Council (IITC): "Declaration of Continuing Independence of the Sovereign Native American Indian Nations," 63, 97–98; earthmaking and, 17
internationalism. *See* Indigenous internationalism; transnational internationalism

Jim Crow, 30

Kauanui, J. Kēhaulani, 207n89
Kellogg, Laura Cornelius, 38, 42
Kelsey, Penelope Myrtle, 214n42
Kenya, 136–37
kinship: extended, 21; gender and, 173–74; as an institution, 79; in Lakota and Dakota life, 76–80; treaty and, 65–66, 80–86
Kymlicka, Will, 107

Ladner, Kiera, 156
LaDuke, Winona, 16
land: abduction and, 122–25; British Columbian land struggle and, 104; culture and, 115–22; as an essential value, 101–2; natural economy and, 119; natural resource extraction and, 120–21, 131, 138–39, 188; as a political concept, 102; property form of, 116–17; Third Worldism and, 127–30
League of Nations, 27–28, 44–45
Ledcie Stechi, 40
Lenin, Vladimir, 158
Lomawaima, Tsianina, 35
Lone Wolf v. Hitchcock (1903), 30, 91
Lummi Nation, 95–96

Macdonald, John A., 151
MacPherson, C. B., 120
making, 199n38
manifestation, 21
Mantena, Karuna, 17
Manuel, Arthur, 133
Manuel, George: abduction and, 122–25; colonial depiction of culture and, 111–12; colonial internationalisms and, 21; First Nations movement and, 102; Fourth Worldism and, 125–40, 187; gender and, 114–15; land as culture and, 115–22; natural resource extraction and, 120–21; new world economic order and, 138–39; 1969 White Paper and, 107–8; resurgence and, 102–4, 110–15, 140; stewardship world order and, 135–39; Tanzanian socialism and, 110–11, 126–30; "worldview" and, 118, 220n28
Maoism, 157
Maracle, Lee, 127; anticolonial internationalism and, 169–70; biography of, 155–56; capitalism and, 158–59; colonial internationalisms, 21; colonial-racial capitalism and, 143–44; cultural nationalism and, 165–66; decolonization and, 142–43, 187; feminism and, 171–78; Fourth Worldism and, 163; gender and, 171–78, 229n80; Marxism and, 143, 182; neocolonialism and, 163–65, 167–68; self-determination and, 157–58, 168–69, 171; sovereignty and, 159–62
Marule, Marie Smallface, 126, 133
Marxism: Indigenous, 141–44, 181–82; syncretic, 224n9; Vancouver Native Study Group and, 157
Mekeel, Scudder, 73
Meriam Report, 204n42
Métis communities, 146–48, 150–52, 154
Milando, Mbutu, 126
Mní wičóni, 1
Montezuma, Carlos, 38, 41–42, 205n47
Monture, Patricia, 179
multiculturalism: resurgence and, 110–15; White Paper, 104–10
My Conversations with Canadians (Maracle), 170–71
My Lai massacre, 53

National Association for the Advancement of Colored People (NAACP), 49
National Congress of American Indians (NCAI), 48, 50

National Council of American Indians (NCAI), 46
National Indian Youth Council (NIYC), 52
nationalism, 159, 165–66
Native People's Caravan of 1974, 158
"Natives Are Part of the Third World" (Maracle), 127
natural economy, 119
neocolonialism, 163–66
New International Economic Order (NIEO), 130–31, 137–38
new world economic order, 138–39
Nickel, Sarah, 129
Nkrumah, Kwame, 128, 164
NODAPL movement, 1–3, 6, 11–12, 183, 195n3
North American Indian Brotherhood, 104
Nyerere, Julius, 110–11, 126, 128, 130–33, 136–37, 222n63

Očhéthi Šakówiŋ, 44
Oklahoma's Poor, Rich Indians, 39–40
Olson, Joel, 209n102
Oppenheim, Lassa, 68, 85
Our Democracy and the American Indian, 38
"Our Sioux People" (Zitkala-Ša), 37

paternalism, 108
patriarchy, 144, 172–80
patriotism, 42–43
Peterson, Helen, 50
Pexa, Chris, 74, 76, 214n40
political slavery, 39
Poor People's Campaign, 52
Posluns, Michael, 102, 111, 118–20, 127. See also *Fourth World, The* (Manuel and Posluns)
possessive individualism, 120
Prashad, Vijay, 126
Pratt, Richard Henry, 41
Prison of Grass (Adams), 146, 149, 164

queer Indigenous feminist politics, 172

race. *See* racism; white supremacism
racial capitalism, 145. *See also* colonial-racial capitalism
racism, 147, 149, 159, 172, 227n37. *See also* white supremacism
Rana, Aziz, 32
Ravensong (Maracle), 180
"Red bourgeoisie," 164–66
"Red capitalism," 166
Reddy, Chandan, 199n38
Red Power Movement, 166; Adams and, 146; decolonization and, 4–5, 144; NARP and, 144; neocolonialism and, 163–68; treaties and, 88. *See also* Canada
reformism, 148
reservations: abolition of, 41; assimilation and, 31; Dawes Severalty Act of 1887 and, 30; termination and, 47; wardship and, 30–31, 36–38, 50
resurgence: abduction and, 122–25; decolonization and, 102–3, 133–34, 140; multiculturalism and, 110–15; self-reliance and, 131; White Paper multiculturalism and, 104–6
Rickard, Clinton, 42
Riel Rebellion, 150–52
Rifkin, Mark, 75
Robinson, Cedric, 145
Roosevelt, Theodore, 30–31
Roper, Rose Marie, 156
Rowse, Tim, 45

Sand Creek massacre, 53
Saskatchewan Native Action Committee (SNAC), 147
Selective Services Act, 41
self-determination (Indigenous): Adams and, 167; anticolonial, 28; anticolonial internationalism and, 169–70; capitalism and, 141; citizenship and, 41–47; cultural freedom and, 111–12; decolonization and, 55–60, 141; Ella Deloria and, 65–66; earthmaking and, 15–16, 18–19; gender and, 172–79; human rights and, 45; Indigenous internationalism and, 20–21; "land back" and, 101; League of Nations and, 27–28, 44; Maracle and, 157–58, 168–69, 171; modes of, 18; NARP and, 157; natural resource extraction and, 120–21, 131,

self-determination (*continued*)
138–39, 188; neocolonialism and,
163–68; NODAPL and, 12; recognition by treaty and, 67–68; as a relation of care for land, 12; resurgence and,
110–15; sovereignty and, 7, 14–15,
183–84; termination and, 47–55; Third World solidarity and, 128; treaties and, 66, 86–100; wardship and, 35–41;
Zitkala-Ša and Deloria and, 60–62.
See also land

self-government (Indigenous): capitalism and, 141; citizenship and, 60; economic models and, 46; Indian Reorganization Act (IRA) and, 71–75

self-reliance, 131–32
settler colonialism. *See* colonialism
settler domination, 39, 42, 64, 84, 156, 189. *See also* colonialism
sexuality, 40
Shackleton, Ron, 126
Shklar, Judith, 33–34
Shulman, George, 59
Simpson, Audra, 210n108
Simpson, Leanne Betasamosake, 20, 113, 115
Singh, Nikhil, 203n21
"Sioux Claims, The" (Zitkala-Ša), 37
slavery, 30, 39
Slotkin, Richard, 57
Smith, Rogers, 33–34, 203n25
socialism: North American Indian, 133; Tanzanian, 110, 131
Society of American Indians (SAI), 35–36, 44
sovereignty: antirelationality of, 7; colonial, 160–61; conceptual logics of, 11–14; decolonization and, 2–4, 188–90; Indian communism and, 42; Indigenous studies and, 7–8; as institution, 8–14; NARP and, 159–60; natural resources and, 137; NODAPL and, 1–2, 12; remapping colonial, 11–15; self-determination and, 14–15; settler colonialism and, 5–11, 14, 54; transnational internationalisms and, 22; treaties and, 92

Speaking of Indians (Deloria), 65, 77, 83, 85
Standing Rock Sioux Reservation. *See* Dakota Access Pipeline (DAPL)
Starblanket, Gina, 70
Stark, Heidi Kiiwetinepinesiik, 70
stewardship world order, 18, 26, 104, 135–39
"Strenuous Life" (speech), 31
Sundogs (Maracle), 180

Tanzania, 110–11, 126–31, 136–37
Taylor, Charles, 107
termination, 47–56, 207nn80–81
theft. *See* abduction
thióšpaye, 77–79, 81
Third World: developmental state and, 17–18; Fourth Worldism and, 135–38; Manuel and, 125–34; Maracle and, 162–63; Red Power Movement and, 144; Tanzania and, 110–11
Thom, Mel, 54
Thunder in My Soul (Monture), 179
Tortured People, A (Adams), 227n50
Trail of Broken Treaties caravan, 66
transnational cosmopolitanism, 201n51
transnational internationalism: definition of, 5; democratic tribal self-government and, 46; Indigenous internationalism and, 19–22; shared oppositional culture and, 162; stewardship world order and, 135–39; Zitkala-Ša and, 45
treaties (specific): Covenant Chain, 66–67; between Dakota and buffalo, 83, 85–86; "peace and friendship," 91; Treaty 6, 152; Treaty of Fort Laramie, 57, 74–76, 85, 94; Two Row Wampum, 66
treaty (concept): collective self-other relations and, 64; "colonial relation" and, 68–69; conceptions of, 66–71; Deloria Jr. and, 57–58, 86–94; earth-making and, 83–84; as instruments of settler-colonial dispossession, 69–70; international status and, 93, 97–98; kinship and, 65–66, 74–75, 77, 80–86;

Lakota and Dakota treaty-making practices, 77, 94–95; protests for repair of violations of, 86, 94; protests to protect hunting and fishing rights from, 86; recognition by, 67–68; relatedness and, 70–71; rights of Indigenous North Americans, 63–64; self-determination and, 66, 99–100; "treaty-covenant relation," 66, 87, 94–99; "treaty relation," 68; trust responsibility and, 97; wardship and, 93, 95, 97

trusteeship, 74

Tully, James, 64, 68–69, 139–40, 211n12

Turner, Dale, 106

"Twenty Points Proposal" (Adams), 88–90, 93

Uhura Na Ujamaa (*Freedom and Socialism*) (Nyerere), 110

Ujamaa, 131–33, 136, 222n63

United Nations (UN): Indigenous self-determination and, 97–98; Indigenous societies and, 20; International Indian Treaty Council (IITC) and, 64, 97–99; natural resources and, 137; World Council of Indigenous Peoples (WCIP) and, 127–28

United States: American universalism and, 203n21; Department of the Interior, 28, 36; Fourteenth Amendment and, 30; imperialism and, 53–60; Indian wars and, 30; Indigenous citizenship and, 29–35; League of Nations and, 27–28; Nineteenth Amendment and, 43; Nixon administration and, 88–89; NODAPL movement and, 1–3, 6, 11–12, 183, 195n3; as a settler society, 30; treaty-making practices and, 67, 86–94; wardship and, 30. *See also* civic inclusion narrative; treaties (specific); treaty (concept)

United States v. Kagama (1886), 30, 91

United States v. Nice (1916), 31–32

United States v. Wong Kim Ark (1898), 30

Universal Congress of the Races in London, 38

Unjust Society, The (Cardinal), 107–8

US Homestead Act of 1862, 154

usurpation, 124. *See also* abduction

Valdez, Inés, 201n51

Vancouver Native Alliance for Red Power (NARP), 144, 156–60, 162–63

Vancouver Native Study Group, 157–58, 163

Venne, Sharon, 128

"villagization," 136

violence, 122–25, 172–74, 177–78; gender-based, 40–41. *See also* abduction

wardship: Canada and, 109; citizenship and, 30–32, 35–41, 43, 49–50 (*see also* citizenship [Indigenous]); Indian Reorganization Act (IRA) and, 71–75; *Oklahoma's Poor, Rich Indians* and, 39–40; termination and, 54–55; treaties and, 93, 95, 97; Zitkala-Ša and, 35–41

Warrior, Clyde, 52

Waterlily (Deloria), 65, 77, 80–83, 214n42

Watkins, Arthur, 48–50

We Talk, You Listen (Deloria), 48

Wheeler-Howard Act. *See* Indian Reorganization Act (IRA)

White Paper liberalism, 106

White Paper multiculturalism. *See* multiculturalism

white supremacism, 28, 146, 148–49, 153, 170–71, 202n7

Whyte, Kyle Pows, 189

Williams, Robert, Jr., 70

Wilson, Woodrow, 27–28, 45, 202nn6–7

WoLakota, 81

Wolfe, Patrick, 197n18

women: colonial-racial capitalism and, 144; decolonization and, 171–80; IRA and, 76; resurgence and, 114–15; suffrage and, 43; wardship and, 40

Worcester v. Georgia (1832), 48

World Council of Indigenous Peoples (WCIP), 17, 127–29, 138

worldmaking, 17

World War I, 42

Wounded Knee, 53, 86, 94

Yellowtail, Robert, 27–28

Zitkala-Ša: assimilation and, 35; citizenship and remedial justice and, 44; citizenship as a necessity and, 42–43; civic inclusion narrative and, 29; freedom and, 28; Indigenous self-government and, 46–47; internationalism and, 45; League of Nations and, 44–45; National Council of American Indians and, 46; *Oklahoma's Poor, Rich Indians* and, 39–40; self-determination and, 60–62; settler ideologies and, 30; Versailles Conference and, 187; wardship and, 35–41, 43; Wilsonian internationalism and, 45

www.ingramcontent.com/pod-product-compliance
Lightning Source LLC
Chambersburg PA
CBHW022044290426
44109CB00014B/982